D1737645

ATLA Monograph Series
edited by Dr. Kenneth E. Rowe

1. Ronald L. Grimes. *The Divine Imagination: William Blake's Major Prophetic Visions.* 1972.
2. George D. Kelsey. *Social Ethics Among Southern Baptists, 1917-1969.* 1973.
3. Hilda Adam Kring. *The Harmonists: A Folk-Cultural Approach.* 1973.
4. J. Steven O'Malley. *Pilgrimage of Faith: The Legacy of the Otterbeins.* 1973.
5. Charles Edwin Jones. *Perfectionist Persuasion: The Holiness Movement and American Methodism, 1867-1936.* 1974.
6. Donald E. Byrne, Jr. *No Foot of Land: Folklore of American Methodist Itinerants.* 1975.
7. Milton C. Sernett. *Black Religion and American Evangelicalism: White Protestants, Plantation Missions, and the Flowering of Negro Christianity, 1787-1865.* 1975.
8. Eva Fleischner. *Judaism in German Christian Theology Since 1945: Christianity and Israel Considered in Terms of Mission.* 1975.
9. Walter James Lowe. *Mystery & The Unconscious: A Study in the Thought of Paul Ricoeur.* 1977.
10. Norris Magnuson. *Salvation in the Slums: Evangelical Social Work, 1865-1920.* 1977.
11. William Sherman Minor. *Creativity in Henry Nelson Wieman.* 1977.
12. Thomas Virgil Peterson. *Ham and Japheth: The Mythic World of Whites in the Antebellum South.* 1978.
13. Randall K. Burkett. *Garveyism as a Religious Movement: The Institutionalization of a Black Civil Religion.* 1978.
14. Roger G. Betsworth. *The Radical Movement of the 1960's.* 1980.
15. Alice Cowan Cochran. *Miners, Merchants, and Missionaries: The Roles of Missionaries and Pioneer Churches in the Colorado Gold Rush and Its Aftermath, 1858-1870.* 1980.
16. Irene Lawrence. *Linguistics and Theology: The Significance of Noam Chomsky for Theological Construction.* 1980.
17. Richard E. Williams. *Called and Chosen: The Story of Mother Rebecca Jackson and the Philadelphia Shakers.* 1981.
18. Arthur C. Repp, Sr. *Luther's Catechism Comes to America: Theological Effects on the Issues of the Small Catechism Prepared In or For America Prior to 1850.* 1982.
19. Lewis V. Baldwin. *"Invisible" Strands in African Methodism.* 1983.
20. David W. Gill. *The Word of God in the Ethics of Jacques Ellul.* 1984.
21. Robert Booth Fowler. *Religion and Politics in America.* 1985.
22. Page Putnam Miller. *A Claim to New Roles.* 1985.
23. C. Howard Smith. *Scandinavian Hymnody from the Reformation to the Present.* 1987.
24. Bernard T. Adeney. *Just War, Political Realism, and Faith.* 1988.
25. Paul Wesley Chilcote. *John Wesley and the Women Preachers of Early Methodism.* 1991.
26. Samuel J. Rogal. *A General Introduction to Hymnody and Congregational Song.* 1991.
27. Howard A. Barnes. *Horace Bushnell and the Virtuous Republic.* 1991.

John Wesley and the Women Preachers of Early Methodism

by

Paul Wesley Chilcote

ATLA Monograph Series, No. 25

The American Theological
Library Association and
The Scarecrow Press, Inc.
Metuchen, N.J., & London
1991

Frontispiece: Susanna Wesley, mother of John and Charles Wesley.

British Library Cataloguing-in-Publication data available

Library of Congress Cataloging-in-Publication Data

Chilcote, Paul Wesley, 1954–
    John Wesley and the women preachers of early Methodism /
by Paul Wesley Chilcote.
        p.   cm. — (ATLA monograph series ; no. 25)
    Originally presented as the author's thesis (Ph.D.)—Duke
University, 1984.
    Includes bibliographical references and indexes.
    ISBN 0-8108-2414-0 (alk. paper)
    1. Women clergy—England—History—18th century.
2. Wesley, John, 1703–1791.   3. Methodist Church—
England—History—18th century.   4. England—Church
history—18th century.   I. Title.   II. Series.
BX8345.7.C45 1991
287'.082—dc20   91-24598

For my mother and father,
Louise and Virgil,
patterns of the faith.

CONTENTS

Abbreviations   vii
Editor's Foreword   ix
Preface   xi

Introduction   1

PART I. THE TRAINING
GROUND FOR WOMEN PREACHERS:
THE EARLY METHODIST REVIVAL, 1739–1760

1. Pioneers, Sustainers, Martyrs   45
2. Lay Leaders in the Methodist Societies   67
3. Communicating the Gospel in All but Preaching   92

PART II. EXPANDING THE ROLE OF
WOMEN TO INCLUDE PREACHING: THE
METHODIST REVIVAL IN FULL FLOWER, 1761–1791

4. A Decade of Experimentation, 1761–1770   117
5. Defining the "Extraordinary Call," 1771–1780   141
6. Official Recognition of Women
   Preachers, 1781–1791   182

PART III. WOMEN PREACHERS IN AN
EVOLVING CHURCH, 1791–1803

7. From Recognition to Repression After Wesley   221

APPENDIXES

A. Biographical Outlines of Methodist Women
   Preachers   253
B. Letters Related to the Question of Women's
   Preaching in Early Methodism   288
C. A John Wesley Letter of September 8, 1761   296
D. A Mary Bosanquet Letter to John Wesley,
   June 1771   299
E. A Joseph Benson Letter   305
F. Selected Invitations to Mary Barritt   309
G. Selected Letters of Encouragement to Miss
   Mary Barritt (Afterward Mrs. Taft)   312
H. A Sermon Register of the Women Preachers   317
I. Text of a Sermon by Mary Fletcher   321
J. Distribution of Women Preachers Throughout
   Britain   328

Selected Bibliography   329
General Index   359
Index of Scriptural References   374

ABBREVIATIONS

Arm. Mag.	*Arminian Magazine: Consisting of Extracts and Original Treatises*, 1778–97, q.v.
Arm. Mag. (B.C.)	*The Arminian Magazine*, 1821– (afterward the *Bible Christian Magazine*), q.v.
Charles Wesley, *Journal*	*The Journal of Charles Wesley*, ed. Thomas Jackson, 2 vols., q.v.
L.Q.R.	*London Quarterly and Holborn Review*, q.v.
Meth. Arch.	Methodist Archives and Research Centre, Rylands Library, University of Manchester
Meth. Hist.	*Methodist History*, q.v.
Meth. Mag.	Continuation of *Arm. Mag.*, 1798–1821
Minutes	*Minutes of the Methodist Conferences*, q.v.
Minutes, Ireland	*Minutes of the Methodist Conferences in Ireland*, q.v.
Moore, *Fletcher*	Henry Moore, *The Life of Mrs. Mary Fletcher*, 6th ed., q.v.

Taft, *Holy Women*	Zechariah Taft, *Biographical Sketches of the Lives and Public Ministry of Various Holy Women,* q.v.
Taft, *Memoirs*	Mary Taft, *Memoirs of the Life of Mrs. Mary Taft,* 2d ed., q.v.
W.H.S.	*Wesley Historical Society, Proceedings*
Wes. Meth. Mag.	*Wesleyan Methodist Magazine,* continuation of *Methodist Magazine,* 1822–1913
Wesley, *Bicentennial Edition*	John Wesley, *Works,* ed. Frank Baker, vols. 27–31, yet to be published, q.v.
Wesley, *Journal*	*The Journal of the Rev. John Wesley,* ed. Nehemiah Curnock, 8 vols., q.v.
Wesley, *Letters*	*The Letters of the Rev. John Wesley,* ed. John Telford, 8 vols., q.v.
Wesley, *Notes*	John Wesley, *Explanatory Notes upon the Old Testament* and *New Testament,* 1st eds., cited by book, chapter, and verse, q.v.
Wesley, *Oxford Edition*	John Wesley, *Works,* ed. Frank Baker, vols. 7, 11, 25, 26, q.v.
Wesley, *Standard Sermons*	*The Standard Sermons of John Wesley,* ed. E. H. Sugden, 2 vols., q.v.
Wesley, *Works*	*The Works of the Rev. John Wesley,* ed. Thomas Jackson, 14 vols., q.v.

EDITOR'S FOREWORD

S INCE 1972, THE American Theological Library Association has undertaken responsibility for a modest
dissertation series in religious studies. Our aim in this
series is to publish two dissertations of quality each year.
Titles are selected from studies in a wide variety of religious
and theological disciplines. We are pleased to publish Paul
Wesley Chilcote's study of John Wesley and women
preachers in eighteenth-century Methodism as number
twenty-five in our series.

Following undergraduate studies in history at Valparaiso
University, Paul Wesley Chilcote studied theology and church
history at Duke University where he received both the M.Div.
and Ph.D. degrees. He has completed postdoctoral study in
Church History at Bristol University in England. He has
taught at Wesley College (Bristol, England), Duke University,
Boston University, and St. Paul's United Theological College
(Kenya, East Africa). His most recent academic post is Tutor
in Church History at the College of Theology of the newly
founded Africa University (Old Mutare, Zimbabwe). Dr.
Chilcote is the author of *Wesley Speaks on Christian Vocation*
(1986), coeditor with Robert E. Cushman of *Theological
Treatises,* forthcoming volume 12 of the Bicentennial Edition
of the Works of John Wesley being published by Abingdon
Press, and author of more than a dozen scholarly articles.

Kenneth E. Rowe
Series Editor
Drew University Library
Madison, NJ 07940

PREFACE

HESTER ANN ROGERS was the first early Methodist woman I encountered by reading her manuscript journals. The more I read about her life and work, and that of other contemporary women of the Wesleyan revival, the more I realized the significance of their influence. Up to the present time, however, no systematic study has appeared in which the role and influence of women is seen as part of and in the light of the larger evangelical revival of the eighteenth century. Few scholars have addressed the question of women preachers in early Methodism and their relationship to the primary founder of that movement, John Wesley. This study is an attempt, therefore, to fill this gap and to recover this important legacy within the Wesleyan tradition. It appears to be long overdue.

I am grateful to my wife, Janet, for her encouragement and patience while a host of early Methodist women have been a part of our family. I also express gratitude to my parents, the Reverend Virgil and Louise Chilcote, who have always inspired me by their commitment to that which is good, and true, and noble in life. They taught me to love my Methodist heritage while always pointing beyond it to the Lord of the Church. A special word of thanks to my daughter, Rebekah, and to my son, Jonathan, who in his death, has taught me more than years of reading ever could.

I stand in the debt of countless other persons in both American and British institutions who have assisted me in my research, guided my thinking, and critically examined my conclusions. Particular thanks are due to the staff members of Duke University Divinity School; Wesley College, Bristol; and the John Rylands Library, Manchester. Financial assistance by the Rotary International Foundation and A Foundation for Theological Education opened doors to the realization of some cherished dreams.

This study reflects the insights and thoughts of many along the way with whom I have discussed the various aspects of this complex theme. Primary among my guides is Dr. Frank Baker. I shall always be grateful for the opportunity of "sitting at his feet" and counting him a valued colleague. To Dr. Robert E. Cushman, theological mentor and friend, I am grateful for the essentially Wesleyan vision of faith seeking understanding. It is my hope that this study will aid in recovering a rich legacy of the Methodist tradition, which we, by and large, have lost. May it both enlarge our understanding and deepen our faith.

INTRODUCTION

THE MOST OBVIOUS REASON for studying the women preachers of early Methodism is that they are there.[1] There is no doubt that women helped to make the Methodist revival of the eighteenth century a powerful religious movement of enduring significance. The women preachers, in particular, exerted an influence which was at once practical and theological. The simple fact that John Wesley and many of the early Methodist leaders sanctioned, and even encouraged, some women to function as preachers under their supervision is striking. In spite of this fact, however, the role and influence of the women preachers of early Methodism have never been fully documented, nor has the unique contribution they made to the eighteenth-century revival of religion been fully appreciated.

WOMEN'S HISTORY

By the very nature of its topic this study represents a venture into the vast and relatively uncharted realm of women's history and is meant to be a contribution, both methodologically and substantively, to this new but increasingly significant area of research. It is only in the course of the past ten or fifteen years that historians have seriously begun to develop women's history as an independent field. As early as 1946, however, Mary Beard, in a monumental study of *Woman as Force in History,* asked herself whether the men who write history consider women something even less

1

important than subjects of men—exactly nothing.[2] Her
irrefutable conclusion was that in spite of their pervasive
influence, women had received vary scant attention from
historians. Today, the prediction of a contemporary re-
viewer, "that no sound historians of the future will neglect
the role of women, as was done in the past," seems closer to
fulfillment than ever before.[3]

"Sexism in historical writing," boldly charges Beth Rosen,
"is much like sexism in daily life. For the most part women
are made invisible."[4] The neglect of historians to recognize
the influence of women or to deal with issues related to the
lives of women is, in large measure, the function of their
ideas about historical significance and social definition. The
problem is twofold. First, historians have judged women by
how far they have participated in, or were allowed to enter,
the arena of traditional power; by how they have helped to
shape the course of political and economic events. Insofar as
women have lived outside this sphere of historical valuation,
they have remained invisible, that is, unimportant and
powerless.[5]

The second aspect of the problem is primarily sociological.

> Theoretical models of society that underlie and guide data
> collection and interpretation are structured in such a way that
> they consider women only insofar as they are attached—in
> some capacity or another—to men. Consequently, significant
> factors or events that pertain primarily to women are
> underrepresented or entirely ignored.[6]

In the writing of Methodist history this focus upon the male
is often manifested in the need to identify significant women
with their husbands.[7]

The male prerogative in the writing of history has
produced other problems as well. Primary among them is the
recovery and utilization of sources in the attempt to
reconstruct the past and even locate women. The marginality
of women has meant that the resources which normally exist
for the historian in a male-dominated culture simply do not
exist for the majority of women. This makes it very difficult
to judge the roles women have assumed and the influence

they have exerted. And with regard to many periods of history, as Berenice Carroll observes, "the very existence of written materials on a woman tells us that she was exceptional."[8]

In this regard, however, eighteenth- and early-nineteenth-century Methodism represents something of an exception, and this for two reasons in particular. First, a large amount of epistolary material is available regarding the early Methodist women, because the age was an age of correspondence.[9] The letters of the early Methodists abound with accounts of their conversions, spiritual experiences, and the progress of the work of evangelism in which some of the women played a major part.[10]

Secondly, Wesley encouraged the early Methodists, and required the leaders of the societies, to record their experiences in journals and diaries, again, for both personal and corporate use. Many of these early manuscript accounts are extant, and many more published in the pages of Wesley's *Arminian Magazine,* or reprinted from the magazine in collections such as Thomas Jackson's *Lives of the Early Methodist Preachers.* These types of resources make the lives of some of the early Methodists, and certainly that of John Wesley, the most fully documented of any age. But even here, with regard to the women, it is necessary to move with great caution, for those sources recorded by men often display a male bias and those written by women were preserved by a male-dominated cultural system.[11]

While the women preachers of early Methodism were by definition exceptional, this study is not intended to be yet another example of what Gerda Lerner has called "compensatory history," or an account of "woman worthies."[12] Far from being a history of exceptional, or even deviant women, the phenomenon of women preachers in the religious revival of the Wesleys represented a natural progression within the context of the Methodist societies. It was a logical extension as well of the Wesleyan theology of religious experience.

This study touches in some measure, therefore, on at least four main areas of women's historiography.[13] It is an institutional history of women in an organization; it is biographical insofar as it relates to the lives of important women; it is a history of ideas about women and their roles; and it is a social history of women in a particular time and place. It is a conscious step toward a more inclusive history of our past. By introducing the women preachers of early Methodism into our historical consciousness, therefore, it is hoped that the more richly textured historical picture which emerges will be beneficial to everyone.

Before we turn our attention directly upon the issue of women preachers in the Wesleyan revival, it will be necessary to examine the appearance of important precursors of these women in the English church, particularly among the various Puritan sects of the previous century, to evaluate the social and religious milieu of the eighteenth century within which they emerged, and to analyze the influence of women upon the life of John Wesley and his appreciation of the role of women in the life of the Church prior to the outbreak of the evangelical revival.

WOMEN PREACHERS IN ENGLAND PRIOR TO METHODISM

Ronald Knox, in his monumental if biased study of enthusiasm, observed that "from the Montanist movement onwards, the history of enthusiasm is largely a history of female emancipation."[14] Early Methodism, according to Knox, represented the ultimate manifestation of this recurring liberationist theme. Whether we agree with Knox's prejudices regarding enthusiasm or not, the fact remains clear that women have proclaimed the Good News they discovered in Christ since the earliest periods of the Church's history. The women preachers of early Methodism hardly represented a new phenomenon in the life of the Christian community, but their historical context and the dramatis personae of the movement made for a unique manifestation of the continuing ministry of women.

Limitations of space make it impossible to afford even the barest outline of the history of the "woman question" in the life of the Church. But a brief examination of the immediate precedents for the women preachers in England, especially during the seventeenth century, bears directly upon the later developments within Methodism. Moreover, the earlier experiences of sectarian women and memories of the previous century determined and conditioned the way in which the activities of the Methodist women, and the movement as a whole, were perceived by the society in general and the religious establishment in particular.

As early as the seventh century women had attained positions of prominence in the infant communities of Anglo-Saxon Christianity. One of the most outstanding of these early figures was Saint Hilda, abbess of Whitby, who in 659 founded a monastery for both men and women, was called "Mother" by all who knew her, and provided important leadership in that critical period of English history.[15] Later in the Middle Ages anticlerical movements tended to exalt the claims of laywomen as well as men, and there is some evidence of actual preaching, for example, by Lollard women.[16] The emphasis placed upon the value of the individual soul, the possibility of direct communion with God, and the reformers' doctrine of the priesthood of all believers rekindled the desire of women to exercise their spiritual gifts in the sixteenth century. Even Luther recognized the radical implications of these ideas and was led to admit, in his treatise on "The Misuse of the Mass," that under some exceptional circumstances, it would "be necessary for the women to preach."[17]

While references to women preachers during the early period of the Reformation are extremely isolated, the tradition of their prominence in the earlier heretical sects of medieval Christendom came to the surface once more with the birth of English Puritanism in the late sixteenth century. The Puritan movement, like the reforming tradition which preceded it and the evangelical revival which followed it, developed within the Anglican church as a means of restoring simplicity in worship, recapturing the spirit of primitive Christianity, and purifying abuses which had crept into the life of the church. Throughout the course of the chaotic seventeenth century, particularly during the period of the Commonwealth when such nonconforming groups as the Anabaptists, Brownists, Familists, Levellers, and Quakers proliferated in an era of boisterous sectarianism, such ideas as the freedom of thought, the believer's rights of conscience, and spiritual equality which had their roots in the Reformation, were pushed to their logical conclusions.[18]

These developments contributed greatly to the increased activity of women in these groups and led to the eventual acceptance of women preachers among many of the sectarian communities. An emphasis upon the conscience or inner spirit, coupled with a conviction of the present activity of the Holy Spirit in the life of the individual, placed in opposition to the institutional church or the letter of the spiritual law as the final seat of authority, led to the eventual overruling of both scriptural and societal prohibitions regarding women. In addition to this, as Geoffrey Nuttall has demonstrated, the rediscovered notion of the "gathered church" and of the importance of shared Christian experience were equally conducive to such an egalitarian ethos:

> The demand that candidates for church membership shall not only possess a personal and conscious Christian experience but be both able and willing to express it in words . . . was a *sine qua non* of any sharing in Church-state . . . . At a deeper level, we may again observe the charismatic assumption behind these exercises. The Holy Spirit who has brought men into a saving experience of Christ will also enable them to bear witness to it.[19]

The practical ramifications of these developments can be discerned clearly in the Puritan rediscovery of the practice of "prophesying."[20]

While John Goodwin simply defined prophesying as "the opening and interpreting the word of God by a proper gift of the Spirit for the work," it was more common for the early Puritan divines to differentiate this activity more clearly from preaching.[21] The Anglican apologist, Robert Baillie, in his *Dissvasive from the Errours of the Time,* affords a more precise definition of this gift as practiced among the Independents:

> About prophesying after Sermon, they are at a full agreement, permitting to any private man of the flock, or to any

> stranger whom they take to be gifted, publickly to expound
> and apply the Scripture, to pray and blesse the people.[22]

According to Nuttall, these prophesyings originated in the Puritan stronghold of Northampton at All Saints' Church in 1571.[23] The major characteristics of this activity of the "gifted brethren," as they were called, included biblical exposition and exegesis, testimony concerning personal Christian experience, and exhortation of the faithful, all of which generally followed the normal preaching.

John Robinson, pastor of the Pilgrim Fathers, affords the locus classicus for a discussion of this subject in his *People's Plea for the Exercise of Prophecy* of 1618.[24] The ends to be obtained through the exercise of this gift included the glorification of God, the development of spiritual gifts, preparation for the ministry, preservation of the purity of doctrine, clarification of doubtful issues, the edification of the church and the conversion of nonbelievers, and the solidarity of clergy and laity. In a later treatise Robinson defends this office by making reference to the Synod of Embden (1571), and demonstrates the egalitarian nature of this charismatic function:

> Into the fellowship of this work are to be admitted not only the
> ministers, but the teachers too, as also the elders and deacons,
> yea, even of the multitude *(ex ipsa plebe)*, which are willing to
> confer their gift received of God, to the common utility of the
> church.[25]

It was but a small step from any person *(ex ipsa plebe)* exercising the gift of prophecy in a service of worship to their entering the pulpit to preach in the more formal sense. And if unordained men were allowed to preach, the next logical step would be the preaching of women as well.[26]

It would appear that the practice of lay and women's preaching originated in Holland at the beginning of the seventeenth century, and it was through this connection that such activities were first reintroduced to England.[27] Arthur Lake, bishop of Bath and Wells, affords evidence regarding the activities of the earliest known English woman preacher in "A Sermon Preached at St. Cvthberts in Welles When

Certaine Persons Did Penance for Being at Conventicles Where a Woman Preached," sometime in the early 1620s.[28] In a letter of February 23, 1637/8, John Bramhall complained to the Archbishop of Canterbury, William Laud, concerning similar extravagancies: "In Mine owne diocess . . . I have had Anababtisticall prophetesses runne gaddinge upp and downe."[29]

Nothing can compare, however, with what took place when the sectaries returned to England in the 1640s. In addition to the famous exploits of Mrs. Attaway, who preached weekly at the General Baptist Church in Bell Alley in London, other women preachers, or "she-preachers" as they were often called, were discovered as far afield as the Holland district of Lincolnshire, as far north as Yorkshire, and in the southern shires as well.[30] Some of these women preached to as many as a thousand onlookers at a time.[31] As late as 1653, a certain "Theodoras" reports the preaching of a lady in a most unusual setting in a letter to Lord Conway:

> Here is start up an audacious virago (a feminine tub preacher) who last Sunday held forth about two hours together within our late Queen's mass chapel at Somerset House, in the Stroud, and has done, so there and elsewhere, divers Sabbath-days of late, who claps her Bible and *thumps the pulpit cushion* with almost as much confidence (I should have said impudence) as honest Hugh Peters himself![32]

The religious establishment, and the vast majority of the Nonconformists as well, regarded the preaching of women as a *reductio ad absurdum*. That such practices transgressed all social and religious conventions of that age John Vickers made abundantly clear in a treatise entitled *The Schismatick Sifted*. It infuriated him

> to see bold impudent housewives, without all womanly modesty, to take upon them (in the natural volubility of their tongues, and quick wits or strong memories only) to prate (not preach or prophesy) after a narrative or discoursing manner, an hour or more, and that most directly contrary to the Apostle's inhibitions.[33]

Some of the antagonistic attitudes exhibited by such opponents, however, were not unfounded. Christopher Hill, for instance, in his examination of the radical ideas which were current during this revolutionary period, observed:

> It seems indeed to have been perfectly simple for a couple to team up together and wander around the country, preaching and presumably depending on the hospitality of their co-religionists.[34]

Right belief, as well as a proper life-style, was something of a preoccupation for the Christian of the seventeenth century, and the common cry inevitably arose that the women preachers proclaim "many dangerous and false Doctrines."[35] The women preachers encountered scorn and abuse on almost every side.

There were voices, however, which spoke up in defense of women's preaching and the place of women in the Church. Samuel Torshell, for instance, in a book proclaiming *The Womans Glorie* (1645), maintained that there was no difference between men and women in the state of grace. "The soul," he exclaimed, "knows no difference of sex."[36] In one of John Rogers' greatest controversial writings, *Ohel or Beth-shemesh* (1653), he devotes an entire chapter to the question of the rights of women in the Church. In a concluding and characteristic passage, he admonishes the women to

> hold fast your liberty; keep your ground which Christ hath got and won for you, maintain your rights, defend your liberties even to the life; lose it not, but be courageous and keep it.[37]

It was the Society of Friends, or Quakers, however, that made the greatest progress toward the realization of sexual equality within the life of a religious community in the seventeenth century. Under the direction of George Fox, this group became the very embodiment of the rights of women to speak in public, to participate in decision-making processes, and to develop and use their gifts.

From its inception, Quakerism asserted the equality of

men and women in spiritual privilege and responsibility.[38] Since all Christians possess the Light of Christ within and are illumined by the Holy Spirit, they maintained that no one should be disqualified from speaking as that Spirit gave them utterance. Women, in fact, figured so prominently among the early Quakers that it was rumored the sect was exclusively female.[39] The first person to accept the views promulgated by Fox was a Baptist woman named Elizabeth Hooten, who in 1648 became the "first publisher of the truth," suffered imprisonment four times in England, and endured the indignities of the barbarous Cart and Whip Act of 1661 when she proclaimed her faith in Boston.[40] Women were also the first to preach the principles of Quakerism in London, at the English universities, in Dublin, and in the New World.[41]

George Fox and his followers stoutly defended the ministry of women by reference to such scriptural texts as Acts 2:17–18, 21:9; 1 Corinthians 11:5; and Joel 2:28–29, and maintained that the Pauline prohibitions were only "local and temporary conditions which have passed away."[42] Fox's *Epistles* resound with the apothegm that women are priests as much as men.[43] And in his famous treatise of 1656, *The Woman Learning in Silence,* Fox proclaimed:

> If *Christ* be in the Female as well as in the Male, is not he the same? And may not the Spirit of *Christ* speak in the Female as well as in the Male? Is he there to be limited? Who is it that dare limit the Holy one of Israel? For the Light is the same in the Male, and in the Female, which cometh from *Christ.*[44]

It was Margaret Fell, however, later to become Mrs. Fox, who produced the most persuasive apology for women's preaching in a small tract entitled *Womens Speaking Justified.*[45] This remarkable woman, correctly styled the "Mother of Quakerism," did more than any single individual to guide and shape the nascent Society of Friends.[46] As in the days of early Christianity when the homes of women often became the focal point for Christian fellowship, the homes of women became the first meeting places of Quaker worship, and Swarthmore Hall, the home of Margaret Fell, became the organizational center and later the world headquarters of the Society of Friends. It was not in this stately mansion, however, but in a Lancaster prison, that Margaret composed what has been called the "pioneer manifesto of women's liberation" in 1666.[47] *Womens Speaking Justified* is an able scriptural defense, not only of the right of women to speak as instruments of the Holy Spirit, but of their ability to participate fully in all aspects of religious life.

In spite of the strength of these convictions among many of the Quaker founders, there was a current of strong disapproval even among Fox's adherents.[48] And as recent studies have shown, the equality that generally obtained with regard to the ministry of men and women did not extend into all realms of life.[49] What is becoming increasingly clear is that Quakerism did not create individuality in women; rather it attracted women who were already autonomous, strong, and assertive.[50] What appealed to these women was the simplicity, the possibility of empowerment in the present moment, the opportunity for full participation, and the sense of adventure which characterized the early Quaker meetings.[51]

While the ministry of women was developed within Quakerism to an unprecedented degree, Fox and his followers were but "irrigating a channel already made."[52] There is no doubt that the activity of preaching taxed seventeenth-century feminine capacity to the utmost, but this is precisely what adds to its significance as a landmark in the movement for giving woman her true place of equal partnership with man.[53] The phenomenon of women's preaching in early Methodism reflects many of these same themes and exhibits strikingly similar characteristics, for which, as we have seen, there were plenty of precedents by Wesley's day, in the history of the Church.

THE SOCIAL AND RELIGIOUS MILIEU OF THE EIGHTEENTH CENTURY

The eighteenth century is most often depicted, at least in its beginnings, as a period of stability and order, the "age of conservatism."[54] By 1700 England had come through the great social upheavals of the Civil War period, had experienced a Glorious Revolution which created new conditions for the exercise of power, and was entering a new age of security. In retrospect, the previous century must have appeared a strange, violent, fanatical world. At the same time, however, the eighteenth century was most certainly an age of transition, a century in which momentous if subtle changes occurred within all the various aspects of English life. Herbert Butterfield, the late Cambridge historian, employed a powerful metaphor in order to capture the spirit of the age:

> One of the vivid impressions left by the history of eighteenth-century England is that of broadening sweep and gathering momentum. It is as though a wave, moving only slowly at first—lightly combing the face of the water—collected from the sea increasing power, and finally arched itself into a thunderous mass.[55]

One of the most vital aspects of this society in transition was the changing and increasing importance of women.[56] To a rather vocal majority the woman's only proper role was that of a dutiful and submissive adjunct to man. These women knew their place and kept it. Richard Steele, for example, whose appreciation for women was generally higher than that of his colleague, Joseph Addison, tersely summarizes the traditional, conservative ideal:

> We have indeed carried Women's Characters too much into public life . . . the utmost of a Woman's Character is contained in domestick life. . . . All she has to do in the World, is contained within the Duties of a Daughter, a Sister, a Wife, and a Mother.[57]

The Ultimate expression of this view came in 1797 with the publication of Thomas Gisbourne's *Enquiry into the Duties of the Female Sex*.[58] But the same sentiments appeared in many works throughout the course of the century, from the great poet Alexander Pope to the late-seventeenth-century pamphlet, *A Discourse of women, shewing their imperfec-*

tions alphabetically, translated from the French at the turn of the century.[59]

Critics of these traditional ideals and caricatures of womanhood were far from silent, however, for as new research is beginning to reveal, the spirit of feminism was irrepressible throughout the century.[60] Daniel Defoe, for instance, made clear his commitment to feminist reform and "argued, directly in his journalism and indirectly in his novels, that women had the capacity to be independent and should be given educational and economic opportunities to become so."[61] From the sophisticated pages of *The Nonsense of Common Sense,* in which Lady Montagu defended women as rational, long-suffering, and courageous creatures, to the anonymous pamphlets, such as *Beauty's Triumph: or, The superiority of the fair sex invincibly proved!* men and women alike were challenging the old conventions of feminine behavior. There is mounting evidence to support the view that "the traditional, conservative ideal of woman had less widespread support and more opposition in the eighteenth century than has been thought."[62] Several interrelated factors contributed to this increased interest in the position of women in society.

For one thing, many of the women of this period founded their hope for liberation in education. Mary Astell, considered by most to be the first English feminist, was the first to articulate this concern in a treatise entitled *A Serious Proposal to the Ladies* in 1694.[63] In this seminal work she advocates a "religious retirement" where women could be educated and given a respite from the social pressures of the world. Improved education naturally meant the opening up of new vistas for women and enabled them to become involved in traditionally male-dominated activities. In particular, women became writers and journalists, and constituted, for the first time in history, an important sector of the reading public.[64] The emergence of these new means of self-expression and employment was but one indicator of the monumental changes that were taking place in English society and leading to greater personal autonomy and self-respect for women.[65]

In 1792 Mary Wollstonecraft, the greatest symbol of

eighteenth-century feminism, published her famous *Vindication of the Rights of Women,* addressing the question of women's political involvement when the subject of human rights was much in the air.[66] The extremely radical nature of this document shocked many, male and female alike, and initiated an intense debate regarding the place of women in society. While the occasional radical feminist voice had failed to shake the stability of the first half of the eighteenth century, by the 1790s English people were beginning to feel the impact of other revolutionary forces, such as industrialization and political radicalism, which were inevitably changing English society.[67] Wollstonecraft's *Vindication,* and more particularly the popular reaction to it, reflects the increasing turbulence of an age in the process of transformation.

In addition to the industrial and political revolutions of the late eighteenth century, one of the greatest forces for change in England was the religious revival, generally known as "evangelicalism." The way in which this movement contributed to or retarded the advance of women in society is a subject of great debate. The positive interpretation advanced by such historians as Wearmouth, for instance,[68] must be placed alongside the antithetical conclusions of those who claim that "the leaders of evangelicalism firmly and clearly opposed the radical demands for equality of the sexes."[69] This negative evaluation is consonant with the tendency to depict Methodism as a counterrevolutionary force for which the maintenance of the status quo figured as a prominent characteristic.

Whether such an analysis is correct with regard to the evangelical movement as a whole, it is difficult to arrive at such a conclusion on the basis of a thorough examination of the material related to the early Methodist women preachers. The question of the liberating or repressing force exerted by religious communities in the lives of women is an extremely complex issue. In its relation to early Methodism it is bound up, not only with the peculiar religious situation of eighteenth-century England, but also with the person of John Wesley.

The quest for peace and moderation which typified English life in the first decades of the eighteenth century is reflected in the religious establishment by an elevation of common sense and a concomitant antipathy to any form of religious "enthusiasm." While religious excitement and the excesses it produced had become repugnant to many, it was the identification of sectarian zealots with the agents of revolution that struck the deepest fear in the hearts of the English people. Dryden succinctly stated this common sentiment in the famous quatrain:

> A numerous Host of dreaming saints succeed;
> Of the true old enthusiastic breed:
> 'Gainst form and order they their power employ
> Nothing to build and all things to destroy.[70]

This fear of civil and religious anarchy led to the ridicule and consequent suppression of the sectaries.

The Church of England had suffered greatly from the turmoil of the seventeenth century. Not only had it lost the Nonconformists on the left with the Act of Uniformity in 1662, but the Glorious Revolution of 1688/9 led to the secession of the Non-Jurors, including the Archbishop of Canterbury, and thereby a large portion of the right was lost as well. Because of these and other factors, the spiritual life of the church was almost moribund in the early eighteenth century, and in spite of many exceptions, the impression of general decay remains. One of the symptoms of this decline in religious fervor was the diminution in the practice of lay preaching.[71] And one consequence of these developments was the virtual disappearance of women preachers.

Even within the Society of Friends, wherein women had experienced the greatest amount of freedom and affirmation, there was marked decline in the activity of women by the beginning of the century. Arnold Lloyd has gone so far as to say that during this period Quaker women "did not enjoy equal status with the men. They had no share in the Yearly Meeting for discipline and took no active part in shaping the discipline."[72] A spirit of quietism pervaded the Society throughout the eighteenth century, entailing a gradual withdrawal from public life and an increasing emphasis upon individualistic piety. Toward the end of the century such quietists as Catherine Phillips and Rebecca Jones traveled extensively throughout the country, but they were exceptions to the rule.[73]

The one great exception to the dearth of women preachers in the early 1700s was May Drummond.[74] Celebrated by such an unlikely figure as Alexander Pope who declared that she "[outdid] Llandaff in doctrine, yea in life,"[75] she was a fluent speaker, and so popular that thousands of people representing numerous persuasions flocked to hear her preach. Crowds were so great at one Quaker meetinghouse that supports had to be added to the galleries to avert possible accident and injury. Numerous panegyrics concerning her life and work appeared throughout the century, the most noteworthy of which was a poem "by a young Lady" printed in the *Gentlemen's Magazine* in 1735:

> No more, O *Spain!* thy Saint *Teresa* boast;
> Here's one outshines her on the *British* coast,
> Whose soul like hers viewed one Almighty end,
> And to that centre all its motions tend,
> Too long indeed our sex, has been deny'd,
> And ridicul'd by men's malignant pride.[76]

Several exotic groups appeared from the end of the seventeenth to the beginning of the nineteenth centuries whose "prophetesses" exhibit striking similarities to the female shamans described by modern anthropology.[77] They are important, not as examples of female preachers—for their activities do not conform to their or this century's criteria for that function—but as charismatic visionaries and spiritual mediums whose experience stunned and often frightened their contemporaries. Moreover, it contributed to the prejudices of many against the public ministry of women.[78]

In 1706 a large group of French Protestants fleeing from persecution arrived in England and began proclaiming the fall of the Roman church. "French prophetesses," such as Betty Gray and "Pudding Pie Moll," aroused the fury of the London mob with their naked, violent orations and immoral conduct. Likewise millennialist groups, such as the Philadelphians founded by Mrs. Leade in 1696, the Shakers led by "Mother Jane" Wardley and Ann Lee, and the Millenarians who followed Joanna Southcott in the early 1800s, witnessed to the continued existence of such visionary strains within the religious communities of English society. All off-shoots of Quakerism, these latter groups became an embarrassment to and were discountenanced by the Society of Friends whose members recognized the inherent pathology of their actions.

WESLEY AND THE INFLUENCE OF WOMEN

Nothing could be further from this world of ecstatic prophetesses and irrational possessions than the restrained, ordered, methodical world of the Epworth rectory. And yet, it was here, in the disciplined environment of his home, that John Wesley received his first lessons concerning the abilities of women and their place in the life of the Church, and this primarily in the example of his mother, Susanna.

It is difficult to exaggerate the influence that Susanna Wesley exerted upon her sons and consequently upon the religious movement which they founded. The numerous studies of her life all draw attention to this important fact.[79] She is preeminently worthy of the title Mother of Methodism, not because derivative hagiography has claimed her as such, but because her pervasive influence is so clearly discernible when the accretions of myth and legend are stripped away. The essential aspects of her character and primary areas of her influence are expressed in Frank Baker's alliterative description of her as "Puritan, Parent, Pastor, Protagonist, Pattern."[80]

Susanna was a daughter of the Puritans, the youngest child in the large family of Samuel Annesley. She was schooled in solid piety by her father, the "Saint Paul of Nonconformity," and stimulated in her learning through frequent encounters with his erudite colleagues. However great the feminist tendency within the Puritan tradition or the impact of such radical personalities as Daniel Defoe upon her young mind, the fact is that "Susanna was what might now be called a liberated woman—because her father was a liberated man."[81] She drank deeply from the wells of English Nonconformity, carried its revolutionary spirit into her own home in spite of her conversion to Anglicanism, and inculcated it with varying degrees of success in the minds of her children.

It was the Puritan Richard Baxter who said that the "chief part of family care and government consisteth in the right education of children."[82] No mother was so indefatigable in her parental responsibilities as was Susanna. In a long letter to her son John, she expressed the extent of her maternal concern:

> There's few (if any) that would entirely devote above twenty years of the prime of life in hope to save the souls of their children (which they think may be saved without much ado); for that was my principle intention, however unskillfully and unsuccessfully managed.[83]

However arguable the theoretical principles of her childrearing practices, there is no doubt that her blending of maternal discipline and affection produced one of the most pious and best educated families in England.[84] Later Susanna would apply her own keen and critical intellect to the defense of her sons' evangelical theology.[85] Moreover, in her style of life, spiritual and intellectual disciplines, theological acumen, and ecclesiastical sensibility she was set forward as the paradigm of the Methodist woman for years to come.[86]

It is her role as pastor, however, that bears most directly upon the subject of this study, for Susanna Wesley represents, in a limited way, the major precursor of the early Methodist women preachers. John Wesley clearly recognized her contribution in this sphere, commenting on the occasion of her death that "even she (as well as her father and grandfather, her husband, and her three sons) had been, in her measure and degree, a preacher of righteousness."[87] She was not only the "priestess of her family," as Abel Stevens has described her, but her ministrations extended beyond the inner circle of the rectory to include the people of Epworth as well. The events which combined to transform private, family devotions into a "society" of the Epworth rectory forekitchen under the direction of the absent rector's wife are well known.[88] But these activities enforced certain principles in the mind of Susanna's impressionable son, not only regarding the nature of the Christian faith itself, but even more particularly concerning God's use of laywomen in the life of the Church and the proclamation of the gospel.

The development of Susanna Wesley's "society" and her activities as its leader bear a striking resemblance to the practices of sectarian women preachers in the previous century and prefigure later theological and practical developments within the Methodist societies as well. The Puritan emphases upon the sanctity of the inner conscience and the present activity of the Holy Spirit in the gradual unfolding of events stand as fundamental principles upon which Susanna's evolving notion of pastoral vocation were based. As early as 1702 she boldly proclaimed this protestant manifesto in a letter to Lady Yarborough: "I value neither reputation, friends, or anything, in comparison of the simple satisfaction of preserving a conscience void of offence towards God and man."[89]

Samuel's prolonged absences from home during the winter months of 1710/11 and 1711/12 intensified Susanna's sense of responsibility with regard to the spiritual nurture of her own family. "I cannot but look upon every soul you leave under my care," she advised her husband, "as a talent committed to me under a trust by the great Lord of all the families."[90] The exigency of her situation finally provided the impetus for a startling revelation:

> At last it came into my mind, though I am not a man, nor a minister of the gospel, and so cannot be engaged in such a worthy employment as they were, yet . . . I might do somewhat more than I do. . . . I might pray more for *the people,* and speak with more warmth to those with whom I have an opportunity of conversing. However, I resolved to begin with my own children.[91]

She thereafter began conducting Sunday evening prayers for her family, enlarged these gatherings when demand necessitated until they took the form of religious services, and continued to conduct her services of "public worship" for the thronging townspeople despite possible repercussions.[92]

The rector's inept and increasingly jealous curate, Inman, finally charged Susanna with conducting a clandestine conventicle and usurping the authority of her husband, which complaints eventually reached Samuel's ears. Susanna responded to Samuel's mild remonstrances by observing that while Inman's services attracted no more than twenty or twenty-five persons, her gatherings could boast between two and three hundred. Moreover, she could point to specific fruit as a product of her labors, to improved relationships among the townspeople, to increased fervor and desire for the things of God. She agreed with Samuel's criticism concerning the impropriety of a woman taking the lead in such matters within the life of the church, but saw no other course of action left open to her.

The strength of her convictions and the justification of her pastoral vocation were set forth in no uncertain terms in a final word to the rector;

> If you do, after all, think fit to dissolve this assembly, do not tell me that you desire me to do it, for that will not satisfy my conscience: but send me your *positive command,* in such full and express terms as may absolve me from all guilt and punishment for neglecting this opportunity of doing good when you and I shall appear before the great and awful tribunal of our Lord Jesus Christ.[93]

The rector wisely acquiesced to the unusual but highly successful practices of his wife which were renewing the religious life of that early society.

A special bond existed between John and his courageous mother.[94] While all of her children received close and affectionate attention, her discernment of John's special gifts and a heightened sense of destiny for this providentially preserved son eventually led to a unique resolution concerning him:

> I do intend to be more particularly careful of the soul of this child that thou hast so mercifully provided for, than ever I have been, that I may do my endeavour to instil into his mind the principles of thy true religion and virtue.[95]

It was only several months after forming this particular resolve that Susanna's call to the care of souls found enlarged expression in the religious services of the rectory. It is not too much to say that "here were sown some of the seeds which later matured into John Wesley's own Methodist societies and his somewhat grudging acceptance of women preachers."[96] It was largely owing to her influence that he seldom wavered in the conviction that no one, even a woman, ought to be prohibited from doing God's work in obedience to the inner calling of her conscience.

It was inevitable that the "femininity of his early environment," as V.H.H. Green has called it, would have abiding consequences in Wesley's life.[97] Alexander Knox, for instance, a distinguished contemporary and ardent churchman, recognized the way in which Wesley was particularly drawn to women:

> It is certain that Mr. Wesley had a predilection for the female character; partly, because he had a mind ever alive to amiability, and partly from his generally finding in females a quicker and fuller responsiveness to his own ideas of interior piety and affectionate devotion.[98]

It is unfortunate that the mention of John Wesley and women usually conjures up distorted images of a succession of abortive relationships, a bungled romance in Georgia, a tragic engagement with Grace Murray, all climaxing in a disastrous marriage to the psychotic widow, Mary Vazeille. A close examination of Wesley's life, however, reveals the erroneous nature of such an impression. On the contrary, it leads to the distinct conclusion that Wesley's relationships with women were both profound and extensive and are directly related to the impact that women were able to have on the Methodist movement.[99]

Women continued to figure prominently in Wesley's life once he left the bounds of his parental home. His relationships with women seem to have been stimulated by a mixture of natural interest and religious concern. While at Oxford he became acquainted with an intriguing circle of women whose friendship often drew him away from his studies into the

idyllic Cotswold countryside and the Stanton rectory.[100] Sally
Kirkham, affectionately known as "Varanese" within the
circle of friends, was certainly the "religious friend" mentioned in Wesley's *Journal*.[101] She became his spiritual
advisor and guide, directed him in his reading of Taylor and
à Kempis's devotional classics which subsequently formed his
view of the Christian life, and proved a great stimulus to the
awakening in him of a heightened sense of call to spiritual
service.

It was in Georgia, however, that Wesley conducted his
initial experiments in the use of women in the life of that
infant, colonial church.[102] The experimental missionary
instituted a number of religious practices, such as the use of
hymns, lay leaders, extemporaneous prayer and preaching,
all of which became prominent characteristics of the
evangelical revival in later years. One particularly controversial practice, which, like the others, was aimed at recapturing
the spirit of the primitive church, was the appointment of
"deaconesses."[103] A number of years later, when Wesley
published his *Explanatory Notes on the New Testament,* he
clearly described the function of such women in the early
church: "It was their office, not to teach publicly, but to visit
the sick, the women in particular, and to minister to them
both in their temporal and spiritual necessities."[104] Wesley
employed at least three women in the exercising of these
responsibilities: Margaret Bovey (afterward Mrs. James
Burnside), Mrs. Robert Gilbert, and Mrs. Mary Vanderplank.[105]

Wesley found precedent for the activities of these women
in two particular sources, both of which exerted a powerful
influence upon the young priest at this time, namely the
primitive church as rediscovered in the work of the
Non-Jurors, and the Moravians, a group of Lutheran pietists
whom Wesley first encountered en route to Georgia. The
radical Non-Jurors, to whom Wesley was indebted, based
their program for spiritual renewal upon the rediscovery of
Scripture as the authoritative source concerning the spirit
and life of the Christian community, and the *Apostolic
Constitutions* as the authoritative record of early church
practice which was universally and constantly received.[106]

Not only had the *Apostolic Constitutions* made provision for deaconesses,[107] but Thomas Deacon's *Compleat Collection of Devotions,* one of Wesley's constant companions in Georgia, contains a description of their duties:

> to assist in the baptism of women, to instruct (in private) children, and women who are preparing for baptism; to visit and attend women in the church, and to correct and rebuke those who behave themselves irregularly there.[108]

Likewise, the Moravian women discharged similar duties among their own sex, both in their newly established community in Georgia and in the Old World from which they had come.[109] One of the distinguishing marks of the Moravian communities was the systematic regimentation of their members involving a strict separation of the sexes. Separated in their communal life primarily "to obviate any disorder," this rule had the inevitable effect of developing the skills of women in the areas of pastoral leadership and oversight.[110] Women leaders were differentiated into various orders such as nurses, widows, deaconesses, and eldresses. The "chief eldress" who oversaw all the women was in a position of great power and influence.[111] Undoubtedly, Wesley learned much more about the employment of women in the church when he later made a pilgrimage to Herrnhut in order to experience firsthand their rediscovery of primitive Christianity.[112]

Women figure prominently in the events of 1738/39, from the famous "evangelical conversion" of May to the organization of "United Societies" directly under the care of John Wesley the following spring. Concerning one of the leaders of a society which had sprung up at Oxford, Wesley wrote: "Mrs. Fox is the very life and spirit (under God) of all the women here that seek our Lord."[113] When Thomas and Elizabeth Fox were anticipating a move from Oxford, Wesley wrote an impassioned letter to persuade them, but particularly Mrs. Fox, to remain:

> The reason against her going hence is as evident as it is weighty: we have no one here like-minded. . . . nor could the

enemy devise so likely a means of destroying the work which is just beginning among them as the taking away from their head.[114]

The great value Wesley placed upon the involvement of women in religious affairs may also be seen in his response to developments in London. When attempts were made to exclude women from some of the society's activities, he exclaimed to the leaders: "I do very exceedingly disapprove of the excluding women when we meet to pray, sing, and read the Scriptures."[115]

Much of Wesley's early appreciation for women's gifts and the utilization of these gifts in the life of the church can be traced to the influence of his mother, to the legacy of the Puritan tradition, to his rediscovery of the practices of the early church, and to his friendship with the Moravians. These factors contributed to the wider space for leadership afforded women in the Methodist societies which were formed later under the Wesleys' direction. The expansion of this leadership to include preaching raises a number of fundamental questions that will be addressed in the pages which follow.

Why is it that women tend to find enlarged opportunity for participation and service in the renewal movements of Christianity, of which the Methodist revival is a prime example? How is the tension between the authority of spiritual gifts or personal charisma and the authority of office or institution resolved with regard to the women preachers of early Methodism? How do the theological and historical dynamics of the Methodist movement enable female preachers to make valuable contributions to the religious revival of the eighteenth century? How does the phenomenon of institutionalization or bureaucratization, with its attendant reversion to patriarchal patterns of leadership, effect the ministry of women within the Methodist tradition?

All of these questions point to a central fact: In the expansion of the role of women within the Wesleyan revival to include the office of preaching and in the consequent developments and debates concerning that phenomenon, history, theology, personality, and ecclesiology combine. They are inextricably interwoven in such a way as to reflect the very nature of the Methodist movement as a whole and its unique position within the history of the Church.

NOTES

1. Dr. Donald G. Mathews ably defends this rationale for historical inquiry in a notable essay entitled "Women's History/Everyone's History," originally delivered as the closing keynote address at the first national conference on the study of Methodist women, convened by the General Commission on Archives and History of the United Methodist Church. It was subsequently published in Hilah F. Thomas and Rosemary Skinner Keller, eds., *Women in New Worlds: Historical Perspectives on the Wesleyan Tradition,* 2 vols. (Nashville: Abingdon Press, 1981), 1:29–47.
2. Mary R. Beard, *Woman as Force in History: A Study in Traditions and Realities* (New York: Macmillan, 1946).
3. R. A. Brown, "Review of Mary Beard's *Women as Force in History,*" *Christian Science Monitor,* April 17, 1946. Following mixed reviews in 1946, this work lay dormant for nearly a quarter of a century, only to be rediscovered through the impetus of the women's movement and was reprinted in 1971. See B. A. Carroll, "Mary Beard's *Woman as Force in History: A Critique,*" in *Liberating Women's History: Theoretical and Critical Essays,* ed. Berenice A. Carroll (Urbana: University of Illinois Press, 1976), pp. 21–46.
4. Beth Rosen, "Sexism in History or, Writing Women's History Is a Tricky Business," *Journal of Marriage and the Family* 33, 3(August 1971): 541. Cf. Dolores B. Schmidt and Earl R. Schmidt, "The Invisible Woman: The Historian as Professional Magician," in *Liberating Women's History,* ed. Carroll, pp. 42–54. For an example of how anonymity has frequently cloaked the contributions of women to the life of religious movements, see Stephen J. Stein, "A Note on Anne Dutton, Eighteenth-Century Evangelical," *Church History* 44, 4(December 1975): 485–91.
5. See A. D. Gordon, M. J. Burkle, and N. S. Dye, "The Problem of Woman's History," in *Liberating Women's History,* ed. Carroll, pp. 75–92; and Mathews, "Women's History/ Everyone's History," pp. 32–33.
6. Margrit Eichler and Carol Avin Nelson, "History and Historiography," *Historian* 40, 1(November 1977): 1.

7. One Methodist historian claims that "the male prerogative is obvious and sometimes insidious" and demonstrates how organs of the various Methodist organizations portray women primarily "as helpmates and dying pious deaths" (Frederick A. Norwood, *The Story of American Methodism* [New York: Abingdon Press, 1974], p. 350).

8. Carroll, *Liberating Women's History,* p.79.

9. See Wesley, *Oxford Edition,* 25:11–28.

10. Ibid., pp. 80–81, concerning the "letter-days" in the early societies. In the very early days of the evangelical revival, as Nehemiah Curnock observed, "Wesley read to the members books of devotion, the Bible, Christian biography, or, as at this period, sermons, thus giving to the conversation which followed a definite and instructive direction. But now, having written the story of his own conversion and various accounts of his personal experience, he induced others—converts in the societies—to write their experiences. Selections from these letters he read in the society-meetings" (Wesley, *Journal,* 2:113; cf. 3:348, 396, 485; 4:259; 6:3).

11. The evidence of such a bias may be illustrated by the exclusion of any reference to the preaching of Diana Thomas, a noted woman preacher of the early nineteenth century, in her biographical sketch published in the *Methodist Magazine.* See William Parlby, "Diana Thomas, of Kington, Lay Preacher in the Hereford Circuit, 1759–1821," *W.H.S.* 14, 5(March 1924): 110–11. Born at Brook Farm, Lyonshall, near Kingston, in 1759, Diana did not become a member of the Methodist Society until the turn of the century, began preaching sometime between 1805 and 1810, and therefore falls beyond the scope of this study. In 1809, however, she was authorized by the Quarterly Meeting and the superintendent to preach in the circuit. In her itinerations she rode thousands of miles on horseback throughout Wales and preached at Pembridge, Wonton, Presteigne, Earisland, Hay, Knighton, Llanvihangel, Ledbury, Ligwardine, Hereford, Clun, Duffrin, Brilley, Talgarth, Pentre, Llansomefried, Builth, Bishopscastle, Chickward, Lyonshall, Maylont, Chinton, Bayley Hill, the Gore, Rhayader, Aberystwyth, Machynlleth, and New Radnor, all of which are mentioned in her journal. See Leslie F. Church, *More about the Early Methodist People* (London: Epworth Press, 1949), p. 172.

12. Gerda Lerner, "Placing Women in History: A 1975 Perspective," in *Liberating Women's History,* ed. Carroll, p. 357.

13. Gordon, Bukle, and Dye, "The Problem of Woman's History," pp. 75–76.

14. Ronald A. Knox, *Enthusiasm: A Chapter in the History of Religion with Special Reference to the Seventeenth and Eighteenth Centuries* (Oxford: Oxford University Press, 1950), p. 140. Viewing this spirit of liberation as one of Methodism's greatest characteristics, Wearmouth claimed Wesley as the father of female emancipation. See Robert F. Wearmouth, *Methodism and the Common People of the Eighteenth Century* (London: Epworth Press, 1945), p. 223. Likewise, Bebb described the founder as "the most outstanding feminist of the eighteenth century" (E. Douglas Bebb, *Wesley: A Man with a Concern* [London: Epworth Press, 1950], p. 140). Cf. Walter Lyon Blease, *The Emancipation of English Woman* (London: Benjamin Blom, 1910), for a general history of this topic.

15. See Beda Venerabilis, *Bede's Ecclesiastical History of the English People,* ed. Bertram Colgrave and R.A.B. Mynors (Oxford: Clarendon Press, 1969), iii. 24–26; iv. 23. Cf. F. L. Cross, ed., *The Oxford Dictionary of the Christian Church* (London: Oxford University Press, 1969), p. 638; and Ida B. O'Malley, *Women in Subjection* (London: Duckworth, 1933), pp. 123–24.

16. Keith Thomas cites such references in the writings of Walter Brute in 1391 and William White in 1428. See "Women and the Civil War Sects," Past and Present 13(April 1958): 46, 58.

17. Martin Luther, *Luther's Works,* Jaroslav Pelikan and Helmut T. Lehmann, gen. eds., 53 vols. (Philadelphia: Fortress Press, 1967), 36:152. John Lambert was burned at the stake in England in 1538 after admitting to this view. See John Foxe, *The Acts and Monuments of John Foxe,* ed. George Townsend and Stephen Reed Cattley, 8 vols. (London: R. B. Seeley and W. Burnside, 1838), 5:207–8.

18. Several classic articles and monographs are of great value in the study of religious women during this period. See in particular Ethyn Morgan Williams, "Women Preachers in the Civil War," *Journal of Modern History* 1, 4(December 1929): 561–69; Thomas, "Women and Civil War Sects," pp. 42–62; Geofrey F. Nuttall, *The Holy Spirit in Puritan Faith and Experience* (Oxford: B. Blackwell, 1946), esp. chap. 5: "The *Inner Life of the Religious Societies of the Commonwealth* (London: Hodder and Stoughton, 1879), pp. 155–57, 341–46. Depending heavily upon these works is Sheila Rowbotham, *Hidden from History* (New York: Pantheon Books, 1974), pp. 8–12.

19. Geoffrey F. Nuttall, *Visible Saints: The Congregational Way, 1640–1660* (Oxford: B. Blackwell, 1957), p. 111.

20. See an erudite discussion of this practice in Nuttall, *Holy Spirit in Puritan Faith*, pp. 75–89.

21. John Goodwin, Πλήρωμα τὸ πνευματικόν, p. 348, cited in Nuttall, *Holy Spirit in Puritan Faith*, p. 75.

22. Robert Baillie, *A Dissvasive from the Errours of the Time* (London: Printed for Samuel Gellibrand, 1645), p. 118.

23. Nuttall, *Holy Spirit in Puritan Faith*, p. 76. It is interesting to note that this town had been a center of Lollard influence in the previous centuries.

24. John Robinson, *The Works of John Robinson, Pastor of the Pilgrim Fathers*, ed. Robert Ashton, 3 vols. (London: John Snow, 1851), 3:281–335. In this treatise Robinson says, with regard to the Pauline prohibitions of 1 Corinthians 14, that the apostle "in restraining women, shows his meaning to be ordinary, not extraordinary, prophesying; for women immediately, extraordinarily, and miraculously inspired, might speak without restraint. Exod. xv. 20; Judges iv. 4; Luke ii. 36; Acts ii. 17, 19" (p. 326).

25. John Robinson, *A Just and Necessary Apology of Certain Christians, No Less Contumeliously Than Commonly Called Brownists or Barrowists* (1625), in *Works,* 3:55, in chap. 8: "Of the Exercise of Prophecy," pp. 5–79. Cf. "On Prophesying and Preaching," in *Mr. Bernard's Dissuasions against Separation Considered,* in *Works,* 2:246–51.

26. This was, in fact, the natural sequence of events which led the Lord Mayor and aldermen of London to petition the House of Lords in January 1646 to prohibit such clandestine activities. It was not until December 1646 that the House of Commons took action against these "preachers," when by a vote of 105 to 57 they resolved that no person should preach or expound the Scriptures in any church, chapel, or other public house unless he be ordained in some Reformed church (*Journals of the House of Commons,* 5:22–23, 34, as cited by Williams, "Women Preachers in the Civil War," p. 564).

27. W. T. Whitley, "The Rise of Lay Preaching in Holland," *Transactions of the Congregational Historical Society* 5, 5(1912); 282–89. Women preachers had been common among the Anabaptists in Germany and the Low Countries as early as the 1520s.

28. Arthur Lake, *Sermons with Some Religious and Divine Meditations,* 3 vols. (London: Printed by W. Stansby for N.

Butler, 1629), 3:67–78. After distinguishing the roles of masters and scholars and enforcing that women have no license to function in the former capacity, Lake berates the penitent parishioners and exemplifies a typical attitude of the clergy: "Certainly you haue . . . shewed your selues vnworthy to be men, that could be so weake as to become Schollers to a woman; I cannot tell how better to resemble your humor, than to the distemperate appetite of girls that haue the Greene-sicknesse, their Parents prouide for them wholsome food, and they get into a corner and eat chalke, and coales, and such like trash: so you that may in the Chvrch haue graue and sound instructions for the comfort of your Soules, in Conuenticles feed vpon the raw, and vndigested meditations of an ignorant vsurping Prophetesse" (p. 78). He concludes his sermon by admonishing that "it is our greatest honour to observe Gods Order." T. G. Crippen tentatively identified this woman with Dorothy (née Kelly) Hazzard, a famous preacher of the Broadmead (Baptist) Church in Bristol. See "A Forgotten Chapter of Early Nonconformist History," *Transactions of the Congregational Historical Society* 1, 3(1902): 192–94. Cf. Leon McBeth, *Women in Baptist Life* (Nashville: Broadman Press, 1979), pp. 29–32. A. C. Underwood, *A History of the English Baptists* (London: Baptist Union Publication Department, 1947), a standard history of this tradition, is nearly silent with regard to the conspicuous contributions of women. On the opposite end of the ecclesiological spectrum from Lake, and yet in the very same vein, the great Bunyon once quipped concerning women: "If she worships in assemblies, her part is to hold her tongue, to learn in silence" (from "A Case of Conscience," quoted in Arnold Lloyd, *Quaker Social History, 1669-1738* [London: Longmans, Green, 1950], p. 107).

29. William E. Collins, *Typical English Churchmen from Parker to Maurice* (London: SPCK, 1902), p. 95.

30. A Puritan minister with Presbyterian sympathies named Thomas Edwards produced the most virulent attack against these women preachers in a diatribe entitled *Gangraena*, the first edition of which cataloged no fewer than 16 varieties of dangerous sectarians, 180 errors, and 28 pernicious practices, to which 34 errors were added in the enlarged edition of 1646. Edwards' works are one of the most important, if biased, sources regarding such women as Mrs. Attaway. See *The First and Second Part of Gangraena; or, A catalogue and discovery of many of the errors, heresies, blasphemies, and pernicious*

practices of the sectaries of this time, 2d ed., corrected and much enlarged, 2 vols. (London: Printed by T. R. and E. M. for Ralph Smith, 1646), 1:116–21, 138, 171; 2:8. A second invaluable source regarding these women was published anonymously in London in 1641 under the title, *A Discoverie of Six Women Preachers in Middlesex, Kent, Cambridgeshire, and Salisbury,* portions of which, in addition to Edwards, have been reprinted in Joyce L. Irwin, *Womanhood in Radical Protestantism, 1525–1675* (New York: Edwin Mellen Press, 1979), pp. 210–14, 214–22. Cf. Thomas, "Women and Civil War Sects," pp. 47, 58.

31. Edwards, *Gangraena,* 1:120.
32. *State Papers Uncalendared,* 813A, paper no. 77, 25 July 1653, as cited in Barclay, *Inner Life of Religious Societies,* p. 157. Barclay affords an interesting catalog of similar references to women preachers throughout this period.
33. Quoted in Julia O'Faolain and Laurel Martines, eds., *Not in God's Image: Women in History from the Greeks to the Victorians* (New York: Harper and Row, 1973), p. 264.
34. Christopher Hill, *The World Turned Upside Down: Radical Ideas during the English Revolution* (London: T. Smith, 1972), p. 255. Likewise, many feared the extremes to which the revolutionary notions propounded by the sects could go, as in 1650 when a "ranter" named Lawrence Clarkson preached a theory of complete sexual freedom. See N. Cohn, *The Pursuit of the Millennium* (London: Secker and Warburg, 1957), pp. 351–71. Cf. W.H.G. Armytage, *Heavens Below: Utopian Experiments in England, 1560–1960* (London: Routledge and Kegan Paul, 1961), chap. 1–3 in particular.
35. Edwards, *Gangraena,* 1:121. Edwards, a staunch Calvinist, criticized the preaching of Mrs. Attaway for its blatant universalism.
36. Quoted in Hill, *World Turned Upside Down,* p. 251.
37. John Rogers, *Ohel or Beth-shemesh. A Tabernacle for the Sun; or, Irenicum Evangelicum, an Idea of Church Discipline* (London: R. I. and G. and H. Eversden, 1653), II. viii. Cf. Edward Rogers, *Some Account of the Life and Opinions of a Fifth-Monarchy-Man. Chiefly Extracted from the Writings of John Rogers, Preacher* (London: Longmans, Green, Reader, and Byer, 1867), pp. 68–70. In 1921 T. G. Crippen discovered a hitherto unknown and fascinating pamphlet from this period entitled *The Females Advocate: Or, An Essay to Prove that the Sisters in every Church of Christ, have a Right to Church-*

Government as well as the Brethren, undated and published anonymously, which addresses itself directly to the Pauline prohibitions in 1 Corinthians 14 and 1 Timothy 2. See T. G. Crippen, "The Females Advocate," *Transactions of the Congregational Historical Society* 8, 2(1921): 96–101.

38. On the place of women in the Society of Friends, see Mabel R. Brailsford, *Quaker Women* (London: Duckworth, 1915); William C. Braithwaite's two classic studies, *The Beginnings of Quakerism* (London: Macmillan, 1912), pp. 12, 44, 157–58, 199–200, 207, 376, 402; and *The Second Period of Quakerism* (London: Macmillan, 1919), pp. 270–87; and Hope Elizabeth Luder, *Women and Quakerism* (Wallingford, Pa.: Pendle Hill, 1974), pp. 11–19.

39. *Clarendon State Papers,* II, p. 323, as cited in Thomas, "Women and Civil War Sects," p. 59.

40. The only biography of Hooten is Emily Manners, *Elizabeth Hooten: First Quaker Woman Preacher* (London: Headley Brothers, 1914), but information concerning her life may be culled from George Fox, *The Journal of George Fox,* ed. Norman Penney, 2 vols. (Cambridge: At the University Press, 1911), 2:32, 463–64; Lloyd, *Quaker Social History,* pp. 108–9; and Ernest E. Taylor, *The Valiant Sixty,* rev. ed. (London: Bannisdale Press, 1951), pp. 39–41.

41. For the pioneering work of women in the spread of Quakerism, see Norman Penney, ed., *"The First Publishers of Truth." Being Early Records (Now First Printed) of the Introduction of Quakerism into the Countries of England and Wales* (London: Headley Brothers, 1907), pp. 79, 209, 219, 244–63. E. E. Taylor identified 8 women preachers of the original 70 publishers of truth in an article entitled "The First Publishers of Truth: A Study," *Journal of the Friends Historical Society* 19 (1922): 66–81. In his *Valiant Sixty,* 4 women's names were added to a reduced list of 66 early preachers (see pp. 40–41, 64–66). The most well known of the early Quaker missionaries was Mary Fisher whose travels took her to the American colonies and in 1658 to Turkey. That women took a share with men in the expanding work of the Society is confirmed by the fact that more than a quarter of the earliest preachers were women. Cf. Geoffrey F. Nuttall, *Studies in Christian Enthusiasm: Illustrated from Early Quakerism* (Wallingford, Pa.: Pendle Hill, 1948), pp. 19–22; Braithwaite, *Beginnings of Quakerism,* pp. 157–58, 207, 402; and Robert J. Leach, *Women Ministers: A Quaker Contribution* (Wallingford, Pa.: Pendle Hill, 1979).

42. See Penney's note, quoting the Quaker theologian, Rowntree, in Fox, *Journal,* 2:463.

43. George Fox, *A Collection of Many Select and Christian Epistles, Letters and Testimonies* (London: Printed and Sold by T. Sowle, 1698), pp. 6, 31, 323, 372. Cf. O'Faolain and Martines, *Not in God's Image,* pp. 265–66.

44. George Fox, *Gospel-Truth Demonstrated, In a Collection of Doctrinal Books* (London: Printed and Sold by T. Sowle, 1706), p. 81; cf. 331, 340, 463, 895.

45. Margaret Fell, *Womens Speaking Justified, Proved and Allowed of by the SCRIPTURES, . . . And how WOMEN were the first that preached the Tidings of the Resurrection of JESUS* (London: Printed in the Year 1666). Cf. her *Touch-stone; or, A Perfect Tryal by the Scriptures* (London: Printed in the Year 1667), being a diatribe against ecclesiastical abuses.

46. See Isabel Ross, *Margaret Fell: Mother of Quakerism* (London: Longmans, Green, 1949), for an excellent and readable account of her life.

47. Leach, *Women Ministers,* p. 8.

48. See Barclay, *Inner Life of Religious Societies,* pp. 344–46.

49. Leach, *Women Ministers,* p. 12.

50. See the penetrating analysis of the Quaker historian Elise Boulding in her *Underside of History: A View of Women through Time* (Boulder, Colo.: Westview Press, 1976), pp. 556–63, 578–83.

51. These four aspects of Quaker spirituality are delineated in Elaine C. Huber, "'A Woman Must Not Speak': Quaker Women in the English Left Wing," in *Women of Spirit: Female Leadership in the Jewish and Christian Traditions,* ed. Rosemary Ruether and Eleanor McLaughlin (New York: Simon and Schuster, 1979), pp. 153–81.

52. Nuttall, *Holy Spirit in Puritan Faith,* pp. 87–89.

53. See this analysis in Braithwaite, *Second Period of Quakerism,* p. 274.

54. For an example of various approaches to interpreting eighteenth-century English society, see in particular Dorothy Marshall, *Eighteenth-Century England* (New York: David McKay, 1962), pp. 29–37; J. H. Whitley, *Wesley's England: A Survey of Eighteenth-Century Social and Cultural Conditions* (London: Epworth Press, 1938), pp. 27–58, 135–60; J. H. Plumb, *England in the Eighteenth Century* (Harmondsworth: Penguin Books, 1953); A. S. Turberville, ed., *Johnson's England: An Account of the Life and Manners of His Age,* 2

vols. (Oxford: Clarendon Press, 1933), 1:1–38, 224–60, 300–335; and Basil Williams, *The Whig Supremacy, 1714–1760* (Oxford: Clarendon Press, 1939), pp. 123–43.

55. Herbert Butterfield, "England in the Eighteenth Century," in *A History of the Methodist Church in Great Britain,* ed. Rupert Davies and E. Gordon Rupp, 4 vols. (London: Epworth Press, 1965–88), 1:23–24.

56. While the topic of eighteenth-century English women has been largely ignored by scholars of the recent past and is just beginning to be developed as an important area of inquiry, several recent studies and a number of older articles and monographs are instructive. See the excellent bibliographical and interpretive essay by Barbara B. Schnorrenberg, "The Eighteenth-Century Englishwoman," in *The Women of England from Anglo-Saxon Times to the Present: Interpretive Bibliographical Essays,* ed. Barbara Kanner (London: Mansell, 1980), pp. 183–228. Cf. Paul Fritz and Richard Morton, eds., *Women in the Eighteenth Century and Other Essays* (Toronto: Samuel Stevens Hakkert, 1976), esp. pp. 73–77, 87–88; Beard, *Woman as Force in History,* pp. 195–203, 320–32; Doris Mary Stenton, *The English Woman in History* (London: Allen and Unwin, 1957), pp. 150–85; and Margaret Phillips and W. S. Tomkinson, *English Women in Life and Letters* (New York: Oxford University Press, 1927), pp. 99–298.

57. *The Spectator* 342 (April 2, 1712), as quoted in Rae Blanchard, "Richard Steele and the Status of Women," *Studies in Philology* 26 (1929): 354. Cf. *Spectators* 4, 10, 85. Samuel Wesley, Jr., John's older brother, reflected this prevalent attitude among the clergy in a lengthy poem entitled "The Battle of the Sexes," subsequently published in *Poems on Several Occasions,* 2d ed., with additions (Cambridge: Printed by J. Benthan, 1743), pp. 15–40.

58. Thomas Gisbourne, *An Enquiry into the Duties of the Female Sex,* 5th ed. (London: Printed by A. Strahan for T. Cadell, Jr., and W. Davies, 1801).

59. See Robert Halsband, "Women and Literature in Eighteenth-Century England," in *Women in the Eighteenth Century,* ed. Fritz and Morton, p. 56.

60. Miriam J. Benkovitz, "Some Observations on Woman's Concept of Self in the Eighteenth Century," in ibid., pp. 37–54.

61. Katherine Rogers, "The Feminism of Daniel Defoe," in ibid.,

p. 3. Contemporary novelists, such as Samuel Richardson and Henry Fielding, exhibited similar concern for the status of women in the society. See Schnorrenberg, "The Eighteenth-Century Englishwoman," p. 190.

62. Jean E. Hunter, "The Eighteenth-Century Englishwoman: According to the *Gentleman's Magazine*," in *Women in the Eighteenth Century,* ed. Fritz and Morton, p. 87.

63. Mary Astell, *A Serious Proposal to the Ladies, for the Advancement of their True and Greatest Interest. By a Lover of Her Sex* (London: Printed for R. Wilkin, 1694). Her *Essay in Defence of the Female Sex. In Which are Inserted the Characters of a Pedant, a Squire, a Beau, a Vertuoso, a Poetaster, a City-Critick, & c.* (London: Printed for A. Roper and E. Wilkinform, and R. Clavel, 1696) is considered to be the first avowedly feminist tract in the English language. For an account of her life, see Florence M. Smith, *Mary Astell, 1666–1739* (New York: Columbia University Press, 1916); and "Mary Astell: A Seventeenth-Century Advocate for Women," *Westminister Review* 149 (January-June 1898): 440–49. It is of great interest to note that the *Proposal,* introduced to John Wesley by Sally Chapone, sparked his lifelong dedication to female education. See Wesley, *Oxford Edition,* 25:285, 286, 289, 301, 316–17. Wesley published his own "Female Course of Study" in the *Arm. Mag.* 3 (1780): 602–4.

64. Robert Halsband has gone so far as to say that the majority of novels published in the eighteenth century were written by women. See "Women and Literature," p. 64.

65. In addition to these factors, Barbara Schnorrenberg addresses the question of significant changes in attitudes about marriage, the family, and law, all of which indicate the century, in "The Eighteenth-Century Englishwoman," pp. 191–198.

66. Mary Wollstonecraft, *A Vindication of the Rights of Women: With Strictures on Political and Moral Subjects* (London: Printed for J. Johnson, 1792). The many biographies on this important figure are judiciously examined in Janet M. Todd, "The Biographies of Mary Wollstonecraft: Review Essay," *Signs: Journal of Women in Culture and Society* 1 (1976): 721–34. Cf. Ellen Moers, "Vindicating Mary Wollstonecraft," *New York Review of Books* 23 (1976): 38–42; O'Malley, *Women in Subjection,* pp. 15–122; and Boulding, *Underside of History,* pp. 580–81.

67. The most important analysis of the impact of industrialization

on the lives of women is Ivy Pinchbeck, *Women Workers in the Industrial Revolution, 1750–1850* (London: Routledge, 1930). For important background material, see Alice Clark, *Working Life of Women in the Seventeenth Century* (New York: E. P. Dutton, 1919), for which there is no equal. In spite of the fact that the French Revolution failed to embrace the feminist program, it was almost inevitable that contemporaries would identify the political statement of feminism with such dangerous, revolutionary ideas. See Schnorrenberg, "The Eighteenth-Century Englishwoman," pp. 201–2.

68. See p. 4 above.

69. Schnorrenberg, "The Eighteenth-Century Englishwoman," p. 199. The relation of the Methodist movement to the changing social order of the eighteenth century is a much controverted issue. Some have argued that the evangelical revival under the leadership of Wesley was effective in bringing about a significant transformation of the English social structure. See Elie Halévy, *England in 1815* (London: E. Benn, 1949), which presents the view that Methodism saved Britain from revolution, and a republication of this thesis in Bernard Semmel. *The Methodist Revolution* (New York: Basic Books, 1973). The most illuminating discussion of the so-called Halévy thesis is afforded in Elie Halévy, *The Birth of Methodism in England,* trans. Bernard Semmel (Chicago: University of Chicago Press, 1971), pp. 1–29. The contrary point of view, maintaining that Wesley and his followers were social conservatives, resisted change, helped to maintain the status quo, and thereby prevented radical social transformation such as was experienced in France, is defended by E. P. Thompson, *The Making of the English Working Class* (New York: Pantheon Books, 1964), and H. E. Hobshawn, *Labouring Men: Studies in the History of Labour* (New York: Basic Books, 1964), esp. pp. 23–33. Cf. J.H.S. Kent, "M. Elie Halévy on Methodism," *W.H.S.* 29, 4 (December 1953): 84–91.

70. *Absalom and Achitophel,* ll. 529–32.

71. An excellent study of this topic has been conducted by J. H. Blackmore, in "Lay Preaching in England from the Reformation to the Rise of Methodism: A Study in Its Development, Nature and Significance" (Ph.D. diss. University of Edinburgh, 1951).

72. Lloyd, *Quaker Social History,* p. 118.

73. Leach, *Women Ministers,* p. 15.

74. For a brief sketch of her life, see William F. Miller, "Episodes

in the Life of May Drummond," *Journal of the Friends Historical Society* 4 (1907): 55–61, 103–14. Cf. Stephen Hobhouse, *William Law and Eighteenth-Century Quakerism* (London: George Allen and Unwin, 1927), pp. 72–75.

75. *Epilogue to the Satires, Dialogue I,* ll. 133–34, in Alexander Pope, *The Poems of Alexander Pope,* gen. ed. John Butt, 11 vols. (New Haven: Yale University Press, 1939–69), 4:308.

76. *The Gentlemen's Magazine: Or, Monthly Intelligencer* 5, 9(September 1735): 555.

77. See I. M. Lewis, *Ecstatic Religion: An Anthropological Study of Spirit Possession and Shamanism* (Harmondsworth: Pelican Books, 1971).

78. On these sects, see Rowbotham, *Hidden from History,* pp. 16–18; and Boulding, *Underside of History,* pp. 582–83.

79. A judicious summary of the biographical material related to her life is provided in John A. Newton, "Susanna Wesley (1669–1742): A Bibliographical Survey," *W.H.S.* 37 (June 1969): 37–41. The most thoroughly documented and incisive study of Susanna is John A. Newton, *Susanna Wesley and the Puritan Tradition in Methodism* (London: Epworth Press, 1968), which ought to be supplemented by the most outstanding popular biography by Rebecca Lamar Harmon, *Susanna, Mother of the Wesleys* (Nashville: Abingdon Press, 1968). These two volumes, taken together, afford more rich detail regarding Susanna's life and are more perceptive with regard to the historical and theological milieu of her day than any of the lives that preceded them. It is surprising that the first complete life of Susanna to be printed, that of John Kirk, *The Mother of the Wesleys: A Biography* (London: H. J. Tresidder, sold by J. Mason, 1864), did not appear until 122 years after her death. Adam Clarke afforded a brief sketch of her life in his *Memoirs of the Wesley Family,* which was originally published in 1832, revised, corrected, and considerably enlarged in 1836 (4th ed., enlarged, 2 vols. [London: W. Tegg, 1860]). Cf. Eliza Clarke, *Susanna Wesley* (Boston: Roberts Brothers, 1891), originally published in 1876; Mabel R. Brailsford, *Susanna Wesley: The Mother of Methodism* (London: Epworth Press, 1938); and G. J. Stevenson, *Memorials of the Wesley Family* (London: S. W. Partridge, 1876).

80. Frank Baker, "Susanna Wesley: Puritan, Parent, Pastor, Protagonist, Pattern," in *Women in New Worlds,* ed. Keller, Queen, and Thomas, 2:112–31. Cf. his "Salute to Susanna," *Methodist History* 7, 3(April 1969): 3–12.

81. Baker, "Susanna Wesley," p. 113. Cf. Newton, *Susanna Wesley and Puritan Tradition*, pp. 19–64; Clarke, *Memoirs of the Wesley Family*, 1:396–98. While the Annesley family was Presbyterian, and therefore of a more conservative persuasion with regard to practices within the church, their home was undoubtedly permeated with the spirit of independence and freedom of thought which characterized the Puritan ethos.

82. Quoted in Newton, *Susanna Wesley and Puritan Tradition*, p. 97.

83. February 21, 1731/2, Wesley, *Oxford Edition*, 25:327. Cf. *Meth. Mag.* 66 (1844): 817–19.

84. On her principles of education and family life, see Wesley, *Journal*, 3:32–39; Wesley, *Oxford Edition*, 25:326–27, 330–31; *Arm. Mag.* 1 (1784): 462–64; and Wesley, *Works*, 7:76–116. The most influential work on education throughout the eighteenth century was John Locke's *Some Thoughts Concerning Education* (London: n.p., 1693), to which Susanna was greatly indebted. Cf. Newton, *Susanna Wesley and Puritan Tradition*, pp. 97–129; and Harmon, *Susanna, Mother of the Wesleys*, pp. 55–65.

85. See Frank Baker, "Susanna Wesley, Apologist for Methodism," *W.H.S.* 35, 3(September 1965): 68–71, concerning her tract entitled *Some Remarks on a Letter from the Reverend Mr. Whitefield to the Reverend Mr. Wesley, in a Letter from a Gentlewoman to her Friend* (London: Printed for John Wesley, 1741).

86. See Baker, "Susanna Wesley," pp. 127–31. Cf. Taft, *Holy Women*, 1:13–18; and Abel Stevens, *The Women of Methodism: Its Three Foundresses, Susanna Wesley, the Countess of Huntingdon, and Barbara Heck* (New York: Published by Carlton and Porter, 1866), pp. 23–55.

87. Wesley, *Journal*, 3:32.

88. The most careful reconstruction and thorough analysis of Susanna's pastoral activities in Epworth, based upon a variety of primary documents, is Baker, "Susanna Wesley," pp. 119–25. Of critical importance are the records afforded by John Whitehead, *The Life of the Rev. John Wesley*, 2 vols. (London: Couchman, 1793, 1796), 1:45–54; and Wesley, *Journal*, 3:32–34. Cf. Clarke, *Memoirs of the Wesley Family*, 2:88–98; Kirk, *Mother of the Wesleys*, pp. 256–65; Harmon, *Susanna, Mother of the Wesleys*, pp. 77–80; Frank Baker, *John Wesley and the Church of England*, pp. 8–10, 342; and O'Malley, *Women in Subjection*, pp. 128–32.

89. Susanna Wesley to Lady Yarborough, March 7, 1702, quoted in Robert Walmsley, "John Wesley's Parents: Quarrel and Reconciliation," *W.H.S.* 29, 3(September 1953): 52. This series of Susanna's letters was published originally in the *Manchester Guardian* on July 2–3, 1953, and subsequently referred to with frequent quotation in Newton, *Susanna Wesley and Puritan Tradition*, pp. 88–93.
90. Susanna Wesley to Samuel Wesley, February 6, 1712, as quoted in Wesley, *Journal*, 3:32.
91. Whitehead, *Life of John Wesley*, 1:47–48, affording a fuller version of the original than that which was edited for publication in Wesley, *Journal*, 3:33.
92. See Whitehead, pp. 48–50, wherein Susanna refers to these complete services in a letter to her husband of February 25, 1712. In these services the Order for Evening Prayer was used as a basic format for the examination of Scripture and comment upon selected "awakening sermons" culled from Samuel's library.
93. Whitehead, *Life of John Wesley*, 1:54.
94. The facts surrounding John's birth, the importance of spacing and birth order, the traumatic event of the rectory fire and John's dramatic rescue, and the special attention given "Jackie" who remained in Susanna's care during the rebuilding of the parsonage, all contributed to the special relationship of mother and son. In *John Wesley and Authority: A Psychological Perspective,* American Academy of Religion Dissertation Series, no. 29 (Missoula, Mont.: Scholars Press, 1979), Robert L. Moore attempts to demonstrate how "patterns of authority relations" affected Wesley's search for selfhood, the development of his theology, and his institutional relationships. Based upon the model of Erik Erikson's psychoanalytic ego psychology, Moore's work flounders in terms of historical methodology and the critical examination of sources. Such psychohistorical research will proceed with greater success, however, as a better critical basis for this scholarship is provided in additional volumes of the definitive *Bicentennial Edition* of Wesley's works.
95. Susanna Wesley, MS Journal, May 17, 1711, Wesley College, Bristol, England. Cf. the citation of Henry Moore, *The Life of the Rev. John Wesley, A.M.,* 2 vols. (London: Kershaw, 1824–25), 1:112. Susanna was always John's closest spiritual advisor. Nowhere is her formative influence revealed more clearly than in the Oxford don's letter seeking the advice of his

mentor in the faith: "If you can spare me only that little part of Thursday evening which you formerly bestowed upon me in another manner, I doubt not but it would be useful now for correcting my heart as it was then for the forming my judgment" (John Wesley to Susanna Wesley, February 28, 1731/2, Wesley, *Oxford Edition,* 25:329).

96. Baker, "Salute to Susanna," p. 10.

97. V.H.H. Green, *The Young Mr. Wesley: A Study of John Wesley and Oxford* (London: Arnold, 1961), pp. 53–54.

98. Printed in Robert Southey, *The Life of Wesley: and the Rise and Progress of Methodism,* new ed., 2 vols. (London: Longman, Green, Longman, Roberts, and Green, 1864), 2:295. Wesley's sister, Hetty, once claimed that her brother liked a woman "merely for being a woman" (cited in Green, *Young Mr. Wesley,* p. 210).

99. This fact may be illustrated by the extent and nature of Wesley's correspondence with women. Frank Baker, editor of the definitive edition of Wesley's letters, comments that "the number of these favoured women correspondents, in a masculine world, serves to emphasize the way in which Wesley was sensitive to the feminine mystique, appreciated female achievements, and encouraged the leadership of women in his societies" (Wesley, *Oxford Edition,* 25:87). These correspondents were characterized by their strong dedication to personal spirituality and alliance to the Methodist societies, their regular engagement in practical religious services, their thoughtfulness, intelligence, and teachability.

100. Wesley was introduced to these women through Robert Kirkham of Merton College, Oxford, a member of the "Holy Club," whose father, the Rev. Lionel Kirkham, was rector of Stanton (Gloucestershire), and whose two sisters, Sally and Betty, figured priminently in the intimate fellowship. The most thoroughly documented study of Wesley during this formative period of his life,wherein his relationships with the Granville and Kirkham families is discussed, is Richard P. Heitzenrater, "John Wesley and the Oxford Methodists, 1725–1735" (Ph.D. diss., Duke University, 1972), pp. 67–68, 112–17. Cf. Green, *Young Mr. Wesley,* pp. 202–26; and Maldwyn Edwards, *My Dear Sister: The Story of John Wesley and the Women in His Life* (Manchester: Penwork [Leeds], n.d.), pp. 18–24.

101. In his brief autobiographical statement, the writing of which was occasioned by the events of May 24, 1738, Wesley writes

concerning the year 1725: "Meeting likewise with a religious friend, which I never had till now, I began to alter the whole form of my conversation, and to set in earnest upon a new life" (Wesley, *Journal,* 1:467). Elsie Harrison afforded incontrovertible evidence that this "religious friend," commonly identified with Betty Kirkham (see Wesley, *Journal,* 1:12–16, 20–28, 52–53), was in fact her sister, Sally (*Son to Susanna: The Private Life of John Wesley* [London: Nicholson and Watson, 1937], p. 66). Wesley later marked April 14, 1725, the day he first met Sally ("Met V[aranese]!") as a red-letter day. See Baker, *John Wesley and the Church of England,* pp. 16–17; cf. Green, *Young Mr. Wesley,* p. 206.

102. As early as February 1733 Wesley was overseeing the activities of a "methodist" group of Oxford townspeople that met at the home of a Miss Potter. By the end of that year, however, the society had become either defunct or independent, and there is no evidence to determine the way in which women were functioning within this group. It is also interesting to note that in his diary, throughout his lifetime, Wesley almost invariably identified such groups by the name of the woman at whose house the meetings were generally held, even if the husband was present and an active member of the assembly. See Heitzenrater, "John Wesley and Oxford Methodists," pp. 212–13, 244, 290, 341. Cf. the letter of John Clayton to John Wesley, September 10, 1733, and the note, in Wesley, *Oxford Edition,* 25:356. For a terse analysis of Wesley's Georgia experience, see William R. Cannon, "John Wesley's Years in Georgia," *Methodist History* 1, 4(July 1963): 1–7.

103. Patrick Tailfer, in his *True and Historical Narrative of the Colony of Georgia,* listed a number of indictments against Wesley by which "all persons of any consideration came to look upon him as a Roman Catholic" (Charleston: n.p., 1741). The third confirmation of this suspicion included his "appointing Deaconesses, with sundry other innovations, which he called Apostolic Constitutions." See Wesley, *Journal,* 1:296; 8:304–7. Cf. Luke Tyerman, *The Life and Times of the Rev. John Wesley, M.A.,* 3 vols. (London: Hodder and Stoughton, 1870–71), 1:147; John Simon, *John Wesley and the Religious Societies* (London: Epworth Press, 1921), pp. 148, 154, 164; and Baker, *John Wesley and the Church of England,* pp. 45, 355.

104. Wesley, *Notes,* Romans 16:1.

105. Wesley, *Journal,* 1:239–46, 272, 276, 314, 329, 337, 364–69, 376, 387. Of Miss Bovey, Wesley wrote: "Here is one woman in America in whom to this day I have found no guile" (1:314). References to Mrs. Gilbert include 1:274, 279, 319, 320, 355, 370. See 1:243, 343, 387, for Mrs. Vanderplank. Regarding these women and their office, see Baker, *John Wesley and the Church of England,* pp. 51, 358. When Charles Wesley hastily returned to England, John found it increasingly necessary to utilize the services of laymen and these women in the pastoral oversight of his unwieldy parish.

106. Wesley, in his studies at Oxford, had benefited from the patristic renaissance of the previous generation. Through John Clayton, tutor of Brasenose College, Oxford, and a devout member of the Holy Club, he was introduced to a radical wing within the Non-Jurors led by Thomas Deacon of Manchester. Wesley naturally warmed to this group and made a particular study of the writings of the Non-Juring divines. See A. W. Harrison, "Wesley's Reading during the Voyage to Georgia," *W.H.S.* 13, 2(June 1921): 25–29. The Non-Jurors considered the *Apostolic Constitutions* to be the most ancient Christian liturgy extant, and while Wesley's faith in the authenticity of this document was shaken in later years, he ever remained loyal to the overall catholic purpose of his Non-Juring friends. On the influence of this group upon Wesley, see in particular Frederick Hunter, *John Wesley and the Coming Comprehensive Church* (London: Epworth Press, 1968), pp. 30–44, and his "Manchester Non-Jurors and Wesley's High Churchism," *L.Q.R.* 172 (1947): 56–61; Luke Tyerman, *The Oxford Methodists* (London: Hodder and Stoughton, 1873), pp. 24–56; and Baker, *John Wesley and the Church of England,* pp. 30–34, 348–50.

107. See chaps. 2. 57; 3. 15, 16; 8. 19, 20.

108. Thomas Deacon, *A Compleat Collection of Devotions, Both Publick and Private* (London: n.p., 1734), pp. 244, 240–46.

109. While an examination of the role of women in Moravianism remains a desideratum, several general studies assist in filling in the background regarding this movement. See Gillian Lindt Gollin, *Moravians in Two Worlds: A Study of Changing Communities* (New York: Columbia University Press, 1967), esp. pp. 67–127; David Cranz, *The Ancient and Modern History of the Brethren,* trans. Benjamin LaTrobe (London: Printed by W. and A. Strahan, 1780), a classic eighteenth-century history of Moravianism; and J. E. Hut-

ton, *History of the Moravian Church,* 2d ed. (London:
Moravian Publications Office, 1909). The inaugural issue of
Christian History is devoted in its entirety to "Zinzendorf and
the Moravians." See in particular *Christian History* 1,
1(1982): 26–31. A. J. Lewis, *Zinzendorf the Ecumenical
Pioneer: A Study in the Moravian Contribution to Christian
Mission and Unity* (Philadelphia: Westminster Press, 1962),
is an excellent biography of the founder. A standard
examination of the relationship between the two movements
is Clifford W. Towlson, *Moravian and Methodist: Relationships and Influences in the Eighteenth Century* (London:
Epworth Press, 1957). this may be supplemented by Martin
Schmidt, *John Wesley: A Theological Biography,* trans.
Norman Goldhawk and Denis Inman, 2 vols. (New York:
Abingdon Press, 1962–66), in which the formative influence
which Continental pietism exerted upon Wesley is clearly
delineated.

110. See Cranz, *History of the Brethren,* p. 115.
111. Anna Nitschmann was elected by lot to this high office when
less than fifteen years of age, later married Count Zinzendorf, and filled her post with great zeal and devotion until her
death. See J. Taylor Hamilton and Kenneth G. Hamilton,
*History of the Moravian Church: The Renewed Unitas
Fratrum, 1722–1957* (Bethlehem, Pa.: Interprovincial Board
of Christian Education, Moravian Church in America, 1967),
pp. 86, 658. Cf. *Christian History* 1, 1(1982): 21.
112. Wesley, *Journal,* 2:19–57.
113. John Wesley to Benjamin Ingham and James Hutton,
November 16, 1738, Wesley, *Oxford Edition,* 25:580.
114. John Wesley to Mrs. Fox, November 24, 1738 in ibid., pp.
588–89. Cf. Wesley, *Journal,* 2:84, 87–88, 92–93, 104–6,
147–51. Regarding other women leaders in Oxford, see
Wesley, *Oxford Edition,* 25:588, 605–6; Wesley, *Journal,*
2:88, 92–93, 102–14, 147–52, 284, 349, 468–77.
115. John Wesley to J. Hutton and Mr. Fox, November 24, 1738,
Wesley, *Oxford Edition,* 25:588.

PART I

The Training Ground for Women Preachers: The Early Methodist Revival, 1739–1760

Mrs. Mary Fletcher, widow of the Rev. J. Fletcher, late vicar of Madeley.

1

PIONEERS, SUSTAINERS, MARTYRS

THE BIRTH OF METHODISM AND THE PREPONDERANCE OF WOMEN

T HE BEGINNING OF METHODISM has always been difficult to date. In his "Short History of the People Called Methodists" of 1781, Wesley distinguished three "rises" of his movement. Each of these points to the religious society as its salient and differentiating feature:

> The first rise of Methodism, so called, was in November 1729, when four of us met together at Oxford; the second was at Savannah in April 1736, when twenty or thirty persons met at my house; the last was at London on [May 1, 1738], when forty or fifty of us agreed to meet together every Wednesday evening, in order to a free conversation, begun and ended with singing and prayer.[1]

It was not until the momentous month of April 1739, however, nearly a year after the formation of the Fetter Lane Society in London and Wesley's Aldersgate experience that certain events led to the consolidation of the so-called United Societies in Bristol.[2] Unlike the religious assemblies in London, these small companies of evangelical Anglicans came under the direct supervision of John Wesley. Dedicated to the renewal of "scriptural Christianity" throughout the land, these *ecclesiolae in ecclesia* rapidly evolved into a vast network of Methodist societies, the superstructure of the Wesleyan revival.

On April 4, 1739, just two days after the scholar-priest had "submitted to be more vile, and proclaimed in the highways the glad tidings of salvation," Wesley recorded the following event in his journal:

> In the evening three women agreed to meet together weekly, with the same intentions as those at London—viz. "to confess their faults one to another, and pray one for another, that they may be healed."[3]

Five days later, in one of a series of letters to James Hutton and the Fetter Lane Society, Wesley identified these early seekers as Mrs. Norman, whose husband apparently owned the land on which Wesley preached his first open-air sermon the previous week, Mrs. Grevil, the spiritually-spasmodic sister of George Whitefield, and a Mrs. Panou.[4] On this same day, April 9, Mrs. Panou's two sisters, Mary Ann Page and Esther Deschamps, were added to the group, and Esther was "by lot chose leader of the band."[5]

Wesley had not the slightest intention of founding a new denomination when he formed these bands and expanded the previously existing societies in Bristol and London. His avowed purpose from the beginning of this monumental work to its end was to reform the moribund Anglicanism of his day, not "to form the plan of a new church," which was the incessant charge he emphatically denied in his *Reasons against a Separation.*[6] The Methodist societies were not brought into being according to any predetermined plan. Rather, in Wesley's mind, they were simply a means for introducing people to God and developed, therefore, according to the exigencies of the moment. They provided a supportive environment within which sincere people could realize their newly discovered life of faith working by love leading to holiness of heart and life.

Personal, religious experience and its power to transform both the individual and the society, therefore, was the spiritual goal upon which Wesley's eyes were firmly fixed. He would utilize almost any method to accomplish this divine mission.

He is perhaps the best example of the ecclesiastical extem-
porizer, not erecting a new denomination around some
particular concern, conviction, or revelation, but doing his
best to fit the old building for its proper task, cleansing here,
repairing or buttressing there, and even adding a new chapel
or transept. He was ready to adopt and adapt any idea which
might help the Church to proclaim the Gospel more effec-
tively.[7]

One important consequence of this basic program of reform
was the substantial involvement of women in the first two
decades of the nascent revival and the development of new
roles for them within the first Methodist societies. Women
early gained the respect and admiration of Wesley's followers as the pioneers, sustainers, and martyrs of the Methodist
cause.

The environment of the Methodist society with its band
and class meetings and its distinctive services of worship,
such as the love feast, proved to be a training ground for the
later women preachers. Within the confines of these
supportive structures early Methodist women felt free to
express themselves and to exercise their gifts in leadership,
prayer, testimony, and exhortation. It is impossible to
understand the phenomenon of women preachers in Methodism apart from these early developments, the roles or
functions of women in the nascent revival, and their place in
the movement as a whole.[8]

When Humphrey Clinker, the Methodist footman-
preacher of Smollett's last and most mellowed novel,
addressed a coach-house gathering, Melford and his uncle
reacted with predictable hostility: "But if we were astonished
to see Clinker in the pulpit, we were altogether confounded
at finding all the females of our family among the audience
. . . and all of them joined in the psalmody, with strong marks
of devotion."[9] The gentlemen's shock, however, is only
symptomatic of the great concern among the critics of
Methodism who interpreted the movement's particular
appeal to women as a revolutionary attack against a
precarious society at its most vulnerable point.[10] In their

minds, it was but a short step from the evangelical
proclamation of freedom in Christ to the feminist plea for
emancipation in society.

A common charge, leveled early against Methodist
women, was the neglect of domestic responsibilities. As early
as 1740, the Reverend James Buller indicted Wesley for
keeping the women in his Bristol society so busy with
religious duties that they could not supplement their
husband's incomes during a period of great economic
depression.[11] The early Methodists were also susceptible to
the same criticism which had been leveled against the
Quakers of the previous century, namely, that their societies
consisted mainly, if not exclusively, of women. In 1741
William Fleetwood summarily dismissed these so-called
perfectionists, observing that "for the most part, their
attendants are silly *Women*."[12] In a scurilous attack upon the
character of Wesley and particular developments within
Bristol Methodism, an anonymous critic estimated that
three-quarters of Wesley's adherents were women.[13] Toward
the end of the century a London bookseller, James
Lackington, caustically wrote of his former spiritual leader,
"I believe that by far the greatest part of his people are
females; and not a few of them sour, disappointed old maids,
with some others of a less prudish disposition."[14]

The fact which the adversaries of Methodism suggested in
their diatribes against the movement becomes obvious when
the evidence is closely examined. The Methodist societies
were, for all intents and purposes, organizations of women.
On Sunday, November 11, 1739, Wesley preached his first
sermon in the ruins of an old foundery in London which he
had secured for the use of those who sought his spiritual
direction. The following summer when dissension over
Moravian quietism finally ruptured the Fetter Lane Society,
Wesley noted the important consequences:

> Our little company met at *The Foundery*, instead of Fetter
> Lane. About twenty-five of our brethren God hath given us
> already, all of whom think and speak the same thing; seven- or
> eight-and-forty likewise of the fifty women that were in band
> desired to cast in their lot with us.[15]

A little more than two years later, in April 1742, Wesley drew up the first list of the Foundery Society's sixty-six leaders. In this group, women outnumbered the men forty-seven to nineteen.[16] A list of Select Society members in February 1744, containing the names of those Methodists who had received remission of sins and whose faith had been tested and proved, reflects a similar proportion of fifty-two women to twenty-five men.[17] The example of the Foundery Society with its 2:1 ratio of women to men is typical of early Methodism as a whole, both in its beginnings and throughout the eighteenth century.[18] There can be no doubt that women wielded tremendous influence during these formative years wherever Methodism was planted and flourished.[19]

FEMALE INITIATIVE IN THE FORMATION AND ESTABLISHMENT OF METHODIST SOCIETIES

Of even greater significance than the preponderance of women in the membership of the societies, however, is the fact that women were conspicuous as pioneers in the establishment and expansion of Methodism. The proliferation of the Wesleyan cluster groups was often the direct consequence of the activity of a woman or group of women. Women invited and hosted the preachers, founded prayer groups and societies on the basis of their own initiative, and propagated and maintained the faith. This fact profoundly affected the general attitudes of Wesley and his adherents concerning the place of women in the movement.

When Wesley was visiting the neighborhood of Halifax in the summer of 1742, Mrs. Holmes of Smith House, Lightcliffe, invited him to preach at her home.[20] Subsequently, Smith House became a chief center for religious revival and greatly contributed to the establishment of Methodism in that general vicinity. About the same time, Wesley honored the request of a poor widow named Goddard and made Chinley a resting place for his itinerants who began regular preaching there.[21] Mary Allinson was the first to open her house to Methodist preachers in Teesdale;[22] the aunt of Mary Denny introduced Methodism to Maldon;[23]

Mrs. Hosmer procured a room for preaching in Darlington;[24] and preaching was reinstated at Normanton only by means of an unnamed woman's persistence.[25]

The initial adherents to the evangelical message preached by Wesley and his itinerants, moreover, were very often women. The famous stonemason preacher of the north, John Nelson, described the events leading to the introduction of Methodism to Leeds: "Now the people from every quarter have flocked to Birstal on the Sabbath, but as yet there came only three from Leeds,—Mary Shent and two other women."[26] Converted under the first sermon they heard, these "three Marys," including Mary Weddale and Mary Maude, formed the nucleus of the first band established in that strategic industrial center, probably before the end of 1742.[27] Across Saint George's Channel, Eliza Bennis, who later became a devoted correspondent and useful advisor to John Wesley on Irish affairs, was the first Methodist in Limerick, converted under the preaching of Robert Swindells, in 1749.[28]

Some women took the initiative in the actual formation of societies with no other authority than their own determination and sense of divine calling. Several years before Wesley's first visit to Macclesfield, Mary Aldersley opened her home, called Shrigley-fold, for religious services and was accustomed to meeting with her friends for prayer, reading of Scripture, and religious conversation.[29] In 1746 Elizabeth Blow crossed the Humber from Grimsby where she had been one of the earliest members and pioneered the founding of Methodism in Hull.[30] Mrs. Martha Thompson, a wealthy widow who possessed a considerable estate at Rufforth, not only opened her own home for preachers, but used her influence to obtain their admission into the cathedral city of York.[31]

Another Martha Thompson, of strikingly dissimilar background and circumstances from her namesake, is credited with the foundation of Methodism in Preston.[32] With the assistance of Sarah Crosby, who would shortly thereafter become the first woman preacher of Methodism, Mrs. Dobinson of Derby became the "principal instrument in introducing our preachers into that town."[33] And this she did in the face of much opposition and discouragement. In this pioneering work, a servant girl, a textile worker, or a housewife was no less acceptable than a woman of social position and influence.[34]

Wealthy women, however, were able to commit not only their lives but their resources to the subsequent development and consolidation of the Methodist societies. The building of chapels was one such contribution. In Macclesfield, Elizabeth Clulow, together with George Pearson, secured a small preaching house for the infant society, and when expansion necessitated a larger chapel, Mrs. Clulow paid for its construction.[35] Mrs. Henrietta Gayer, wife of the clerk to the House of Lords for the Irish Parliament, was converted in 1772, set apart a room in her house known as the "Prophet's Chamber" for the preachers, secured the erection of the first chapel in Lisburn in 1774, was instrumental in planning the construction of the Donaghadee chapel, and after her husband's death devoted the totality of his estate to Christian work.[36]

The first Methodist in Sevenoaks was Mrs. Amy George who had walked to Shoreham in order to invite Wesley to preach at her home, subsequently designated the "Pilgrim's Inn." She built a chapel at the back of her business premises which Wesley opened on December 12, 1774.[37] He was impressed with the great hall which Miss Harvey had built in her hometown of Hinxworth in Hertfordshire.[38] She had taken a lively interest in the prosperity of Methodism and built several other chapels at her own expense in Baldock, Stevenage, and Biggleswade, all of which she settled on the Methodist plan. At her death she left a legacy of three thousand pounds to support the Methodist cause.[39] Wesley maintained an intimate contact with these pioneers and patrons who were greatly respected within their societies. It was not uncommon for him to place reliance on such leaders who had proved themselves worthy of his trust, even in those areas traditionally dominated by men.[40]

The pioneering work of Mrs. Dorothy Fisher illustrates the formative influence exerted by a woman at all the various levels of a new society's development.[41] While her story comes from the last quarter of the eighteenth century, it is representative and serves as an example of how Methodism grew in its early days and how women quite often stood on the cutting edge of its expansion. Dorothy was converted under Wesley's preaching in London and joined the society there in 1779. About the year 1784 she moved to Great Gonerby in Lincolnshire, opened her house to preaching because of the great accommodation it afforded, and in 1786 purchased a small stone building to be fitted up for a chapel, principally at her own expense. A small group of Methodists at Sturton had heard of Dorothy's piety and thought that the state of religion in Lincoln could be immeasurably improved if she were to make her residence there.

The prime mover in this missionary venture, Sarah Parrot of Bracebridge, walked twenty-seven miles to Mrs. Fisher's home, placed the proposition before her, and Dorothy, concluding that it must be a call from God, consented, settled her affairs, moved to Lincoln, procured a suitable residence, and invited the traveling preachers to take the city into their round at the close of 1787. The following January, Wesley wrote to Lancelot Harrison expressing his hopeful expectations:

> I am glad sister Fisher is settled at Lincoln, and that you have begun preaching there again. Hitherto it has been
>   A soil ungrateful to the tiller's toil; But possibly it may now bear fruit.[42]

A small society was formed in an old lumber room near Gowt's Bridge, consisting of four women, Mrs. Fisher, Sarah Parrot, Hannah Calder, and Elizabeth Keyley. The newly planted society did bear fruit, and Dorothy subsequently built a chapel with an adjoining residence which was later entrusted to the care of the Methodist Conference. Thus Methodism was established in that cathedral city as it had been planted in many other places throughout the British Isles. The extent to which women were permitted to assume the initiative in the societies, and to function as pioneers and sustainers of the Methodist cause, often gave them a working equality with their male counterparts. The atmosphere created by their activities and witness became more and more conducive to the expansion of their roles.

Another aspect of the involvement of women in the Wesleyan revival contributed greatly to the increased valuation of their presence and activity in the societies during this formative period and thereby paved the way to a greater acceptance of later developments. The women bore witness to the faith, and that not only in terms of their personal experience and the practical expression of the transforming gospel in their lives, but also in their courageous endurance of persecution, and for a limited number, martyrdom.

According to Wesley, the first witness of the great salvation, or sanctification, in Bristol was Ann Steed.[43] In his published *Journal,* Wesley juxtaposes John Johnson's account of Judith Beresford's death with that of a man who "died as stupid as an ox."[44] He identified Elizabeth Longmore as the "first witness of Christian Perfection" in the strife-ridden community of Wednesbury, whose "whole life was answerable to her profession, every way holy and unblameable."[45] And years earlier, in the midst of the Fetter Lane controversy, when many were being persuaded that they had no faith and were casting away their confidence in God, the responsibility of the faithful to bear witness to the life of God within them, both male and female alike, must have been indelibly impressed upon Wesley's mind by the profound nature of his mother's response:

> I know that the life which I now live, I live by faith in the Son of God, who loved me, and gave Himself for me; and He has never left me one moment, since the hour He was made known to me in the breaking of bread.[46]

Some women were called to defend their faith in even more drastic circumstances and thereby gained the profound respect of their male associates. Following the Wednesbury riots of October 1743 Wesley asked Joan Parks if she was frightened when the mob took hold of her:

She said, "No; no more than I am now. I could trust God for you as well as for myself." . . . I asked if the report was true that she had fought for me. She said "No; I knew God would fight for His children."[47]

When a mob attacked John Healy as he began to preach in the Irish village of Athlone, an unnamed Methodist woman swore that a priest's servant who was brandishing a knife would not cut up his victim. In spite of continued whippings that afterward led to her death, she stood guard over the evangelist until help finally came.[48]

Not all of the Methodist women held to the pacifist point of view, as may be illustrated by the case of Hannah Davenport. When a mob attempted to force its way into her home where she was protecting Thomas Hanby, "she seized an axe, and taking her stand in the door-way, declared she would cut down the first who dared to approach."[49] No one entered. The witness of the lives and deaths of these early women contributed to the generous acceptance of their activities within the life of their societies.

THE LEADER'S RESPONSE TO THE WOMEN PIONEERS

During these early and formative years prior to the convening of the first Methodist Conference of preachers in 1744, very little information is available concerning the question of women preachers per se. The leaders were only beginning to formulate a view of their peculiar mission and develop a sense of their particular identity, much less articulate answers to the highly complex questions of ecclesiology and ministry. What was clear in their minds at this point, however, was that Methodism was first and foremost a reforming movement within the Church of England. Allegiance to Anglicanism, therefore, was an essential aspect of its evolving self-understanding.

One particular concern for them was the striking resemblance Methodism bore, not only to some of the older Nonconforming sects, but to some of the recent and more radical movements. The paroxysms associated with early

Methodist revivalism troubled Wesley because of their similarity to those of the French Prophetesses and Jansenist convulsionaries.[50] The frequent association of such phenomena with women had a restraining effect upon the widening sphere of their influence as the Wesleys sought to free themselves from the incessant charge which so greatly prejudiced the minds of many against their movement, namely, enthusiasm.

Tension between the normative place and influence of women in the Methodist societies and the unwarranted identification of certain irregularities with fanatical enthusiasm on the part of the Angelican establishment was exacerbated by developments in London. Some of the members of the Methodist society came under the strong influence of French Prophetesses. On June 7, 1739, Charles Wesley had an interview with one of these women at the home of a Methodist who had succumbed to her alluring influences. "She lifted up her voice," he declared, "like a lady on the tripod, and cried out vehemently, 'Look for perfection; I say absolute perfection!' . . . She concluded with an horrible hellish laugh; and endeavoured to turn it off."[51]

Several days later, one of her adherents told Charles that she could "command Christ to come to her in what shape she pleases; as a dove, an eagle, &c."[52] John Wesley had previously encountered a prophetess of this kind in January of 1739 and was impressed neither with her contortions nor her words.[53] When he returned to London, having been in Bristol since March, and discovered that these prophetesses had been particularly successful among the women of the Fetter Lane Society, he found it necessary to warn them "not to believe every spirit, but to try the spirits, whether they were of God."[54] He perceptively recognized the dangers of guilt by association.

There is no evidence that women preached in the Methodist societies in this early period. It is of great interest to discover, however, that this charge was leveled against the movement as early as 1740 by an early opponent, the Reverend William Bowman. In his pamphlet entitled *The Imposture of Methodism Display'd*, this Yorkshire vicar unleashed his fury at so-called enthusiastic innovations:

A Third Mark of Imposture propagated by these mad
Devotionalists is their teaching, *That it is lawful and expedient
for mere Laymen, for Women, and the meanest and most
ignorant Mechanics, to minister in the Church of Christ, to
preach and expound the Word of God, and to offer up the
Prayers of the Congregation in the public Assemblies.*[55]

He proceeded to demonstrate how this practice was
"neither reasonable nor scriptural, contrary to the plain
Institutions of Christ and his Apostles, condemn'd by the
universal Voice of All Antiquity, and a dangerous and
unwarrantable Innovation."[56] Ironically, it was precisely for
these reasons that Charles Wesley forbade the "preaching"
of a woman when he examined the society at Evesham in
May 1743:

The Society walk as becometh the Gospel. One only person I
reproved; not suffering her any longer, notwithstanding her
great gifts, to speak in the church, or usurp authority over
the men.[57]

Despite the indictments of an opponent such as Bowman,
it is clear that the Wesleys were very much opposed to
women taking such a monumental step and thereby trans-
gressing the boundaries established by both society and
church. John and Charles Wesley were both devoted
Anglican priests and did their best to keep within the limits
set by the laws and regulations of their church, including
those which restricted the activities of women. This conservative attitude is clearly reflected in two of John Wesley's
publications. In both of these apologetic writings Wesley
sought to discuss "objectively" controversial issues surrounding the revival, dismiss erroneous allegations leveled at
the movement, and dissociate the Wesleyan revival in
principle and practice from sectarian movements that he
believed were aberrations of the gospel. Wesley was anxious
to disprove allegations concerning women preachers at this
early stage, both in his interest for truth and for fear of
undesirable associations.

While little controversial literature was issued throughout
the century by Methodists and Quakers against each other,

misunderstandings and tensions between the two groups began to mount as early as the 1740s.[58] In February 1748 Wesley wrote a letter to a Methodist who had joined the Quakers, apparently Stephen Plummer of Paulton near Bristol, outlining in fifteen propositions the essentials of the Christian faith according to Robert Barclay's *Apology for the True Christian Divinity,* and pointing out the differences between Quakerism and Christianity. Soon after, Wesley published this epistle under the title, *A Letter to a Person lately join'd with the People call'd Quakers.*[59]

Wesley had little quarrel with Barclay theologically, excluding his understanding of justification, but took issue with his doctrine of the ministry under his tenth proposition. In particular, he rejects the Quaker notion "that we judge it noways unlawful for a woman to preach in the assemblies of God's people." In defense of the prohibition of such activities, Wesley marshals the two classic Pauline texts, 1 Corinthians 14:34–35 and 1 Timothy 2:11–12, enjoining the silence of women in the church, which he understands from the context to mean women in general. Moreover, public teaching, he maintains, necessarily implies usurpation of male authority. He employs standard arguments to counter Barclay's additional scriptural defenses, so-called:

> "But a woman 'laboured with Paul in the work of the gospel.'" Yea, but not in the way he had himself expressly forbidden.
>
> "But Joel foretold, 'Your sons and your daughters shall prophesy.' And 'Philip had four daughters which prophesied.' And the Apostle himself directs women to prophesy; only with their heads covered."
>
> Very good. But how do you prove that prophesying in any of these places means preaching?[60]

Wesley's position in this document is clear: he refused to countenance the public preaching of women.

The second document related to this issue, also an open letter, was the product of an exchange between Wesley and George Lavington, bishop of Exeter, and addressed the charge of enthusiasm which the prelate had leveled against Methodism.[61] In a scurrilous tract entitled *The Enthusiasm of*

Methodists and Papists Compared, the first installment of which was published anonymously in March 1749, Lavington charged that *"Women and boys* are actually employed in this ministry of *public preaching."*[62] This allegation, reminiscent of William Bowman's earlier charge, Wesley summarily dismissed in his *Second Letter to the Author of the Enthusiasm of Methodism, &c.* in 1751. "Please tell me where?" he retorts. "I know them not, nor even heard of them before."[63]

There is no question that Lavington expressed many of the opponents' fears concerning the large place given to women in early Methodism. In a characteristically virulent vein, he claimed, "Tis observable in *Fact,* that a *Multiplicity of Wives,* and promiscuous Use of Women has been the *Favorite Tenet* of most Fanatical Sects!"[64] Nothing, however, could have been further from Wesley's vision of the Christian life or of his mission to reform the church than such lascivious and irresponsible innuendo. Nevertheless, the great extent to which women were permitted to assume the initiative in the societies and function as pioneers and leaders often gave them a working equality with men. And this is what the guardians of society and church so greatly feared. A wealth of factors combined both in the founder and the movement to create a climate conducive to this acceptance and empowerment of women, the most important of which were the extraordinary nature of the revival, the general environment of the societies, and Wesley's evolving theology of the Church and ministry.

NOTES

1. Wesley, *Works,* 13:307.
2. Two societies, those of Nicholas Street and Baldwin Street, had been active in Bristol. On May 9, 1739, Wesley secured property in the Horsefair to build a room to make adequate provision for the tremendous influx of new members. This "New Room," the first Methodist chapel, became the focus of Wesley's energies as the spiritual director of these United

Societies. This term later became applied to all other societies acknowledging allegiance to the Wesleys. See Wesley, *Journal,* 2:194–230; Baker, *John Wesley and the Church of England,* pp. 75–77.

3. Wesley, *Journal,* 2:174.
4. Wesley, *Oxford Edition,* 25:625–28. Cf. *Arm. Mag.* 6 (1789): 240–45; and *W.H.S.* 2 (1900): 5–6.
5. Ibid., p. 631. At five that evening a second band of six women was formed under Anne Williams. Cf. *W.H.S.* 5 (1906): 4.
6. Wesley, *Works,* 13:225.
7. Frank Baker, "John Wesley's Churchmanship," *L.Q.R.* 185, 4(October 1960): 271–72.
8. While the following chapters are particularly concerned with developments during the years between 1739 and 1760, strict chronology will not be adhered to at all times due to the continuing significance of certain roles and functions of women that originated in this formative period. Since the offices of band and class leader, for instance, continued throughout the course of the eighteenth century, illustrative material has been drawn from this larger period.
9. Tobias Smollett, *The Expedition of Humphrey Clinker* (Harmondsworth: Penguin Books, 1978), p. 169.
10. See Donald H. Kirkham, "Pamphlet Opposition to the Rise of Methodism: The Eighteenth-Century English Evangelical Revival under Attack" (Ph.D. diss., Duke University, 1973), pp. 217–28, whose analysis of relevant primary documents has been closely followed herein.
11. James Buller, *A Reply to the Rev. Mr. Wesley's Address to the Clergy* (Bristol: S. Farley, 1756), p. 25. See similar criticisms in *The Mock-Preacher: A Satyrico-Comical-Allegorical Farce* (London: C. Corbette, 1739), pp. 15–16; [Samuel Weller], *The Trial of Mr. Whitefield's Spirit in Some Remarks upon his Fourth Journal,* (London: T. Gardner, 1740), pp. 35–36; and *A Plain and Easy Road to the Land of Bliss* (London: W. Nicholl, 1762), p. 65.
12. William Fleetwood, *The Perfectionists Examined; or Inherent Perfection in this Life, no Scripture Doctrine, To which is affix'd, the Rev. Mr. Whitefield's Thoughts on this Subject, in a Letter to Mr. Wesley* (London: J. Roberts, 1741), p. 2.
13. An Impartial Hand, *The Progress of Methodism in Bristol: or, The Methodist Unmask'd,* 2d ed. (Bristol: J. Watts, 1743), p. 20.
14. James Lackington, *Memoirs of the Forty-five First Years of the*

Life of James Lackington, the Present Bookseller in Finsbury Square, London, new ed. (London: By the Author, 1794), p. 123. Cf. James Bate, *Quakero-Methodism; or A Confutation of the First Principles of the Quakers and Methodists* (London: John Carter, [1740]).

15. July 23, 1740, Wesley, *Journal,* 2:371.

16. These earliest extant society lists are recorded in George J. Stevenson, *City Road Chapel, London, and Its Associates* (London: George J. Stevenson, [1872]), pp. 28–39. It is important to note that Stevenson incorrectly refers to these lists as "class lists" when, in fact, they are clearly "band lists." Prior to 1743 there were no "class lists," and many errors have sprung from this misnomer. When spoken of as "society" records, these lists properly refer to the "select society," i.e., the grouping together of the members of the "band societies."

17. The bands, at this time generally composed of six or seven members, were separated into four classifications: single men, married men, single women, and married women. Fifty-seven of the eighty-five leaders in the list of band members for June 1745 were women.

18. The strength of this claim becomes increasingly evident upon examination of the extant society lists from this period. Early records of the society in Bristol afford corroborative evidence, a spot check of Wesley's manuscripts, dated September 29, 1770, revealing a total membership of 901 in 54 classes, composed of 592 women and 309 men, all illegible or questionable names being counted as men. The earliest list for the Frome Society, that of June 1759, contains the names of 25 women and 13 men. The occupations of the working women included card-setters (4), spinners (4), scribbler (1), shoe-maker (1), and map maker (1) (Stephen Tuck, *Wesleyan Methodist in Frome, Somersetshire* [Frome: Printed by S. Tuck, 1837], p. 35). The earliest records extant, not merely for the Glamorgan Circuit, but for Methodism in Wales, are lists for the eleven societies formed in that region prior to Wesley's death. Dated 1787, these lists include the names of 101 women and 49 men. The seven members of the Newport Society were all women (Idwal Lewis, "Early Methodist Societies in Glamorgan and Monmouthsire," *Bathafarn* 11 [1956]: 57–59). Likewise, another Newport Society, on the Isle of Wright, was composed of only women according to the records of 1762 (John B. Dyson, *Methodism in the Isle of Wight: Its Origin and Progress down to the Present Time* [Ventnor, Isle of Wight:

George M. Burt, 1865], pp. 60–61). Earlier that same year, on May 26, 1762, Wesley recorded that "in the afternoon we got well to Galway [Ireland]. There was a small society here, and (what is not common) all of them were young women" (Wesley, *Journal,* 4:505). While exclusively female societies were rare, and there were exceptions to the general preponderance of women, such as the religious revival at Everton in 1759 which, according to Wesley, attracted three times as many men as women (*Journal,* 4:317–18), or the exclusively male societies of the Bradford area (see W. W. Stamp, *Historical Notices of Wesleyan Methodism in Bradford and Its Vicinity* [Bradford: Henry Wardman, n.d.], pp. 62–63), the general impression of a large female majority in the membership throughout the British Isles remains. It is interesting also to note that Donald G. Mathews's examination of the Old South revealed that about 64 percent of each congregation was female, a statistic which nearly matches that of early Methodism in Britain (see *Religion in the Old South* [Chicago: University of Chicago Press, 1977], pp. 102–24).

19. One must be cautious so as not to fall into a dangerous trap when analyzing and evaluating statistics regarding sex ratios within the Methodist societies. While records show that the membership of early Methodism was then (as possibly now) on a proportion of two women to one man, such numerical preponderance does not *necessarily* imply twice the influence. Despite the socioreligious impediments of the eighteenth century, however, the influence of women within Methodism, more often subliminal than apparent, was certainly pervasive. It is noteworthy, for example, that Wesley's diaries throughout this early period indicate that he spent much more time with women than with men, and necessarily so. Whereas, in the balance, women *may* not have exerted an influence greater in proportion or quality to that of Methodist men, the great value which was placed upon their presence within the societies (in contrast to the general cultural attitude) carried with it an inherent power of affecting others.

20. June 2, 1742, Wesley, *Journal,* 3:16; cf. 6:16, 102, and 3:297. According to James Everett, Mrs. Holmes was the only Methodist in the area (*Wesleyan Methodism in Manchester* [Manchester: S. Russell, 1827], p. 52). Cf. *W.H.S.* 7 (1910): 169–73; John Simon, *John Wesley and the Methodist Societies* (London: Epworth Press, 1923), p. 76; and Schmidt, *John Wesley,* 2:74.

21. Wesley, *Journal,* 3:142n.
22. Anthony Steele, *History of Methodism in Barnard Castle and the Principal Places in the Dales Circuit* (London: George Vickers, 1857), p. 41.
23. Leslie F. Church, *The Early Methodist People* (London: Epworth Press, 1948), p. 40. Cf. Wesley, *Journal,* 4:249, 289.
24. George Jackson, *Wesleyan Methodism in the Darlington Circuit* (Darlington: Printed and sold by J. Manley, 1850), p. 17. Cf. George Smith, *History of Wesleyan Methodism,* 2d ed. rev., 3 vols. (London: Longman, 1862), 1:279–80.
25. Thomas Cocking, *The History of Wesleyan Methodism in Grantham and Its Vicinity* (London: Simpkin, Marshal, 1836), pp. 173–74, regarding the influence of Mary Kerry; cf. *Meth. Mag.* 37 (1814): 188. For a representative selection of references to women who invited or hosted Methodist preachers, see Wesley, *Journal,* 5:435, 447, 450, 473, 479; 6:40–41, 52, 66, 283, 286. For the influence of Mary Carey in Donaghadee in the establishment of Irish Methodism, see C. H. Crookshank, *History of Methodism in Ireland,* 3 vols. (Belfast: R. S. Allen, Son and Allen, 1885), 1:46–47; cf. 1:200, 241, 252, 297, 407–8; 2:44, 114–15.
26. Thomas Jackson, ed., *The Lives of the Early Methodist Preachers. Chiefly Written by Themselves,* 4th ed., 6 vols. (London: Wesleyan Conference Office, 1875), 1:60.
27. J. E. Hellier, "The Mother Chapel of Leeds," *Methodist Recorder Winter Number* 35 (Christmas 1894): 62–63; John Lyth, *Glimpses of Early Methodism in York and the Surrounding District* (York: William Sessions, 1885), p. 24; George West, *Methodism in Marshland* (London: Wesleyan Conference Office, [1886]), pp. 21–22; Smith, *History of Wesleyan Methodism,* 1:221. A similar society of three women was formed by Wesley in the village of Gamblesby between 1749 and 1751 (see G. H. Bancroft Judge, "The Beginnings of Methodism in the Penrith District," *W.H.S.* 19, 7[September 1934]: 153–60). Cf. the account of the three women who formed the first society in Gonersby, in Cocking, *Methodism in Grantham,* pp. 143–44. For Ruth Blocker, the pioneer of Methodism in Briestfield, see John R. Robinson, *Notes on Early Methodism in Dewsbury, Birstal, and Neighbourhood* (Batley: J. Fearnsides and Sons, 1900), pp. 32–33.
28. C. H. Crookshank, *Memorable Women of Irish Methodism in the Last Century* (London: Wesleyan-Methodist Book-Room, 1882), pp. 20–30; Wesley, *Letters,* 4:82, 220–21, 228; 5:6, 24,

56, 137, 142, 150, 188, 190, 193, 242, 268, 283, 290, 298, 314, 321, 337, 343; 6:6, 16, 23, 40, 55, 68, 76, 79, 243. Cf. Crookshank, *History of Methodism in Ireland,* 1:48, 240–41, 287; and 2:153–54 concerning other women pioneers.

29. Benjamin Smith, *The History of Methodism in Macclesfield* (London: Wesleyan Conference Office, 1875), pp. 17–19.

30. See *Meth. Mag.* 60 (1837): 885–99, where a full account of the early history of Hull Methodism is given. Cf. J. H. Grubb, "The Conference Town," *Wes. Meth. Mag.* 121 (1898): 483–94; George Lester, *Grimsby Methodism (1743–1898) and the Wesleys in Lincolnshire* (London: Wesleyan-Conference Book-Room, 1890), p. 48; Wesley, *Journal,* 4:20n; and John S. Simon, *John Wesley and the Advance of Methodism* (London: Epworth Press, 1925), p. 228.

31. Lyth, *Methodism in York,* pp. 53–54. Cf. *Arm. Mag.* 6 (1783): 471; and Wesley, *Journal,* 4:66n. Lyth further notes that it was to the zeal, determination, and consistency of Hannah Harrison and Ruth Hall in particular that "the successful establishment of Methodism in this locality is greatly indebted" (p. 64). These two women later emerge as influential women preachers. See Appendix A.

32. John Taylor, *The Apostles of Fylde Methodism* (London: T. Woolman, 1885), pp. 8–17; J. W. Laycock, *Methodist Heroes of the Great Haworth Round, 1734–1784* (Keighley: Wadsworth, Rydal Press, 1909), pp. 198–200; W. Pilkington, *The Makers of Wesleyan Methodism in Preston* (London: Charles H. Kelly, 1890), p. 14; W. F. Richardson, *Preston Methodism's Two Hundred Years* (Preston: Printed at Adelphi Chambers by Henry L. Kirby, 1975), pp. 9–15; and Edwards, *My Dear Sister,* pp. 45–50.

33. A. Seckerson, "An Account of Mrs. Dobinson," *Meth. Mag.* 26 (1803): 557–66. Cf. *Meth. Mag.* 24 (1801): 274; and 53 (1830): 786.

34. See Wellman J. Warner, *The Wesleyan Movement in the Industrial Revolution* (London: Longmans, Green, 1930), pp. 264–65.

35. Smith, *Methodism in Macclesfield,* pp. 45–46, 149–50. Cf. Tyerman, *Life of John Wesley,* 3:8. This chapel was completed in 1764, and it is important to note that the society placed its trust in the judgment and integrity of this woman. The deed was transferred to Martha Ryle from her husband on December 30, 1780, with a trust deed properly executed soon thereafter.

36. Crookshank, *Memorable Women,* pp. 36, 116–24; Crookshank, *History of Methodism in Ireland,* 1:286–87.
37. Thomas Brackenbury, "Methodism in Sevenoaks," *Methodist Recorder Winter Number* 41 (Christmas 1900): 91–93; Wesley, *Journal,* 3:265; 6:53. The appellation "Pilgrim's Inn" became a familiar epithet designating houses of hospitality for the Methodist itinerants. See F. F. Bretherton, *Early Methodism in and around Chester, 1749–1812* (Chester: Phillipson and Golder, 1903), pp. 62–65, regarding the home and hospitality of Mrs. Mary Lowe, and her memoirs in *Meth. Mag.* 32 (1809): 187–91, 229–39.
38. Wesley, *Journal,* 6:362; 7:35, 40, 216, 337. According to Bretherton, Mrs. Mary Bealey of Radcliffe near Manchester "built at her own expense what was considered to be at the time the prettiest Chapel in Methodism" (*Methodism in Chester,* pp. 194–95). It was not uncommon for a woman of means to erect a chapel at the scene of her conversion, as did Miss Richardson of Ryefield; see Crookshank, *History of Methodism in Ireland,* 2:160; cf. *Wes. Meth. Mag.* 67 (1844): 633–35.
39. *Wes. Meth. Mag.* 52 (1829): 289–92; cf. Wesley, *Journal,* 6:362n.
40. In 1777 Wesley entrusted the building program of the chapel at High Wycombe to his faithful correspondent Hannah Ball. See Wesley, *Letters,* 6:258; and Joseph Cole, ed., *Memoir of Miss Hannah Ball, of High-Wycombe, in Buckinghamshire,* revised and enlarged by John Parker (London: Published by John Mason, 1839), pp. 137–48.
41. Abraham Watmough, *A History of Methodism in the Neighbourhood and City of Lincoln* (Lincoln: Printed by R. E. Leary; sold by J. Mason, 1829), pp. 21–25. Cf. Cocking, *Methodism in Grantham,* pp. 217–26; Wesley, *Journal,* 7:412–13; *Letters,* 7:326–27; and *Wes. Meth. Mag.* 48 (1825): 290.
42. Watmough, op. cit., p. 24. This letter of January 18, 1788, apparently escaped the attention of Telford in his edition of Wesley's letters. The original was in the hands of Harrison's daughter, Mrs. Belton of Walkeringham, when Watmough produced his history.
43. Wesley, *Journal,* 2:511; 4:532. Wesley preached her funeral sermon on October 28, 1762.
44. Ibid., pp. 204–10. Wesley often pointed to Miss Beresford as a primary exemplum of his doctrine of perfect love.
45. Ibid., 5:356; cf. 4:367–70 for an account of her religious experience.

46. November 10, 1739, Wesley, *Journal,* 2:315.
47. Ibid., 3:103.
48. Simon, *John Wesley and the Advance of Methodism,* pp. 63–64. Another one of the early women martyrs was Mary Bird, who, after a number of murderous threats was struck on the side of the head with a stone and killed on June 20, 1743 (see Simon, *John Wesley and the Methodist Societies,* pp. 129–30). In the early years of the revival the Methodists were particularly susceptible to persecution. The journal of John Nelson frequently refers to the assaults of rioters and records the tragic event of his wife's miscarriage which resulted from the cruel and inhumane treatment of the mob (see Jackson, *Lives of Early Methodist Preachers,* 1:150–65). Cf. Wesley, *Works,* 13:143, 169–233. There were outbreaks of mob violence as early as 1739 in Bristol and 1740 in London. The rioting was more sustained, however, in the Midlands. Darlaston, Walsall, Bilston, Nottingham, Derby, and Newark all became centers of rioting, and Wednesbury was virtually under mob law during 1743 and 1744. See the chapter, "Persecution and Triumph," in Church, *More about Early Methodist People,* pp. 57–98.
49. J. B. Dyson, *A Brief History of the Rise and Progress of Wesleyan Methodism in the Leek Circuit* (Leek: Printed by Edward Hallowes, [1853]), p. 11.
50. See Knox, *Enthusiasm,* pp. 356–71; Sidney Dimond, *The Psychology of the Methodist Revival: An Empirical and Descriptive Study* (Oxford: Oxford University Press, 1926), pp. 116–18; and Church, *More about Early Methodist People,* pp. 59–62.
51. Charles Wesley, *Journal,* 1:152.
52. Ibid., p. 153.
53. Wesley, *Journal,* 2:136–37. "I went," wrote Wesley, "(having been long importuned thereto) about five in the evening, with four or five of my friends, to a house where was one of those commonly called French prophets. After a time she came in. . . . Her head and hands, and, by turns, every part of her body, seemed also to be in a kind of convulsive motion. This continued about ten minutes, till, at six, she began to speak (though the workings, sighings, and contortions of her body were so intermixed with her words, that she seldom spoke half a sentence together)." According to Curnock's conjecture, this prophetess was a Mary Plewit of London.
54. June 13, 1739, in ibid., p. 220.

55. William Bowman, *The Imposture of Methodism Display'd* (London: Joseph Lord, 1740), p. 27.

56. Ibid., p. 28.

57. Charles Wesley, *Journal,* 1:307. His allusion to the Pauline prohibitions is evident. It is also noteworthy that Charles Wesley frequently referred to the Methodist societies as "churches." Cf. Simon, *John Wesley and the Methodist Societies,* p. 118.

58. See Frank Baker, *The Relations between the Society of Friends and Early Methodism* (London: Epworth Press, 1949), pp. 3–16 in particular.

59. This publication passed through no fewer than three editions that same year, and was subsequently reprinted in the famous *Preservations against Unsettled Notions in Religion.* John Telford, who tentatively identified the recipient of this letter as Thomas Whitehead, reprinted the *Letter* in Wesley, *Letters,* 2:116–28. Cf. Wesley, *Works,* 10:177–88. A definitive analysis of this document will be afforded in Wesley, *Bicentennial Edition,* vol. 13. For evidence supporting the identification of Plummer as the Quaker convert, see Frank Baker, "Wesley Bibliography," *W.H.S.* 21, 6(June 1938): 156.

60. Wesley, *Letters,* 2:119–20.

61. See the definitive text of Wesley's open letters to Lavington in Wesley, *Oxford Edition,* 11:353–429.

62. [George Lavington], *The Enthusiasm of Methodists and Papists Compared. Part II* (London: J. and P. Knapton, 1749), p. 126.

63. Wesley, *Oxford Edition,* 11:406.

64. [Lavington], *Enthusiasm of Methodists. Part II,* p. 161.

2

LAY LEADERS IN THE METHODIST SOCIETIES

LEADERSHIP ROLES FOR WOMEN IN THE EVOLVING MOVEMENT

O NE OF THE SALIENT FEATURES of early Methodism was its capacity to create its own leadership from within. The early pioneers who were responsible for the initiation of new societies naturally assumed positions of leadership, and the large extent to which women functioned in this sphere was a major factor contributing to the inclusiveness and vitality of the movement. Methodism afforded a variety of opportunities for leadership to those who were disenfranchised and provided a sense of empowerment for those who stood impotently on the periphery of English society, namely, the masses of working-class and common people and women.

This leveling sentiment which the critics of Methodism so greatly feared was an inherent aspect of the evangelical preaching of Wesleyan itinerants. "Very far from being an anodyne," claims Wearmouth, "the urgent and compelling message of the Methodists was a summons to put spiritual sloth aside and accept duties and responsibilities and to play a full part in the arena."[1] Not only was faith to be expressed in works, but individual talents were to be developed as a sacred trust from God. The general environment of the Methodist society, therefore, was conducive to the cultivation of women's as well as men's skills and to their consequent empowerment for ministry.

By the middle of the 1740s the nascent revival had weathered the initial storms raised by persecuting mobs and unsympathetic clergy. Its leaders had also become sensitive to the tension between their own evangelical urge and loyalty to the Church of England.[2] The leadership of the movement by this time had evolved into three rather well-defined sections. At the top was John Wesley, surrounded by a small group of Anglican clergy or "Ministers," including his brother Charles. Directly beneath them and under their vigilant surveillance was a group of lay preachers, "Helpers" or "Assistants," who devoted their full time and energy to the supervision of the societies and the continued expansion of Methodism into previously unevangelized areas.

The third and largest group of leaders included the local, or nonitinerating preachers, leaders of small groups, sick visitors, stewards, and housekeepers.[3] It was within this sphere that women found the widest range of opportunity and exerted their greatest influence upon the nascent revival. Those areas of leadership and participation which proved to be most significant as a training ground for the later women preachers were the offices of band and class leader, and sick visitor.

Following the model of older Anglican religious societies and the Moravian communities, Wesley subdivided his Methodist societies into small, homogeneous groups of four or five persons of the same sex and marital status. The primary purpose of these "bands" was intense personal introspection coupled with rigorous mutual confession for those who were "pressing on to perfection."[4] The *Rules of the Band-Societies,* which Wesley had drawn up during the Christmas of 1738, emphasize this intimate, confessional design.[5] While admission into these small cell groups was dependent only upon an earnest desire to be saved, the penitential discipline administered upon all and by all was intense.

At Bristol on February 15, 1742, the desire to liquidate the debt on the New Room led to another major subdivision in the societies. The well-known suggestion of one Captain Foy concerning the "proper method for discharging the public debt" was adopted, and it was agreed that "the whole society would be divided into little companies or classes—about twelve in each class."[6] While a rather mundane concern, therefore, provided the initial impetus for these developments, Wesley immediately seized upon this financial expedient as an opportunity for the improvement of pastoral care and oversight within his rapidly expanding network of societies.[7] These classes, usually composed of twelve persons of both sexes, were divided topographically or according to the exigencies of membership and leadership, and soon began to meet weekly for fellowship of a somewhat less intensive nature than that of the bands.

Wesley appointed the men and women who were responsible under him for the spiritual oversight of the members of these bands and classes. Profoundly aware of the perils of numerical success, he was determined to maintain as close a contact with his followers as possible. His perception of the practical value of suggested arrangements and his organizational genius were important factors contributing to Wesley's unprecedented ability to maintain personal contact with his growing constituency.

It was the band and class leaders, however, who stood nearest to the rank and file of the movement, and for this reason they occupied a strategic position within the societies. They were drawn from every conceivable sector of the English society.[8] And they exerted a powerful influence upon the development of the Methodist institution. An examination of the inner structure of the societies reveals that the movement was sustained by a vast network of trained, functioning laypersons who viewed their roles, not as passive recipients for whom ministry was performed, but as active, ministering servants who cared for one another.[9] While in the eighteenth century it was strange for such offices to be occupied by the uneducated and impoverished, it was an even greater anomaly that a large number of the leaders should be women.[10]

Such leaders had to be persons of spiritual and emotional maturity. Not only were they highly visible as representatives of the Methodist movement, but they were charged with the pastoral oversight of souls under their care. A number of personal characteristics were necessary in order to discharge this sacred responsibility.[11] The first prerequisite was a clear understanding of God's saving grace and the way of salvation as an experienced reality in their lives. Integrally related to this primary attribute was a concomitant desire to transmit this saving knowledge and experience to others.

Trustworthiness and personal integrity were conspicuous and indispensable qualities for these roles, as is evidenced by the numbers who were quickly removed from their offices because of lapses in these specific areas. The primary function of these leaders was to assist their Methodist brothers and sisters in a common quest for holiness by means of exhorting, rebuking, or offering advice according to the exigencies of each particular situation. Many of the women were well suited by nature for this kind of spiritual nurturing, and some, such as Eliza Bennis, exercised their office with such sensitivity and discernment that the preachers refused to allow them to resign.[12]

Since segregation both by sex and marital status was a basic principle of the band meeting, leadership was based primarily upon one's ability to empathize with the spiritual and temporal struggles of the members. Mutual ministry and the sharing of spiritual concerns were fundamental aspects of the nurture which took place within the bands. Wesley attempted to secure leaders, therefore, from among the members in the first instance, and very often a natural leader was already present in the person who had gathered the others. But sometimes he chose other leaders, and there were many instances of one leader providing pastoral guidance for several bands.

The Methodist class, however, represents a different category. For the class meeting was normally a kind of "family" gathering, where old and young, women and men, might be present, and where the male community leader functioned most often as the natural leader of the group. Wesley or one of his itinerants, moreover, would fairly frequently be present at a class, and almost always at a quarterly gathering of all the classes in a society for the purpose of examining the membership and distributing class tickets. In the course of time, in those societies which were large enough to have some degree of segregation in the class structure, rarely was a man allowed to lead an exclusively female class, apart from the preacher.[13] Women did find themselves, however, at the head of men's classes in a number of isolated situations.

In October 1776, Wesley wrote to one of his favorite correspondents, Mrs. Dorothy Downes, expressing his views concerning the propriety of such an arrangement:

> As to the question you propose, if the leader himself desires it and the class be not unwilling, in that case there can be no objection to your meeting a class even of men. This is not properly assuming or exercising any authority over them. You do not act as a superior, but an equal; and it is an act of friendship and brotherly love.[14]

Mrs. Hainsworth, another wife of an itinerant preacher, found herself in a similar situation many years later in Rakefoot. According to a historian of Methodism in the north, she "showed a vigour of understanding, quick intelligence, and force of will, which fitted her for a foremost position in the Society. No wonder that she became a leader, and—somewhat against her will—a leader of men."[15]

Entry into this noble office often produced powerful effects upon the lives of those called to it and elicited the best qualities in some of the finest women of the day. Wesley recalled the model afforded by Jane Muncy in London:

> From the time that she was made a leader of one of two bands she was more eminently a pattern to the flock: in self-denial of every kind, in openness of behaviour, in simplicity and godly sincerity, in steadfast faith, in constant attendance on all the public and all the private ordinances of God.[16]

Such experiences were made possible for women because of the very nature of the small groups within the societies and the atmosphere they naturally tended to create. All members of the bands and classes were expected to give utterance to their thoughts, desires, and experiences. Women, as well as men, were encouraged and exhorted to "speak freely" concerning the state of their souls or any subject that was of significance to their pilgrimage in the faith.

Mrs. Elizabeth Taylor was noted for the breadth of her knowledge and the depth of her wisdom. She always expressed herself in a very plain and familiar manner, both within and outside the context of the class meeting. "The propriety of her observations," remarked her husband, "was generally evident and striking."[17] She was well versed in a wide range of theological topics and seldom feared venturing her opinion on controversial subjects. In Frances Pawson's characteristic words of approbation concerning the women leaders who had influenced her life, one of whom is honored as Methodism's first woman preacher, it is easy to discern the importance of the small groups in the revival and the way in which these institutions helped to pave the way for the enlarged activity of women in the societies: "I cannot repeat all the good things I heard from Mrs. Crosby, Mrs. Downes, and others. I can only add, that those little parties, and classes, and bands, are the beginning of the heavenly society in this lower world."[18]

Another office in which the early Methodist women excelled was that of sick visitor. In a letter to his brother, dated April 21, 1741, Wesley describes the institution of this office in London: "I am settling a regular method of visiting the sick h[ere]. Eight or ten have offered themselves for the work, who are like to have full employment."[19] In his lengthy letter of 1748 to the Reverend Vincent Perronet, published as *A Plain Account of the People Called Methodists,* Wesley describes the office in further detail:

> It is the business of a Visitor of the sick, to see every sick person within his district thrice a week. To inquire into the state of their souls, and to advise them as occasion may require. To inquire into their disorders, and procure advice for them. To relieve them, if they are in want. . . . Upon reflection, I saw how exactly, in this also, we had copied after the primitive Church. What were the ancient Deacons? What was Phebe the Deaconess, but such a Visitor of the sick?[20]

While it was not their privilege to teach in public, these persons were called to minister to the sick in both their temporal and spiritual necessities.[21] Moreover, Wesley's analysis of Matthew 25:36, "I was sick, and ye visited me," elicited one of his most radical statements, not only concerning the working equality of women in the life of the Church, but of their legitimate and noble place in the order of creation as well:

> "But may not *women,* as well as men, bear a part in this honourable service?" Undoubtedly they may; nay, they ought; it is meet, right, and their bounden duty. Herein there is no difference; "there is neither male nor female in Christ Jesus." Indeed it has long passed for a maxim with many, that "women are only to be seen, not heard." And accordingly many of them are brought up in such a manner as if they were only designed for agreeable playthings! But is this doing honour to the sex? or is it a real kindness to them? No; it is the deepest unkindness; it is horrid cruelty; it is mere Turkish barbarity. And I know not how any woman of sense and spirit can submit to it. Let all you that have it in your power assert the right which the God of nature has given you. Yield not to that vile bondage any longer! You, as well as men, are rational creatures. You, like them, were made in the image of God; you are equally candidates for immortality; you too are called of God, as you have time, to "do good unto all men." Be "not disobedient to the heavenly calling." Whenever you have opportunity, do all the good you can, particularly to your poor, sick neighbour. And every one of *you* likewise "shall receive *your* own reward, according to *your* own labor.[22]

This new undertaking not only produced immediate benefits, such as the saving of lives, the healing of sickness, the prevention of pain, and the removal of want, but it had a more abiding consequence in providing yet another important training ground for the later women preachers. Activity in this sort of benevolent service afforded countless opportunities for discussion of the life of faith, plain and open relations with other people, and, on occasion, evangelization by means of casual conversation and exhortation. When the visitation of the sick was gradually and naturally expanded to include work in the prisons among the unenlightened, evangelistic activities such as personal testimony conjoined with the reading of Scripture and exhortation specifically aimed at conversion received the approbation of Wesley and his ordained colleagues.[23]

GRACE MURRAY: A PROTOTYPE FOR FEMALE LEADERSHIP

In this early period Grace Murray stands out as a model of the Methodist woman. Her indefatigable labors and her standing as one of the celebrities of early Methodism demonstrate the heights to which a woman could rise if she were capable and dedicated. She first appears in connection with the Foundery Society in London where she is listed as one of the early band leaders in 1742.[24] Her *Memoirs* afford a glimpse of this early entry into the life of the unfolding revival:

> Mr. *Wesley* made me a *Leader of a Band;* I was afraid of undertaking it, yet durst not refuse, lest I should offend God. I was also appointed to be one of the *Visitors of the Sick,* which was my pleasant work.[25]

In October 1742, following the loss of her husband at sea, she returned to her mother's home in the north, and found there a larger sphere of usefulness. She was appointed one of the first class leaders of the newly established society at Newcastle, and entered fully into the pioneering work:

> Mr. *Wesley* fixed me in that part of the work which he thought proper; and when the House was finished, I was appointed to be the *Housekeeper.* Soon also, the people were again divided into *Bands,* or small select Societies; women by themselves, and the men in like manner. I had full a hundred in *Classes,* whom I met in two separate meetings; and a *Band* for each day of the week. I likewise visited the *Sick* and *Backsliders.* . . . We had also several Societies in the country, which I regularly visited; meeting the women in the day time, and in the evening the whole society. And oh, what pourings out of the Spirit have I seen at those times! It warms my heart now while I relate it.[26]

Soon after, an even wider sphere of action presented itself. "She travelled," according to her son, "by Mr. *Wesley's* direction, through several of the northern counties, to meet and regulate the female societies; afterwards she went over into *Ireland* for the same purpose."[27] Vigilant in these itinerant labors, frequently traveling without any companion, she became noted, not only for her evangelical conversation and prayers, but also for her equestrian skills.[28] While Stamp asserts that "she never indeed attempted to preach," he affirms that Wesley was accustomed to speak of her as his "right hand."[29]

In the important document concerning his relationship with Grace Murray, Wesley greatly commends her labors: "I saw the work of God prosper in her hands. . . . she was to me both a servant and friend, as well as a fellow-labourer in the Gospel."[30] Her varied duties as band and class leader, visitor of the sick, housekeeper, traveling companion, and itinerant "regulator" of the women's groups, all of which entailed no small amount of care and responsibility, she discharged with zeal and fidelity. Women, such as Grace Murray, functioned, in effect, as subpastors, leading the Methodist family in their simple acts of worship and service.

WESLEY'S VIEW OF THE CHURCH AND MINISTRY

The later phenomenon of women preachers within Methodism, while directly related to the conducive environment of the societies, must also be viewed within the context of Wesley's evolving conception of his own role in the revival, his theology of the Church, and his view of the ministry of the laity. For Wesley, theology and the practical life of the Church were inextricably interrelated: "His practices modified his theology, and his changed theology led him into new practices."[31] In this first phase of the revival there was naturally no intimation of a separate or specifically Methodist ministry differentiated from that of the Church of England. From the outset of the revival, however, Wesley clearly recognized the exceptional nature of his position.

In a letter to his anxious brother, written nearly three

months after his initial submission to, what was considered, the contemptible practice of field preaching, Wesley affords an important *apologia* for his actions:

> And to do this I have both an ordinary call and an extraordinary. . . . Perhaps this might be better expressed in another way. God bears witness in an *extraordinary manner* that my *thus exercising* my ordinary call is well-pleasing in his sight.[32]

While his ordinary call was conferred by the hands of a bishop, the extraordinary call, so he maintained, was being continually validated by the testimony of the Holy Spirit.[33] The spiritual fruits resulting from such novel activities in an extraordinary situation were positive proof of divine blessing. This basic conception was to have far-ranging implications; not only did it bear directly upon the practice of lay preaching which developed during the first two decades of the revival, but it supplied the basic rationale for the inclusion of women in these activities in later years.

The unfolding of Wesley's self-understanding during these early years reflects a tension in his mind about the nature of the Church. His adult life was characterized by an attempt to maintain a dynamic balance between two fundamentally different views of the Church. On the one hand, Anglicanism represented the apostolic or institutional Church, linked to its originative event by means of tradition and historical consciousness. The Wesleyan societies, on the other hand, embodied what might be called a charismatic view of the Church. The emphasis of this latter principle fell upon the faithful few, a fellowship of believers, and the living faith they held in common.[34] Wesley believed that these seemingly antithetical views were in fact compatible, and both could be enthusiastically embraced in their dialectical tension so long as the Methodist societies remained within the Church of England.

What is important, however, is that as early as 1746 Wesley tended to view the Church more and more in essentially functional rather than institutional terms. Nowhere is this conviction more clearly expressed than in his important correspondence with the pseudonymous John Smith. In his letter of June 25, 1746, he enunciates this view of the Church in response to charges of anarchism:

> I would inquire, What is the end of all *ecclesiastical order*? Is it not to bring souls from the power of Satan to God? And to build them up in His fear and love? *Order*, then, is so far valuable as it answers these ends; and if it answers them not it is nothing worth. . . . wherever the knowledge and love of God are, *true order* will not be wanting. But the most *apostolical order* where these are not is less than nothing and vanity.[35]

"Thus, during the first decade of the revival," claims Baker, "Wesley had formulated views of the Church and ministry that were charismatic rather than authoritarian, and therefore held within them the seeds of sectarianism."[36] These views, moreover, hold within them the key to his later acceptance of women preachers.

THE EMERGENCE OF MALE LAY PREACHERS AND EXHORTERS

One of the first indications that these dissident seeds had taken root, at least from the point of view of Wesley's critics, was the early appearance of lay preachers within the Methodist societies.[37] Lay preaching was a logical and natural extension both of the leveling principle and activities within the societies and the implicit theology of the movement. While Wesley's field preaching was probably more "irregular" in its transgression of the territorial cure of souls than the practice of lay preaching in the societies, for which there was strong precedent in the primitive Church, the employment of laymen to preach was regarded by many antagonists as the first serious aberration of Anglican discipline.[38] The rise of itinerant lay preaching transgressed both of these ecclesiastical conventions. The invasion of parishes by unordained preachers was a particular irritation, as one critic made abundantly clear:

> The Methodist Preacher came to an Anglican parish in the
> spirit, and with the language of a missionary going to the most
> ignorant heathens; and he asked the clergyman to lend him his
> pulpit, in order that he might instruct his parishoners for the
> first time in the true Gospel of Christ.[39]

The origin of the lay preachers, and Wesley's grudging
acceptance of them, is a primary example of the way in which
his pragmatic churchmanship was inextricably related to his
burning desire to proclaim a certainly unconventional gospel.
In this particular development, it is not surprising that
Wesley proceeded "cautiously, however, bit by bit as he felt
compelled rather than according to a carefully planned and
timed schedule."[40] Wesley's acceptance of lay preachers in
this early stage of the revival is of quintessential importance
to this study, because the privilege of preaching later
extended to a limited number of women in the 1760s directly
parallels that accorded to laymen. Wesley would also justify
his subsequent actions for the same reasons.

The Anglican priest accepted the services of laypersons as
leaders within the societies without hesitation, just as he had
committed pastoral responsibility to laypersons in Georgia.
But his assent to the activities of Methodist lay preachers,
such as the three Thomases, Maxfield, Richards, and
Westall, depended, as did his own unique calling, upon the
"extraordinary" nature of the ecclesiastical situation. Wesley
made this abundantly clear in his famous sermon (178), "The
Ministerial Office," in which he described the itinerant lay
preachers of the 1740s as "*extraordinary messengers,* raised
up to provoke the *ordinary* ones to jealousy."[41] Extraordinary circumstances demanded unusual action and responses.
Kent explicates the principle that was clear for Wesley:

> In such a moment God Himself is not limited by the rules of
> His Church, but is free to act through His chosen servants;
> when Christ's messengers find themselves at a loss, He
> Himself empowers them to turn from the normal pastoral
> system and themselves choose and appoint men to do what
> must be done.[42]

These early preachers were distinguished, therefore, from other contemporary lay evangelists both by their unswerving commitment to Wesley and his Arminian soteriology and their firm resolve to stay within the Established Church. Justification for the use of unordained preachers was to be found, not only in the unequivocal command of God to proclaim salvation in Christ, but also in the increasing necessity of pastoral oversight in the expanding movement.[43] "Neither the spread of the Methodist societies," claims Baker, "nor their proliferation into a connected network of evangelical pockets throughout the land would have been possible without the itinerant lay preachers."[44]

While in these early years of the revival the lay preachers drew their authority directly from Wesley, who sanctioned their calling and commissioned them for their work, their increasing success and the popularity of their preaching and pastoral oversight tended to create a de facto authority. In time, this principle of self-authentication contributed to an evolving ministerial self-consciousness. The principles at work here were to profoundly affect Wesley and his followers' attitudes toward the women who later assumed similar responsibilities.

The aspiring lay preachers had to evidence a number of marks in order to satisfy Wesley's stringent requirements. The Conference of 1746 struggled with the question of a Methodist lay ministry and developed a threefold test regarding "those who believe they are moved by the Holy Ghost and called of God to preach.":

> 1. Do they know in whom they have believed? Have they the love of God in their hearts? Do they desire and seek nothing but God? And are they holy in all manner of conversation?
> 2. Have they *Gifts* (as well as *Grace*) for the work? Have they (in some tolerable degree) a clear sound understanding? Have they a right judgment in the things of God? Have they a just conception of the *salvation by faith?* And has God given them any degree of utterance? Do they speak justly, readily, clearly?

3. Have they success? Do they not only so speak as
generally either to convince or affect the hearts? But have any
received remission of sins by their preaching? a clear and
lasting sense of the love of God? As long as these three marks
undeniably concur in any, we allow him to be called of God to
preach. These we receive as sufficient reasonable evidence
that he is moved thereto by the Holy Ghost.[45]

Those who possessed these three characteristics of conversion (or grace, gifts, and fruit) were then placed "on trial" for
one year before being admitted into "full connection," at
which time they were further examined by the conference.[46]

A call was the essential qualification for the lay preachers,
the authenticity of which was tested by the marks.[47] A strong
emphasis was placed upon the dynamic interaction and
present activity of the Holy Spirit, both to confirm and
actualize the call. David Shipley has described the vocation
of preaching in early Methodism, therefore, as "a response
to the act of God in bestowing 'the call to preach' and the
personal presence of the Holy Spirit to assure the sole source
of power for the actualization of that 'call'."[48]

While the call normally consisted of both an inward call
from God and an outward call of the church, symbolized in
the act of ordination, both of which Wesley himself could
claim as an ordained priest of the church, it is clear that for
him only the inward call was essential. "I allow, that it is
highly expedient, whoever preaches in His Name should
have an outward as well as an inward call," he emphasized in
his "Caution against Bigotry," "but that it is *absolutely
necessary,* I deny."[49]

Wesley took this argument one step further in a defensive
reply to the criticisms of the Reverend Thomas Adams:

It is true that in *ordinary* cases both an *inward* and an *outward*
call are requisite. But we apprehend there is something far
from "ordinary" in the present case. And upon the calmest
view of things, we think they who are only called of God, and
not of man, have *more* right to preach than they who are only
called of man, and not of God.[50]

This position, of course, not only opened the door for the activities of laymen, but it afforded a consistent and incontrovertible justification for their labors. Moreover, if the call was genuine, the fruit produced as a result of the preaching was considered the equivalent of an outward call.[51]

Wesley's acceptance of the lay preachers was dependent, moreover, upon two fundamental distinctions which he clearly delineated toward the close of his life in the all-important sermon, "The Ministerial Office." With regard to the first distinction, Wesley appealed to the Old Testament and the dual offices of priest and preacher:

> In ancient times the office of a Priest and that of a Preacher were known to be entirely distinct. . . . From Adam to Noah, it is allowed by all that the first-born in every family was of course the Priest in that family, by virtue of primogeniture. But this gave him no right to be a Preacher, or (in the scriptural language) a Prophet. . . . For in this respect God always asserted his *right* to send by whom he *would* send.[52]

Wesley, therefore, viewed his lay preachers as prophets not as priests.

Likewise, from the New Testament he drew a second distinction between pastors and evangelists:

> I do not find that ever the office of an Evangelist was the same with that of a Pastor, frequently called a Bishop. . . . I believe these offices were considered as quite distinct from each other till the time of Constantine.[53]

While the pastor presided over the flock and administered the sacraments, it was the special province of the evangelist to assist him and preach the Word. The early Methodist lay preachers, viewed as prophets (preachers) and evangelists, therefore, required no formal episcopal sanction for their activities. These itinerant preachers were not only called but personally chosen by Wesley who then took full responsibility for them and fitted them as best he could for their work.[54]

The selection of these "sons in the gospel" tended to

evolve naturally, with candidates progressing by the logic of events from the lower levels of leadership in classes and bands, through a number of intermediate stages, to their eventual status as preachers.[55] This natural progression may be seen in the complaint of an anonymous critic:

> No sooner does a person commence Methodist; than he may hope to rise through all the different gradations of the Society, and may even aspire to become in time a travelling preacher.[56]

The general pattern which began to emerge was that of a personal impression or call, often received with reluctance or even furious resistance, growing in intensity, leading to consultation with fellow members of the society, public testimony and prayer, followed by a venture into preaching *ad probandam facultatem,* the fruits of which justified the sower in continuing to sow and reap.[57] Not infrequently circumstances forced ultimate submission to a call and helped to clarify it at the same time. Leslie Church suggests the following general impression:

> It was natural that the class member, accustomed to giving his testimony in what was a family circle, should wonder whether he ought not to bear his witness in the world outside. Often, when such thoughts were in his mind, someone suggested that he should exhort. Sometimes the suggestion was strong enough to amount to a commissioning which brought what had been a vague sense of possibility to a definite divine call, interpreted through a human suggestion or even command.[58]

Given the fact of female preponderance in the societies, it is not surprising to find the same general pattern influencing the lives of women as well as men.

One of the intermediate stages between the private prayer and testimony of the small groups and the public exposition of Scripture in preaching, alluded to in the preceding quotation, is that of exhortation. The position of "exhorter" is an interesting class of leadership within the Methodist system, not only because of its elusory relation to the "local preacher"—the lay preachers of Methodism who were engaged in some form of secular employment and, therefore, did not "travel" or itinerate in the Connection, but functioned as "worker/preachers"—but also because of the large number of early Methodist women who functioned in this capacity.[59]

This peculiar office seems to have arisen out of the extenuating circumstances created by the impressment of Methodist lay preachers for the royal navy in Cornwall, a particularly effective way of surpressing the movement. According to some reports, this practice left scarcely a lay preacher at liberty in the entire county.[60] In the absence of the lay preachers, the societies continued to meet and certain of the leaders not only admonished the members in their several classes but also "gave an exhortation" to larger groups.

Exactly when this practice began to develop is difficult to determine, but as early as 1746, when Charles Wesley journeyed into Cornwall, he discovered four such exhorters at Gwennap:

> I talked closely with each, and find no reason to doubt their having been used by God thus far. I advised and charged them not to stretch themselves beyond their line, by speaking out of the Society, or fancying themselves public teachers. If they keep within their bounds as they promise, they may be useful in the church: and I would to God that all the Lord's people were Prophets, like these![61]

A year later when John examined the stewards of all the Cornish societies, he found no fewer than eighteen such laborers in the county and after examination found thirteen of these well suited for the work. These he advised to "be helpful when there was no preacher in their own or the neighbouring societies," and admonished to "take no step without the advice of those who had more experience than themselves."[62] While the activities of the exhorters fell short of preaching, in the usual sense of the term, they were expected to demonstrate the same qualities as the lay preachers, and their calling was tested likewise by the graces, gifts, and fruits they exhibited.

What differentiated the exhorter from the lay preacher

was that the lay preacher "took a text." This simple phrase had become synonymous with the transition from exhorting to preaching by 1770. In her study of the contribution of local preachers, who were sometimes described as exhorters, Margaret Batty suggests that exhorting consisted of "reproving sin, pleading with sinners to flee from wrath to come, describing his own experience in those matters and testifying to his present joy."[63] Over time, these exhortations apparently assumed a somewhat rigid form, held together around these particular aspects of the Christian life. Some exhorters found themselves as permanent substitutes for seldom-arriving traveling preachers, particularly in the more isolated areas. A common practice developed of reading one of Wesley's sermons or other devotional material, interjecting comments or personal applications as particular situations merited.[64] Women who functioned in this capacity were receiving invaluable experience in the art of evangelical proclamation. The distinction between exhorting and preaching, moreover, was a fine line soon crossed by an impassioned speaker, man or woman.

NOTES

1. Wearmouth, *Methodism and Common People,* p. 221.
2. See Baker, *John Wesley and the Church of England,* pp. 106–19.
3. For the organization of the early societies and their evolving structure, see Baker's chapter, "The People Called Methodists, 3. Polity" in Davies and Rupp, *History of the Methodist Church,* 1:213–55. Cf. Simon, *John Wesley and the Methodist Societies,* pp. 214–21.
4. On the nature of the bands, see Davies and Rupp, *History of the Methodist Church,* 1:189–91, 218–25; and Baker, *John Wesley and the Church of England,* pp. 51–61, 75–79.
5. Wesley, *Works,* 8:272–73. These regulations included five questions asked of everyone at every meeting: "(1) What known Sin have you committed since our last Meeting? (2) What Temptations have you met with? (3) How was you delivered? (4) What have you thought, said or done, of which you doubt whether it be a Sin or not? (5) Have you nothing you

desire to keep secret?" Cf. Wesley, *Journal,* 3:201; and *Standard Sermons,* 2:299–301, 305.

6. Wesley, *Journal,* 2:528; cf. *Works,* 8:252–53; 13:259; and *W.H.S.* 3:64–65.

7. Upon his return to London, he divided the societies there into classes as "there could be no better way to come to a sure, thorough knowledge of each person." And on April 25, 1742, he described this as "the origin of our classes at London, for which I can never sufficiently praise God, the unspeakable usefulness of the institution having ever since been more and more manifest" (Wesley, *Journal,* 2:535). Cf. Davies and Rupp, *History of the Methodist Church,* 1:222–25; Baker, *John Wesley and the Church of England,* pp. 77–78, 87.

8. Warner, *Wesleyan Methodism in Industrial Revolution,* pp. 261–62. Cf. David L. Watson, "The Origins and Significance of the Early Methodist Class Meeting" (Ph.D. diss., Duke University, 1978), pp. 317–20; and P. D. MacKenzie, "The Methodist Class Meeting: A Historical Study" (Th.M. thesis, St. Andrews University, 1969), pp. 74–79.

9. An able defense of this conclusion has been provided by James L. Garlow, "John Wesley's Understanding of the Laity as Demonstrated by His Use of the Lay Preachers" (Ph.D. diss., Drew University, 1979).

10. See p. 49 above. It is important to differentiate clearly between band and class meetings and the nature of their respective leadership, for the general preponderance of women in the early Methodist societies does not necessarily imply a preponderance of women at both levels of leadership. The overwhelming number of women band leaders was due to the need for them in the sexually segregated band units. Since there were more women than men in most societies, band leadership was preponderantly feminine. Many of these women, however, possessed innate pastoral talent which contributed greatly to their stature within the society. But it is very doubtful whether there were near as many women class leaders as there were men. Most of the family-oriented classes were sexually mixed, and most of these small groups were led by men, including, of course, a large number of ministers and itinerants who functioned in this capacity.

11. A descriptive analysis of this office is afforded in Garlow, "John Wesley's Understanding of Laity," pp. 197–201.

12. Crookshank, *Memorable Women,* p. 24.

13. See Watson, "Origins of Class Meeting," p. 317. David

Watson's unqualified assertion that "at no time was a man allowed to lead a female class" was based upon Stevenson's supposition to that effect (*City Road Chapel*, p. 29) and must be read cautiously in the light of these important qualifications.

14. Wesley, *Letters*, 6:233; cf. *Journal*, 6:130.

15. William Jessop, *An Account of Methodism in Rossendale and the Neighbourhood* (Manchester: Tubbs, Brook, and Chrystal, [1880]), p. 293. A John Hargreaves enrolled himself in her class and felt that he had acted wisely as she "stood spiritually and intellectually head and shoulders above every other member of the Society." Jessop subsequently reveals his own prejudices regarding the proper place of women: "Although it may be very plain, according to Scripture, and the fitness of things, that women are not born to rule, the economy of Methodism has wisely provided for the employment of female-leaders, thereby affording to devout and intelligent women one of the most useful and honourable spheres to be found in the universal church. . . . There is, however, such an incongruity in men's meeting with female leaders, as must prevent it from coming into general practice; but there are some exceptional instances in which a female stands out in a Society so distinctly superior to all the rest of the members that the incongruity is reduced to a minimum."

16. July 31, 1741, Wesley, *Journal*, 2:483.

17. D. Taylor, *A Sermon Occasioned by the Death of Mrs. Elizabeth Taylor, Who Departed This Life October 22, 1793* (London: Printed for the Author, 1794), pp. 68–69.

18. Joseph Sutcliffe, *The Experience of the Late Mrs. Frances Pawson, Widow of the Late Rev. John Pawson* (London: Printed at the Conference Office, by T. Cordeux, 1813), p. 84.

19. Wesley, *Oxford Edition*, 26:55–56; cf. *Letters*, 2:306; and *Journal*, 2:448, 453–54.

20. Wesley, *Works*, 8:263.

21. See Wesley, *Notes*, Romans 16:1.

22. Sermon 98: "On Visiting the Sick," Wesley, *Works*, 7:125–26.

23. On the work of Sarah Peters, see pp. 95–96 below.

24. It is not within the scope of this study to discuss the controverted issue of John Wesley's relationship with this early Methodist woman, and particularly their aborted engagement. On the life and work of Grace Murray, see William Bennet, *Memoirs of Mrs. Grace Bennet* (Macclesfield: Printed and sold by E. Bayley, 1803). Considerable attention was drawn to the relation between these two Methodist celebrities

by Nehemiah Curnock in his article, "The Loves and Friendships of John Wesley," *Methodist Recorder Winter Number* 43 (Christmas 1902): 21–32, which sympathized greatly with Mrs. Murray (see also some modification of his views in the editorial notes, Wesley, *Journal*, 3:284, 367, 371, 395, 416–40). At best, it is difficult to harmonize some of his statements with those more sympathetic to Wesley in Tyerman, *Life of John Wesley*, 2:42–57, who is followed by Stevens, both in *Women of Methodism*, pp. 114–28, and in *The History of the Religious Movement of the Eighteenth Century Called Methodism*, 3 vols. (London: Wesleyan Methodist Book Room, 1878), 3:406–12. The study of J. Augustin Leger, *John Wesley's Last Love* (London: J. M. Dent & Sons, 1910) is an attempt to provide a full and accurate reconstruction of the relationship based on all the pertinent documents and previous studies. More recent studies have opened new areas of debate concerning this intriguing couple. See Simon, *John Wesley and the Advance of Methodism*, pp. 107–14, 138–45; and Frank Baker, "John Wesley's First Marriage," *L.Q.R.* 192, 4(October 1967): 305–15.

25. Bennet, *Memoirs of Grace Bennet*, p. 11. Cf. Stevenson, *City Road Chapel*, p. 29.

26. Ibid. pp. 13–14. Cf. William W. Stamp, *The Orphan-House of Wesley; With Notices of Early Methodism in Newcastle-upon-Tyne* (London: Published by J. Mason, 1863), pp. 42–53. Sarah Ryan, who was appointed housekeeper at the New Room, Bristol, and also managed the school at Kingswood from 1757 to 1761, functioned in the same capacity in the southwestern center of Methodism. A. G. Ives describes her similar responsibilities, which included "meeting a hundred persons every week in Methodist class or band, and also making excursions into the country around Bristol" (*Kingswood School in Wesley's Day and Since* [London: Epworth Press, 1970]), pp. 50–51. See Wesley's letters of November 8 and 22, 1757, to Mrs. Ryan, providing instructions and establishing regulations for the office of housekeeper, in Wesley, *Letters*, 3:239–41.

27. Bennet, *Memoirs of Grace Bennet*, p. 19. Elsewhere her son claims that she "was the principal person employed by [Wesley] to organize the female classes of his connection" (see William Bennet, *A Treatise on the Gospel Constitution* [London: Sold by B. I. Holdsworth, 1822], p. 8). Cf. Wesley, *Journal*, 3:284, 367, 371–75, 416–40, 515.

28. See the interesting anecdote in T. P. Bunting, *The Life of Jabez Bunting, D.D.*, 2 vols. (London: T. Woolmer, 1887), 1:5.

29. Stamp, *The Orphan-House*, p. 48.

30. Wesley's MS account is preserved in the British Library and has been accurately reproduced with narrative and notes in Leger, *Wesley's Last Love.* Cf. Stevens, *Women of Methodism*, p. 118.

31. Baker, *John Wesley and the Church of England*, p. 137.

32. John Wesley to Charles Wesley, June 23, 1739, Wesley, *Oxford Edition*, 25:660.

33. For this view Wesley was very possibly indebted to the influential Anglican divine, Richard Hooker, whose similar views are expressed in the seventh book of his *Laws of Ecclesiastical Polity*. See Baker, *John Wesley and the Church of England*, pp. 64–65.

34. There is no need to describe Wesley's ecclesiastical odyssey here in detail, as that service has been rendered elsewhere. See in particular, Baker, *John Wesley and the Church of England*, pp. 137–59.

35. Wesley, *Oxford Edition*, 26:206.

36. Baker, *John Wesley and the Church of England*, p. 113.

37. A vast literature has been devoted to this important topic. See in particular, Henry Bett, *The Early Methodist Preachers* (London: Epworth Press, 1935); Maldwyn Edwards, *Laymen and Methodist Beginnings* (Nashville: Methodist Evangelistic Materials, 1963); Baker, *John Wesley and the Church of England*, pp. 79–84. Several dissertations of value touch this area, such as James Simpson Wilder, "Early Methodist Lay Preachers and Their Contribution to the Eighteenth-Century Revival in England" (Ph.D. diss., University of Edinburgh, 1948); Blackmore, "Lay Preaching in England"; and Garlow, "John Wesley's Understanding of the Laity." On the question of the first lay preacher, see Frank Baker, "Thomas Maxfield's First Sermon," *W.H.S.* 27, 1(March 1949): 7–15.

38. Ecclesiastical law stipulated that "only a deacon ordained to the ministry of the Word was entitled to venture upon the authoritative exposition of Holy Scripture" (Baker, *John Wesley and the Church of England*, p. 79). Cf. Kirkham, "Pamphlet Opposition to Methodism," pp. 168–75; and John Kent, *Jabez Bunting, the Last Wesleyan: A Study in the Methodist Ministry after the Death of John Wesley* (London: Epworth Press, 1955), p. 10.

39. Cited in A. M. Lyles, *Methodism Mocked: The Satiric Reaction to Methodism in the Eighteenth Century* (London: Epworth Press, 1960), p. 28.
40. Baker, "John Wesley's Churchmanship," p. 271.
41. Wesley, *Works,* 7:277.
42. Kent, *Jabez Bunting,* p. 13.
43. See Kent's analysis, "The Extraordinary Messengers of God," in *Jabez Bunting,* pp. 7–16.
44. Baker, *John Wesley and the Church of England,* p. 81. Likewise, Garlow observes that "the lay preachers sustained Methodism. A permanent structure could not have been built by Wesley alone, not merely because of the extraordinary growth of the societies, but because very few clergy would provide leadership. Thus lay preachers became the vehicles by which England was evangelized" ("John Wesley's Understanding of the Laity," pp. 66–67).
45. John Bennet's Copy of the Minutes of the Conferences of 1744, 1745, 1747 and 1748; with Wesley's Copy of those for 1746," in *Publications of the Wesley Historical Society* (London: Published for the Wesley Historical Society by Charles H. Kelly, 1896), p. 35.
46. These questions retained their essential form after 1766 and may be found in Wesley, *Works,* 8:325–26.
47. See Leslie F. Church, "The Call to Preach in Early Methodism," *L.Q.R.* 179 (July 1954): 185–91; E. Fay Bennett, "The Call of God in the Ministry of John Wesley: A Study of Spiritual Authority in Methodist History," (diss., Southwestern Baptist Seminary, 1963); Garlow, "John Wesley's Understanding of the Laity," pp. 82–84.
48. David C. Shipley, "The Ministry in Methodism in the Eighteenth Century," in *The Ministry in the Methodist Heritage,* ed. Gerald O. McCulloh (Nashville: Board of Education, Methodist Church, 1960), p. 16.
49. Wesley, *Standard Sermons,* 2:119; cf. *Works,* 13:200.
50. October 31, 1755, Wesley, *Oxford Edition,* 26:610–11; cf. the momentous letter of September 24, 1755, to Rev. Samuel Walker concerning the question of separation from the Church of England (26:592–96), as well as the strong defense of lay preaching afforded in his *Appeals to Men of Reason and Religion* (11:28–30, 292–302).
51. Garlow suggests that "Wesley's insistence upon 'fruit' in his potential lay preachers was not in keeping with the Anglican procedure of securing priests in eighteenth-century

England. . . . Wesley's preachers were not separated from the common folk by ordination. Their 'authority,' whatever it might be, existed not in orders, but in moral and spiritual accomplishments" ("John Wesley's Understanding of the Laity," p. 81); cf. p. 84. While this may be true, a precedent for such a view existed within Anglicanism itself and Wesley could have appealed to Hooker on this very point: "Men may be extraordinarily, yet allowably, two ways admitted into spiritual function in the Church. One is when God himself doth of himself raise up any whose labour he useth without requiring that men should authorize them; but then he doth ratify their calling by manifest signs and tokens himself from heaven" (*Ecclesiastical Polity*, VII, xiv, 11). The profound influence which Susanna exerted upon her son at this point must also be acknowledged. It is well illustrated in the well-known story of her restraining Wesley from silencing the "first Methodist lay preacher," Thomas Maxfield. Baker reconstructs this epochal event: "Wesley cried, 'Thomas Maxfield has turned preacher, I find!' To which his mother calmly replied: 'John, you know what my sentiments have been. You cannot suspect me of favouring readily anything of this kind. But take care what you do with respect to that young man, for he is as surely called of God to preach as you are. Examine what have been the fruits of his preaching: and hear him also yourself.' As John did so he would recall a childhood memory of his own mother discoursing to a crowd of parishioners in the rectory at Epworth" (*John Wesley and the Church of England*, p. 83). Cf. Baker, "Thomas Maxfield's First Sermon," pp. 7–15.

52. Wesley, *Works*, 7:274.
53. Ibid., pp. 275–76.
54. See Douglas R. Chandler, "John Wesley and His Preachers," *Religion in Life* 24, 2(Spring 1955): 241–48.
55. See the illuminating survey of biographical details of the "first race" of Methodist preachers afforded by Warner in *Wesleyan Movement in Industrial Revolution*, pp. 248–67. Cf. Church, "Call to Preach," pp. 185–91; and Watson, "Origins of Class Meeting," p. 320.
56. *A Review of the Policy, Doctrines and Morals of the Methodists* (London: J. Johnson, 1791), p. 8.
57. "To demonstrate capability." Cragg notes that Wesley was "appealing to the example of the Reformed churches, but he was unquestionably aware of the use of *facultas* in churches of

the Catholic tradition" (Wesley, *Oxford Edition*, 11:298). Cf. Frederick A. Norwood, "The Shaping of Methodist Ministry," *Religion in Life* 45, 3(August 1974): 348–49; Garlow, "John Wesley's Understanding of the Laity," p. 83; and Church, "Call to Preach," pp. 186–87.

58. Church, "Call to Preach," p. 189.
59. The striking similarity between this role and the practice of "prophesying" in the puritan tradition is one of tremendous import. See pp. 6–7 above.
60. See Simon, *John Wesley and the Methodist Societies*, pp. 238–39.
61. June 30, 1746, Charles Wesley, *Journal*, 1:419. Cf. Duncan Coomer, "The Local Preacher in Early Methodism," *W.H.S.* 25, 3(September 1945): 33–42; Garlow, "John Wesley's Understanding of the Laity," pp. 208–11; Davies and Rupp, eds., *History of the Methodist Church*, 1:236–37. Exhorters have also been identified in Yorkshire at Todmorden in 1749.
62. July 9, 1747, Wesley, *Journal*, 3:307. Cf. Jackson, *Lives of Early Methodist Preachers*, 3:295–96; 5:222.
63. Margaret Batty, "The Contributions of Local Preachers to the Life of the Wesleyan Methodist Church until 1932, and to the Methodist Church after 1932 in England" (M.A. thesis, University of Leeds, 1969), p. 38.
64. Ibid., pp. 35–36.

3

COMMUNICATING THE GOSPEL IN ALL BUT PREACHING

D URING THE FIRST DECADES of the Wesleyan revival, women became engaged in a number of modes of public speaking. As we have seen, the fact of general female preponderance, the effects of the pioneering and sustaining labors of women, the peculiar character of the Methodist societies, and the extraordinary nature of their mission, all combined to create an environment conducive to the expansion of female leadership roles in the revival. In this early period, women employed three particular means of communicating their newly discovered faith which proved to be stepping-stones or intermediate stages to the actual proclamation of the gospel in formal preaching. While each of these modes—public prayer, testimony, and exhortation—are distinct in terms of function, in practice they are often inseparable.[1] Each is grounded in the evangelical urge to save souls and, because it is primarily a charismatic activity, finds its ultimate warrant in the present and enabling work of the Holy Spirit.

PRAYING IN PUBLIC

For many of the early Methodist women public prayer was their first experience in public utterance. They undoubtedly felt a great amount of freedom to pray in the small, family-oriented groups within the societies. Often women founded prayer meetings which augmented the Methodist system of classes and bands. The evangelistic orientation of such groups is clearly reflected in A. B. Seckerson's account of Mary Prangnell's activities on the Isle of Wight:

> She became exceedingly desirous that others should partake of the same blessing, and this she diligently laboured to promote, by forming prayer meetings in various parts of the neighbourhood, and attending them at every opportunity without neglecting her duties as a wife and a mother.[2]

Sarah Moore, who received her first membership ticket in 1749 at eleven years of age and led the first class meeting at Hallam when only seventeen, was noted for walking "from her home in Sheffield to Bradwell to hold prayer-meetings in the house of Isabella Furness and Margaret Howe, of that High Peak village."[3]

Women were often encouraged to venture forth in such activities as the instruments of revival, as was the case with one Isabella Wilson:

> Hitherto, though urged to it, Miss Wilson had refrained from exercising herself publicly in the cause of religion, but hearing, from the late Mr. Percival, of the revival which had taken place in Yorkshire some years ago, in which it had pleased God particularly to own the prayer-meetings; and seeing her relations brought into Christian liberty, and the work prospering around her, from earnest supplications in private, she proceeded to pray more openly for such as were in distress of soul, and not in vain; the Lord often graciously answered for himself. Her mode of praying was not loud, yet fervent, and her faith remarkably strong in a present Saviour for a present salvation.[4]

"And she was more and more willing," claims her biographer, "to be accounted a fool if she might be the means of glorifying God, and helping others."[5] This recurring sentiment is echoed in the life and labors of Anne Warren, whose husband testified that

> she clearly saw that she was likely to be of little or no service to the church of Christ, till she was willing to lay all her notions of honour and respectability at the foot of the cross, and to be willing to be accounted "a fool for Christ's sake." This

referred chiefly to her reluctance to engage in public prayer, in the company of other females, and in her own family.[6]

The prayers of the women reflected a wide range of styles and forms, as may well be expected, extending from the exotic and abstruse to the ingenuous and profound. In his *Journal,* Wesley relates a very interesting specimen of a prayer, that, in spite of its peculiarity, seems to have affected him greatly:

> The fire kindled more and more, till Mrs. ——— asked if I would give her leave to pray. Such a prayer I never heard before: it was perfectly an original; odd and unconnected, made up of disjointed fragments, and yet like a flame of fire. Every sentence went through my heart, and I believe the heart of everyone present. For many months I have found nothing like it. It was good for me to be here.[7]

Some of the women, such as Sarah Crosby, were highly gifted in the art of prayer. On the occasion of her death, Frances Pawson recalled one of her unique qualities: "She used to begin prayer with the simplicity of a little child, and then rise to the language of a mother in Israel. Thus she prayed with the Spirit, and with understanding."[8] Toward the close of the century no figure was so renowned for her exertions in public prayer as was Ann Cutler, affectionately known as "Praying Nanny."[9]

In the advertisement to William Bramwell's account of her life and work, Zechariah Taft says that "her peculiar call from Heaven appears to have been chiefly the exercise of *importunate believing prayer.*"[10] Following her conversion she began to exercise her gifts in public and became more convinced about the authenticity of her calling:

> She began to pray in meetings and several were awakened and brought to God. The effects of her labours were manifest. . . . Her manner and petitions were strange to numbers, as she prayed with great exertion of voice and for *present blessings.* She would frequently say, "I think I must pray. I cannot be happy unless I cry for sinners. I do not want any praise: I want nothing but souls to be brought to God. I am reproached by

most. I cannot do it to be seen or heard of men. I see the world
going to destruction, and I am burdened till I pour out my soul
to God for them."[11]

While her public prayers were generally very short, the
extent and intensity of her personal devotional life was
unparalleled. It was characterized by frequent and often
lengthy periods of private prayer, as many as twelve to
fourteen such times each day, in addition to usual nocturnal
orisons. "For prayer," testified Bramwell, "I never expect to
see her equal again."[12]

The work of Sarah Peters in the London prisons during the
early years of the revival affords an excellent example of the
evangelistic application of prayer and its natural transformation into testimony and exhortation in such circumstances.[13]
Wesley observes that "it was her peculiar gift and her
continual care, to seek and save that which was lost; to
support the weak, to comfort the feeble-minded, to bring
back what had been turned out of the way."[14] The
evangelistic urge of this Foundery Society band leader may
be illustrated, moreover, by one of her own characteristic
statements: "I think I am all spirit; I must be always moving,
I cannot rest, day or night, any longer than I am gathering in
souls to God."[15] When Silas Told began his pioneering work
among the condemned malefactors in London's Newgate
Prison, he found an able and willing assistant in Sarah. In
October 1748, when religious services were organized for the
inmates by these Methodists, Sarah proved indefatigable:

> Six or seven of those who were under sentence of death came.
> They sung a hymn, read a portion of scripture, and prayed.
> Their little audience were all in tears. Most of them appeared
> deeply convinced of their lost estate. From this time her
> labours were unwearied among them, praying with them and
> for them, night and day.[16]

She visited all of the prisoners in their cells, sometimes
going alone, sometimes in the company of one or two others.
She "exhorted them, prayed with them, and had the comfort
of finding them every time more athirst for God than
before."[17] In these efforts she was instrumental in the

conversion of a number of souls who courageously bore witness to their newfound faith in the face of death. When John Lancaster, one of the first converts, entered the press-yard to be executed, he saw Sarah, "stepped to her, kissed her, and earnestly said, 'I am going to paradise to-day. And you will follow me soon.'"[18] His prophecy was fulfilled, when two weeks later, she died from the "prison fever," contracted as a result of her labors. In these types of exercises the thin line between prayer and exhortation, or even scriptural exposition and preaching, often became blurred.

THE TESTIMONY OF METHODIST WOMEN

The similarity between Wesley's charismatic view of the church, or at least of his societies within the church, and the Puritan notion of a "gathered church" has been suggested by a number of scholars.[19] One of the primary characteristics of the Puritan church which later became prominent in Methodism was an emphasis upon testimony. "Though Wesley did not make the testimonial of one's experience a requirement of admission as had the Congregationalists," observes Monk, "the testimonial became a significant feature of the Methodist societies."[20] The necessity of religious self-expression within the small groups of early Methodism served to train an articulate laity and became an important factor in the spread of the gospel through both male and female instrumentality.

It was natural, and therefore not uncommon, for the sharing of personal testimonies to follow immediately a regular service of preaching. During an extended tour of Wales, after preaching on August 13, 1746, at Llan-saintffraid, Wesley records that one of the women

> could not refrain from declaring before them all what God had done for her soul. And the words which came from the heart went to the heart. I scarce ever heard such *a preacher* before. All were in tears round about her, high and low; for there was no resisting the Spirit by which she spoke.[21]

This particular incident is noteworthy, not only because of the response of overwhelming approbation it elicited from Wesley, but also because of the explicit enunciation of the charismatic theme it affords.

What the early Methodists experienced, they felt compelled to share. And Wesley firmly believed that God, through the power of the Holy Spirit, would enable those who had received salvation to bear witness to the transforming work of Christ in their lives. Moreover, the evidence that God "owned" this type of witness was substantial. At the close of a service at Athlone, in Ireland, a Mrs. Glass responded to his call to "give yourself, soul and body, to God," and bore witness before all the congregation in a way that "pierced like lightning."[22]

Other occasions of public worship and Christian fellowship provided an appropriate context for testimony, afforded women a unique opportunity to exercise their gifts, and contributed to the development of their skills in communicating the gospel. From the outset of the revival, Wesley intended all such activities to be ancillary to the Church of England. "Means of grace" soon developed, however, which supplemented the public worship of the Established Church and the more intimate fellowship of the bands and classes. In time, the early morning preaching service, the love feast, the watchnight service, and the covenant service all became distinctive features of the Methodist revival.[23] Wesley characteristically adopted and adapted these services from the sources that appealed to him the most, namely, the primitive Church, the Moravian societies, the Puritan tradition, and his beloved Church of England. Of all these services, it was the love feast that afforded women the greatest opportunity for self-expression.

These love feasts, patterned after the *agape* of the early Church and the contemporary Moravian services, became an extension of the class and band meetings in Methodism and involved the simple symbolic act of eating and drinking together.[24] The first Methodist love feast was apparently held by the women of the Bristol Society on April 15, 1739.[25] Baker succinctly describes the essential nature of these gatherings for Christian fellowship and nurture:

> Scores of references to love-feasts in eighteenth- and nine-teenth-century diaries and journals testify to the fact that though the common meal was of real importance as a symbol of Christian family life, and though prayer and singing were inseparable from such occasions, the focal point was testimony, the spiritual "sharing" to which the taking of food and drink together was the symbolic prelude.[26]

Wesley attested to this charismatic nature of the gatherings and to the ability of the Holy Spirit to equip the faithful as the instruments of divine love. "I have seldom heard people speak with more honesty and simplicity," he said, "than many did at the love-feast which followed. I have not seen a more unpolished people than these; but love supplied all defects."[27] This charismatic principle involving the testimony of the Holy Spirit finds full expression in the well-known Wesley verse:

> Poor idiots He teaches to show forth His praise,
> And tell of the riches of Jesus's grace.
> No matter how dull the scholar whom He
> Takes into His school, and gives him to see;
> A wonderful fashion of teaching He hath,
> And wise to salvation He makes us through faith.[28]

That this principle should apply to women as well as men was self-evident, at least in the mind of John Wesley. And he enforced this view at a love feast in the West Riding of Yorkshire which was remembered to the end of the century:

> I hastened back to the lovefeast at Birstall. It was the first of the kind which had been there. Many were surprised when I told them, "The very design of the lovefeast is free and familiar conversation, in which every man, yea, every woman, has liberty to speak what ever may be to the glory of God."[29]

The supreme value of the love feast for the women lay in its open fellowship and its Christian expression of freedom and equality. In contrast to the intimate dialogue of the small fellowship groups, the love feast provided a more public sphere for the exhibition of women's talents and the open expression of their faith. "Small wonder," says Baker, "that heightened emotions, renewed vows of dedication, and even conversions, were frequent at the love-feasts."[30]

The joint meeting of the bands also proved to be a fruitful context for these experiences. In a characteristic and now familiar vein, Wesley recorded the events of a combined band meeting at the Norwich Foundery:

> While a poor woman was speaking a few artless words out of the fullness of her heart, a fire kindled and ran, as flame among the stubble, through the hearts of almost all that heard; so, when God is pleased to work, it matters not how weak or how mean the instrument.[31]

Likewise, at the meeting of bands at Whitby, the influence of pent-up emotions was evident as "one plain woman cried, and spoke, and cried again, so that they were in tears on every side."[32] In a letter to Mrs. Bennis, Wesley emphasized the beneficial effects of such testimony and explained why everybody ought to declare what God has done for his soul: "Those who are saved from sin should freely declare it to believers," he advocated, "because nothing is a stronger incitement to them to seek after the same blessing."[33]

For some of the women, as may well be expected, participation in such testimonials and testifying to the present activity of God in their lives before a large, albeit sympathetic, group necessitated a great amount of courage. The public expression of personal experiences was an activity seldom entered into lightly, and often, only after a long period of inner turmoil. Sarah Crosby carefully copied a portion of Jane Cooper's personal diary into her Letterbook, which deals with important experiences during the final year of her short but eventful life.[34] This record typifies the experience of many Methodist women who became engaged in public speaking.

The pattern of preliminary apprehensiveness, eventual submission to the impulse to speak, and the consequent sense of satisfaction and spiritual approbation which the account exemplifies could be multiplied many times over with regard to the experience of the early Wesleyan women. The breakthrough for Jane Cooper came on January 15, 1762:

Went to Lon^n on Friday to the Meeting. Mr. M^d desired any to Speak who had not before declared the goodness of God. I was convinced I ought to Speak but fear'd I sh^d bring a reproach upon the Cause by my foolishness was tempted to think I sh^d fall down in a fit if I began & that I knew not how to order my Speach aright. but the L^d said "take no thou^t how or what you shall Speak for in that hour it Shall be given you. . . ."

. . . I felt an awful sense of God while Speaking & sat down with emotion that Spoak to my Heart well don good & faithfull Servant. My Soul was so well Satisfied with the approbation of Xt. I neither wish'd nor fear'd what man thou^t of me. I only pray'd they might receive the truth in the Love of it lest their Souls Sh^d Suffer loss. I am content to be vile let God be glorified & it sufficeth.[35]

As in the case of many other women, Miss Cooper's venturing upon this activity, and not so much the activity as the manner of her discourse, produced an initial wave of opposition. This particular case illustrates how such ostracism was often interpreted as a divine seal upon the labors of the persecuted faithful:

In going home I heard that Mr. B. Said I made an exhortation for half an hour on friday. what will not prejudice report My God lay not fully to His Charge. Thou knowest whose words I spoke & for what cause I did so. all hail my Saviour's hallow' d Cross! Now I begin to be a deciple if all men Speak evil of me for thy sake. Make me Steady to Stand reproach & give cause for it.[36]

In the minds of some, apparently, the testimonial exertions of women came perilously close to transcending the limits of their sex. What was of primary importance to these female witnesses, however, was the satisfaction of preserving a conscience void of offense toward God.

FEMALE EXHORTATION WITHIN THE METHODIST SOCIETIES

While exhortation resembled preaching in many ways, this activity fell short of true preaching, as we have seen, by virtue of its definition.[37] It consisted primarily of reproving sin, pleading for the sinner to repent and be saved, and testifying to one's own experience. The exhorters, therefore, did not actually proclaim the gospel by "taking a text"; rather, their function was to invoke a response from those who had already heard the Good News.

While the origins of this office apparently reside in the lack of authorized lay preachers in certain regions and the exigencies of similar situations, the practice of exhorting is also closely related to and a prominent feature of the Methodist *ars moriendi*.[38] "I should not wonder if a *dying* saint were to prophesy," exclaimed John Wesley in a letter to his brother. "Listen to Sally Colston's last words!"[39] The deathbed exhortation of Elizabeth Maxfield, wife of Wesley's first "son in the gospel," is exemplary:

> Some young people came to see her, and she exhorted them, very earnestly to turn to the Lord in the time of their youth. All were affected much, at what she said to them, as she let no one go out of her company without entreating them to trust in the Lord with all their hearts.[40]

Wesley encouraged women to exhort their fellow Methodists in a variety of contexts, from the intimacy of casual conversation to the formality of public services of worship. He emphasized the importance of this activity to one young lady who was particularly gifted in this sphere:

> I believe you do not willingly lose any opportunity of speaking for a good Master. I apprehend you should particularly encourage the believers to give up all to God, and to expect the power whereby they will be enabled so to do every day and every moment. I hope none of your preachers speak against this, but rather press all the people forward.[41]

Several months later he advised her to "snatch all the opportunities you can of speaking a word to any of your neighbours," and encouraged her to "exhort the believers to go on to perfection."[42]

Exhortation was a natural co-implicant of Wesleyan evangelical theology, therefore, and obtained a distinctively close relationship to the doctrine of "perfect love" or Christian Perfection, the flying goal toward which all Methodists pressed in this life. Thus Wesley viewed the formal gathering of the society at Newcastle as an appropriate occasion for such exertions:

> One means of retaining the pure love of God is the exhorting others to press after it. When you meet on a Sunday morning, I doubt not but this will be the chief matter both of your prayers and conversation. You may then expect to be more and more abundantly endued with power from on high, witnessing that He is faithful and just both to forgive us our sins and also to cleanse us from all unrighteousness.[43]

It was only natural that prayer and testimony should evolve, by the logic of events, into exhortation, especially within the context of the public prayer meetings. This natural progression is evident in the life of a young Yorkshire lass, Ann Thompson, who had been converted under the preaching of a woman:

> Some time after her conversion, she began to exercise in the public prayer meetings, and now and then, to give a word of exhortation. Finding that in proportion to her endeavours for the salvation of others her own happiness increased;—and seeing that her labours were acceptable to the people and owned of God, she began to multiply her exertions.[44]

Penelope Newman, a bookseller from Cheltenham who later became a renowned woman preacher, began to exhort in prayer meetings soon after she united with the Methodists. Through these activities she was instrumental in the conversion of the man she would marry, Jonathan Coussins, who thereafter became one of Wesley's noted itinerants.[45] One of Ann Cutler's exhortations is described in some detail by William Bramwell:

> In the evening we had a public prayer meeting in the chapel. She then stood upon one of the forms and gave us an exhortation, which was well approved. She was uncommonly

earnest for precious souls. The zeal she had for them seemed to be unparalleled. There were many singularly blessed of God.[46]

By means of such exertions, Methodism was founded in Barnard Castle in about 1747 by Catherine Graves. After traveling with George Whitefield in Scotland, she returned to the Dales, instituted a prayer meeting in that market town, became the leader of a class, and exhorted the small assemblies when they gathered together.[47]

While exhortations were also common in the classes and bands[48] and occasionally served an evangelistic function outside of the societies,[49] they most frequently followed the preaching of an itinerant, just as "prophesying" had followed the preaching of Puritan ministers in the previous century. In a letter to Zechariah Taft, Mary Holder explained the nature of her exhorting:

> My method, as you know, was to give a word of exhortation after my dear husband had finished his sermon, or to pray, as I felt led by the spirit of God: and I must say, the Lord has owned and blessed my feeble efforts, to the spiritual profit of some precious souls.[50]

Likewise, after Sarah Drury of Doncaster was made a class leader, "she began to exhort sinners to turn to the Lord. This she always preferred doing, after some friendly preacher had ended his sermon."[51]

Many of the women were extremely reticent about exercising themselves in such a public manner, both for personal reasons and for the sake of the movement. In spite of a tremendous conviction regarding her duty to call sinners to repentance, Sibyll Best expressed great ambivalence in the face of taking such a step:

> On her first obtaining the salvation of God, she felt much for sinners, and cried, and prayed for them before God in private. She saw it her duty *now* to pray for them and to exhort them in public; but the latter she felt, as if she durst not attempt; partly from natural timidity and bashfulness, and partly

because she knew this would not be well received by some whom she thought she dared not to offend.[52]

Fearful of "grieving the spirit of God," she eventually resolved to embrace the first opportunity for such service and was assured that the Holy Spirit would assist her in her labors.

The spiritual turmoil experienced by Judith Land of Norfolk typifies the struggle of many women to reconcile an unequivocal sense of duty or calling with the social and religious norms of the day:

> Feeling an increasing love for perishing sinners, and an earnest desire for their salvation, she ventured in public to give a word of exhortation, which the Lord owned with his blessing. She began to feel this more and more her duty: indeed the salvation of her own soul seemed closely connected with her striving to save the souls of others; she became greatly alarmed at this, especially when she considered her want of judgement and ability; on this ground she endeavoured to excuse herself, and stifled those convictions, until the anguish of her soul became intolerable. . . . She had no peace until she consented to *exhort sinners to repent and turn to God:* so [as] soon as she obeyed God in this, her peace returned. She is never so happy as when exercising in these labours of love, knowing that this is the will of God concerning her. Hitherto the Lord has owned her labours, hereby testifying that she is not deceived.[53]

The strength of a woman's convictions concerning the necessity of her warning and exhorting sinners was usually enough to enable her to withstand the onslaught of ridicule and abuse that inevitably came her way. But when pressed to defend their cause, these women exhorters could say with the father of Methodism:

> Shall I, for fear of feeble man,
> The Spirit's course in me restrain?—
> Or, undismay'd in deed and word,
> Be a true witness for my Lord?

> The love of Christ doth me constrain
> To seek the wandering souls of men;
> With cries, entreaties, tears, to save,
> To snatch them from the gaping grave.
>
> For this let men revile my name;
> No cross I shun, I fear no shame:
> All hail, reproach! and welcome pain!
> Only thy terrors, Lord, restrain.[54]

Of all the women of the nascent revival, no woman came closer to preaching in the formal sense of the term than did Alice Cross of Booth-Bank in Cheshire.[55] She introduced Methodism to Booth-Bank in 1744 by inviting the itinerants to her home to preach. A pulpit was erected in the largest room of her house and a small society formed. She served as the leader of this small band of Methodists for many years and developed a reputation for the way in which she provided hospitality for common beggars and earnestly exhorted them to seek the salvation of God. As a result of her labors, Booth-Bank became the center of Methodism in Lancashire and Cheshire, her farmhouse being licensed for preaching even before a Methodist chapel was built in Manchester.

Tyerman says that "Alice had been a rude, uncultivated creature, but had a dash of the heroine in her constitution."[56] John Pawson left a fascinating manuscript account of her work which Everett subsequently published in his history of Methodism in Manchester. He attests to the nature of her activities:

> When they happened to be disappointed of a preacher, she herself would occupy the pulpit. While hearing a sermon, I never saw her sit down. She took her stand beside the pulpit, and turned her face to the wall, so that she never saw who was there till the service was over.[57]

William Stamp helped to clarify this somewhat enigmatic statement in a subsequent article concerning John and Alice Cross:

> Mrs. Byrom, of Liverpool, whose ancestors formed part of the original society in this place, observes, that, "when the Preacher who was expected to fill the little pulpit was by any means prevented from coming, Alice invariably supplied his lack of service, but *never entered the pulpit!*[58]

Unfortunately, no other information is available concerning this would-be female preacher. What is clear is that Alice was functioning as a technical exhorter, at the very least, as early as the mid-1740s, and even perhaps as a "local preacher" if the "sermon" referred to in Pawson's account was indeed hers. If she did "preach" in the formal sense, however, there is no confirmation of the fact by Wesley.[59]

In 1759 Wesley advised an unknown, and apparently gifted, woman concerning the stewardship of her talents:

> In one word, be anything but a trifler, a trifler with God and your own soul. It was not for this that God gave you
> "A mind superior to the vulgar herd." No, Miss———, no! but that you might employ all your talents to the glory of Him that gave them. O do not grieve the Holy Spirit of God! Is He not still stirring within you?[60]

If pushed to its logical extreme, the principle expressed in this statement could be used to sanction even the preaching of women. While the Wesleys could not as of yet accept such a step, the door was certainly ajar, and continuing to open.

Indeed, in spite of his general prohibition, as early as 1755, in an important document which Wesley prepared for the conference of that year, he seems to allow for the possibility of women's preaching in exceptional cases. He distinguishes between authority to preach and authority to administer the sacraments, and finds precedent for this view in the practices of the early Church:

> Evangelists and deacons preached. Yea, and women when under extraordinary inspiration. Then both their sons and their daughters prophesied, although in ordinary cases it was not permitted to "a woman to speak in the church."[61]

Moreover, some Methodists were profiting from the ministrations of women preachers from other traditions, such as Mary Peisley, a well-known Quaker minister from Ireland, who was offered the hospitality of the Methodist chapel in Norwich in 1753.[62] And Methodist women themselves were being allowed to assume roles within the Wesleyan societies that the Church had seemingly always reserved for men. They were determined to employ all the talents that God had given to them.

NOTES

1. On these modes as preliminary to preaching, see E. K. Brown, "Women of the Word," in *Women in New Worlds,* ed. Thomas and Keller, 1:70–73, and his "Wesley and Women Preachers," *Circuit Rider* 6, 1(January 1982): 6–7.
2. Anthony Seckerson, *Memoirs of the Experience, Life, and Death, of Mrs. Mary Prangnell, of Merston, in the Isle of Wight* (Newport: Published by W. W. Yelf, 1827), p. 7. Cf. Dyson, *Methodism in the Isle of Wight,* pp. 134–38. Dyson reports that Mary often took a leading part in these exercises and developed a reputation as a great woman of prayer. In addition to her public ministrations she was known "to spend a greater part of the night in this holy exercise, pleading with God for her children, the members of her class, and for the salvation of souls" (p. 137). She was Elizabeth Wallbridge's class leader, the woman who became immortalized in the nineteenth century as "the dairyman's daughter." See Legh Richmond, *The Dairyman's Daughter* (Edinburgh: Oliphant Anderson and Ferrier, 1869); Benjamin Carvosso, "The Dairyman's Daughter," *Wes. Meth. Mag.* 61 (1838): 102–9; and Dyson, *Methodism in the Isle of Wight,* pp. 189–226.
3. J. J. Graham, *A History of Wesleyan Methodism in Sheffield Park, Sheffield* (Sheffield: Sir W. C. Leng, 1914), pp. 12–13. It is noteworthy that late in life Wesley blamed the dissipation of religious fervor on the dissolution of such prayer meetings; see e.g., *Journal,* 7:276.
4. John Pipe, "Memoir of Miss Isabella Wilson," *Meth. Mag.* 31 (1808): 461. Her biographer further notes that while the preachers were setting forth full salvation "from the pulpit, and

by various publications, she strove to cast her mite into the sacred treasury, by meeting classes, holding meetings for prayer, visiting the sick, by epistolary correspondence, and spiritual conversation when in company with others" (p. 462).

5. Ibid., p. 462.
6. Samuel Warren, *Memoirs and Select Letters of Mrs. Anne Warren: With Biographical Sketches of Her Family*, 2d ed. (London: Printed for the author, sold by John Mason, 1832), p. 44.
7. September 17, 1764, Bath, Wesley, *Journal*, 5:94.
8. Sutcliffe, *Experience of Frances Pawson*, pp. 104–5. Mrs. Elizabeth Mortimer, a devoted friend and colleague, recognized this unique gift and "used to say, that she could descend to the capacity of a child, and then rise again to expatiate on the deep things of God, with those that had attained the highest state of grace." On the occasion of their first meeting, Sarah had advised her to pray with simplicity. Cf. Brown, "Women of the Word," p. 72.
9. Like Sarah Crosby, Ann Cutler would later appear as one of early Methodism's exceptional women preachers. See pp. 102–3, 225–26 herein.
10. William Bramwell, *A Short Account of the Life and Death of Ann Cutler*, new ed. with appendix by Z. Taft, containing *An Account of Elizabeth Dickinson* (York: Printed by John Will, 1827), p. 2.
11. Ibid., p. 6. She received much criticism concerning the manner of her praying. While recognizing the validity of the complaints lodged against her, she rejoined: "I have tried to pray differently, but am always less confident. I would do anything to please if it did not hurt my own soul: but I am in this way the most free from wanderings, and have the greatest confidence" (p. 11).
12. Ibid., p. 11.
13. John Wesley published an account of her labors several years following her death in November 1748 as a part of his seventh published journal of 1754. See Wesley, *Journal*, 3:381–87. This was reprinted toward the end of his life as "Some Account of Sarah Peters," *Arm. Mag.* 5 (1782): 128–36. Cf. Silas Told, *An Account of the Life and Dealings of God with Silas Told, Late Preacher of the Gospel*, 3d ed., corrected (London: George Whitfield, 1786); *London Magazine* (1748): 426–67; Tyerman, *Life of John Wesley*, 2:27–29; Simon, *John Wesley*

and the Advance of Methodism, pp. 127–28; and Church, *More about Early Methodist People,* pp. 196–99.
14. *Arm. Mag.* 5:128.
15. Ibid.
16. Ibid., p. 129.
17. Ibid., p. 130.
18. Ibid., p. 134.
19. Wesley was a master at the art of plastic synthesis, and in the development of his societies borrowed from a number of traditions. Simon, for instance, in his *Wesley and the Religious Societies* and *Wesley and the Methodist Societies,* stresses the affinity between Wesley's societies and those of Anglicanism. Towlson has emphasized the influence of Moravianism. On the question of Methodist affinity with Puritanism, see Duncan Coomer, "The Influence of Puritanism and Dissent on Methodism," *L.Q.R.* 175, 4(October 1950): 346–50; Horton Davies, "Epworth's Debt to Geneva—A Field of Research," *Livingstonian* (1960): 5–6; John A. Newton, *Methodism and the Puritans* (London: Dr. Williams's Trust, 1964); A. Skevington Wood, "John Wesley's Reversion to Type; The Influence of His Nonconformist Ancestry," *W.H.S.* 35, 4(December 1965): 88–93; and Robert C. Monk, *John Wesley: His Puritan Heritage* (New York: Abingdon Press, 1966), esp. pp. 211–218. In this last work, Monk delineates a number of characteristics of the gathered Church, drawn primarily from the analysis afforded in the works of Geoffrey Nuttall, which are consonant with Methodist self-understanding. These include the view of the Church as a fellowship of mutually concerned individuals, acceptance of holiness as the aim of Church life, an insistence upon freedom of opinion, and the close discipline required of members.
20. Monk, *Puritan Heritage,* p. 212.
21. Wesley, *Journal,* 3:250 (emphasis added).
22. June 17, 1749, in ibid., p. 405.
23. See Church, *More about Early Methodist People,* pp. 210–88.
24. An authoritative examination of the development and decline of the Methodist love feast is afforded in Frank Baker, *Methodism and the Love-Feast* (London: Epworth Press, 1957). For a brief survey, see Church, *More about Early Methodist People,* pp. 237–42.
25. See Wesley's letter of April 21–26, 1739, Wesley, *Oxford Edition,* 25:635. A love feast for the men was held subse-

quently on May 29, 1739, at the Baldwin Street Society (Wesley, *Journal,* 2:186).

26. Baker, *Methodism and the Love-Feast,* p. 25.
27. September 4, 1776, Axminster, Wesley, *Journal,* 6:126.
28. Quoted in Wesley, *Journal,* 7:49, in relation to a love feast held in London on February 6, 1785.
29. July 19, 1761, Wesley, *Journal,* 4:471. Cf. 4:439–41; 5:304; Warren, *Memoirs of Anne Warren,* p. 44; and Church, *Early Methodist People,* p. 56. On this particular occasion, a spiritual flame was kindled that "ran from heart to heart, especially while one was declaring, with all simplicity, the manner wherein God, during the morning sermon (on the words, 'I will, be thou clean,') had set her soul at full liberty."
30. Baker, *Methodism and the Love-Feast,* p. 26. See the vivid description of such an event in Stamp, *Methodism in Bradford,* p. 42.
31. January 30, 1761, Wesley, *Journal,* 4:432.
32. June 17, 1770, in ibid., 5:371.
33. March 29, 1766, Wesley, *Letters,* 5:6; cf. 6:94, 127–28.
34. Wesley had a very high estimate of Cooper's character and writing. See his anonymous publication of *Letters Wrote by Jane Cooper: To which is Prefixt, some Account of Her Life and Death* (London: Strahan, 1764); cf. Jane Cooper, "Christian Experience," *Arm. Mag.* 5 (1782): 408–9, 489–90; and Wesley, *Journal,* 4:539. Born at Higham in Norfolk in 1738, she died at the young age of 25 in November 1762. The portion of her diary copied by Sarah Crosby covers the period between January 9, 1762, and March 13, 1762. See Sarah Crosby, MS Letterbook, 1760-1774, Perkins Library, Duke University, pp. 108–19.
35. Crosby, MS Letterbook, pp. 111–13.
36. Ibid., p. 114.
37. See pp. 83–84 above.
38. This is an area of interest that still requires much research. The Methodists were certainly indebted to the characteristic expression of Anglican spirituality with regard to the "rules and exercises of holy dying," embodied in the devotional classics of Jeremy Taylor, which works profoundly influenced the young Wesley and helped to form his view of the Christian life.
39. February 8, 1763, Wesley, *Letters,* 4:202. Cf. Wesley, *Journal,* 6:75; and the account of Elizabeth Vandome, who, on her deathbed "exhorted them all to live near to God" (5:298).

40. *A Short Account of God's Dealings with Mrs. Elizabeth Maxfield, Wife of the Rev. Thomas Maxfield* (London: Printed by J. W. Pasham, 1778), p. 30.
41. John Wesley to Jane Hilton, March 1, 1769, Wesley, *Letters,* 5:128.
42. John Wesley to Jane Barton, November 1, 1769, in ibid., p. 151.
43. John Wesley to Elizabeth Ritchie, June 23, 1774, in ibid., 6:94. While Wesley thought exhortation was an important means of encouraging his adherents to full conformity to the image of Christ, he also recognized that many received remission of sins through the exhortative ministries of women, and thereby began their pilgrimage of faith. For examples, see Wesley, *Journal,* 7:91; Crookshank, *History of Methodism in Ireland,* 1:55, 389; and Crookshank, *Memorable Women,* pp. 28–29.
44. Taft, *Holy Women,* 2:219.
45. See W. A. Green, "Jonathan and Penelope Coussins," *W.H.S.* 34, 3(September 1963): 58–60; *Meth. Mag.* 29 (1806): 290–92, 296, 344; and Taft, *Holy Women,* 1:291.
46. Bramwell, *Account of Ann Cutler,* p. 21.
47. See Steele, *Methodism in Barnard Castle,* pp. 16–18; Harold Beadle, "Methodism in Barnard Castle and Upper Teesdale before 1800," *W.H.S., Northeast Branch* 21 (March 1974): 4–8; "The Highest Market Town in England," *Methodist Recorder Winter Number* 41 (Christmas 1900): 84; and Wesley, *Journal,* 4: 29n. Church remarks how in 1753 when Whitefield visited the town he discovered that the Methodist women were known locally as "lilty-pattens" because of the wooden pattens they wore to the preaching house each morning (*More about Early Methodist People,* p. 136).
48. See Sarah Stevens' account of her exhortation in a letter to her husband, dated June 26, 1794: "Last evening we assembled together to meet in class; when several who were not members, desired permission to come and be with us during our meeting, which was granted. I found great enlargement of heart while *speaking to the people;* and was led in a particular manner to *exhort* them to look for a present blessing, and to venture on Christ by faith" (Taft, *Holy Women,* 1:162–63).
49. See the account of Jane Treffry, who "went to the hospital and spoke to a large company of sick and dying," in Richard Treffry, Jr., *Memoirs of Mrs. Jane Treffry* (London: Published by John Mason, 1830), pp. 94–96.

50. February 11, 1825, Taft, *Holy Women,* 1:128; cf. 1:100.
51. Ibid., p. 249.
52. Ibid., p. 97.
53. Ibid., p. 201. For other examples of female exhorters in the eighteenth and nineteenth centuries, see 1:50, 91, 143, 151, 246; 2:180, 182, 188.
54. This hymn, sometimes entitled "The Faithful Ambassador," was John Wesley's translation of the hymn by Gerhard Tersteegen (1697–1769), and appeared in *A Collection of Hymns for the Use of the People Called Methodists,* no. 279. A textual analysis of this hymn is afforded in Wesley, *Oxford Edition,* volume 7.
55. This remarkable woman (not to be confused with Alice Crosse [née Booth] of Hoo Hoyle, whose first husband was Samuel Sutcliffe and who later married John Crosse, vicar of Bradford) was probably born in 1709, married a Cheshire farmer by the name of John Cross, and died at her home in Booth-Bank on May 29, 1774. For the primary sources concerning her life and work, see Appendix A. It is very possible that the first Methodist Quarterly Meeting in Cheshire was held at the Cross home in 1752. On this question, see Wesley F. Swift, "Early Methodism in Northwich," *W.H.S.* 22, 2(June 1939): 38–45; *W.H.S.* 7:78–79; and *Wes. Meth. Mag.* 66 (1843): 376. Their home is pictured in Wesley, *Journal,* 3:297, and *W.H.S.* 7: facing p. 75.
56. Tyerman, *Life of John Wesley,* 1:546.
57. Everett, *Methodism in Manchester,* p. 65. Tyerman, following this account, states that "Alice herself would occupy the pulpit, and, with faithful energy, declare the truth as it is in Jesus" (*Life of John Wesley,* 1:546). Likewise, E. A. Rose, in *Methodism in Cheshire to 1800* (Wilmslow: Published by Richmond Press, [1979]), p. 33.
58. *Wes. Meth. Mag.* 66 (1843): 27 (emphasis added). This testimony would seem to indicate that Pawson's statement to the effect that she "occupied the pulpit" was simply a euphemism for her supplying the lack of the preacher's services. It was common for later women preachers of the 1770s to refuse offers to occupy pulpits, taking their place, instead, beside the pulpit or on some other elevated platform. This was also the usual protocol of Quaker women preachers and other dissenting females of the previous century.
59. Wesley visited the home of John and Alice Cross in 1747 and spoke of the little society meeting in their house as a "quiet

and loving people," but makes no mention of her activities. See Wesley, *Journal,* 3:296.
60. February 21, 1759, Wesley, *Letters,* 4:51–52.
61. Baker, *John Wesley and the Church of England,* p. 333. The manuscript copy of this address, "Ought We to Separate from the Church of England?" in the hand of John Nelson, has been published in its entirety as an Appendix in Baker's book, pp. 326–40. Baker points out that in his translation of 1 Corinthians 14:35, Wesley correctly alters the "women" of the Authorized Version to "woman." It should also be noted that Wesley adumbrates a view here which he fully explicated in his later sermon, "The Ministerial Office." See p. 81 above.
62. See *Some Account of the Lives and Religious Labours of Samuel Neale, and Mary Neale, Formerly Mary Peisley, Both of Ireland,* new ed., enlarged, ed. A. R. Barclay (London: C. Gilpin, 1845), pp. 325–26. In a letter to her cousin, James Pim, July 24, 1753, Mary Peisley wrote: "I was obliged to make a visit to a large congregation of the people called Methodists at their place of worship, who behaved with great moderation, and some of them discovered a Christian love and tenderness; their speaker left the assembly to us, sat quietly by us all the time, and bid us act according to our freedom, which led us to silence for near an hour, a thing I believe very uncommon to them."

PART II

*Expanding the Role of
Women to Include
Preaching: The Methodist
Revival in Full Flower,
1761–1791*

Mrs. Mary Taft. Engraved by W. Holl from an original painting.

4

A DECADE OF EXPERIMENTATION, 1761–1770

I N THE SUMMER OF 1763, Samuel Johnson, the staunch High Churchman and quick-witted conversationalist, remarked to his faithful Boswell: "Sir, a woman's preaching is like a dog's walking on his hinder legs. It is not done well; but you are surprised to find it done at all."[1] Unlike his noted contemporary, Wesley's initial prejudice against the preaching of women gradually dissipated as, step by step, in response to the exigencies of extraordinary situations, he followed the internal promptings of the Holy Spirit, always testing them with the authority of Scripture, reason, experience, and tradition. His attitude toward the whole question began to change over the course of the revival's third decade, just as his views on lay preaching were necessarily transformed a generation earlier. From 1761 to 1770 the roles of women in the movement continued to expand in a logical and natural progression, and, while their numbers were not large, a small group of women began to emerge as Methodism's first women preachers.[2]

Had the question not arisen of its own accord, it is probable that Wesley would never have contemplated the use of women in preaching. Undoubtedly, the same could have been said with regard to the male lay preachers. In the early nineteenth century, Zechariah Taft would employ this very argument and take it one step further:

> Mr. Wesley, in the former part of his life, was opposed to women preaching, but never so much an enemy to it as he was to *lay preaching;* but no sooner was he convinced that God was with them, that sinners were converted by them, than he not only ceased to forbid them, but gave them encouragement.[3]

As we shall see, the same dynamics that were operative in Wesley's acceptance of the first lay preachers were to be reduplicated in the cases of certain exceptional women.

The same distinctions that Wesley had employed in earlier years would prove to be of critical importance once again. And while subtle distinctions, or even apparently sharp ones—such as that between giving a short "exhortation" in a service and preaching from a text—often became blurred in the heat of the moment, it was only through such experiences and experimentation that a clearer definition of the practices and roles of women could emerge.[4] Of primary importance is the fact that Wesley never conceived of lay preaching, male or female, as a right to be seized; rather, it was a gift of God to an exceptional few to be exercised with a profound sense of responsibility.

SARAH CROSBY: FIRST AUTHORIZED WOMAN PREACHER

While a number of early women, such as Alice Cross, Catherine Graves, or even Grace Murray, came very close to preaching, the first woman to receive Wesley's informal authorization for activities in this sphere was Sarah Crosby.[5] Unfortunately, very little is known about the early life of this significant figure. Born on November 7, 1729 (New Style), apparently in the Leeds area, she was converted on October 29, 1749. One result of this transformation was an insatiable desire to proclaim her newfound faith to others. She recorded:

> I was 20 years old within a week, when God revealed his Son in my heart, and now I thought all my sufferings were at an end. I laboured to persuade all with whom I conversed, to come to Christ, telling them there was love, joy, peace, &c. for all that come to him.[6]

She heard both Whitefield and Wesley preach in London during that winter and joined the Foundery Society in October 1750, becoming a leader of a class some two years later.[7]

Sarah's husband, the man who had introduced her to Wesley's writings, apparently deserted her after a marriage of about seven years, on February 2, 1757.[8] A new chapter in Sarah's life opened the following May, therefore, when she met Mary Bosanquet and formed with her one of the most significant friendships of early Methodism. Mary, a somewhat perplexed youth at the time, sought the spiritual counsel of her Methodist friends, and in her journal recalls this initial encounter with the elder Mrs. Crosby. She records the compelling nature of her ingenuous testimony:

> I received a message from Miss Furley, (now Mrs. Downs,) that on such a day Mrs. Crosby would be at her house. I went to meet her in the spirit of prayer and expectation. She simply related what God had done for her soul.[9]

Later that summer Sarah settled in Christopher's Alley, in Moorfields, not far from the Foundery, where she resided with a circle of women including Mrs. Sarah Ryan, Mary Clark, and occasionally Miss Bosanquet.[10] The work of these women among the poor and indigent of London was soon to become famous.

Sarah had been subject to strong religious impressions from the days of her childhood. Activities in the London Society, however, intensified her eagerness to exhort others to repentance and faith, a desire which was the natural consequence of her experience of conversion. Indeed, she seems to have been consumed by this sense of duty:

> From the love I felt to those I knew to be equally fallen from original righteousness with myself, I often desired to be instrumental in turning them to God, and never had a moment's peace any longer than I endeavoured to aim at this wherever I came.[11]

While her spiritual experience was one of ecstatic ups and downs, the more intimate her knowledge of salvation became, the more her desire to declare the work of God was accentuated. After having assumed the responsibilities of a class leader she received a vision of Jesus while in prayer, "and he spake these words to my heart, *'Feed my sheep.'* I answered, 'Lord, I will do as thou hast done; I will carry the lambs in my bosom, and gently lead those that are with young.' ''[12] It was by means of gradual steps, therefore, that Sarah progressed from testimony in her class to the more public witness of preaching.[13]

She experienced something of a call to preach, or the glimmer of such a call, in conjunction with a profound awakening of God's grace in her life, all of which she related to Wesley in a letter:

> I felt my soul as a vessel emptied, but not filled. Day and night I was amazed at the blessed change my soul experienced; but I said nothing to any one, because I was not, as yet, sure what the Lord had done for me; though I had always promised, if the Lord would but fully save me, I would declare his goodness although I believed it would expose me to various exercises, both from Ministers and people.[14]

In March 1760, she experienced that fullness of salvation upon which her calling seems to have been contingent. In her manuscript Letterbook, on a separate page dated from the time of the experience, she describes the ecstasy of the total self-emptying which God wrought in her soul:

> Who after many a Winters Night & Summers Day had brought me to a Period, even to make one hearty renunciation of *all! all!* O! what doth that imply? . . . I am determined to be all the Lord's, yea and My God hath taken me for His own forever.

The next month, she wrote from Leeds to a friend, asserting both the primacy of God's grace in salvation and the prerogative of the Spirit to work where God wills:

> That it is the work of the Lord I am *sure*. He is undoubtedly pouring out his Spirit upon many. Let *us* join to pray that he may pour it out more abundantly; If God will work who shall hinder?[15]

She was apparently ripe for preaching, and a special occasion of spiritual outpouring was not long delayed.

In 1759 a young woman by name of Dobinson acquiesced

to Sarah Crosby's entreaties to participate in her class meeting, was converted largely through the instrumentality of her conversation and prayers, and joined the Foundery Society.[16] At the commencement of 1761, this zealous new Methodist and her husband moved from London to Derby with the express intention of forming a Methodist society there. In this enterprise they were supported through the presence and assistance of Mrs. Crosby.[17] Not only did this venture lead to the establishment of a society, but it marks the beginning of women's preaching as well.

Twenty-seven people were present at the class meeting on Sunday evening, February 1, which Mrs. Crosby and her convert had set into operation upon their arrival. And Sarah records with some embarrassment the events of the following week:

> Sun. 8. This day my mind has been calmly stayed on God. In the evening I expected to meet about thirty persons in class; but to my great surprise there came near two hundred. I found an aweful, loving sense of the Lord's presence, and much love to the people: but was much affected both in body and mind. I was not sure whether it was right for me to exhort in so public a manner, and yet I saw it impracticable to meet all these people by way of speaking particularly to each individual. I, therefore, gave out a hymn, and prayed, and told them part of what the Lord had done for myself, persuading them to flee from all sin.[18]

Sarah knew that she had come perilously close to preaching and immediately wrote to her spiritual mentor seeking his advice concerning this unconventional course of events. Baker points out that Wesley "does not seem to have been unduly worried, for his answer was not despatched until three days after he had received her letter, on February 14."[19] In the meantime, on Friday, February 13, she addressed a large congregation once again and seems to have been more and more confirmed in the suitability of her actions:

> In the evening I exhorted near two hundred people to forsake their sins, and shewed them the willingness of Christ to save: They flock as doves to the window, tho' as yet we have no

preacher. Surely, Lord, thou hast much people in this place! My soul was much comforted in speaking to the people, as my Lord has removed all my scruples respecting the propriety of my acting thus publickly.[20]

This inner conviction was strengthened by Wesley's reassuring letter:

London, February 14, 1761

My Dear Sister,
    Miss Bosanquet gave me yours of Wednesday night. Hitherto, I think you have not gone too far. You could not well do less. I apprehend all you can do more is, when you meet again, to tell them simply, "You lay me under a great difficulty. The Methodists do not allow of women preachers; neither do I take upon me any such character. But I will just nakedly tell you what is in my heart." This will in a great measure obviate the grand objection and prepare for J. Hampson's coming. I do not see that you have broken any law. Go on calmly and steadily. If you have time, you may read to them the *Notes* on any chapter before you speak a few words, or one of the most awakening sermons, as other women have done long ago.[21]

This event, and Wesley's qualified approval of Sarah Crosby's actions, marks the beginning of his acceptance of women preachers. The more stringent aspect of Wesley's churchmanship made it impossible for him at this point to admit to the use of the term "preacher" in such cases, but the close association of reading portions of his notes on the New Testament and speaking a few words to a large assembly is highly suggestive of preaching in a more technical sense.[22] Sarah took Wesley's advice concerning the practices of "other women long ago," an unmistakable reference to the activities of his mother in the Epworth rectory, and on Good Friday, March 20, "read a sermon on the occasion to several persons, who were met together, and went to bed weary but happy in God." Likewise, on Easter, she felt the Lord very present as she "prayed and exhorted many sinners to turn to God."[23]

During the fall of 1761 Wesley found it necessary to advise Grace Walton who had apparently encountered a situation similar to that at Derby. Wesley's defective letter is dated September 8, 1761, from London:

> If a few more Persons come when you are meeting, [you may] either enlarge four or five Minutes on [y^e] Question you had [or give] a short Exhortation (perhaps for five or six minutes) [and then] sing & pray: This is going as far as I think any Woman [should do.] For the Words of the Apostle are clear. I think & [?as] always, [that his] meaning is this: "I suffer not a woman to teach in a [public congr]egation, nor thereby to usurp Authority over the man." [The man] God has invested with the Prerogative: whereas teaching . . .[24]

Wesley's close adherence to a rigid interpretation of Saint Paul's directive to Timothy is quite clear and consistent with his notes on the text to which he alludes.[25] His note on the prohibitive statement of 1 Corinthians 14:34 is more explicit, but distinctive in its admission of certain exceptions, a fact upon which later women will earnestly take their stand:

> "Let your women be silent in the churches." —Unless they are under an extraordinary impulse of the Spirit. "For," in other cases, "it is not permitted them to speak"—By way of teaching in publick assemblies. "But to be in subjection"—To the man whose proper office it is to lead and to instruct the congregation.[26]

MARY BOSANQUET AND THE LEYTONSTONE ORPHANAGE

The years 1761 to 1763 were characterized by explosive revival and were thrilling for the Methodist societies in London. In April 1761 Sarah Crosby returned from her pioneering labors in Derby to contribute to the expansion of Methodism in the metropolis. Little is known about her labors during this period, but from her letter of January 28, 1763, we know that she was fully employed throughout the latter half of 1762:

> I have been 5 mounths at Canterbury, which has been much for my own good, & the good of many. there has been a great revival, & quickening among the peopel. when I have an Opportunity, I will send you the Coppy of the account, Mr. W[esley] desired me write Him.[27]

From the same letter, written upon her return to London, we know that she was concerned about the confusion created by the excesses of certain "simple brethren" and supported Wesley in his attempts to restrain the fanaticism of Maxfield and Bell.[28] But more importantly, her return provided the occasion for her to renew her friendship with Mary Bosanquet and her female companions.

Mary was born into a wealthy family on September 1, 1739, at Leytonstone in Essex, outside of London.[29] Having been greatly impressed by a Methodist servant in her household, at the tender age of seven she determined to become one of them, regardless of the cost. She was deeply moved by the writings of Mrs. Lefevre and even had the opportunity of meeting this influential woman shortly before the latter's death.[30] She moved in London Methodist circles from an early age, and shortly after her first encounter with Mrs. Crosby, she met Mrs. Sarah Ryan, who immediately took her under her wing. Mary confided to her journal:

> The more I conversed with Mrs. Ryan, the more I discovered of the glory of God breaking forth from within, and felt a strong attraction to consider her as the friend of my soul. I told her the past sins, follies, and mercies of my life, and received a similar account from her.[31]

During the summer of 1757, when she was eighteen, she immersed herself in the life of the Methodist society and deepened her relations with the little company of believers in Moorfields while her parents spent their holiday in Scarborough.

Mrs. Ryan, a leading spirit within early Methodism who became one of Wesley's most intimate correspondents, was on the opposite end of the socioeconomic spectrum from Miss Bosanquet. Born of poor parents on October 24, 1724, she was stirred by the preaching of George Whitefield at the age of seventeen, later heard Wesley at the suggestion of Sarah Crosby, and joined the Foundery Society.[32] In the face of severe opposition due to Mrs. Ryan's doubtful reputation, Wesley placed his full confidence in her and appointed her housekeeper at Bristol in 1757.[33]

In the years immediately following, Wesley wrote more perhaps to her than anyone else, a fact which incurred the jealous wrath of his unstable and paranoid wife, who, on one occasion referred to her in the presence of Wesley's preachers as a whore with three living husbands.[34] Wesley's reliance on her proved to be well-founded, however, for during his visitation of the societies around Bristol in the winter of 1757/58 he discovered that Kingswood School, now under her administration, was "at length what I have so long wished it to be—a blessing to all that are therein and an honour to the whole body of Methodists."[35]

In the meantime, Miss Bosanquet's connections with Methodism were producing tensions within her family which inevitably led to something of an ultimatum. Mary's father, irritated by her associations with such enthusiasts and the changes he had observed in her life, said to her:

> "There is a particular promise which I require of you, that is, that you will never, on any occasion, either now, or hereafter, attempt to make your brothers what you call a Christian." I answered, (looking to the Lord,) "I think, Sir, I dare not consent to that."[36]

Resigning herself to the fact of this apparently irreconcilable situation and moved by deep convictions, Mary, having obtained her majority, left her luxurious home. Thereafter she entered into a new course of unostentatious but active devotion and benevolence.

Taking lodgings in two unfurnished rooms in Hoxton Square, she committed herself to a plan of ministry and service, endeavoring to avoid the company of single men whenever possible, to lay out her time by rule, and to fix her mind on the example of Christ, leading a mortified life. In 1762 Mary was fortified by the arrival and support of her old friend, Mrs. Ryan, who had left her position in Bristol because of her declining health. In spite of her weakened condition, Sarah, whom Wesley would later refer to as Mary's twin soul, labored indefatigably with her companion and friend in this semimonastic conclave.[37]

In the year 1763, both the extent of their activities and the sphere of their influence was widened extensively. At this time, a house in her possession, close to her family home in Leytonstone, became vacant. She consulted her father, with whom she had been partially reconciled, about the possibility of moving to "The Cedars," as the residence was called. He made no objection, only adding that "if a mob should pull your house about your ears, I cannot hinder them."[38] And so, on March 24, 1763, the wealthy and cultured Miss Bosanquet and Mrs. Ryan, the erstwhile domestic servant, moved to Leytonstone, with the express intention of establishing an orphanage and school on the basis of Wesley's own prototype at Kingswood.

Wesley kept this model Christian community, combining vibrant personal piety and active social service, under his personal surveillance, and on December 1, 1764, expressed his optimism and great expectations concerning its progress: "M[ary] B[osanquet] gave me a further account of their affairs at Leytonstone. It is exactly *Pietas Hallensis* in miniature. What it will be does not yet appear."[39] This "further account" supplemented the pamphlet that she had published under Wesley's auspices in November.[40] It may possibly be related to an improperly identified manuscript in the Methodist Archives bearing the title, "An Account of the Rise & Progress of the Work of God in Latonstone, Essex, 1763," which is in Mary Bosanquet's unmistakable hand.[41]

After much careful deliberation they determined to take in none but the most destitute and friendless. The children who were chosen often came "naked, full of vermin, and some afflicted with distemper." At first the family consisted of Mary, Sarah, a maid, and Sally Lawrence, Mrs. Ryan's niece of about four years of age who had been taken from the side of her mother's coffin to their house.[42] With the addition of five more orphans and confronted with the problem of Mrs. Ryan's failing health, a pious young woman, named Ann Tripp, was secured as a governess for the children.[43] They formed themselves into a tightly knit community, adopted a uniform dress of dark purple cotton, and ate together at a table five yards long. Over the course of five years they sheltered and cared for thirty-five children and thirty-four adults. Through their labors, what might have become an elegant home "became a school, an orphanage, a hospital and a kind of *beguinage* for poor widows."[44]

Mary's journal bears testimony to the course of events which led her to become engaged in activities similar to those of Sarah Crosby several years before:

> In order to supply the want of public means, (which we could not have but when we went to London,) we agreed to spend an hour every night together in spiritual reading and prayer. A poor woman with whom I had formerly talked, came to ask if she might come in, when we made prayer. We told her at seven every Thursday night she should be welcome. She soon brought two or three more, and they others, till in a short time our little company increased to twenty-five. . . . Some few were offended, and came no more; but most appeared under conviction, and those we appointed to meet on Tuesday night, reserving the Thursday for the public meeting, which still kept increasing, and in which we *read a chapter,* and sometimes *spoke from it.*[45]

By this time the women felt that it would be expedient to apply to Wesley for a preacher. Their plan was approved, Mr. Murlin sent the following Sunday, and within a fortnight a new society with twenty-five members was formed. The women, primarily Mary and Sarah at first, continued their Thursday evening public services, which included the reading and exposition of Scripture, and in spite of the opposition that began to arise, addressed the large assemblies that flocked to The Cedars.

During the summer months of 1765, Wesley had been incessantly traveling, writing, and preaching throughout Ireland. When the annual conference was convened in Manchester on August 20, no fewer than ninety-two itinerant preachers were stationed in thirty-nine circuits. Among the many questions put before the conference was a query concerning one of the Pauline prohibitions related to the women. The question was asked, "But how can we encourage the women in the Bands to speak, since 'It is a shame for women to speak in the Church?' I Cor. xiv. 35." Wesley provided his own reply:

> I deny, 1 That *speaking* here means any other than speaking as a *public teacher*. This St. Paul *suffered not,* because it implied "usurping authority over the man." 1 Tim. ii. 12. Whereas *no authority* either over man or woman is unsurped, by the *speaking* now in question. I deny, 2 That *the Church* in that text, means any other than the great congregation.[46]

In spite of the official position of the conference, Sarah Crosby continued persistent in her labors, apparently with the approbation of her spiritual leader. In a letter she addressed to an unidentified woman prior to the conference, she sets forth her own views on this subject:

> I think I do use the little Strength I have in Instruct[g] the Ignorent reclaiming the wicked reliev[g] the Pain of those who suffer in body or mind. I am generely some way or other imploy[d] in some of these works. I am not concious of any willfull omissions. Lord correct me wh[re] I go astray! Unless my not speaking amoung the B[g] may be stiled omissions However. I have broke throu[g] that Sometime agoe and been blesst in Speaking. I do not think it wron[g] for women to speak in public provided they speak by the Spirit of God.[47]

It is not clear exactly when Sarah Crosby became directly connected with the Leytonstone orphanage and its work, but as early as September 1766 Wesley was sending letters to her at that address.[48] From that point on, the lives of the three women, Mary and the two Sarahs, became inextricably interwoven. On February 12, 1767, Wesley was delighted by the effective ministry of the community, and after preaching at Leytonstone exclaimed: "Oh what a house of God is here! Not only for decency and order, but for the life and power of religion! I am afraid there are very few such to be found in all the King's dominions."[49] In May of that year, somewhat displeased at Mrs. Crosby for not having heard from her in some time, Wesley wrote from Sligo, encouraging her in her labors:

I hope your little family remains in peace and love and that your own soul prospers. I doubt only whether you are so useful as you might be. But herein look to the anointing which you have of God, being willing to follow wherever He leads, and it shall teach you of all things.[50]

CROSS HALL, YORKSHIRE

In a year's time, Sarah and the entire Leytonstone community were led in fact into new areas of service, the scope of which was continually expanding. Mary had been advised frequently to move to some part of Yorkshire and purchase a farm. Such a move would relieve some of the financial pressures which proved to be a constant burden and would provide a more conducive environment for the raising of her children. She was also concerned about Mrs. Ryan's health which was rapidly deteriorating.[51] The arrival of Richard Taylor from Yorkshire, and his offer to assist them in such a resettlement, seemed to be a providential sign. Convinced that this was God's will, on June 7, 1768, she set out with her friend Ryan, Ann Tripp, sister Crosby, and their family of dependents and orphans.

They made the arduous journey north to a strange land, wild and sparsely populated, with few roads and none of the comforts of civilization, nevertheless one of the distinctive centers of early Methodism. Yorkshire boasted nearly one-third of all the Methodist chapels by 1770. The small company stayed with Mrs. Taylor's parents until early August, when they found a suitable house at Gildersome in the West Riding of Yorkshire. Mary's hopes that the change of air might benefit Sarah Ryan were crushed, however, on August 17, 1768, when her "twin soul" died at the age of forty-three. She was buried in the Leeds Old Churchyard, and her original epitaph reflects both the character and simplicity of this one "Who lived and died a Christian."[52]

Their new residence, a farmhouse known as Cross Hall, near Morley and in the general vicinity of Leeds, soon became a vital center of Methodist worship and witness. Sarah Crosby had spent some time in Yorkshire previously, and several who had been affected by her words in the past now agreed to meet with them fortnightly for prayer. Miss Bosanquet recalls the consequences:

> One and another begged to join in our Wednesday night meetings, and our number increased to about fifty, all of whom were ardently desiring, or sweetly brought into, that liberty. When we grew too numerous, (for they began to come from many miles round,) I advised those who were able, to gather a meeting of the same kind near their own homes. This was attended with many blessings. We sometimes visited those infant meetings, and they increased and spread as well as ours.[53]

Mary, as she frequently said, had many occasions to praise God for the wisdom of their resettlement to Cross Hall and rejoiced in the fact that "many a soul has been born in her, and many sweet seasons did we know with the Lord."[54] Wesley, still quite sensitive about the issue of women preachers deemed it necessary to provide Sarah Crosby with more explicit advice concerning their extended activities. Having been detained from embarking for Ireland, he wrote to her from Chester on March 18, 1769:

> I advise you, as I did Grace Walton, formerly, (1) Pray in private or public as much as you can. (2) Even in public you may properly enough intermix *short exhortations* with prayer; but keep as far from what is called preaching as you can: therefore never take a text; never speak in a continued discourse without some break, about four or five minutes. Tell the people, "We shall have another *prayer-meeting* at such a time and place." If Hannah Harrison had followed these few directions, she might have been as useful now as ever.[55]

This letter affords Wesley's first precise definition of the preaching office as it relates to women. Just as he had advised the early lay preachers, now, some three decades later, he cautioned the women to avoid what appeared to be "preaching," namely, "taking a text" and "speaking in a continued discourse," in order to maintain the integrity of his expanding movement. It is clear that he was a little anxious about the activities of Sarah Crosby and Mary Bonsanquet and was not yet prepared radically to modify his own views. He was still attempting to differentiate testimony and exhortation from formal preaching, and sincerely believed that such a fine distinction would obviate the "grand objection." This confidence, however, proved to be mistaken. During the ensuing years, Cross Hall, the headquarters for the pioneering work of women in the north, became the focal point for discussions related to this potentially volatile issue.

OTHER ASPIRING WOMEN PREACHERS

The evangelistic activities associated with the small conclave of women at Cross Hall were reduplicated elsewhere as women sought to express their faith actively and openly. Hannah Harrison, the aspiring young preacher about whom Wesley voiced his disapproval in his letter to Mrs. Crosby, is a representative of these concurrent developments. First mentioned by Wesley as a "blessed woman" in his letter to Miss Ann Foard, an exceptional and promising Southwark Methodist,[56] Hannah was particularly useful as an agent of reconciliation at Beverley, where, as Tyerman recounts, the itinerants, or Culamite preachers as they were called, were often besieged by furious mobs.[57] To Miss Jane Hilton, the young Yorkshire Methodist and faithful correspondent both before and after her marriage to William Barton, Wesley wrote on November 26, 1768:

> There seems to have been a particular providence in Hannah Harrison's coming to Beverley, especially at that very time when a peace-maker was so much wanting; and it was a pledge that God will withhold from you no manner of thing that is good.[58]

The "Account of Mrs. Hannah Harrison" which appears in the *Methodist Magazine* of 1802 fills in some of the details about her life as culled from the testimony of John Pawson, an unnamed friend, and the subject herself, but makes no mention of her preaching labors.[59] While many of the facts concerning her life remain a mystery, she seems to have been born in York in 1734, was convinced of sin through the ministration of Jonathan Maskew in November 1750, experienced forgiveness in May of the following year and a profound deepening of her faith while receiving the Lord's Supper at some subsequent point.[60] A well-educated lady of the middle class, she was instrumental in the establishment of Methodism in York.[61]

According to the report of Taft:

> She held many public meetings at *Malton,* and in that neighbourhood; one of our aged and respectable friends, frequently speaks of the pleasure and profit, he and others derived from those opportunities.[62]

It was under her ministry that John Atlay, one of Wesley's itinerants, was awakened.[63] She apparently left her native Yorkshire after many years of service in order to finish her course in London, where she often made excursions into the country during the summer months, and died on December 19, 1801.[64]

Mrs. Eliza Bennis, who had founded Methodism in Waterford and was the first adherent of Wesley's in Limerick, functioned for a number of years, in all but name, as Wesley's "Assistant" in Ireland. No evidence is available to support the claim that she assumed the role of a preacher, but there is no doubt that her responsibilities and activities would have led her into situations conducive to such ministrations. Wesley encouraged her as a co-laborer of Richard Bourke, a man of unwearied diligence and patience who had entered the itinerancy in 1765, and hoped that they would "faithfully endeavour to help each other on." "Remember you have work to do in your Lord's vineyard," he reminded her, "and the more you help others the more your soul will prosper."[65]

Indeed, Mrs. Bennis supervised the activities of the circuit. In a letter of July 8, 1770, she wrote to Wesley:

> I hope you will not think me presumptuous in dictating, but I find my soul knit to these poor sheep. . . . Brother Bourke, at my request, has taken Clonmel into the circuit, and doubt not

but there will be good done there; but as this has caused an entire alteration in the circuit from the former plan, I have to request your forgiveness for my officiousness; if you disapprove, it can be re-altered.[66]

Far from castigating her for what some might have considered to be a flagrant usurpation of authority by a woman, Wesley fully approved her modification of the circuit plan and continued to seek her counsel on all such matters.[67]

Similar encouragements were forthcoming for youthful Peggy Dale, another of Wesley's favored correspondents and the niece of Miss Margaret Lewen, a wealthy benefactress who had become enamored of Methodism through the influence of the Leytonstone women. During the winter of 1769 he wrote to Miss Dale in emphatic tones:

> There is one rule which our Lord constantly observes,— "Unto him that hath shall be given." "Unto him that *uses* what he hath!" Speak, therefore, as you can; and by-and-by you shall speak as you would. Speak, though, with fear; and in a little time you shall speak without fear. Fear shall be swallowed up in love![68]

While Wesley's exhortation in this particular instance most certainly referred to less formal opportunities of witness-bearing, the implications of his statement, both in terms of the principle and practice of preaching, would have been obvious to the conscientious women who aspired to fulfill a strong sense of calling.

During the summer of 1770, Wesley was apparently excluded from a parish church because the congregation thought he had allowed Sarah Crosby to preach at Huddersfield.[69] In spite of the fact that Mrs. Crosby disavowed her engagement in such an activity in that particular instance, Wesley replied with little concern that "He did not mind that, for He had Places enough to preach in." It was becoming increasingly clear that the question of women's preaching was an issue that required more immediate attention on the part of the Methodist leadership. Indeed, it was Mrs. Crosby's supposition that "our Preachers will have it up at the Conference." And she expressed her great interest to Mr. Mayer, as one might well expect, "Concerning what passes on that Head." Unfortunately, no record of the conference's deliberations on this issue has been preserved. It is clear, however, that the experimentation of the 1760s provided a strong impetus for the clarification of women's roles within the Wesleyan revival, and particularly those of aspiring women preachers.

NOTES

1. Under the date of July 31, 1763, in George Birkbeck Hill, ed., *Boswell's Life of Johnson,* revised and enlarged by L. F. Powell, 6 vols. (Oxford: At the Clarendon Press, 1934), 1:463.
2. This particular decade is marked as a period of spectacular growth in the Methodist societies. According to the third edition of Myle's *Chronological History of Methodism,* which is generally reliable, by 1770 there were 108 preaching houses in England. Nearly three-quarters of these were built between 1760 and 1770. In the two epoch years, 1766 and 1770, 16 and 26 new chapels were opened respectively. See William Myles, *A Chronological History of the People Called Methodists,* 3d ed., enlarged (London: Sold by the author, 1803), pp. 323–40. Statistics drawn from the fourth edition (pp. 427–45) are comparable, but somewhat more inflated. See *W.H.S.* 9:42; and Church, *Early Methodist People,* pp. 55–56. Wesley's correspondence during this period also indicates the large part played by women in the spiritual life and development of the societies; see e.g., Wesley, *Letters,* 4:229–322.
3. Z. Taft, *The Scripture Doctrine of Women's Preaching: Stated and Examined* (York: Printed for the author, by R. and J. Richardson, 1820), p. 16.
4. Some of the women were not sure, for instance, of exactly how close they had come to transcending the limitations of their sex in any given situation. The delineation of acceptable parameters was yet to be established, and terms such as "preaching," "speaking," or "exhorting" were often employed haphazardly and with little precision by many people. It is not surprising, therefore, as we shall see, that women should consult Wesley in order to determine whether they had "preached" or not.
5. For primary and secondary works related to her life and work, consult Appendix A. No less than 24 of John Wesley's letters

to her are extant, the earliest letter dated June 14, 1757. The full text of these letters, now available only in Wesley, *Letters* (21 letters), *W.H.S.* 19:173–74 (1 letter), and Crosby, MS Letterbook (2 letters), will appear in Wesley, *Bicentennial Edition,* vols. 27–31. Cf. Nolan B. Harmon, gen. ed., *The Encyclopedia of World Methodism,* 2 vols. (Nashville: United Methodist Publishing House, 1974), 1: 607.

6. "The Grace of God Manifested, in an Account of Mrs. Crosby, of Leeds," *Arm. Mag.* 29 (1806): 420–21.

7. In "John Wesley and Sarah Crosby," *W.H.S.* 27, 4 (December 1949): 76–82, Frank Baker corrects the many inaccuracies both in Ann Tripp's account of her death (*Arm. Mag.* 29:610–17) and in A. W. Harrison, "An Early Woman Preacher—Sarah Crosby," *W.H.S.* 14, 5(March 1924): 104–9.

8. *Arm. Mag.* 29:564. This fact is drawn from her diary entry of February 2, 1773 which reads: "It is sixteen years this day, since my husband went from me, and from that time I have believed I should see him no more in this world." Previous writers have misinterpreted this reference to mean the death of her husband, which misunderstanding is clarified by previous hints of estrangement from her husband (see Baker, "Wesley and Crosby," pp. 76–77).

9. Moore, *Fletcher,* p. 27.

10. Ibid., pp. 28–29. Mary referred to this residence as "a little Bethel."

11. *Arm. Mag.* 29:466–67.

12. Ibid., p. 470.

13. See Baker, "Wesley and Crosby," p. 78.

14. *Arm. Mag.* 29:472–73.

15. MS Letter, April 30, 1760, Meth. Arch.

16. Seckerson, "Account of Mrs. Dobinson," p. 558.

17. Ibid. Cf. G. Arthur Fletcher, "Derby—The Old Chapel in St. Michael's Lane," *W.H.S.* 15, 4(December 1925): 109–10. This project was evidently planned over the course of several months as a letter from Mrs. Crosby to a Sarah Moor (of Sheffield?), dated September 1760, London, would indicate: "I shall set out for Derby about a month hence, but cannot tell you where to direct to. Perhaps you will see Mr. H[ampson] again first, who may be able to inform you, or bring me a letter" (quoted in Everett, *Methodism in Sheffield,* pp. 153–54). Everett tentatively identified Hampson, who was the itinerant later appointed to that circuit.

18. *Arm. Mag.* 29:518. This account, very reminiscent, both in

general impression and detail, of Susanna Wesley's Epworth experiences, has become part of early Methodist legend through constant repetition. See Wesley, *Journal,* 4:525; Tyerman, *Life of John Wesley,* 2:398–99; John S. Simon, *John Wesley: The Master Builder* (London: Epworth Press, 1927), pp. 292–94; Stevens, *Women of Methodism,* pp. 79–85; Smith, *History of Wesleyan Methodism,* 1:420–21; Church, *More about Early Methodist People,* pp. 149–52; A. B. Lawson, *John Wesley and the Christian Ministry: The Sources and Development of His Opinions and Practice* (London: SPCK, 1963), pp. 176–77; Thomas M. Morrow, *Early Methodist Women* (London: Epworth Press, 1967), pp. 13–14; Edwards, *My Dear Sister,* pp. 91–94; Brown, "Women of the Word," pp. 75–76.

19. Baker, "Wesley and Crosby," p. 78.
20. *Arm. Mag.* 29:518.
21. Wesley, *Letters,* 4:133. In actuality, another preacher, a Mr. G——h, came to her relief rather than Mr. J. Hampson. Cf. *Arm. Mag.* 19:519. This is the first of many letters related to women preachers in early Methodism, and therefore stands as a piece of extremely important documentation. A list of these letters has been compiled in Appendix B: "Letters Related to the Question of Women's Preaching in Early Methodism."
22. "The modern reader of this letter," claims Kent Brown, "may be inclined to think Wesley is telling her it is all right to preach as long as she doesn't call it 'preaching.' Actually he is telling her it is all right to 'witness' to God's work in her heart. 'Preaching' in the technical sense he would have her avoid" (Earl Kent Brown, "Standing in the Shadow: Women in Early Methodism," *Nexus* 17, 2 [Spring 1974]: 27). Wesley's advice, it seems to me, goes beyond a simple approval of personal testimony (witness); and while he clearly emphasizes the testimonial nature of her activities, he does not prohibit preaching in a more formal sense.
23. *Arm. Mag.* 29:164.
24. The letter clearly lacks a strip down the left margin of the first page. Telford attempted to reconstruct the letter with only partial success. See Wesley, *Letters,* 4:164. A later transcript in the hand of E. H. Bryant is somewhat fuller than Telford's, but still unsatisfactory. See Appendix C for a detailed reconstruction of this important letter.
25. The text, of course, is 1 Timothy 2:12: "For I suffer not a woman to teach, nor to usurp authority over the man, but to be

in silence." Wesley's *Notes,* published in 1755, laconically express his view: "12. 'To usurp authority over the man'—By publick teaching." His note on verse 13 indicates "that Woman was originally the inferior."

26. Wesley, *Notes,* 1 Corinthians 14:34.
27. Sarah Crosby to Mr. Oddie, at the New Room, in the Horse Fair, London, January 28, 1763, Meth. Arch.
28. See Wesley, *Journal,* 4:535–38.
29. Bibliographical details may be consulted in Appendix A.
30. Very little hard biographical data is available upon Mrs. Lefevre (?1723–56), a devout woman who was held in high esteem by the Methodist leaders. She appears to have been converted and became a Methodist only two or three years prior to her death. Her husband published ninety of her letters, the writings referred to here, *Letters upon Sacred Subjects, by a person lately deceased* (London, 1757), which Wesley reprinted and abridged in 1769 under the title, *An Extract of Letters by Mrs. L****. See Wesley, *Oxford Edition,* 26:540, 541, 546–47, 551, 553, 573–74, for related letters to Wesley.
31. Moore, *Fletcher,* p. 29.
32. See her "Account," being an autobiographical sketch of her spiritual pilgrimage in a letter to Wesley, in *Arm. Mag.* 2 (1779): 296–310. Cf. Appendix A.
33. See Wesley, *Journal,* 4:243–44, 274; Wesley, *Letters,* 3:239–41; Tyerman, *Life of John Wesley,* 2:109–10, 285–89, 297; and Edwards, *My Dear Sister,* pp. 50–57.
34. In the tangled skein of her early life, Sarah had married a profligate bigamist who subsequently deserted her, and wedded an Irish sailor named Ryan, who, after cruel treatment of her, went to sea. When it appeared that he was lost at sea she returned to and married an Italian, Solomon Benreken, to whom she had been previously engaged.
35. January 4, 1758, Wesley, *Journal,* 4:247. Cf. E. Ralph Bates, "Sarah Ryan and Kingswood School," *W.H.S.* 38, 4 (May 1972): 110–14.
36. Moore, *Fletcher,* p. 33.
37. Mrs. Ryan expressed her feelings concerning the prospect of assisting her in her work in a letter: "It seems to me as if the Lord had laid your burden on me, as he once committed the care of Mary to Joseph, and afterwards to the favoured disciple." She concluded by quoting the hymn: "Jesus, to thy preserving care/My choicest blessing I commend;/ Receive,

and on thy bosom bear,/The soul whom thou has made my friend" (Moore, *Fletcher,* p. 43).

38. Ibid., p. 45.
39. Wesley, *Journal,* 5:102. Education was a particular emphasis of Continental Pietism which asserted that the Church ought to reassume responsibility in this sphere. To this end, Francke's Orphan-school in Halle, shaped in part by the model created by Duke Ernest the Pious in Gotha, gave classical expression to this aspiration. Wesley's foundation of Kingswood School near Bristol was an integral part of this lineage. See Schmidt, *John Wesley,* 2:175–86. The following year, on December 12, 1765, Wesley recorded: "I rode to Leytonstone, and found one truly Christian family: that is, what that at Kingswood should be, and would, if it had such a governess" (*Journal,* 5:152).
40. [Mary Bosanquet], *A Letter to the Rev. Mr. John Wesley. By a Gentlewoman* (London: Sold at the Foundery, in Upper Moorfields, 1764), actually dated November 8.
41. Miss Elizabeth Ritchie was originally identified as the authoress, but the volume is presently cataloged under Sarah Ryan. In addition to the "Account," this small duodecimo volume includes the record of a diary in Miss Bosanquet's handwriting, the entries of which, concluding on Jany 11, –65 are followed by fragments last dated Aug. 24, 1768. Journal entries in an unidentified hand follow several blank pages. From this account we know that Mary commenced her labors in Hoxton Square in February 1761.
42. Sally lived with Mary Bosanquet, her adopted mother, until her death on December 3, 1800, and like her aunt and foster mother became useful as a preacher. See pp. 199–200 below and bibliographical data in Appendix A.
43. She was converted under the preaching of Thomas Maxfield, later settled in Leeds, and at the time of her death in 1823 was one of the oldest leaders of the society there.
44. Church, *More about Early Methodist People,* p. 189.
45. Moore, *Fletcher,* pp. 46–47 (emphasis added).
46. *Minutes,* 1:52.
47. Sarah Crosby to Mrs.————, July 7, 1765, MS Letterbook, pp. 37–38.
48. Wesley, *Letters,* 5:25–26. Telford observes that "the Leytonstone circle was disposed to be critical of Wesley's spiritual experience." This letter of September 12, 1766, written from St. Ives, Cornwall, was in response to such criticisms. Cf. the letters to Mrs. Ryan, 5:17-18.

49. Wesley, *Journal,* 5:195.
50. May 2, 1767, Wesley, *Letters,* 5:46. Later that fall, on the evening of November 20, 1767, Wesley preached once more at Leytonstone and expressed his yearning to visit there more often. "How good would it be for me to be here," he wrote, "not twice in a year, but in a month!" (*Journal,* 5:239).
51. On May 14, 1768, Mrs. Crosby wrote in her journal: "This was a day of fatigue in outward employment, but I had inward rest. In the night, Sister R. was taken very ill; but soon our Lord poured a spirit of prayer on us all. I believed before, but now I was assured we should go to live in Yorkshire" (*Arm. Mag.* 29:564).
52. Moore, *Fletcher,* p. 73. The bodies of Sarah Crosby and Ann Tripp would later be laid to rest along with this aspiring woman preacher. The inscription on the subsequent tomb at St. Peter's churchyard, Leeds, simply read: "Here lieth the body of Mrs. Sarah Ryan, who departed this life August 17, 1768, aged 41 years, who lived many years a burning and shining light, and finished her course with joy" (J. E. Hellier, "Some Methodist Women Preachers," *Methodist Recorder Winter Number* 36 [Christmas 1895]: 66; Hellier, "Mother Chapel of Leeds," p. 65; Baker, "Wesley and Crosby," p. 82). There is an obvious discrepancy regarding her age as given in the inscription and that calculated from her date of birth, October 20, 1724 (*Arm. Mag.* 2:296). The accuracy of this date is corroborated elsewhere, and Moore was correct, having claimed that she died in "the forty-fourth year of her age" (p. 72), two months prior to her forty-fourth birthday.
53. Ibid., p. 77.
54. Ibid., p. 80.
55. Wesley, *Letters,* 5:130. Cf. pp. 123, 136, 296–98 herein.
56. August 8, 1767, Newcastle, Wesley, *Letters,* 5:59–60. Born in Southwark in 1741, Ann joined the Methodist Society when twenty years of age and married a Southwark undertaker named John Thornton in 1772. She died at Bath on March 18, 1799.
57. See Tyerman, *Life of John Wesley,* 2:502.
58. Wesley, Letters, 5:113.
59. *Meth. Mag.* 25 (1802): 318–23, 363–68. Joseph Benson, editor of this publication at the time, was a noted antagonist to women's preaching, and silence concerning the subject's accomplishments in this sphere may have been the result of his editorial work. Taft affords a brief sketch of her life in *Holy Women,* 1:203–4. Cf. Appendix A.

60. Ibid., pp. 319–21.

61. See Lyth, *Methodism in York,* pp. 64–68.

62. Taft, *Holy Women,* 1:204.

63. Ibid. Cf. Hellier, "Some Methodist Women Preachers," p. 67; Jessop, *Methodism in Rossendale,* p. 94. Atlay figured prominently in the lengthy controversy over the Deed of Declaration in 1784 (see Moore, *Life of John Wesley,* 2:329).

64. *Meth. Mag.* 25:368. Her funeral sermon was preached by Joseph Benson on December 27, 1801. There is not a little confusion over her identity, Taft noting in the margin of his personal copy of *Holy Women:* "Is this the person whose life is published in the Method. Mag. for 1802, see p. 318 the smaller work" (1:203). Elements of the two biographical sketches— e.g. attestation to the loss of her sight as a youth and her subsequent recovery—seem to support a common identity. Telford identified her as the wife of Lancelot Harrison, a colleague of Thomas Rankin and William Brammah in Lincolnshire. There is no conclusive documentary evidence, however, to support this conjecture. According to the *Meth. Mag.,* her maiden name was Harrison, her father probably being Ebeneezer Harrison, a brewer of York. Likewise, there is no evidence of her having been married.

65. John Wesley to Eliza Bennis, September 18, 1769, Bristol, Wesley, *Letters,* 5:150.

66. Ibid., p. 193.

67. See ibid., pp. 193–94; cf. 5:190–91; 283–85, 343–44; 6:23. Mrs. Bennis later emigrated to Philadelphia with her husband where she died in 1802.

68. November 17, 1769, London, in ibid., p. 157. Miss Dale married Edward Avison of Newcastle on March 4, 1773, and died shortly thereafter in November 1777, aged thirty-three.

69. Sarah Crosby to Mr. Mayer, Stump Cross, July 13, 1770, Meth. Arch. In this letter, directed to Portwood Hall, Near Stockport, Cheshire, Sarah writes: "Mr. W. gives me the same advice that you do, & I heard of no Complaints made to him about us, only Mrs. [*sic*] wo^d not let him preach in his Church, because he had lent a Female Preach, tho this was not true, for I only met the Class at Hu[dder]s field !" Cf. Brown, "Women of the Word," p. 75.

5

DEFINING THE "EXTRAORDINARY CALL," 1771–1780

T HE DECADE OF THE 1770s represents a critical period in the history of Methodism. Throughout the course of these years Wesley became increasingly aware of the direction in which the movement under his leadership was headed. The failure of incessant attempts at reconciliation with the evangelical elements within the religious establish-ment inevitably led him to turn his attention more fully to ensuring the perpetuity of Methodism and its witness, preferably within, but if necessary distinct from, the life of the Church of England.[1] To this end, it was necessary to introduce new elements into the advancing movement as the societies became increasingly consolidated. And as Baker has demonstrated, while Wesley attempted to march with the leaders of the Anglican church, he "had his eyes so firmly fixed on his spiritual goal that he never realized how far he had strayed from the remainder of the column."[2]

A CRUCIAL TRANSITION IN WESLEY'S VIEW

The transformation of Wesley's attitude toward the women preachers during this critical period, and the consequent expansion of their labors and influence within the Methodist societies, cannot be fully understood apart from the context of these general developments. Furthermore, it is not surprising to discover that during the course of these years, Wesley expressed his mature, explicit, and definitive opinion on this question. Decreased anxiety concerning the stability of his bond with the Church of England made it easier for

Wesley to countenance the development of additional irregularities as long as they promoted the cause of evangelical Christianity.

The case of Sarah Crosby, as we have seen, clearly demonstrates the cautious progression of Wesley's thinking in this regard.[3] In 1761 he discreetly approved her actions in Derby and admonished her to speak in public about her Christian experience or to read edifying literature to her assemblies as his mother had done at Epworth. In 1769 he agreed that she might even deliver short exhortations, carefully avoiding what appeared to be preaching by frequently interrupting her discourse and never taking a text. During the years that immediately followed, these developments came to a head, however, and it became increasingly clear to Wesley that he must accept an occasional woman preacher by virtue of an "extraordinary call."

Exactly when this transformation took place is difficult to determine, but it would seem to be directly related to the activities of Mary Bosanquet and his attempt to accommodate the case of this exceptional woman and her co-workers. During the summer of 1771 she wrote to Wesley, seeking his advice and direction concerning the work in which she and Sarah Crosby had become engaged.[4] Marked by sound and prudent judgment and cogent argumentation, this lengthy letter represents the first serious defense of women's preaching in Methodism. Mary argues that on the basis of her examination of Scripture, women were occasionally called of God to preach in extraordinary situations.

Employing lines of argumentation similar to those which characterized Margaret Fell's *Womens Speaking Justified* nearly a century before, Miss Bosanquet carefully considers the classic statements of Saint Paul in 1 Timothy 2 and 1 Corinthians 14 and addresses six objections that had been raised concerning their specific activities.

Her first conclusion is that the so-called prohibitive passages refer to specific situations in which certain women were meddling with church discipline and government and do not apply, therefore, either to women in general or preaching in particular. Furthermore, a literal interpretation of these scriptural texts would contradict the apostle's admonitions concerning the necessity of women prophesying with their heads covered, in 1 Corinthians 11:5. In her view, the objection that the speaking of women should be limited to times of a "peculiar impulse" placed too severe a limitation upon the gracious activity of God. The Almighty could as easily inspire a servant to speak "two or three times in a week, or day" as "two or three times in her life."

Mary rejects the notion that preaching "is inconsistent with that *modesty* the Christian religion requires in *women* professing godliness," pointing to the examples of Mary, the woman of Samaria, the handmaid of 2 Samuel 20, and Deborah, all of whom both were characterized by purity and humility and publicly declared the message of the Lord. Finally, to those who object that all these were extraordinary calls, a claim for which Miss Bosanquet, in their judgment, possessed no authority, she retorts:

> If I did not believe so, I would not act in an extraordinary manner.—I praise my God, I feel him very near, and I prove his faithfulness every day.

Miss Bosanquet's letter, if not itself serving as a catalyst in the transformation of Wesley's opinions, elicited one of his most definitive statements defending the legitimate nature of her unique calling. It is noteworthy that his response should assert, not only an apostolic precedent for this innovation in particular, but also for Methodist irregularities in general:

Londonderry, June 13, 1771

My dear sister,

I think the strength of the cause rests there, on your having an *Extraordinary Call.* So, I am persuaded, has every one of our Lay Preachers: otherwise I could not countenance his preaching at all. It is plain to me that the whole Work of God termed Methodism is an extraordinary dispensation of His Providence. Therefore I do not wonder if several things occur therein which do not fall under ordinary rules of discipline. St. Paul's ordinary rule was, "I permit not a woman to speak in the congregation." Yet in extraordinary cases he made a few exceptions; at Corinth, in particular.[5]

This important letter demonstrates how Wesley was struggling to accommodate the preaching of women, which was apparently owned of God, to the pattern of his ecclesiastical system. His acceptance of an "extraordinary call" as a divine sanction for the boldly innovative actions of Mary Bosanquet and her circle was a difficult but monumental step for him to take. This acknowledgment of the exceptional means by which God was revivifying the Church of England, the same basic rationale upon which Wesley had justified his own irregularities and those of his lay itinerants, now enabled him to allow and even encourage similar activities among women, regardless of the revulsion of the Church or the State.

In an accompanying letter to Sarah Crosby, Wesley advised that her discourses should be based on Scripture texts. "Reading a chapter or part of one and making short observations," he suggested, "may be as useful as any way of speaking."[6] Such a use and application of Scripture is significant because it placed the speaker under a new restraint, namely, the necessity of dealing with the specific doctrines brought out by the "texts."

While Wesley's advice to Mary Stokes, a devout and trusted leader of Methodism in Bristol, later to become a noted preacher within the Society of Friends, was somewhat less specific, it was no less ardent:

> In order to speak for God, you must not confer with flesh and blood, or you will never begin. You must vehemently resist the reasoning devil, who will never want arguments for your silence.[7]

And the following month he admonished her:

> Set aside all evil shame, all modesty, falsely so called. Go from house to house; deal faithfully with them all; warn every one; exhort every one. God will everywhere give you a word to speak, and His blessing therewith.[8]

The extraordinary cases appeared to be less isolated than many, including Wesley, realized. Throughout the course of the decade, the number of women preachers quickly increased and their influence began to be felt throughout the British Isles.

ANN GILBERT: FIRST CORNISH WOMAN PREACHER

About the same time that Wesley was conferring with the Cross Hall women about their work, Mrs. Ann Gilbert commenced her labors as the first woman preacher of her native Cornwall.[9] When "Captain Dick" Williams, one of the first itinerants to visit that area, prayed and preached in Gwinear in 1743, Ann was convinced that "the Methodists were a people going to heaven." It was not until 1760, however, that a society was established in her community. At her first opportunity she united herself with the "Methodies" and soon became exemplary both in her devotion to the Society and in her diligent use of the means of grace. In her own words, she narrates the occurrence of a significant chain of events nearly a decade later: "One blessed fruit of the work which God had wrought in me, was a more than usual concern for the salvation of poor sinners . . . steadfast to this day."[10]

Some time later she was called upon to address a meeting of the young people and said that she "was so filled with the peace and love of God, that I could not but exhort and intreat them to repent."[11] The extraordinary consequences which accompanied her exertions led to an important resolve:

> These tokens for good so encouraged me, that I promised the Lord, if he would give me strength, to use it to his glory; and blessed be his Name, he has enabled me to continue to the present day. . . . by owning my pour labours in the conversion of many sinners.[12]

On one occasion, perhaps during his visitation of the society in August 1773 or that of the following summer, she consulted Wesley on the subject of her speaking in public. After hearing her statement, he is reported to have tersely replied: "Sister do all the good you can."[13]

Taft attests to the fact that Ann believed her commission had come from the highest authority. In a marginal notation he affords the following pertinent anecdote:

> I have been informed that however opposed to womens Preaching the preachers were who were appointed to that Circuit, they were soon convinced that *Ann Gilbert* was eminently *holy* and *useful,* but on one occasion a person informed her that the new preacher had given it out that he would silence her . . . & her answer on hearing this was "if Mr.———, can produce more converts than I, I will give it up.[14]

The itinerant, soon convinced of her calling wisely acquiesced and received her as a co-laborer. Mrs. Gilbert was welcomed into the Methodist chapels of western Cornwall, and one of the itinerants affords a unique eyewitness account of one of these occasions in a letter to Miss Mary Barritt, dated 1798:

> I had the pleasure of hearing Mrs. Ann Gilbert preach in the Chapel at Redruth, to about 1400 people. She had a torrent of softening eloquence, which occasioned a general weeping through the whole congregation. And what was more astonishing she was almost blind, and had been so for many years.[15]

EXPANDING FRONTIERS IN THE SOUTH AND NORTH

Mrs. Bathsheba Hall, a conscientious member of the Methodist Society in Bristol, gave vivid expression to the tension many women felt at this period between the evangelical duty to communicate their faith and an inveterate reticence that disdained publicity:

> The Lord is reviving his work at *Bedminster.* I feel my soul much engaged in it. And yet I tremble, lest I should not be diligent therein. I know, I must improve my Lord's talent. I had rather be obscure. But I dare not. O my God, help me to fight thy battles.[16]

The great extent to which Methodist women did in fact transcend the limitations placed upon them by both the Church and the society remained one of the salient characteristics of the Wesleyan revival throughout this period. The facts are clear. The revival that broke out at Weardale in the summer of 1772 was spearheaded by a schoolmistress, Jane Salkeld.[17] On February 14, 1776, Wesley made a similar discovery:

> I preached at Shoreham. How is the last become first! No society in the country grows so fast as this, either in grace or number. The chief instrument of this glorious work is Miss Perronet, a burning and a shining light.[18]

To Elizabeth Ritchie, his enterprising convert of Otley, he wrote:

> You give me a pleasing account of the work of God which seems to be dawning about Tavistock. It is probable you was sent thither for this. . . . I am not content that you should be pinned down to any one place. That is not your calling. Methinks I want you to be (like me) here and there and everywhere. Oh what a deal of work has our Lord to do on the earth! And may we be workers together with him![19]

Wesley realized how the life of many of his societies depended on the indefatigable labors of key women. This became all too apparent when they were removed or relocated. On March 3, 1774, he preached at Leytonstone, only to find that the society had shrunk to five or six members, remaining but "a shadow of that which was for some years a pattern to all the kingdom!"[20] When Jane Salkeld married and was prohibited from meeting with the young people, the remains of that select society "fell heaps upon heaps."[21] Wesley was livid about similar developments concerning an exceptional young woman, Ann Bolton, whom Wesley termed the "sister of my choice:"

> Ever since that madman took away her office in Witney from Nancy Bolton, Witney Society has dropped; such as Wycombe Society would do if you took away Hannah Ball from them.

> She has all Hannah's grace, with more sense. See that she be
> fully employed. You have not such another flower in all your
> gardens.[22]

Wesley was not unaware of the peril within which women
placed themselves as a result of their aggressive evangelical
behavior. Taft attests to such persecutions:

> Madame Perrott preached the word of life to all who would
> hear, in private houses, both in town and country; and while
> thus engaged she was sometimes pelted with mud, and
> otherwise very roughly and cruelly treated.[23]

To Miss Martha Chapman, however, Wesley enunciated the
principle upon which all of their labors were to be founded:

> If you speak only faintly and in-directly, none will be offended
> and none profited. But if you speak out, although some will
> probably be angry, yet others will soon find the power of God
> unto salvation.[24]

And so, he exhorted Mary Bishop, the proprietor of
private schools in Bath and later Keynsham near Bristol, to
conquer her natural reserve.[25] "Take up your cross; when the
occasion offers, break through," he admonished her,
"speak, though it is pain and grief unto you."[26] To Eliza
Bennis, his "functioning Assistant" in Limerick he wrote:

> I fear you are too idle: This will certainly bring condemnation.
> Up and be doing! Do not loiter. See that your talent rust not:
> rather let it gain ten more; and it will, if you use it.[27]

In these direct, forcible, and pithy expressions, Wesley
reveals a basic attitude that is epitomized in his message to
Miss Bishop: "I lament over every pious young woman who
is not as active as possible."[28] While not all of these women
preached, they all participated in the same spirit that led a
number to take that ultimate step.

One such woman who became "as active as possible" was
Miss Penelope Newman.[29] She owned a bookseller's shop in
Cheltenham and was apparently converted there under the

preaching of John Wesley sometime between 1766 and 1771.[30] She became a woman of deep piety, taught in the society, led two classes and a select band, and remained a faithful correspondent of Wesley, informing him of the progress of the work of God in and around Cheltenham. In February 1773 she confided to him:

> Soon after I came from Bristol, I could not be satisfied with doing so little for God. This caused me to intreat him day and night to point out something more for me to do for his glory.[31]

Two years later Wesley advised her that "Wherever the good Providence of God makes a way for you to help ye neighbours, you must not let slip the opportunity."[32]

She followed Wesley's advice with great enthusiasm, and, as Tyerman reports, "devoted herself wholly to the work of God, making visits to adjacent towns and villages, and, like S. Crosby and others, occasionally giving public exhortations."[33] Wesley held a very high opinion of her qualifications and usefulness and continued to encourage her in these pious endeavors around Cheltenham, Tewkesbury, and the environs, writing in the winter of 1778:

> You do well, as often as you have opportunity, to make little excursions among your neighbours. You have already seen the fruit of your labour of love; and more fruit will follow. . . . Work your work betimes; and in His time He will give you a full reward.[34]

She was instrumental in the conversion of her mother and her future husband and son in the gospel, Jonathan Coussins, one of Wesley's itinerants from 1780, who "sometimes pleasantly observed that he married his mother" on this account.[35] After her marriage in October 1782, however, she curtailed her public exercises substantially as a result of declining health and the considerable afflictions of her husband.

In the life of Jonathan Coussins, the work of the women preachers of the south and the north conjoin in a peculiar fashion, for not only was he converted through the instrumentality of his future wife, but he was greatly influenced by the witness of Mary Bosanquet as well. Richard Waddy recalls that in 1778, "he had the happiness of hearing Mrs. Fletcher give an exhortation at Bath, and at that time felt power to give up his whole soul to God, in a way he never had done before."[36] Long before this, however, Mary and her sister soul, Sarah Crosby, had been vigilant in their labors in Yorkshire. In Miss Bosanquet's journal, under the date February 2, 1773, we discover the first explicit reference to a sermon text appropriated by a Methodist woman preacher: "I went this day to A——. Had a good time in speaking from those words, 'O Nebuchadnezzar, we are not careful to answer thee in this matter.' "[37]

Several weeks later Mary availed herself of an opportunity to address a small gathering at a public inn and at a large house the following morning on one of her journeys.[38] The unconventional activities in which she engaged often evoked unpredictable responses and planned itineraries had to be altered frequently in order to accommodate the exigencies of the moment. Such was the case when Mary visited fashionable Harrogate later in 1773:

> After a few days, I was asked to go to Pannal, (about a mile from Harrogate,) in order to hold a meeting at the house of a poor woman, who had taken the Preachers in once or twice; at which I found many had been offended, and threatened much, so that I did not know what sort of treatment I was likely to meet with. Nevertheless I did not dare to refuse. We had a profitable time, and all was quiet. Two days after, I heard that some of the chief opposers were much affected; Glory be to God![39]

Some of the gentlemen who were staying in the inn where she lodged unanimously requested that she meet with them in the great ball-room.[40] "This was a trial indeed!" Mary confessed. "It appeared to me I should seem in their eyes as a bad woman, or a stage-player; and I feared they only sought an opportunity to behave rudely."[41] On the contrary, they were so affected as to invite her return the following Sunday, at which time a larger company assembled, including some of the socially elite of High-Harrogate.

Mrs. Spencer, a member of the Society of Halifax, remembered hearing Miss Bosanquet preach in the old chapel on one occasion and noted that "she would not ascend into the pulpit, but stood upon the stairs," a fact which the early historians of Methodism emphasized without hesitation.[42] Indeed, many were the conflicts, and many were the taunts she received as a result of her labors. Moreover, her reluctance to cause any offense often led her to question the prudence of her actions. On December 17, 1773, she wrote:

> Last Friday I went to Leeds to meet some classes. O how much do I suffer for every meeting I propose! The enemy follows me hard with such buffeting fears and discouragements as I cannot express. However, I determined to go, and leave the event to God.[43]

Speaking in public created so much anxiety for her that she set apart a whole day for prayer in order to determine why she was so held in bondage concerning it. Her journal reflects the intensity of her anguish:

> It cannot be expressed what I suffer:—it is only known to God what trials I go through in that respect. Lord, give me more humility, and then I shall not care for anything but thee! There are a variety of reasons why it is such a cross. The other day one told me, "He was sure I must be an impudent woman; no modest woman, he was sure, could proceed thus!" Ah! how glad would nature be to find out,—Thou, Lord, dost not require it![44]

The fruit of her labor, however, proved to be a constant confirmation of her calling, and in the midst of struggle she could proclaim:

> I had a clear conviction, God brought me to Yorkshire, and that I had a message to this people; and that notwithstanding the darkness which hung over my situation, I was at present where God would have me.[45]

While Mary Bosanquet seemed indefatigable in her labors, in the mid-1770s her friend and colleague, Sarah Crosby, began a whirlwind campaign across the difficult and

trackless Yorkshire moors and dales, beginning her long
itinerations that would continue for some twenty years.
Upon her return to Cross Hall on January 26, 1773, Mrs.
Crosby wrote somewhat apologetically to her spiritual
mentor concerning his letter of the previous October:

> I own I have been long Silent to y^r Important Questions; tho'
> not for want of regard, but travelling, and many engagements,
> Prevented my Having the Quiet, undisturb'd Time, for
> Reading over the plain Acct. of perfection, &cc.[46]

Indeed, throughout this period, she became particularly well
known and her services in such demand in the North and
West Ridings of Yorkshire that it was not uncommon for her
to hold as many as four meetings a day, addressing as many
as five hundred persons who had eagerly gathered to hear
her.[47] In her journal she recorded the events of a typical day
in 1774:

> We had a lively prayer meeting at five, a good band meeting
> at ten, and another at two; at five, Mrs. C. walked with me to
> Beeston; at seven, the house was full of people, and they
> obliged me to get into their little desk. I had great liberty in
> speaking, and felt my Lord exceedingly precious.[48]

In an extremely important letter to a friend and aspiring
woman preacher, written in July of that year, Sarah describes
the essential interrelation of her religious experience and the
divine imperative to preach God's grace:

> I hope My Dear Friend will Be glad to hear, that our Lord
> continues to pour out His Spirit amongst us. . . . And what is
> astonishing even to ourselves is, that our Lord is doing this
> great work, by the most *Simple* means. Many are thirsting for
> full salvation in L [?] & various other places. We have had
> some sweet meetings, and My Jesus often says, "Behold a
> [Proof?] cometh."
> As for Myself my Dear, I know not what to say, but that,
> the Immeasurable Comfort swells my own Transported
> Breast! For He renewth my strength as the Eagle: I live in a

Holy Astonishment before My God: while He fills My Soul with Divine Power, and the *simplicity* of a little Child, & never was so continually fill'd, yea overflow'd, with love before. Indeed My Lord shews me the reason was Because I Hearken'd *too much* to the Voice which Said, hold thy peace; keep Thy Happiness to thyself. (Tho not Enough to please them neither.) But He now forbids me, to Hide, the Light He gives, under a Bushel. And the more Simply I witness for God, the more Does He witness in my Heart, & others too, Glory be to His Dear Name forever. "O let my Mouth be fill'd with thy Praise, while, all the day long I publish thy Grace, &cc.[49]

Later that month she traveled with Wesley, her "dear Father in the Gospel," by easy stages to Robin Hood's Bay and then on to Scarborough. From there she ventured out on her own on a three-week campaign including stops at Guisborough, Newton, Stokesley, Potto, Bransdale, Highton-Dale, Gillamore, Lastingham, Bilsdale, and Northallerton. At nearly every one of these towns and villages she met the people at five in the morning and often held meetings in the afternoon and evening. The events of Sunday, July 24, at Guisborough, are exemplary:

I spent an hour at five, with as many as could come,—had a very solemn meeting at the preaching house, at half past eight; I believed it would be a good time, and so it was. The people came from many places round about. By one o'clock, four or five hundred were gathered together, with whom I had a very solemn time, and much of the presence of God. I met the class at five, and another public meeting at seven,—there were more present than before. I am astonished at the strength of body my Lord gives me; I ascribe it all to him.[50]

On one occasion toward the end of her itinerary, in spite of a hoarse voice and aching limbs, she spoke to between five and six hundred people in the rain "in a field, because no house could contain the people." Concluding her labors at Whitby, weary in body, she seemed all the more strengthened in her resolve to improve her talent:

> I had a very good time, and a house full of people. In the
> evening I went up to the top of the hill, *and was so sensible*
> *when praying alone, that I was doing my master's blessed will,*
> *in going among the people that no outward voice could have*
> *strengthened* the conviction. My spirit rests herein.—In the
> arms of divine love.[51]

Reflecting upon her experiences in a letter to her friend,
Mrs. Cayley, written from Whitby that following October,
she confessed that she was "truly, & literally, alone with
Jesus, in the midst of Multitudes, as tho' Standing before His
almighty Throne. . . . My Lord often Imploys me in Speaking
to Multitudes; but my great[st] Imployment is, to bear the
Burthens of Perticular Souls."[52] Seldom confined exclusively
to the responsibilities of her many public ministries, Sarah's
schedule was often filled with extra meetings of a more
intimate nature and her time devoted to much personal
conversation and pastoral direction as well.

And so, like Wesley, having parted company with leisure,
she was at Sheriff Hutton on Sunday, November 20, engaged
once again in her familiar routine:

> I rose at five, and praised my God. The weather was very
> severe. I met the people at six, and met the class at nine,—and
> held a public meeting at ten.—I had a good time, and still a
> better at two,—and concluded the day with a prayer meeting.
> I have cause to praise the Lord, for bringing me hither; for his
> *presence* has been a paradise unto me.[53]

And when visiting York two days later, she "was pained to
find that none in this City rise to meet together to worship
God at five."[54]

In the midst of these labors, having preached in chapels,
houses, barns, and open fields, Sarah says: "I was as sure that
I was employed by my Lord and doing his will, as of my own
life."[55] Upon her return to her headquarters at Cross Hall in
December 1774, her schedule hardly slackened and included
visits to Middleton and Churwell, near Leeds, to Halifax, to
Killinghall and Pannal, near Harrogate, and to Bradford
where a crowd of *"quakers, baptists, church folks,* and
methodists" was so great that they feared the collapse of the

meetinghouse galleries.[56] Her experiences in that place not only awed and inspired her, but humbled her as well:

> On sunday evening while I was standing up in the great preaching house, surrounded by upwards of *two thousand* souls, my good Lord, who never leaves those who trust in him, brought to my remembrance the time wherein he shewed me, that if I could talk to as many souls as could possibly hear me to the end of my life, it would be but a little handful compared with what the whole world contained.[57]

Mrs. Crosby's success was unquestionable, and despite widespread prejudice against women preachers, many of the Methodist leaders were cooperative and even provided opportunities for her to exercise her exceptional talents. On May 2, 1775, she dined with John Pawson, one of the three preachers stationed at Leeds who appeared to be sympathetic to her cause:

> He told me that he had heard that I had meetings at the preaching house at Halifax and Bradford, and that they were filled with people, and said *I was very welcome to have my meetings at the preaching house in Leeds if I pleased,* for which I thanked him.[58]

Frances Mortimer, the future wife of this prominent itinerant, had had the opportunity of hearing Sarah on December 1, 1774, and recorded her impressions with great delight in her journal:

> Mrs. Crosby expounded the 13th chapter of the first epistle to the Corinthians. She explained the characters of divine charity, or love, with a simplicity I had never heard before. Her heart and words acted in concert. Every sentence was impressive, and carried conviction to the heart. . . . my soul panted for that love on which she so delightfully expatiated.[59]

Sarah Crosby's reputation as a remarkable preacher soon preceded her wherever she went and her indefatigable public labors led Taft to exclaim "that this apostolic woman was an *itinerant,* yea, a *field preacher.*"[60]

ELIZABETH HURRELL: ANOTHER HERALD OF THE NORTH

In a letter written by Mrs. Marshall, a faithful and zealous Methodist of Parkgate, near Guiseley in Yorkshire, to Mrs. Hopper, wife of an illustrious preacher, a new figure is introduced into the circle of women preachers of Yorkshire, namely, Miss Elizabeth Hurrell:

> I have taken a little round with Mr. Wesley; I have had a good profitable time. My old friend Miss Hurrell, was along with me at Keighley, Haworth, Bingley, Bradford, Dawgreen, Birstall, Leeds, and Ledsham, and Mrs. Crosby at some of the places. I was also most of two days and a night at Miss Bosanquet's, and indeed she seems to have all the qualifications of a gentlewoman and Christian.[61]

Miss Hurrell was apparently awakened under the ministry of the Reverend Mr. Berridge of Everton.[62] Preaching with Wesley's approval, her labors proved to be very useful, particularly in the northern counties of Yorkshire, Lancashire, and Derbyshire, where she traveled extensively.

In a letter to Mrs. Crosby, written from Derby on May 18, 1779, Elizabeth reveals something of her industrious round:

> I arrived with God's blessing on saturday week, where I have *full employ,* and here I believe it is the Lord's will I should be for a season; but rest now satisfied, and wait the Lord's direction.
>
> If nothing prevent, I intend going from hence to *Sheffield, Doncaster, York,* and stop a little at *Pocklington, Beverly, Driffield,* and from thence to *Scarborough,* and then where the Lord pleases to appoint.[63]

Taft claims that "she possessed a wonderful ability of conveying her ideas and feelings, with scriptural accuracy," and her preaching "often manifested such a strength of thought, and felicity of expression, as were irresistibly impressive."[64] Among those who were "brought to the knowledge of the truth" through her instrumentality were

William Warrener (the first Methodist missionary to the West Indies), Henry Foster (a Wesleyan itinerant who died after laboring seven years in the Connection), and John Lancaster (a local preacher at Pickering and Burlington).

In spite of the impressive effects of her widespread labors, at some point she decided to desist from preaching. In a letter of June 1780, she confessed to a friend, "I have been employed very little for the LORD, I fear I am too bad for the LORD to use."[65] Exactly what led her to this decision must be left to conjecture, but Taft afforded a number of possibilities:

> Some have attributed it to the influence some persons of property had over her, who were opposed to her public labours, and [have thought that] she gave up the work of the ministry to retain their confidence and friendship; others have supposed that the loss of some considerable property at Whitby, and the effect it had upon her mind was the occasion; while others suppose she sunk beneath the *heavy cross* connected with the public exercises of *females*.[66]

Whatever the reason or combination of circumstances, in retrospect she deeply lamented the decision, and disparingly cried, "I am going to die. . . . O that I had my time to live again, I would not bury my talent as I have done."[67]

To return to 1775, however, an event of some importance revolves around this active woman and reveals the tensions that were beginning to emerge over the question of women preachers. In a letter to Joseph Benson, the assistant recently appointed to Newcastle, Wesley notes:

> John Fenwick has sent me a minute account of the manner how Miss Hurrell came to speak in the room at Sunderland; and Alexander Paterson has given me a particular narration of what occurred on Sunday the 22nd instant. It seems—this much is plain at least—that she has no more place at Sunderland; and I doubt whether we may not add, nor at any place in the Newcastle Circuit.[68]

It was undoubtedly to this event that Wesley referred in a conciliating letter to Sarah Crosby the following month:

Betsy Hurrell will do no harm if she comes to Leeds again. I suppose it was for her sake chiefly that aweful event was permitted. And it has had the effect which was designed. She was greatly humbled on the occasion.[69]

The clouded facts surrounding this "aweful event" would seem to be related to a direct confrontation between Miss Hurrell (and her supporters) and Joseph Benson, who was emerging as a primary antagonist of the women preachers. Some time earlier in 1775, Robert Empringham, Benson's colleague in Newcastle, complied with the wish of Fenwick and solicited signatures for a petition on behalf of Miss Hurrell.[70] According to Benson, this step was directly calculated to make Wesley believe that some of the itinerants had opposed her both violently and publicly. Countering this allegation, Benson assured Wesley that he had never spoken a word against her in public:

> If I have mentioned my objections to her proceedings in *private,* it has been to very few individuals, and that with great calmness and moderation; and the same I may affirm of Mr. Smith, Cownley, Lowes, and others with us.[71]

One such privately communicated criticism, apparently related to this incident or the controversy surrounding it, must certainly be the draft of a virulent letter in the handwriting of Joseph Benson which has been preserved in the W. L. Watkinson Collection at the New Room, Bristol.[72] "Passing over some things less material," writes Benson, "I hasten to assure you I am very sorry you should be so far overseen as to allow any *female* whatsoever to take your place in the pulpit." Such an action is contrary to "conscience," he maintains, for the apostle Paul (in 1 Corinthians 14:34) enjoins "the absolute necessity of imposing silence on women in the congregation." Any transgression of this rule, therefore, is inexcusable.

> Now dear friend, can you tell me why those who set aside this command[t] of the L[d] do not set aside all his other command[ts]? Can you tell me why those daring females, who seem to have stript themselves of the chief ornament of their sex, I mean

chaste & humble modesty & made themselves naked to their shame do not also commit fornication, & adultery, get drunk & swear? . . . They have effrontery enough, to ascend a pulpit & harange a promiscuous congregation for an hour together, when they are by God himself expressly forbid to so much as speak (by way of teach^g) in an public assembly.

Benson denied that there was any want of preaching, for God "raises up preachers of ye superior sex," and even if such were lacking, this would give no excuse to women for "breaking a plain command of God." He can discern no other motivation in them other than pride, self-love, and a concern for their own honor:

Having already disregarded X^t & his inspired Apostles, & now counter to the stream of all antiquity 'tis no wonder if they sh^d pour contempt on the order of M^r W^y & his preachers.

While Benson falls short of ranking the women preachers "wth the lew'd & impudent whores & actresses at Corinth," he discerns within their actions an underlying satanic design aimed at destroying the Wesleyan revival. Fearful of the worst, Benson prophetically concludes:

I wish M^r W^y & the Brethren w^d take the matter into serious consideration. It is now high time to do it.—If it is winked at for a few years, we shall have female preachers in abundance, more I dare say then men. . . . till behold the sexes have changed places, the woman is become the head of the man, the men almost all, learn in subjection & the women teach wth authority! These things ought not so to be!

MARGARET DAVIDSON: FIRST IRISH WOMAN PREACHER

Whereas the Benson episode in the north of England seemed a harbinger of intensified conflict over the "woman question" throughout the Connection, the sphere of women's influence was just beginning to open up in Ireland. Mrs.

Bennis continued to advise Wesley concerning developments there and directed the activities of the societies at Limerick and Waterford.[73] In county Down the work of Methodism was greatly advanced by the evangelical preaching of the Reverend Edward Smyth and the assistance of his wife, Agnes.[74] But the first woman preacher in Ireland was Margaret Davidson, a blind and somewhat disfigured native of Ballybredagh in Killinchy who had become intimately related to this enterprising couple.[75]

Margaret appears to have been introduced to Methodism under the preaching of James Oddie about 1758.[76] Despite a treacherous journey of seven miles, this blind girl determined to make her way to the nearest society at Comber, the third place into which Methodism was introduced in the county of Down. After two attempts and two failures she was finally received very warmly by Hudson, the preacher, and the small band of Methodists on the occasion of her third effort. On May 1, 1765, she was present to hear Wesley preach at a service at Newtownards and retained a vivid memory of the experience: "After preaching, he took me gently by the hand and said, 'Faint not, go on, and you shall see in glory!' These words left a lasting impression on my mind."[77]

Two years later she was advised to move to Lisburn where she remained for seven years and became one of the fourteen Methodists (chiefly women) of that town. It was here that she began to exercise the unusual gifts she possessed, especially in prayer, and her sphere of usefulness was gradually enlarged. She visited among her neighbors, prayed with them, and occasionally assisted at public services. Like many of her female colleagues, she wished to avoid giving any possible offense and was careful, therefore, never to "presume to stand up as an exhorter, lest any should take an occasion to say that I assumed the character of a preacher, which might have hurt the cause of God."[78] She entered into the work of the great revival which took place at Ballinderry in the winter of 1769/70, however, and rendered valuable assistance in that extraordinary situation. And in 1776, when she met Reverend and Mrs. Smyth at Derryaghy, she became closely identified with the revival at Ballyculter.[79]

Having been invited to spend some time with the Smyths, she accompanied the preacher to a meeting at Dunsford, where he insisted that she address the assembly. The effects of her clear intellect and retentive memory, her great fluency and fervor of speech, and the simplicity of her witness were immediate. Smyth considered it advisable to leave her to work among the people. Regular evening meetings were arranged and many flocked to hear the blind preacher present her message. Within a month no fewer than one hundred persons had experienced a powerful spiritual awakening in their lives. According to Margaret, her general approach in these proceedings was "to draw inferences from their own catechism and from the hymns with which they were affected."[80] Before she left, a number of classes were formed and societies established all over the district. She received many invitations to preach thereafter and managed to itinerate a few weeks each year in spite of her blindness.

METHODISTS AND QUAKERS

In December 1777 Mary Bosanquet journeyed into the west country, was led to speak with great freedom at a lovefeast at Bath, and remained there until the following April.[81] This extended visit was anticipated by Wesley who wrote to Mrs. Crosby concerning it. In this important letter of December 2, 1777, Wesley not only emphasizes the value of their labors as his co-workers, but reiterates his mature view of their preaching as an "extraordinary call." He also explicitly differentiates his opinion on this question from that of the Society of Friends:

> I hope you will always have your time much filled up. You will, unless you grow weary of well doing. For is not the harvest plenteous still? Had we ever a larger field of action? And shall we stand all or any part of the day idle? Then we should wrong both our neighbour and our own souls.
>
> For the sake of retrenching her expenses, I thought it quite needful for Miss Bosanquet to go from home. And I was likewise persuaded (as she was herself) that God had

something for her to do in Bath and Kingswood; perhaps in
Bristol too, although I do not think she will be called to speak
there in public.

The difference between us and the Quakers in this respect is
manifest. They flatly deny the rule itself, although it stands
clear in the Bible. We allow the rule; only we believe it admits
of some exceptions. At present I know of those, and no more,
in the whole Methodist Connexion. You should send word of
what our Lord is doing where you go to, dear Sally.[82]

Proselytizing between the two groups continued throughout this period with notable conquests on both sides. Some
Methodist women defected to the Society of Friends,
however, not only for the attractions of Quaker mysticism,
but because of the Society's avowed egalitarianism.[83] The
first woman preacher to defect in this way was Mary Stokes,
a trusted Methodist leader at Bristol, who left her position in
1772 to join the Friends' Meeting in the Friars, nearly
opposite the New Room in the Horsefair.[84] Later, Mary
became "one of the greatest and most influential of the
women preachers of the eighteenth century."[85]

Born in Bristol in 1750, she passed through an intense
period of devotion to Methodism and began her public
ministry as early as 1771. On October 12 of that year she
confided with Thomas Rankin about her religious experience
and the divine confirmation of her labors:

While I have been speaking, I have felt such divine
communications of his love, such rays of approbation, from
him, that with ecstasy I have cried, "Jesus is precious! My
God, and my ALL!"[86]

Mary was an intimate friend of John Wesley, who did
everything in his power to keep her from joining the
Quakers. In his last letter to her he entreated her to read his
Letter to a Quaker and expressed his fear that she was
unwittingly teetering "on the brink of a precipice."[87] The
quality of her faith and life, however, which endeared her to
Wesley are unmistakable:

> She was intensely religious, possessed a remarkable gift in ministry, and was fused through her entire being with a burning passion for the conversion of souls. "I sometimes feel," she used to say, "that I could fly even to distant lands to proclaim the gospel of life and salvation."[88]

While Wesley failed to retain her within the circle of Methodism, there is no question that her Quaker conversion had a strong reciprocal influence on her adopted Society. Jones claims that "wherever we get a glimpse of her message, it throbs with an evangelical passion."[89] The central thrust of her evangel was "Preach Christ crucified. . . . Proclaim not only what He would do within us by His Spirit, but also what He hath done without us, the all-atoning sacrifice which should never be lost sight of!"[90] She brought a new strain of evangelical preaching into Quaker worship when the antievangelical forces of mysticism, rationalism, and Deism were exerting a strong influence upon that Society. On the question of her balanced perspective and the influence of her preaching, Jones observes:

> She brought with her into the Society of her adoption a fervour and a dynamic quality in every way like that which marked the founders of Methodism. . . . She struck a new note in Quaker preaching, but she was so deeply imbued with all that was best in the Quaker spirit that her hearers hardly suspected what a change of emphasis marked her glowing messages. She was a gentle revolutionist, transforming people who had no idea they were being transformed.[91]

Throughout the course of this decade the Quaker witness in Bristol was reviving and led to a number of conversions besides that of Mary.[92] John Helton, a popular Methodist preacher succumbed to the allurements of Barclay's *Apology,* converted to Quakerism, and in 1778 published a formidable reply to Wesley's famous thirty-year-old *Letter to a Quaker.*[93] In this irenic pamphlet Helton attempts to demonstrate how Wesley had altered his views on a number of critical issues. Having closely examined those Quaker principles to which Wesley had objected in 1748, Helton "found reason to conclude that he now sees things more clearly, and has therefore changed his mind with regard to the seventh proposition on Justification, and the tenth on Women's preaching."[94]

First of all, Helton counters Wesley's previous prohibition of female preaching on the basis of scriptural precedent, showing how the Pauline injunctions which Wesley employs for his defense (1 Corinthians 14:34 and 1 Timothy 2:12) only "*seem* to serve the purpose; but that they are not used in their true signification."[95] The heart of Helton's argument is that throughout the New Testament "prophesying" and "preaching" are synonymous and that the evidence overwhelmingly supports the validity of women who function in this capacity.[96] In support of his view that prophesying in these critical passages means "preaching in the common acceptation of the word," he elicits the aid of the noted biblical commentator, Matthew Henry:

> In his comment on prophecy, he says, "By the Spirit they shall be enabled to foretell things to come, and to preach the Gospel, without distinction of sex, not only your sons, but your daughters."[97]

In the end, however, Wesley's errant preacher claims that a shorter method might have been taken to demonstrate that women's preaching is lawful, namely:

> There are several female teachers in the Methodist Society; and hence I concluded, in the beginning of this Letter, that the objector has changed his sentiments in this particular. If he has not, there seems a manifest inconsistency in his suffering women to preach.[98]

While Wesley had in fact changed his mind regarding women preachers, the main point of contention was his insistence that such gifted women were exceptions to the apostolic rule, extraordinary and not ordinary instruments of God's grace. He was content to leave the matter where it stood and did not even venture to print a formal reply to Helton's pamphlet.[99]

There can be no doubt, however, that in his wider acceptance of women as extraordinary messengers of the gospel he acted partly under the influence of the Society of Friends.

THE "WOMEN OF ISRAEL" IN YORKSHIRE

The affect which many of these women preachers had upon their hearers is well illustrated by an anecdote concerning William Varty of Penrith. In May 1776 this enterprising young man was on a business venture to Leeds, and a friend persuaded him to hear a lady preacher in one of the Methodist chapels, probably in Baildon. The preacher was Mary Bosanquet, and in her journal she writes about the event under the date, May 5, 1776:

> I had a meeting some days ago at B——, where an odd circumstance occurred. I observed (as I was speaking on these words, "The Master is come, and calleth for thee") a gentleman among the congregation who looked with great earnestness. . . . He told me he was building a house for an Assembly; but he would go home and turn it into a Preaching-house, if I would come and speak in it, that his neighbours might get the light he had got. . . . Satan made use of this occurrence to bring me into discouragement respecting public speaking; but some years after I heard a most pleasing account of this gentleman,—that he had indeed turned his Assembly-house into a Methodist Preaching-house, and that himself and family were joined to the Society.[100]

This incident proved to be only the beginning of an extraordinary summer and fall for Mary Bosanquet. On Tuesday, June 11, 1776, she seems to have returned to the place of Varty's conversion, but because of extenuating circumstances found it necessary to become a field preacher:

> We stood in an open place, with some serious people from other parts, and some of the careless inhabitants. However, all behaved well, and I found liberty in enforcing those words, "Acquaint now thyself with God, and be at peace; hereby good shall come unto thee!"[101]

Despite the overwhelming approbation she received and the support of the Methodist leadership, she was often beset by intense doubts concerning the propriety of her actions. On August 30 she confided to her diary:

> Yesterday it was given out for me to be at————. For a whole month it lay on my mind. None, O my God, but Thyself, knows what I go through for every public meeting. I am often quite ill with the prospect.[102]

She continued to preach in barns, however, and to renew her covenant with various societies, pleading all the while in the words of Solomon, "Ah, Lord! how shall I, who am but a child, go in and out before this Thy chosen people."

One of the most significant days in the life of Mary Bosanquet was September 17, 1776, when she preached to several thousand people at Goker and Huddersfield. Her journal account of this experience is certainly the most well-known description of the preaching of a woman in the Wesleyan revival, and as such, has become an inextricable part of Methodist hagiography. It is of quintessential importance because it affords many details regarding the circumstances surrounding the event, the setting and nature of the audience, the texts and outline of the sermon preached, and Miss Bosanquet's feelings regarding the dynamics involved in her exceptional labors. It would be impossible to improve upon her own simple account of her experience that day:

> Last Sabbath morning I went, according to appointment, to Goker. I arose early, and in pretty good health. The day was fine, though rather hot. About eleven we came to Huddersfield, and called on Mrs. H. She had asked me to lodge there on my return, and have a meeting, saying, many had long desired it, and there would be no Preacher there on that day. I felt immediately the people laid on my mind, and that I had a message to that place; and said, "If the Lord permit, I will." She then said, "We will give it out at noon." We rode forward. Benjamin Cock met us, and kindly conducted us over the moors. When we came to his hut, all was clean, and victuals enough provided for twenty men! But I was so heated

with ride, (nearly twenty miles,) and with the great fire on which they so liberally cooked for us, that I could not eat. My drinking nothing but water seemed also quite to distress them. They said, the meeting had been given out in many places, and they believed we should have between two and three thousand people. That I did not believe; but there was indeed such a number, and of such a rabble as I scarce ever saw. At one we went out to the rocks, a place so wild that I cannot describe it. The crowd which got round us was so great, that by striving which should get first to the quarry, (where we were to meet,) they rolled down great stones among the people below us, so that we feared mischief would be done. Blessed be God, none was hurt. I passed on among them on the top of the hill, not knowing whither I went. Twice I was pushed down by the crowd, but rose without being trampled on. We stopped on the edge of a spacious quarry, filled with people, who were tolerably quiet. I gave out that hymn, "The Lord my pasture shall prepare," &c. When they were a little settled, I found some liberty in speaking to them, and, I believe, most heard. As we returned into the house, numbers followed, and filled it so full we could not stir. I conversed with them, but could not get much answer. They stood like people in amaze, and seemed as if they could never have enough. Many wept, and said, "When will you come again?" We then set off for Huddersfield. I felt very much fatigued, and began to think, how shall I be able to fulfill my word there? As we rode along, Brother Taylor said, "I think I ought to tell you my mind. I wish we could ride through Huddersfield, and not stop; for I know there are some there who do not like women to speak among them, and I fear you will meet with something disagreeable." I looked to the Lord, and received, as it seemed to me, the following direction: If I have a word to speak for him, he will make my way; if not, the door will be shut.

Upon her arrival she made an interesting discovery:

But few of the principal persons had any objection, and the people much desired it; beside, as it had been given out at noon, there would be a great many strangers, whom it would not be well to disappoint. It was then agreed, that we should have the meeting in the house, where they usually had the preaching; but when we came here, the crowd was very great,

and the place so hot, that I feared I should not be able to speak
at all. I stood still, and left all to God. A friend gave out a
hymn; during which, some fainted away. Brother Taylor said,
"I perceive it is impossible for us to stay within doors: the
people cannot bear the heat, and there are more without than
are within." We then came out. My head swam with heat; I
scarce knew which way I went, but seemed carried along by
the people, till we stopped at a horse-block, placed against a
wall, on the side of the street, with a plain wide opening before
it. On the steps of this I stood, and gave out, "Come, ye
sinners, poor and needy," &c. While the people were singing
the hymn, I felt a renewed conviction to speak in the name of
the Lord. My bodily strength seemed to return each moment.
I felt no weariness, and my voice was stronger than in the
morning, while I was led to enlarge on these words, "The Lord
is our Judge, the Lord is our Lawgiver, the Lord is our King,
he will save us." . . . Deep solemnity sat on every face. I think
there was scarce a cough to be heard, or the least motion,
though the number gathered was very great. So solemn a time
I have seldom known; my voice was clear enough to reach
them all; and when we concluded I felt stronger than when we
began.[103]

Mary was always sensitive about the way in which her
actions were perceived, mainly because she did not want the
means she employed to proclaim God's love to become a
hindrance to those who had not experienced it yet. While she
felt a definite sense of divine confirmation "when standing on
the horse-block in the street at Huddersfield," she realized
how ridiculous she must have appeared to many of her
contemporaries. "Therefore, if some persons consider me as
an impudent woman," she conceded, "and represent me as
such, I cannot blame them."[104] And yet, she offered an
articulate defense of her actions, in her journal, answering
several of her critic's questions.

To those who admonished her to take "a round" and
thereby assume the status of a traveling preacher, she
responded by saying that this was not her calling; rather, she
had many other duties and cares of which they knew nothing.
She was content to follow God's guidance as opportunities

for preaching arose. Some critics complained that she was hypocritical in describing her assemblies as "meetings" when, in fact, they were services of worship and preaching. This, she said, suited her design best, however, because it was less ostentatious, left her at liberty to speak more or less as she felt herself led, and gave her opponents less cause for offense. To those who advised her to become a Quaker, she retorted that she was convinced of God's active presence among the Methodists and therefore resolved to "stick to them like a leech" regardless of the consequences. "I do nothing," she advised her Methodist critics, "but what Mr. Wesley approves; and as to reproach thrown by some on me, what have I to do with it, but quietly go forward, saying, 'I will be still more vile,' if my Lord requires it!"[105]

Sarah Crosby continued indefatigable in her labors, frequently joining her talents with those of Miss Bosanquet or Miss Hurrell, and in spite of her self-abnegation for failing to improve "either my time, or talents, as I wish I had." In contrast, her diary reveals a clear glimpse of the extent of her manifold activities during the year 1777. On the last day of that year she recorded:

> Thou hast enabled me, from the first of last January to the fourth of this month (December), to ride 960 miles, to keep 220 public meetings, at many of which some hundreds of precious souls were present, about 600 private meetings, and to write an 116 letters, many of them long ones; besides many, many conversations with souls in private, the effect of which will, I trust, be "as bread cast on the waters." All glory be unto him, who has strengthened his poor worm.[106]

In a letter to her friend Mary Woodhouse, later Mrs. Holder, she describes the work occasioned by her having been detained at Bridlington:

> I have been amazed indeed; but it is the Lord, who will send, by whom he will send. It seems a moment of mercy, a time of love to the people of Bridlington, glory be to God! The dew drops have fallen upon them, but it appears as if a shower was coming down.[107]

In her journal, Mrs. Holder, who often assisted her itinerant husband by exhorting after he had preached, describes Sarah's excursions throughout North Yorkshire:

> After some months Mrs. Crosby came again to Scarborough, and Miss Hurrel came with her; and they were the means of many flocking to the house of God. Their labours *publicly* and *privately* were blest in town and country to numbers of precious souls. Mrs. Crosby, continued to come to Whitby several times for some years. She stayed with us in my father's house many weeks, and was a pattern of holiness in all manner of conversation. Her life and labours of love were of great use to many a soul, and *I bless God that I ever saw her* . . . her *advice, reproof, instruction,* and *example* were rendered exceedingly useful.[108]

Throughout the closing years of this decade, Elizabeth Hurrell was also particularly useful at Beverley where the society seemed to be in a constant state of turmoil. On October 28, 1777, Wesley wrote concerning her to Mrs. Barton, with high hopes that "good will result from Miss Hurrell's visit. She has been of use to many."[109] She returned the following year and received Wesley's approbation: "It is well you spent a little time at poor Beverley. The little flock there stands in need of all the help we can give them. Hardly any Society in England has been so harassed as they have been from the very beginning."[110]

The work of these women in Yorkshire was admired and sanctioned by many of the leaders of the Wesleyan revival, lay and clergy alike. A letter written by the Reverend John Fletcher to the woman who was later to become his wife and co-worker at Madeley, Miss Bosanquet, affords one of the strongest statements of approval from one of the most venerated figures of early Methodism and Wesley's designated successor:

> My Christian love waits upon Mrs. Crosby, Miss Hurrel, and Miss Ritchie, I hope the Lord binds you each day closer to Himself and to each other, and enables you to see and experience the glory of the promise made to the daughters and handmaids, as well as to the sons and servants of the Lord.

> Oh, what a day when we shall all be so filled with power from
> on high, as to go forth and prophesy, and water the Lord's
> drooping plants and barren parched garden with *rivers of
> living water flowing from our own souls.*[111]

Wesley's own views on this question changed radically over
the course of this decade, as we have seen, but he never
permitted women's preaching to become a general practice.
Each woman's claim to possess an extraordinary call to
proclaim the gospel was judged on its own merits, just as each
lay preacher's calling was evaluated on the basis of his gifts,
grace, and fruits. That Wesley maintained strict control over
the activities of aspiring women preachers is evident from his
forceful letter to George Robinson, written from Manchester
on March 25, 1780: "I desire Mr. Peacock to put a final stop to
the preaching of women in his circuit. If it were suffered, it
would grow, and we know not where it would end."[112]

Far from representing a regression in Wesley's attitude
toward the exceptional women of Methodism, this letter
simply reaffirms the principle upon which all of his decisions
concerning ecclesiology were based, a principle which had
come more clearly into focus during the 1770s. This view of
the exceptional nature of the Wesleyan revival and the
validity of extraordinary means in this unique dispensation of
God's grace is succinctly expressed in Zechariah Taft's
analysis of the relationship between John Wesley and his first
authorized woman preacher, Sarah Crosby:

> She was one of those females to whom the Lord had given a
> dispensation to publish the glad tidings of salvation by Jesus
> Christ. Nevertheless, he did not wish her, or any other female
> to assume the title and character of a preacher, as he
> considered their call, not an *ordinary,* but an *extraordinary*
> one, and knowing the strong prejudice which prevailed in the
> minds of men in general, and of some of his own connexion
> against such a ministry, he gave *such* cautions to sister Crosby,
> and other female preachers with whom he corresponded,
> which, if attended to, *he* believed would be a means of
> softening the prejudices of his differing brethren, and yet
> increase and perpetuate the benefit which would accompany
> and follow their public ministrations.[113]

In the final decade of his life, however, the number of such exceptional cases was greater than he or any of the Methodist leaders anticipated. It was difficult for Wesley to admit the Crosbys and the Bosanquets and prohibit the ministry of other extraordinary messengers who happened to be women.

NOTES

1. This shift toward "denominationalism" in Wesley's thinking or strategy is reflected in subtle albeit significant changes in the wording of the *Minutes*. For instance, in 1770 and from then on, the words "tending to a separation" became "sliding into a separation from the Church" (*Minutes*, 1:540–41). Cf. Baker, *John Wesley and the Church of England*, pp. 197–99.
2. Baker, "John Wesley's Churchmanship," p. 273.
3. Baker, *John Wesley and the Church of England*, pp. 203–4.
4. This letter, simply dated 1771 from Cross Hall, near Leeds, is reproduced in its entirety in Appendix D. Sarah Crosby copied her colleague's letter along with Wesley's response in her MS Letterbook, pp. 55–61. It would seem that Zechariah Taft was the first to publish this text in his apologetic tract, *The Scripture Doctrine of Women's Preaching* (pp. 19–21) in 1820 and subsequently reprinted it as an appendix to Bramwell's *Account of Ann Cutler* (pp. 34–37) seven years later. Henry Moore was apparently unaware of this important document, but Jabez Burns, probably relying on Taft, reprinted the letter in his *Life of Mrs. Fletcher* (London: J. Smith, 1843), pp. 164–67.
5. Meth. Arch., correcting Wesley, *Letters*, 5:257. Cf. Baker, *John Wesley and the Church of England*, p. 204. There has been much confusion over the identity of the recipient of this letter. In Joseph Nightengale's *A Portraiture of Methodism* (London: Longman, Hurst, Rees, and Orme, 1807), p. 454; Myles, *Chronological History*, p. 99; and Tyerman, *Life of John Wesley*, 3:112 (who quotes from the manuscript letter), the recipient is correctly identified as Mary Bosanquet. John Simon, in *John Wesley, The Master Builder*, p. 292, followed the mistake of Taft, *Holy Women*, 2:57–58, in identifying Sarah Crosby as the recipient. This error was also perpetuated in Wesley, *Works*, 12:356, later surfaced in Harrison's biographical sketch of Mrs. Crosby (*W.H.S.* 14:107), and reappeared recently in Brown, "Standing in the Shadow," p. 27, although

this was subsequently corrected in his "Women of the Word," p. 75. The confusion very probably arose from the fact that this letter was written on the same sheet as one of the same date to Mrs. Crosby, who resided with her at Cross Hall in Yorkshire. Both letters were published by Telford in his standard edition of the *Letters,* 5:257–58.

6. Wesley, *Letters,* 5:257–58. Apparently referring to the incident in which Wesley was debarred from preaching in a parish church because of his attitude concerning women, he concludes: "I doubt whether at *that particular time* it was advisable for you to go to Huddersfield. But it is past. All that you can do now (if you have not done it already) is to write lovingly to Mr. A[tlay] and simply inform him of those facts, concerning which he was misinformed before. It is not improbable he may then see things clearer; but if he do not, you will have delivered your own soul. And whatever farther is said of you is *your* cross. Bear *it,* and it will bear *you.*"

7. January 1772, Wesley, *Letters,* 5:302.

8. February 11, 1772, London, in ibid., p. 305. See pp. 162–63 below.

9. Consult Appendix A for pertinent references.

10. "The Experience of Mrs. Ann Gilbert, of Gwinear, in Cornwall," *Arm. Mag.* 18 (1795): 44.

11. Ibid., p. 45.

12. Ibid.

13. Taft, *Holy Women,* 1:49.

14. Ibid., pp. 50–51. Noted in Taft's own hand in his personal copy.

15. Ibid., p. 51. She was apparently blinded in or about the year 1754. It is impossible to determine exactly when this event of preaching at Redruth took place. Ann died on July 18, 1790, at her home in Gwinear.

16. "An Extract from the Diary of Mrs. Bathsheba Hall," *Arm. Mag.* 4 (1781): 373.

17. Wesley, *Journal,* 5:469.

18. Ibid., 6:97.

19. May 8, 1774, Wesley, *Letters,* 6:84.

20. Wesley, *Journal,* 6:11.

21. Ibid., p. 25.

22. John Wesley to Francis Wolfe, January 11, 1775, Luton, Wesley, *Letters,* 6:136.

23. Taft, *Holy Women,* 1:171. Very little is known about this aspiring woman preacher other than the fact that she was one of the first Methodists on the Isle of Jersey.

24. February 25, 1774, Near London, Wesley, *Letters*, 6:74, here speaking specifically about the doctrine of Christian Perfection.
25. November 30, 1774, Reigate, in ibid., pp. 138–39.
26. April 1, 1773, Dublin, in ibid., p. 23.
27. Ibid.
28. December 26, 1776, London, in ibid., pp. 245–46.
29. See Appendix A for bibliographical details. James Bartram, a Wesleyan local preacher turned Congregationalist minister, who knew her family, informs us that she was "a sister of Mr. Thomas Newman, a substantial Mercer, Draper, and Tailor in Cheltenham" (*W.H.S.* 25:87).
30. The probable dates coincide with his visits on March 18 and October 10, 1766, and March 16, 1768, with August 1, 1771, being the most likely. See Richard Green, *An Itinerary in Which are Traced the Rev. John Wesley's Journeys from October 14, 1735, to October 24, 1790* (Burnley: Printed by B. Moore, n.d.).
31. February 21, 1773, Cheltenham, *Arm. Mag.* 29:171.
32. April 22, 1775, Portarlington, *W.H.S.* 25:87.
33. Tyerman, *Life of John Wesley*, 2:560.
34. November 1, 1778, London, Wesley, *Letters*, 6:329.
35. Taft, *Holy Women*, 1:291. Coussins was born at Reading in Berkshire on January 2, 1757, converted in 1776, entered the itinerancy in 1780, and was appointed to the Gloucester Circuit in 1782 and 1783 where he met and married Penelope and served with Robert Empringham among others. On October 13, 1805, he died at Diss, in Norfolk, after twenty-five years service in the itinerant ministry.
36. *Arm. Mag.* 29:295. Mary had not yet actually married John Fletcher. Taft affords greater detail concerning this encounter: "That eminent female, visited Bristol and Bath, with an intention to warn sinners of their danger, and to lead believers into the full enjoyment of their Christian privileges. Mr. Cousins went to hear her preach, and to him she proved a Priscilla indeed." Wesley wrote to Mary Bosanquet on February 23, 1778, concerning her work in Bath and Bristol: "Who knows but the illness of Miss Bishop might be permitted for this very thing—that you might have a more dear and open way to help the women at Bath forward? What you have to do at Bristol does not yet appear, Providence will open itself by-and-by. I am glad Philly [sic] Cousins retains her confidence. See that she has something to do" (Wesley, *Letters*, 6:306–7).

37. Moore, *Fletcher,* p. 98. See Appendix H for a list of sermon texts employed by the women preachers.
38. Moore, *Fletcher,* pp. 98–99.
39. Ibid., pp. 99–100.
40. Joanna Dawson and Arnold Kellet have identified this venue as the ballroom of the White Hart Motel in Harrogate, in *People and Places in Yorkshire Methodism* (a souvenir booklet of the W.H.S. Exhibition, Harrogate Conference, 1971), p. 6.
41. Moore, *Fletcher,* p. 100.
42. J. U. Walker, *A History of Wesleyan Methodism in Halifax* (Halifax: Hartley and Walker, 1836), pp. 135–36. Cf. Smith, *History of Wesleyan Methodism,* 1:362–63; and J. Robinson Gregory, *A History of Methodism,* 2 vols. (London: Charles H. Kelly, 1911), 1:114–15.
43. Moore, *Fletcher,* p. 103.
44. May 28, 1775, in ibid., p. 107.
45. Ibid., pp. 107–8.
46. Sarah Crosby to John Wesley, Crosby, MS Letterbook, p. 48.
47. On her labors during this period, see Church, *More about Early Methodist People,* pp. 150-53; Morrow, *Early Methodist Women,* pp. 16–21; and Brown, "Women of the Word," pp. 79–80, all of whom draw their accounts from her journal.
48. April 6, 1774, Taft, *Holy Women,* 2:63. Pulpits during the eighteenth century were generally large enough to stand in, often called "desks," or described disparagingly as "tubs." In this instance, Mrs. Crosby broke from the convention of many women preachers, both Quaker and Methodist, who preferred to take their stand alongside rather than in the pulpit.
49. Sarah Crosby to Elizabeth Hurrell, Cross Hall, July 2, 1774, Crosby, MS Letterbrook, pp. 69–71.
50. Taft, *Holy Women,* 2:69.
51. Ibid., p. 75.
52. Crosby, MS Letterbrook, p. 75.
53. Taft, *Holy Women,* 2:76.
54. Ibid., p. 77.
55. March 22, 1775, in ibid., p. 78.
56. Ibid., pp. 82–83.
57. Ibid., p. 84.
58. Ibid. The place to which she was invited was evidently the famous Old Boggard House (see Hellier, "Some Methodist Women Preachers," p. 66). Pawson, twice elected president of the Methodist Conference, and one of his colleagues at Leeds, William Brammah, were supportive of the women preachers.

59. Sutcliffe, *Experience of Frances Pawson,* p. 33.
60. Taft, *Holy Women,* 2:24.
61. Parkgate, July 16, 1772, Charles A. Federer, "Parkgate, Near Guiseley, Yorkshire," *W.H.S.* 5 (1906): 240–41. Cf. Laycock, *Methodist Heroes in Haworth Round,* p. 300. For a very interesting letter from Mrs. Ann Ray to Miss Hurrell, Newington, September 2, 1769, see *Meth. Mag.* 44 (1821): 361–362. See Appendix A for related bibliographical data.
62. See the account in Taft, *Holy Women,* 1:175–81; 2: 101–3; and various letters in Wesley, *Letters,* 6:169, 184–85, 192, 269, 286.
63. Taft, *Holy Women,* 1:178–79.
64. Ibid., p. 181.
65. Ibid.
66. Ibid., pp. 177–78. Bracketed portions indicate the editorial revisions in Taft's personal copy.
67. Ibid., p. 178. She appears to have moved to Queen Square, London, in 1780, where Wesley visited her in 1788 and 1790 at her home in Upper Gower Street.
68. October 30, 1775, London, Wesley, *Letters,* 6:184–85. Wesley had made reference to Fenwick, a strong advocate of the women preachers, in a letter to Christopher Hopper of February 1, 1775: "Surely it cannot be that you should find in the house at Newcastle an account which John Fenwick sent me, and that you should send it back to him" (*Letters,* 6:137–38.)
69. November 29, 1775, Norwich, in ibid., p. 192. Two years later, on July 29, 1777, he wrote in a similar vein to Mrs. Barton: "I believe, if Miss Hurrell were to spend a little time with you, it might be of great use to many" (*Letters,* 6:269).
70. See ibid., p. 184, for Telford's analysis.
71. Quoted from Benson's MS Life, 1:376, as cited in Wesley, *Letters,* 6:184n. Cownley and Lowes were both seasoned preachers and well acquainted with Newcastle Methodism.
72. See Appendix E for the full text of the letter, including Benson's erasures, here omitted for clarity. This hitherto unpublished letter was conjecturally dated circa 1773/4, but the coincidence of events and internal evidence support a later date, perhaps the summer or early fall of 1775, necessarily subsequent to Benson's stationing in Newcastle, but prior to Wesley's letter to him of October 30. A date of October 1775 would seem to present the fewest difficulties. The unidentified recipient, most certainly a fellow itinerant, is less easily identified, but would seem to be Robert Empringham, who

may have had responsibility for the services at the Sunderland Society as a preacher in the Newcastle Circuit. The difficulty here is in the necessity of Benson's writing thus to a colleague in the circuit, unless he conceived the letter to be a formal censure of his activities. Perhaps John Fenwick was the intended recipient, or another preacher who relinquished his pulpit to Miss Hurrell in the vicinity. There is no evidence to demonstrate that this draft was ever actually posted.

73. See Wesley, *Letters*, 5:343–44. In his letter of November 3, 1772, Wesley sought her advice concerning the proper stationing of preachers in these circuits. The sentence alluding to this fact was omitted from early editions of Wesley's works, but restored in Telford's standard edition.

74. Smyth, the nephew of Dr. F. A. Smyth, archbishop of Dublin, was removed from his curacy for preaching Methodist doctrines, thereafter entered wholly into the work of the revival, organizing meetings for instance at Dunsford and Downpatrick, traveling throughout Ireland, and holding services both in chapels and the open air. Agnes frequently held prayer meetings and exhorted with her husband's approval. Crookshank records one such occasion: "Mrs. Smyth, having visited a family, a member of which had died, found a large number of persons assembled in the house. Her first impulse was to remain silent; but, when she thought of the many souls there were before her, perhaps perishing for lack of knowledge, she felt constrained to speak to them . . . a duty from which she shrank, but again rose the thought, 'If I omit it, the conviction of remissness in my duty will be insupportable' " (*Memorable Women*, pp. 126–39).

75. See the major sources on her life and work in Appendix A.

76. According to Church, "as she groped her way to the edge of the crowd, he was announcing a hymn:

> Ye blind, behold your Saviour come;
> And leap, ye lame, for joy.

It seemed to her a direct message from God" (*More about Early Methodist People*, p. 173).

77. Quoted in Crookshank, *Methodism in Ireland*, 1:182. Cf. Wesley, *Journal*, 5:113.

78. Edward Smyth, ed., *The Extraordinary Life and Christian Experience of Margaret Davidson, as Dictated by Herself* (Dublin: Dugdale, 1782), p. 97.

79. Ibid., pp. 97–99.
80. Ibid., p. 97. Cf. Brown, "Women of the Word," p. 71.
81. See Moore, *Fletcher,* pp. 125–28.
82. Wesley, *Letters,* 6:290–91. Regarding this letter George Smith observed: "It is evident, therefore, that Wesley did not merely connive at female preachers; he gave them his direct and formal sanction, when, as in these two cases, he was convinced they were called of God" (*History of Wesleyan Methodism,* 1:420–21). Both Bath and Kingswood tended to be more sympathetic to the ministry of women. The influence of the Countess of Huntingdon, who had founded and maintained a large federation of Calvinistic Methodist societies, may explain the openness of the Methodist communities at Bath. In Kingswood, women had long functioned in positions of leadership at the school (e.g., Mrs. Ryan). Bristol, boasting the oldest Methodist chapel in Britain and maintaining its role as one of the major centers of early Methodism, tended to be more conservative in its views. Bristolian Methodists also found it necessary to compete against a strong Quaker presence which may have tempered their views about the propriety of women preachers.
83. The irony of this situation is that while the Quakers appeared to be more egalitarian in their acceptance of women preachers, the local leadership of the movement retained a decidedly masculine, if not antifeminist, predisposition. In Methodism, on the other hand, women were given a working equality with men in positions of societal leadership from the outset of the revival, but the acceptance of women as preachers was much more gradual. The utilization of women in the two similar movements was reversed, as it were, in terms of the areas of responsibility, Methodism emphasizing equality on the local level with women preachers as exceptions to the general rule, and Quakerism accepting women ministers with a paternalistic bias, largely unacknowledged, among the rank and file. See Leach, *Women Ministers,* p. 12, where this historian says: "Unfortunately the equality which permitted preaching and traveling in the ministry did not extend into all realms of life. To assume that men and women were equal in the Society of Friends at this early time is questionable." Cf. Braithewaite, *Second Period of Quakerism,* pp. 273–87; Lloyd, *Quaker Social History,* pp. 110–25. Concerning Quakerism in the mid-nineteenth century, Elizabeth Isichei writes: "The equality of men and women in Quakerism was more apparent than

real, but the powers open to women were so large compared with their restricted role in other religious—or, for that matter, secular—organizations in Victorian England, that they deserve to be regarded as one of the most striking elements in Quaker organization" (*Victorian Quakers* [London: Oxford University Press, 1970], pp. 107–10).

84. She was born to Joseph and Mary Stokes on June 6, 1750, later joined the Methodist Society at the New Room, becoming an intimate friend of Elizabeth Johnson, was married to Robert Dudley of Clonmel, Ireland, with whom she bore two children, resided in London from 1820, and died at her home at Peckham on September 24, 1823, being interred in the Friends' Cemetery near Bunhill Fields. On her life, see Elizabeth Dudley, ed., *The Life of Mary Dudley*, (London: Printed for the editor, and sold by J. and A. Arch, 1825); Taft, *Holy Women*, 2:149–77; Rufus M. Jones, *The Later Periods of Quakerism*, 2 vols. (London: Macmillan, 1921), 1:63–64, 198–99, 210–11, 237–42, 274–78; and Joseph Smith, *A Descriptive Catalogue of Friends' Books*, 2 vols. (London: Joseph Smith, 1867), 1:546.

85. Jones, *Later Periods of Quakerism*, 1:198.

86. Mary Stokes, "The Experience of Miss Mary Stokes, in a Letter to Mr. Tho. Rankin," *Arm. Mag.* 18 (1795): 101.

87. August 10, 1772, Sheffield, Wesley, *Letters*, 5:334–35; cf. 5:230, 302, 305; and Wesley, *Journal*, 6:185, 254.

88. Jones, *Later Periods of Quakerism*, 1:277. This missionary desire was fulfilled in her life when she traveled throughout the continent of Europe with Sarah Grubb, her Quaker colleague, in 1787–88 (see Dudley, *Life of Mary Dudley*, pp. 42–72). Cf. Sarah Grubb, *Some Account of the Life and Religious Labours of Sarah Grubb*, ed. Lindley Murray (Dublin: Printed for R. Jackson, 1792), pp. 157–65.

89. Ibid., p. 278; cf. pp. 68, 76, 87–88, 210–11, 230–42.

90. [Dudley], *Life of Mary Dudley*, p. 286. Cf. *An Extempore Discourse, Spoken at a Public Meeting, Held at the Friends' Meeting House, at Epping* (London: Printed for R. Hunter, 1823).

91. Jones, *Later Periods of Quakerism*, 1:278.

92. See Baker, *Friends and Early Methodism*, pp. 18–20.

93. Helton's reply consisted of an octavo pamphlet of sixty-six pages, entitled *Reasons for Quitting the Methodist Society; Being a Defence of Barclay's Apology* (London: Printed by J. Fry, 1778). See the letters exchanged between Wesley and Helton in Wesley, *Letters*, 6:278, 285, 288, 309, 318.

94. Helton, *Reasons for Quitting,* p. 5.

95. Ibid., p. 17.

96. Employing the standard line of argumentation, which in Quakerism may be traced back to Margaret Fell, he marshals the classic texts to support his interpretation, namely, Joel 2:28; Acts 20:9; Phil. 4:2; Rom. 16:11; 1 Cor. 11:4–5; 14:3–5, 31; Exod. 7:1–2; Acts 15:33 and Luke 1:67; 2:38.

97. Helton, *Reasons for Quitting,* p. 22.

98. Ibid., p. 23.

99. One of Wesley's preachers, John Fenwick, whom we have encountered previously as a protagonist of Elizabeth Hurrell's labors, produced a poignant rebuttal entitled *Appeal to All Men of Common Sense* in 12 pages. See Baker, *Friends and Early Methodism,* p. 19.

100. Moore, *Fletcher,* p. 113. The memoirs of Robert Gate, a businessman of Penrith, fill in some of the details. Apparently, Varty joined the only available Methodist society in the area, a small meeting at the home of Betty Benson in Gamblesby. According to Gate's biographer, the building utilized for preaching which he constructed "had been designed for an hctel, but through hearing Miss Bosanquet preach, he changed his purpose concerning the whole, and converted the remainder of the building into shops, one of which was afterwards occupied by Mr. Gate" (George G. S. Thomas, *The Life of Mr. Robert Gate, with some Notices of Early Methodism in the Penrith Circuit* (London: Elliot Stock, 1869), pp. 31–38. Cf. Judge, "Methodism in Penrith District," pp. 155–56.

101. Ibid., p. 114.

102. Ibid., p. 115.

103. Ibid., pp. 117–19. Cf. Church, *More about Early Methodist People,* pp. 142–45.

104. Ibid., p. 120.

105. Ibid. It is very probable that she was consciously mimicking Wesley's own words occasioned by his venture into field preaching (2 Samuel 6:22), a phrase which long continued to be used in Methodist circles (see Wesley, *Journal,* 2:172).

106. *Meth. Mag.* 29:567. See this frequently quoted passage in Baker, "Wesley and Crosby," p. 79; Harrison, "Early Woman Preacher," p. 107; Church, *More about Early Methodist People,* p. 153; Hellier, "Some Methodist Women Preachers," p. 66; Morrow, *Early Methodist Women,* p. 21; and Brown, "Women of the Word," p. 80.

107. July 9, 1778, Crosby, MS Letterbook, p. 65.
108. Taft, *Holy Women,* 1:104. During one of these visits to Scarborough, Isabella Mackiver was converted under her preaching. She recounts the deep impression made by her visit. "Sarah Crosby of Leeds came to Scarborough. She was going to have a young women's band meeting at six o'clock in the morning, which they invited me to attend. It proved a profitable opportunity to me, and I afterwards joined the Society, for which I have abundant cause of thankfulness. I remember her saying to us that she enjoyed such a sense of the Lord's presence that—

> Not a cloud did arise
> To darken the skies
> Or hide for a moment
> Her Lord from her eyes.

(Susan C. Brooke, "The Journal of Isabella Mackiver," *W.H.S.* 28, 8[December 1952]: 161).
109. Wesley, *Letters,* 6:286.
110. December 9, 1778, Dover, in ibid., p. 331; cf. p. 329.
111. Luke Tyerman, *Wesley's Designated Successor: The Life, Letters, and Literary Labours of the Rev. John William Fletcher, Vicar of Madeley, Shropshire* (London: Hodder and Stoughton, 1882), pp. 400–401. This is one of the very few explicit statements of Fletcher on the question of women preachers. The obvious biblical allusion is to Acts 2:28 in which the prophet Joel is quoted. On July 15, 1776, Wesley wrote to the third woman mentioned in the letter, Miss Ritchie of Otley, encouraging her to be fully employed: "The word of our Lord to you is, 'Feed My lambs.' Methinks I see you giving yourself up, as far as possible you can, to that blessed work; carrying the weak, as it were, in your bosom, and gently leading the rest to the waters of comfort" (Wesley, *Letters,* 6:225).
112. Wesley, *Letters,* 7:8–9. John Peacock served as his assistant at Grimsby.
113. Taft, *Holy Women,* 2:24.

6

OFFICIAL RECOGNITION OF WOMEN PREACHERS, 1781–1791

THE DECADE PRIOR to Wesley's death in 1791 witnessed a great flowering of the activities of women preachers within Methodism. From Cornwall to the North Yorkshire moors, and in Ireland as well, women's voices were raised in proclamation of the gospel they felt called of God to preach. As a result of Wesley's changing attitude about the role of female preachers in his movement and the testimony of many witnesses to the abundant fruit of their labor, the English Methodist Conference was eventually led to recognize officially a number of these exceptional women. In these later years, when Wesley was asked why he encouraged certain of his female devotees in this practice, the elderly sage replied simply, "Because God owns them in the conversion of sinners, and who am I that I should withstand God."[1]

FROM CROSS HALL TO MADELEY

In the spring of 1780, when the youthful Robert Roe heard Mary Bosanquet at Leeds, she greatly exceeded his expectations. "So much wisdom, dignity, and piety, joined to so much childlike simplicity," he wrote, "I never saw before."[2] This characteristic approbation is all the more significant when juxtaposed with Mary's own evaluation of her labors. On February 15, 1781, for instance, she confided to her journal:

> I am going to———. It is a fine opportunity for speaking to a number of the most lively souls, out of various societies; and they begin to inquire all around when I will come. O my God,

how these things break me to pieces! What an unworthy worm! If they knew me, how could they be astonished, that the Lord should work by such a one as me! But thou canst do whatever seemeth thee good![3]

For thirteen years Mary had labored at Cross Hall, caring for the many children under her charge and frequently preaching upon the request of societies throughout the northern counties and beyond. On June 8, 1781, the day after the thirteenth anniversary of her coming to Yorkshire, Mary received a remarkable letter from the Reverend John Fletcher that would lead her into a new and unforeseen relationship and a widening sphere of activity. In this letter, Fletcher, one of Methodism's most capable protagonists and one of Wesley's most trusted friends, spoke of his growing admiration and secret affection for Miss Bosanquet.[4] Having refused repeated offers of marriage from various suitors, Mary was now prepared to unite with the vicar in a unique partnership of mutual service and love.[5] She sold her Yorkshire farm, settled all of the remaining children of the orphanage, and was married to Fletcher on Monday, November 12, 1781, at Batley Church.[6]

The couple remained at Cross Hall until January 2, 1782, when they set out for the vicarage at Madeley.[7] While John Valton rejoiced over this marriage, he fully realized that he would be deprived of a valued assistant in Yorkshire. "Mr. Fletcher," he confided to his journal, "stole hallowed fire from my people, by taking away Miss Bosanquet to Madeley."[8] Wesley voiced a similar concern in a letter to Mrs. Downes, dated December 1, 1781, from London:

> Mr. and Mrs. Fletcher made an excellent beginning, and I trust they will increase with all the increase of God. Now let all of you that remain in the neighbourhood arise up and supply her lack of service. Be instant in season, out of season, that all may know you have caught her mantle![9]

There is no question that Yorkshire's loss was Madeley's gain.

On the first Sunday that the Fletchers were at Madeley, John introduced his bride to the people and boldly proclaimed, "I have not married this wife for myself only, but for your sakes also."[10] The following summer, in response to Mary's exuberant letter of July 7 concerning the expansion of her labors, Wesley expressed his great satisfaction at hearing "that the work of our Lord prospers in your hands."[11] Wesley's only apprehensiveness concerning Mary's new situation was similar to that expressed in a letter to the Cotswold preacher Penelope Newman on the eve of her marriage to Jonathan Coussins:

> I have often been concerned at your being cooped up in a corner; now you are likely to have a wider field of action. Only the danger will be lest, when you have more opportunity you should have less desire of doing good.[12]

Whereas Penelope found it necessary to curtail much of her work after her marriage, Mary's work continually expanded. "My spiritual sphere of action is different," she wrote on September 12, 1782. "I have in many respects, a wider call for action than before."[13]

John and Mary Fletcher functioned, for all practical purposes, as co-pastors of his parish throughout the course of their brief marriage. Methodist preachers had preached in Madeley Wood on previous occasions, but they had never been able to make inroads into the community. The evangelically oriented parishioners apparently refused to meet in classes and bands under itinerant supervision.[14] This situation changed radically, however, upon Fletcher's return, and largely through the instrumentality of his wife. The townspeople were extremely receptive to Mary's ministrations. "My call is also so clear," she was soon able to confirm, "and I have such liberty in the work, and such sweet encouragement among the people."[15] And throughout the autumn of 1784 she "found great liberty both in public and private meetings."[16]

This felicitous arrangement was terminated prematurely, however, by the untimely death of the well-loved vicar on Sunday evening, August 14, 1785.[17] In the depths of her grief, Mary wrote:

My loss is beyond the power of words to paint. I have gone through deep waters but nothing to this. Well I want no pleasant prospect but upward, nor anything whereon to fix my hope but immortality. . . . The sun of my earthly joys is set forever.[18]

Mary's sense of the continued presence of her "most sympathizing and heavenly friend," however, soon transformed her grief into renewed dedication to God and to the mission they held in common.[19] Shortly after her husband's funeral, she recorded in her diary:

I found the dear children which my beloved Partner had left behind, laid upon my mind. . . . Therefore, before another week passed, I saw I must act among them, and meet the people the same as before;—and, though very ill and filled with sorrow, the Lord enabled me to do so,—showing me the only way to bear the cross profitably, was so to carry it as if I carried it not.[20]

William Tranter's personal reminiscences of Methodism in Madeley include a remarkable chronicle of Mary's continued work.[21] Before his death, Fletcher had opened several new places of worship in the vicinity of Madeley. A tithe barn on the premises had been fitted up for preaching and provided adequate space for the regular preaching of itinerants and the evangelical curate. "Here, also," observes Tranter, "Mrs. Fletcher, after the removal of her holy husband to his heavenly rest, held her meetings for exposition of the Scripture, religious experience, and prayer."[22] In later years, Mary had a seat elevated a step or two above the level of the floor in this and the other chapels of the neighborhood so she could address the large crowds with greater ease.[23]

Through her various labors Mary contributed greatly to the cultivation of a vital faith among the inhabitants of the parish. Tranter describes her activities in some detail:

Tribes were seen going up from all the neighbouring places early on the Sabbath morning, for Mrs. Fletcher's nine o-clock meeting, full of joy, or of joyous expectation of having gracious manifestations from their Lord.

On a week-day evening service, it was not unusual to see the room crowded with attentive and delighted hearers, while this blessed woman was expounding, generally, some historic portion of Scripture. . . . The effect produced was often truly astonishing. . . . It was not uncommon to see two, three, or more Clergymen, pious and able men, from neighbouring and even distant parishes, among the congregation at these evening lectures.[24]

During the years following her husband's death, Mary not only continued her regular preaching services within the bounds of the parish, but extended her influence to Coalbrookdale, Coalport, and other surrounding villages where she was uniformly received by expectant and delighted crowds. Mary's own words convey the rich quality of her experience at Madeley and her profound sense of Christian vocation:

I never was in any situation in which I had so much opportunity of doing good, (according to my small abilities,) as in this place, and that in various ways, public and private; and to many who live at a distance also. These are providentially thrown in my way, and I find such clear leadings of the Spirit in conversing with them, that (painful as many circumstances are) I am constrained to say, If I choose for the work of God, *here* I must abide and fix my home.[25]

ELIZABETH TONKIN: CORNISH PREACHER

Thomas Shaw, in his *History of Cornish Methodism*, claims that "women preachers were all but unknown" in that region.[26] One shining light who followed directly in the footsteps of Cornwall's first woman preacher, however, was Elizabeth Tonkin.[27] Born on May 9, 1762, at the important evangelistic center of Gwinear, she came under the influence of devoted Methodists early in life and was invited to attend the society class meeting in 1778. Ann Gilbert, who had already gained something of a reputation as a preacher in Cornwall, befriended the impressionable sixteen-year-old. She exerted a formidable influence upon Elizabeth through her leadership of the class and her exemplary activities as a female evangelist. Elizabeth found in her a mentor whose Christian experience was both sane and joyful.[28] It was not until 1782, however, after she had moved to the parish of Feock, that Elizabeth was persuaded to take up the mantle of her paragon and friend.

When she arrived at her new home on the advent of her twentieth birthday, there was no Methodist society established in the vicinity. Elizabeth applied for preachers, and through her instrumentality, regular preaching was extended to that area of the vast and expanding circuit. Her son describes the circumstance that laid upon her the necessity of preaching:

> One sunday evening the preacher appointed for Feock was prevented from attending, by the recent death of his daughter, and no other was sent to supply his place. . . . some called on my mother to speak to them, which she at first refused to do, saying she had never so engaged in her life. However, she at last consented to give out a hymn, and pray with them, hoping this would satisfy them; and when she had done this, she strove to dismiss them, but the attempt was vain; they still persisted in their request, and told her plainly if she did not speak to them they would not go away for the night.[29]

She capitulated to their demands, and "the power of God came down among them." In spite of Elizabeth's efforts to dissuade her hearers, they published that she would preach again the next Sunday. And so, Elizabeth received her call to preach as had many of her female antecedents, by the clamors of the congregation. Thus she was propelled into a new phase in her life, exhorting her hearers to repentance and continual growth in grace as opportunities presented themselves to her.

When the traveling preacher in charge of the circuit, Joseph Taylor, was apprised of her "irregular activities," he simply chose to overlook them. And when he later met the aspiring preacher, he is said to have greeted her by remarking, "Well Betsy, I did not open your mouth, and I will not shut it."[30] Elizabeth frequently encountered strong prejudice and opposition, however, as was the case when she began to preach regularly in Roseland where she traveled on business. But her persistent efforts resulted in nothing less than a revival, the establishment of classes, and within her lifetime, the foundation of seven societies and chapels. While the majority of her labors were confined to the regions surrounding Falmouth and Veryan bays in the Truro, Saint Mawes, and Saint Austell circuits, the influence of her ministry was felt throughout Cornwall.

In December 1785 she married a Mr. Collett who supported her in her work and played some part in extending her influence. Richard attested to the fact that his mother's new responsibilities as a wife and parent brought with them no slackening of her perseverance:

> For nearly twenty years, she frequently held meetings in the neighbouring places on the Lord's-day, and sometimes on the working-day evenings also; but never to the neglect of her domestic duties; for whenever she thus engaged she ordered her family concerns also, that we were never deprived of one comfort on her account.[31]

This dual devotion to home and evangelistic ministry was rekindled when Elizabeth moved with her husband to Veryan in 1786 and once again at Saint Erme where, in May 1804, she spoke in public for the last time.[32]

Unfortunately, in the nineteenth century, when the tide of opinion within Methodist circles turned against the preaching of women, much of Elizabeth's story was lost in the historical consciousness of her spiritual progeny. When Richard Collett's account of her life was sent to Jabez Bunting, the editor of the *Methodist Magazine,* by an eminent Wesleyan minister who had been intimately acquainted with the family for some thirty years, it never came to print. The editor did not wish to publish the life "lest it should be a precedent to young females in the connexion, who are ready to step into the work."[33] The testimony of a son, however, stands as an appropriate tribute and amaranthine portrait of this persistent witness:

> In conversing about the deep things of God, she greatly excelled; being ever ready out of the good treasure of her heart to bring forth good things. But while her lips fed many,

nothing like ostentatious display, ever appeared in her deportment. When opportunities for speaking to the use of edification, could be obtained, she chose rather to be thought singular, or unsociable, or deficient in capacity, than to incur the guilt of speaking idly.[34]

THE WOMEN PREACHERS OF NORFOLK AND SUFFOLK

During this same period, the activities of a newly emerging group of women preachers were beginning to receive attention in Norfolk and Suffolk. When Wesley's itinerary took him through these counties in the fall of 1781, he was amazed by the following remarkable discovery:

> I went to Fakenham, and in the evening preached in the room built by Miss Franklin, now Mrs. Parker. I believe most of the town was present.
>
> *Tues.* 30.—I went to Wells, where also Miss Franklin had opened a door, by preaching abroad, though at the peril of her life. She was followed by a young woman of the town, with whom I talked largely, and found her very sensible, and much devoted to God. From her I learnt that, till the Methodists came, they had none but female teachers in this county; and that there were six of these within ten or twelve miles, all of whom were members of the Church of England.[35]

Unfortunately, nothing else is known about this band of Anglican evangelists who were sympathetic to the Methodist cause. Wesley was impressed with their work, and this encounter served to confirm his opinion regarding the validity of such activities.[36]

Whether these women exerted a direct influence upon their Methodist sisters, or vice versa, is impossible to determine. There is every possibility that the original impetus for their preaching came from the revivalistic fervor of growing Methodism in that region and a number of Methodist women who were active locally about the same time. This whole question aside, by the mid-1780s, a number of female preachers in the Norwich Circuit had developed something of a reputation. And standing in the vanguard was a young lady named Mary Sewell.[37]

Very little is known about Mary's early life in the small village of Thurlton. Taft attests to the fact that she joined the local Methodist society "when she was but young in years" and began to preach when she was twenty.[38] Perhaps William Lamb, uncle of the Methodist biographer Charles Atmore, was present at the inception of her ministry when he "heard a Miss Sewell give an exhortation in a small home in the village."[39] Apparently, her address was instrumental in removing his prejudices about the Methodist people.

Mary had a similar effect upon Adam Clarke, one of the greatest scholars of early Methodism, when he visited the circuit in 1784. He had been cautioned concerning several celebrated female preachers who were active there and entered into his work with considerable prejudice against their ministry. When in Thurlton, he went directly to the home of Mary Sewell and interrogated her concerning her call. She responded to his queries by referring him to the places where she had preached in the circuit and requested that he inquire among the people concerning her gifts, graces, and fruit. Upon further investigation, Clarke found her ministry to be both scriptural and sound.[40] On April 28, 1784, he heard her preach on the classic Wesleyan text, Ephesians 2:8, and left this remarkable account of her proclamation of God's saving grace:

> I have this morning heard Miss Sewell preach; she has a good talent for exhortation, and her words spring from a heart that evidently feels deep concern for the souls of the people; and, consequently, her hearers are interested and affected. I have formerly been no friend to female preaching; but my sentiments are a little altered. If God give to a holy woman, a gift for exhortation and reproof, I see no reason why it should not be used. This woman's preaching has done much good; and fruits of it may be found copiously, in different places in the circuit. I can therefore adopt the saying of a shrewd man, who having heard her preach, and being asked his opinion of the lawfulness of it, answered, "An *ass* reproved Balaam, and a *cock* reproved Peter, and why may not a *woman* reprove sin!"[41]

While Mary once risked her life by facing the mob at Yarmouth when she testified to her faith, she was welcomed in many villages throughout Norfolk and Suffolk. She is reported to have preached in the open air at "Soddon . . . and at Lowestoft; at Long-Stratton, Wortham, Melless, Lopham, and at Beccles."[42] The oldest register that has been preserved from Yarmouth, which then formed part of the Norwich Circuit, contains the names of the Methodist preachers for 1785. It is noteworthy that on the second page of the record, we find "Sister Mary Sewell" included among the names of the "local preachers."[43]

Like so many of the early Methodist preachers, male and female alike, Mary spent herself in her preaching. In a personal gloss to his sketch of her life in *Holy Women,* Taft testified to the ardor of her spirit:

> Miss Sewell did not revolt at the idea of singularity, and having once assumed the character of a separatist from the world, she supported it with inflexible stability. She was unmovable in the practice & profession of the gospel, & as the natural consequence, made great proficiency in divine things. Her attainments in religion were not of the ordinary kind.[44]

Mary Sewell, as has been indicated, was not alone in her work in the Norwich Circuit. Shortly after Adam Clarke heard her preach in the spring of 1784, he had the opportunity of hearing one of her colleagues, a Mrs. Proudfoot. A brief paragraph recalling her sermon from Exodus 3:3, "And the bush was not burnt," constitutes the only remaining testimony to her life and labors. It provides but a meager glimpse into the world of this female preacher:

> She spoke several pertinent things, which tended both to conviction and consolation; and seems to possess genuine piety. If the Lord choose to work in this way, shall my eye be evil because He is good? God forbid! Rather let me extol that God, who, by contemptible instruments, and the foolishness of preaching, saves those who believe in Jesus. Thou, Lord, choosest to confound the *wisdom* of the world by *foolishness,* and its *strength* by *weakness,* that no soul may glory in thy presence; and that the excellency of the power may be seen to

belong to Thee, alone. Had not this been the case, surely *I* had never been raised up to call sinners to repentance.[45]

It was the activities of women such as these that led some ministers to deprecate the preaching of women at the momentous conference convened at Leeds in 1784. On that occasion, Wesley continued to defend the practice in extraordinary situations. And one old veteran, Thomas Mitchell, reminded his colleagues of a somewhat embarrassing point, and perhaps the source of their uneasiness. "I know not what you would do with the good women," he instructed the antagonists, "for all the fish they catch they put into our net."[46]

SARAH MALLET OF LONG STRATTON

One of the most celebrated of these female "fishers" was another preacher of the eastern counties by the name of Sarah Mallet. Her ministry is crucial and represents an important triumph for the women preachers of Methodism. In events which surrounded her life and work, the leadership of the movement finally and officially recognized the role of female preachers in the life of the evangelical revival.

John Wesley visited Long Stratton on Monday, December 4, 1786, and was surprised to learn that a young girl he had heard about by virtue of her uncommon fits and a celebrated preacher were one and the same person. The elderly preacher, who was always intrigued by phenomena he could only partially understand, was captivated by the testimony which Sarah Mallet had to bear:

> I found her in the very house to which I went, and went and talked with her at large. . . . Of the following relation, which she gave me, there are numberless witnesses.
>
> Some years since it was strongly impressed upon her that she ought to call sinners to repentance. This impression she vehemently resisted, believing herself quite unqualified, both by her sin and her ignorance, till it was suggested, "If you do it not willingly, you shall do it whether you will or no." She fell into a fit, and while utterly senseless, thought she was in the

preaching-house in Lowestoft, where she prayed and preached for near an hour, to a numerous congregation. She then opened her eyes, and recovered her senses. In a year or two she had eighteen of these fits, in every one of which she imagined herself to be preaching in one or another congregation. She then cried out, "Lord, I *will* obey Thee; I *will* call sinners to repentance." She has done so occasionally from that time; and her fits returned no more.[47]

This remarkable young lady was born at Loddon in Norfolk on February 18, 1764.[48] When Methodist preachers began itinerating throughout that area, the Mallet family came under their influence. Apparently, all of them received membership tickets a day or two prior to Sarah's departure to Long Stratton on January 3, 1780, where she resided with her uncle. During the course of the next several years, Sarah was shifted back and forth between her parental home and that of her uncle. As Mary Sewell preached frequently at both Loddon and Long Stratton during these years, there is little doubt that the impressionable Sarah came under her formidable influence.

On May 28, 1781, on a visit to Hadderson, she experienced the first of many seizures she was to have. Her uncle describes the unusual occurrence:

At breakfast, she was suddenly struck, went into another room, and lay down on the bed. She immediately lost her senses, and lay as dead until three in the afternoon. When she came to herself, she said, she had seen two angels, who took her where she had a full view of the torments of the damned: and afterwards, of the happiness of the blessed into which she asked, if she might not enter? But was answered, "Not yet: she had work to do upon earth."[49]

As time passed, she began to see more clearly the work she was to do. In March of 1785 she explained:

It was imprest on my mind, to speak in public for God: and those words were continually before me, *Reprove, rebuke, exhort!* Nor could I by any means drive them out of my thoughts. But I could not bear the thought, having been in time past no friend of women's preaching. I therefore resolved never to do any such thing, be the consequence what it would. From the moment it seemed as if the powers of darkness overwhelmed my soul: and I was forced to withdraw from the family, and pour out my soul before God.[50]

She returned to her uncle's home in Long Stratton on May 10, 1785, in a somewhat confused state of mind. Increasingly convinced of her call to preach, she continued to reason against the conviction of her heart; profoundly concerned about the plight of her neighbors, she did not know how to begin, being held back by fear and shame. Her health began to fail, and by the fall she was so weak that there was little hope for her life.[51] On December 15, 1785, she began having seizures once again. William Mallitt narrates the events of Christmas Day when one of the Methodist preachers was in their company:

> Mr. *Byron* came to my house, who entering the room and seeing her sitting in the chair, and looking like one dead, he was so struck that he thought he should not be able to preach. Meantime she thought herself to be in the preaching house at *Lowstoff,* before a large congregation; and that she took her text from Rev. iii. 20. *Behold, I stand at the door and knock.* This discourse she preached in Mr. *Byron's* hearing. The next day she preached again in Mr. *Byron's* hearing, on John vii. 37. She continued to preach in every following fit, speaking clear and loud, though she was utterly senseless.[52]

She preached in this manner some sixteen additional times over the course of the next several weeks. On January 15, 1786, Sarah's uncle invited members of the society to come and hear her, and by the end of the month as many as two hundred people were crowding into their home to witness this unusual phenomenon.[53] Through the means of this "affliction," Sarah claimed that God opened her mouth.[54] She determined to concede, therefore, to the demands of God's call and began her public ministry at the local Methodist chapel in February 1786.

From this time, according to her report, her strength continually increased. And despite her fears at the thought of preaching she persevered. "These words," she wrote, "had followed me for near a year, 'Ye shall be hated of all men for my name's sake': and so did those, 'Fear not; for I am with thee: be not afraid: for I am God.' "[55] She was appointed to speak in her uncle's house every other Sunday evening and began to experience "great peace in my soul and more nearness to God" than ever before. Several weeks after Wesley's visit, on Christmas Day 1786, Sarah had the experience of losing her senses of sight and hearing while she was preaching. Having recovered but a few hours later, she proclaimed that if she had many lives, she would "give them all for him who gave his own life for me!"[56]

When Sarah entered into this public work, according to her journal, "Mr. Wesley was to become a father and a faithful friend."[57] There is no question that the encouragement he gave to her was more decided than that recorded in any other case. And Wesley was influential in winning for her the full support and authorization of the Manchester Conference of 1787. Sarah's journal affords details regarding this momentous occasion:

> When I first travelled I followed Mr. Wesley's counsel, which was, to let the voice of the people be to me the voice of God;—and where I was sent for, to go, for the Lord had called me thither. To this counsel I have attended to this day. But the voice of the people was not the voice of some preachers. But Mr. Wesley soon made this easy by sending me a note from the Conference, by Mr. Joseph Harper, who was that year appointed for Norwich.[58]

This note is probably the single most important piece of documentary evidence concerning the women preachers of early Methodism. This unique document is, in fact, an official authorization for her to preach, and reads simply:

> We give the right hand of fellowship to Sarah Mallet, and have no objection to her being a preacher in our connexion, so long as she preaches the Methodist doctrines, and attends to our discipline.[59]

This action evidently diminished the opposition she encountered from fellow itinerants on her journeys throughout Norfolk and Suffolk, the nature and extent of which she reveals in her journal:

My way of preaching from the first is to take a text and divide it, and speak from the different heads. For many years when we had but few Chapels in this Country, I preached in the open air and in barns—and in waggons. After I was married I was with my husband in the preachers plan, for many years. He was a Local Preacher thirty-two years, and finished his work and his life well.

I am glad some of our preachers see it right to encourage female preaching. I hope they will all, both Local and Travelling Preachers, think more on these words "quench not the Spirit," neither in themselves nor others. "Despise not prophesyings," no, not out of the mouth of a child,—then would they be more like Mr. Wesley: and I think more like Christ.[60]

The profound effect which Miss Mallet exerted upon Wesley with regard to the ministry of women in the evangelical revival is evident from their correspondence. Wesley wrote to her from Bristol on October 6, 1787, expressed his great desire to see her again, and encouraged her to keep her heart with all diligence.[61] Later in the winter he warned her: "Beware of pride! Beware of flatterers! Beware of dejections! But above all beware of inordinate affections!"[62] In the same letter he expressed his concern for her financial situation, saying "I know that neither your father nor uncle is rich; and in *travelling up and down* you will want a little money."[63]

In a letter of August 2, 1788, Wesley offered to obtain necessary books for "Sally" just as he had assisted his other itinerants in the pursuit of learning.[64] He afforded advice concerning the necessity of humility and answered a question about the need to be licensed as a nonconforming preacher:

But you are in far greater danger from applause than from censure; and it is well for you that one balances the other. But I trust you will never be weary of well doing. In due time you shall reap if you faint not. Whoever praises or dispraises, it is your part to go steadily on, speaking the truth in love. I do not require any of our preachers to license either themselves or the places where they preach.[65]

On one occasion, Wesley came to Sally's defense when she had preached in Norwich, apparently without observing the appropriate protocol:

London, February 21, 1789

My Dear Sister,
As your speaking at Mr. Hunt's was not a premeditated thing, I see no harm in it, and indeed you was so hedged in by a concurrence of circumstances that I do not know how you could well avoid it. Perhaps there was some end of Divine Providence (not known to us) to be answered thereby. Therefore I am not at all sorry that it so fell out. But you must expect to be censured for it.
But I was a little surprised a while ago when one speaking of you said, "Sally Mallet is not so serious as Betty Reeve." I thought Sally Mallet was serious as any young woman in Norfolk. Be wary in all your actions, and you will never [want] any assistance which is in the power of, my dear Sally,

Yours affectionately,
John Wesley[66]

Elizabeth Reeve, whom Wesley mentions in this letter, was one of Sarah Mallet's converts and kept her brother's house at Redgrave in Suffolk. Miss Mallet had visited and preached in this little village and left behind a small band of followers. Her ministrations engendered a strong sense of vocation in Betty, who then began to preach as well.[67] When Wesley learned of these developments, he asked Sally to bring her to Diss in order to talk with her about her religious experience and work. Having been satisfied with regard to her motives and her call to preach, he encouraged her in her efforts to proclaim the gospel.[68] She was instrumental in raising a little society in Redgrave and, according to Taft, "continued to preach as long as she could be helped into the pulpit."[69]
Wesley followed the progress of these sister preachers with affectionate interest. From Canterbury he wrote to Miss Mallet on December 15, 1789, offering her technical advice

about homiletical skills and the appropriate manner of conducting services of worship:

> It gives me pleasure to hear that prejudice dies away and our preachers behave in a friendly manner. What is now more wanting in order to recover your health you yourself plainly see. Be not at every one's call. This you may quite cut off by going nowhere without the advice of Mr. Tattershall. Never continue the service above an hour at once, singing, *preaching,* prayer, and all. You are not to judge by your own *feelings,* but by the word of God. Never scream. Never speak above the natural pitch of your voice; it is disgustful to the hearers. It gives them pain, not pleasure. And it is destroying yourself. It is offering God murder for sacrifice. Only follow these three advices, and you will have a larger share in the regard of, my dear Sally,
>
> Yours affectionately,
John Wesley[70]

A year later, only several months prior to his death, Wesley scrawled a final letter of encouragement to her which concluded: "For has not God given me to you for a tender guard of your youth? And I believe you will find few that will watch over you more tenderly."[71] While little is known of her efforts to proclaim the gospel after Wesley's death, her own words serve as a fitting tribute to this important early woman preacher:

> The same Lord that opened my mouth, and endued me with power, and gave me courage to speak His Word, has through His grace enabled me to continue to the present day. The Lord has been, and is now the comfort and support of my soul in all trials. And, thank God, I have not run in vain, neither laboured in vain. There are some witnesses in heaven and some on earth.[72]

MARY FLETCHER'S COMPANIONS AND THE "FEMALE BRETHREN" OF LEEDS

In March of 1787 Wesley journeyed to Bristol where he found Mrs. Fletcher busily engaged. She met with as many of the classes and society gatherings as time and strength permitted, having been encouraged by her spiritual mentor to do all the good she could during her brief stay. "Her words were as fire," Wesley reported, "conveying both light and heat to the hearts of all that heard her."[73] On the evening of Sunday the eighteenth, when Mrs. Fletcher declared the steadfast love of God at a love feast at the New Room, Wesley could not help but comment on the improvement in her manner of speaking. "It is now smooth, easy, and natural," he observed, "even when the sense is deep and strong."[74]

Mary Fletcher functioned as an important model for many women who were attracted by her magnetism and patterned their own ministries after her dynamic life and work. This was especially true in the case of Sarah Lawrence, who as servant, or rather adopted daughter, of the unwavering preacher, was Mary's constant companion throughout the course of her life.[75] Perhaps no one was so intimately acquainted with Mary's life of devoted service and disciplined ministry as was her "beloved Sally."

Sarah Lawrence was the orphaned niece of Mary's friend and colleague, Mrs. Ryan, and became a part of the Leytonstone family when but a little girl in the early 1760s.[76] Raised, therefore, in one of the most eminent schools of Christian piety in England, first in the London orphanage and then at Cross Hall in Yorkshire, it was natural for Sarah to commit herself to the evangelical message of the Wesleys and his female devotees. She joined the society when nearly eighteen and was confirmed as a devoted Anglican at the old parish church in Leeds.

Mrs. Fletcher recognized and nurtured the unique talents which her adopted daughter possessed. Following a profound religious awakening during the winter of 1778, Mary expressed hopes that Sally would follow in her own footsteps:

> Soon after a visible concern arose in her mind, more forsible than ever, for the souls of the people and in particular of the rising generation. And such a gift was then given her for children, as I have hardly seen in any one, and a love like that of a parent.[77]

Her work with the children and her efforts to relieve the hardships of the sick led to the deterioration of her own health. She persevered in her labors, however, frequently exhorting her neighbors to repent and change.[78] "For reproving sin, and inviting to the means of grace," proclaimed Mrs. Fletcher, "few could equal her."[79]

At Madeley, Sarah began meetings in one of the most profligate areas within the parish, visited door to door, and on at least one occasion, extended her evangelism to a number of persons in the local public house. Mary describes the expansion of her ministry and the development of her style:

> She began meetings in different places, on which numbers attended. Her method was, after singing and prayer, to read some life, experience, or some awakening author, stopping now and then, to explain and apply it as the Lord gave her utterance. And several, who are now lively believers in our connexion, were brought in through that means.[80]

When mining operations commenced in the small village of Coalport, several miles across Sutton-Common from Madeley, Sarah was strongly importuned to go and establish meetings there as well. Here she preached every other Sunday evening for four years.[81] "Her word was amazingly received by numbers," proudly declared Mrs. Fletcher, "and deeply did they lament when she could no longer meet with them as usual."[82]

The other women who had at one time formed a closely knit circle around Mary Bosanquet continued to preach with Wesley's approval, primarily throughout the northern regions. In 1781, when John Fletcher removed Mary to her new home in Madeley, Sarah Crosby and Ann Tripp seem to have taken up residence in Leeds. According to J. E. Hellier, they lived in a small house adjoining the parent chapel of the original society in Leeds, known locally as the Old Boggard House.[83] On April 3, 1785, Wesley wrote to Mrs. Crosby from Manchester and expressed his pleasure regarding her "full Employment" in the circuit, despite her lack of strength.[84] Together with Ann, she assumed leadership of a strong and influential band of women preachers known as the "Female Brethren."[85] Whereas the unconscious contradiction in their title might have brought a chuckle to some, these women proved intrepid in their challenge of processes that had been dominated traditionally by men.

When the English Conference was convened at Leeds in July of 1789, they exerted their influence with regard to the important matter of circuit appointments. The stewards of the societies in Leeds had filed a petition for Dr. Adam Clarke to be stationed in that circuit. Crowds of people flocked to hear him preach twice at the conference on the last Sunday of July. The Female Brethren, however, sent a counter petition begging the conference that he might not be appointed.[86] Wesley yielded to the wishes of the women. When Clarke's name was put down for Halifax, however, he encountered the same note of disapprobation from the women of Yorkshire. "Dr. Clarke was learned," they said, "but he was dull," and once more he was displaced. The voice of the women prevailed.[87]

LESSER-KNOWN WOMEN PREACHERS

While preachers such as Sarah Crosby, Sarah Mallet, and Mary Fletcher were clearly exceptional in terms of their status throughout the Methodist Connection, there were other, lesser-known women who rose up spontaneously throughout the course of the 1780s. A large number of these anonymous women and their stories are lost to the historian forever. And many women preached, although they were never officially recognized as preachers or authorized by the conference in their labors as was Miss Mallet. In the case of a small number of these women, their names and some facts about their lives have been preserved.

Ellen Gretton, for instance, was the daughter of a clergyman who had pioneered the work of Methodism in Grantham in the late 1770s.[88] Apparently, she never entered a pulpit but preferred to deliver her addresses "seated and with her bonnet on." John Wesley anticipated the influence she would be able to exert on the small village south of Grantham to which she subsequently moved:

> I am glad to hear that regular preaching is already begun at Skillington; we have no time to lose. If a few should be awakened there, I doubt not the work will increase, and perhaps you will have a larger sphere of action than ever you had yet. Meantime be faithful in that which is little![89]

And several months later, when Ellen married William Christian, Wesley admonished her to pursue her calling. He reminded her, moreover, of an important prototype in that work:

> In the new sphere of action to which Providence has called you, I trust you will find new zeal for God and new vigour in pursuing every measure which may tend to the furtherance of His kingdom. In one of my mother's letters you may observe something resembling your case. She began only with permitting two or three of her neighbours to come to the family prayers on Sunday evening. But they increased to an hundred, yea above an hundred and fifty. Go humbly and steadily on, consulting the Assistant in all points, and pressing on to perfection.[90]

Mrs. Mary Gilbert, one of the early Methodist missionaries to Antigua, continued the work of her husband, Francis, following his untimely death. Her niece narrates the events subsequent to her return to missionary work in the summer of 1781:

> My zealous aunt, finding the fields white to harvest, and almost without a labourer, overcame her natural diffidence, and not only met a class of white, and another of coloured women, but opened her house on Friday evenings, for females of all colours, coloured and black men. . . . These meetings commenced with singing and prayer, a chapter was then expounded, and she closed as she began.[91]

On another island, the Isle of Jersey, lived a Miss Bisson of St. Heliers, whose experience and piety had deeply impressed Wesley on several of his visits to that outpost. On

February 16, 1787, he wrote to Robert Brackenbury, his representative stationed there with Adam Clarke, and expressed his desire for "our sister [to] preach in private houses."[92]

Wesley, an extremely perceptive leader of an ever-growing movement, was especially cognizant of the isolated work of these women in the promotion of the gospel and the expansion of the evangelical revival.[93] His mature view on the question of women preachers is well illustrated by his relationship with a noted woman preacher who commenced her labors just as his seemingly interminable career was coming to its end.

ALICE CAMBRIDGE OF BANDON, IRELAND

C. H. Crookshank, the distinguished historian of Methodism in Ireland, once suggested that female preaching was never very popular among the Irish people. While Margaret Davidson, the remarkable blind preacher of county Down, had proclaimed the gospel to spellbound congregations throughout the course of the 1770s,[94] there does seem to have been a peculiarly vehement resistance to such irregularities in Ireland. For a woman to preach in that country, dominated as it was by Roman Catholicism and stringent Reformed traditions, required an extra measure of courage. Nothing, however, was to deter Alice Cambridge of Bandon. Her exemplary career stands as one of the great legacies of Irish Methodism.[95]

Her evangelistic work began when her experience in the Methodist band meeting brought her so rich a peace that she could not contain the good news concerning her discovery. Like so many of her predecessors in the work, she felt an earnest desire to bring others to a similar experience, and first exhorted her former companions to repent. Believing that it was her manifest duty to spread the message of God's grace, Alice began to pray, and consequently, to speak in public. She established meetings in various parts of the town, and her sphere of usefulness was greatly enlarged when invitations for her to hold services began to arrive from towns and villages such as Kinsale, Youghal, and Cappoquin, as well as the larger cities of Cork, Limerick, and Dublin.[96]

Opposition to her irregular activities soon arose, however, and to Alice's great consternation she was condemned by both secular officials and Methodist leaders alike. Distressed by the disapprobation of her co-laborers, she wrote to Wesley for advice and received the following reply:

> I received your letter an hour ago. I thank you for writing so largely and so freely; do so always to me as your friend, as one that loves you well. Mr. Barber has the glory of God at heart; and so have his fellow labourers. Give them all honour, and obey them in all things as far as conscience permits. But it will not permit you to be silent when God commands you to speak: yet I would have you give as little offence as possible; and therefore I would advise you not to speak at any place where a preacher is speaking at the same time, lest you should draw away his hearers. Also avoid the first appearance of pride or magnifying yourself. If you want books or anything, let me know; I have your happiness much at heart.[97]

The fact that Wesley penned this letter of encouragement only a month prior to his death led G. J. Stevenson to claim that "in this he left a dying testimony in favour of female preaching."[98]

Crookshank described Miss Cambridge as remarkably neat, plain, and Quaker-like in appearance. According to Taft she was a stout woman, and, while her accent was pleasing and her enunciation clear and distinct, she possessed extraordinary vocal powers. Modest in manner and indomitable with regard to her call, she possessed the requisite gifts for a ministry of public preaching. Apparently, the predominant theme of her preaching was the goodness of God, which she gratefully acknowledged as the source of her peace and life.[99] While she assumed none of that superiority to which her talents and usefulness might have entitled her, in the years following Wesley's death her work became so successful that it served as a perennial source of embarrassment for her male colleagues who increasingly questioned the propriety of such activities in Ireland.[100] The same debate would soon be raging across Saint George's Channel in English Methodism.

COURAGE IN THE FACE OF
MOUNTING OPPOSITION

During the 1780s great strides were made within Methodism toward a fuller realization of a female ministry as an integral part of the evangelical revival and movement. The official authorization of Sarah Mallet by the Conference of 1787 certainly represents a monumental step in the history of Methodism. And the widespread support of such women as Mary Fletcher, Elizabeth Tonkin, the preachers of Norfolk and Suffolk, and the Female Brethren of Leeds is indicative of the great flowering of their activities throughout this period. But, as has been intimated from time to time, a stormy protest was gathering momentum.

In Taft's personal copy of *Holy Women,* on a blank page adjacent to his account of the life and work of Alice Cambridge, he reflected upon the effects of the opposition she had encountered from men she would have preferred to embrace as colleagues. His annotation reveals something about the nature and character of these women that must not be overlooked:

> By far the greater part of those who ought to hold up their hands, have either frowned upon their labours, or spoken of them with coldness & indifference. The trial of many pious women has caused them to triumph over the sneers of the ungodly; but how strange that they cannot be subject to the divine requirements without also setting at nought the counsels & admonitions of their Christian bretheren. To stand in the face of the Philistines is a cross at the sight of which many have trembled, but to have to labour under the displeasure of the herald of God is almost intolerable. Nothing except the approval of God, could give so much life & energy to female exertions in the Church, as the countenance of their bretheren in the Lord. And nothing but the frown of Jehovah, could so effectually cramp their operations, as the disapprobation of those who are stiled the Ambassadors of Christ.

On June 20, 1790, the first woman preacher of Methodism, Mrs. Sarah Crosby, wrote the following letter of encouragement to an aspiring preacher—a potential colleague—and described the central conviction that had sustained her life and ministry:

> When we know we have our Lord's approbation, we should stand, like the beaten anvil to the stroke; or lie in his hands, as clay in the hands of the potter. Through evil report, and good, we pass, but all things worketh together for good, to them that love God. Speak and act, as the spirit gives liberty, and utterance; fear not the face of man, but with humble confidence, trust in the Lord; looking unto him who is able, and willing to save to the uttermost, all that come unto God by him.[101]

Thus was the mantle passed from one woman to the next.

NOTES

1. Cited in Church, *More about the Early Methodist People,* p. 137. Details concerning the time, place, and circumstances of this statement are undetermined.
2. *Arm. Mag.* 7 (1784): 470.
3. Moore, *Fletcher,* p. 137.
4. See Moore, *Fletcher,* pp. 139–41. Fletcher had met Mary some twenty-five years before and when he wrote this letter had not seen her for fifteen years. Their mutual secret affection and subsequent romance is one of the classic stories of the Methodist heritage. John William Fletcher, originally Jean Guillaume de la Fléchère (1729–1785), was born at Nyon, Switzerland, and educated at the University of Geneva. He came under the influence of the Methodists while serving as a tutor in Shropshire, was diverted from a military career, and sought Holy Orders within the English church. In 1757 he was ordained both deacon and priest, assisted Wesley for some time as a clerical colleague, and thereafter accepted the living of Madeley, Shropshire, in 1760. He was a faithful parish priest, transformed that populous industrial area into an evangelical center, and was widely revered as a genuine saint. Fletcher became the primary spokesman for Wesley and the Arminian Methodists when the controversy with the Calvinist evangelicals began in 1771. His classic series of "Checks to Antinomianism" stands as a lasting tribute to the force and clarity of his argument

and the piety and charm of his personality. On his life and work, see Tyerman, *Wesley's Designated Successor; Letters of the Rev. John Fletcher,* ed. Melville Horne (New York: Lane and Scott, 1849); *The Works of the Rev. John Fletcher,* 2d Am. ed. (New York: Published by John Wilson and Daniel Hitt, J. C. Totten, Printer, 1809); James Wiggins, *The Embattled Saint: Aspects of the Life and Thought of John Fletcher,* Wesleyan Studies No. 2 (Macon, Ga.: Wesleyan College, 1966); and David C. Shipley, "Methodist Arminianism in the Theology of John Fletcher," Ph.D. diss., Yale University, 1942.

5. It is not surprising that Mary sought the advice of her spiritual mentor, John Wesley, concerning this flowering relationship with John Fletcher. After consulting with her about the proposal, he approved of it entirely. See Wesley, *Works,* 11:329; cf. a letter written at Cross Hall by Sarah Crosby to Elizabeth Mortimer, in *Wesley: Autograph Letters and Manuscripts,* Meth. Arch., p. 56.

6. Under this date, John Valton wrote in his MS Journal: "How I was surprised when I came this morning to Cross Hall and found the Rev. Mr. John Fletcher and Miss Mary Bosanquet just returned from church with a few select friends. They had chose this day in preference as being their preaching night. Such a holy couple were scarce ever paired. O what a blessed day we had! Nothing but the voice of prayer and praise was heard. . . . Jesus was at the marriage feast indeed, and turned our water into wine, and, I believe, filled all the water-pots" (J. C. Nattrass, "Excerpts from John Valton's MS Journal," *W.H.S.* 8 [1912]: 22). In a letter of December 26, 1781, Fletcher spoke of his increasing regard for his wife: "Had I searched the three kingdoms I could not have found one brother willing to share gratis my weal and woe and labours, and complaisant enough to unite his fortunes to mine. But God has found me a partner, a sister, a wife, to use St. Paul's language, who is not afraid to face with me the colliers and bargemen of my parish until death part us" (see Tyerman, *Wesley's Designated Successor,* pp. 145–65). Of their marriage, Samuel Bradburn, one of the great orators of Methodism, is once to have said: "Such a pair,—I am inclined to think there never was a holier or happier couple since Adam ate the forbidden fruit" (quoted in Edwards, *My Dear Sister,* p. 95). Cf. the colorful account of a Yorkshire farmer's recollections of their marriage and ministry, in *W.H.S.* 8 (1912): 29.

7. Moore, *Fletcher,* p. 142. Cf. Wesley, *Journal,* 6:345n. Sarah

Lawrence accompanied the Fletchers as a well-pleasing part of their newly established family.

8. Jackson, ed., *Lives of Early Methodist Preachers*, 6:102. Cf. Robinson, *Methodism in Dewsbury*, p. 65.

9. Wesley, *Letters*, 7:94-95.

10. Tyerman, *Wesley's Designated Successor*, p. 502. Similarly, Moore notes that before their marriage, the would-be husband counseled his wife-to-be: "My dear, when you marry me, you must marry my parish" (*Fletcher*, pp. 178–79).

11. July 12, 1782, Birmingham, Wesley, *Letters*, 7:128.

12. October 1, 1782, Bristol, in ibid., p. 143. Cf. pp. 186–88 above.

13. Moore, *Fletcher*, pp. 143–44.

14. See Tyerman, *Wesley's Designated Successor*, p. 503. Cf. Wesley, *Journal*, 6:345, where Wesley mentions the pains that were taken by the Fletchers to prevail on the people to join the society.

15. Moore, *Fletcher*, p. 154.

16. Ibid., p. 156.

17. The immediate cause of his death seems to have been a fever contracted through his visitation of ailing parishioners. His death was felt as a grievous blow, not only by bereaved people of Madeley parish, but by the leaders of the evangelical revival, and particularly John Wesley. At that time, Wesley was in the west of England and unable to see him or to attend his funeral. As soon as possible, however, he published a sermon in memory of him and took as his text the same passage that his brother Charles had used at the death of their mutual friend and colleague, Rev. Vincent Perronet of Shoreham: "Mark the perfect man, and behold the upright: For the end of that man is peace" (Psalms 37:37). His sermon represents one of the most remarkable tributes to an exceptional man: "Many exemplary men have I known, holy in heart and life, within fourscore years, but one equal to him I have not known,—one so inwardly and outwardly devoted to God. So unblamable a character in every respect I have not found either in Europe or America; and I scarce expect to find another such on this side of eternity" (Wesley, *Works*, 7:449). This sermon (pp. 431–49) was dated October 24, 1785, from Norwich. Cf. Tyerman, *Life of John Wesley*, 3:464.

18. Moore, *Fletcher*, pp. 158–60.

19. After Fletcher's death, Mary published a treatise entitled *Thoughts on Communion with Happy Spirits*, printed in

Birmingham without a date, in which she explained her opinions concerning the communion of the saints and continued participation with those who have died in the faith.

20. Moore, *Fletcher,* p. 174.
21. *Wes. Meth. Mag.* 60 (1837): 900–903. Cf. Stevens, *Women of Methodism,* pp. 66–67; and Church, *More about Early Methodist People,* pp. 145–46.
22. Ibid., p. 901. Joseph Benson, whom we have encountered previously as an outspoken opponent of female preaching, preached himself in this barn on a subsequent visit to the region: "I rode hither to see the pious widow of my much-esteemed friend Mr. Fletcher. I found her, if possible, more devoted to God, and filled with his love, than ever. And what a pattern for good works, and those of all kinds, done to the bodies and souls of men! What a couple were they! And how mysterious the providence that separated them! I preached in the evening in the barn she has fitted up for a preaching-house. It will hold about three hundred hearers: it was thoroughly filled, and we had a refreshing season together" (Richard Treffrey, *Memoirs of the Rev. Joseph Benson* [London: Published by John Mason, 1840], p. 131). Another prominent Wesleyan itinerant, Joseph Entwisle, preached there and provided a detailed description of the building: "I preached in the Tythe Barn, adjoining to the vicarage, which was furnished by Mr. and Mrs. Fletcher. Hundreds of people were stowed together, insomuch that I could scarcely squeeze through them to the desk. The barn seems to have been built two hundred years; it is open to the roof, thatched with straw, and all the windows, except one, are made of oiled paper. . . . It is easy to preach here: I could have continued all night" (quoted in Stevens, *Women of Methodism,* pp. 71–72; cf. Church, *More about Early Methodist People,* pp. 145–46).
23. Ibid. Cf. Stevens, *Women of Methodism,* pp. 64–65. The curate, Mr. Melville Horne, was sympathetic to her cause, fully supported her in her labors, and not only allowed her to remain in the vicarage house, but, in later years, charged her with the responsibility of selecting a new curate when he assumed a chaplaincy in Sierra Leone.
24. Ibid., pp. 901–2.
25. Moore, *Fletcher,* p. 178.
26. Thomas Shaw, *A History of Cornish Methodism* (Truro: D. Bradford Barton, 1967), p. 58. Apparently unfamiliar with the

pioneering work of Ann Gilbert in the 1770s, he mistakenly asserts that Elizabeth Tonkin was "the first, and for years the only woman preacher in the main stream of Cornish Methodism."

27. For resources on her life and work, see Appendix A.
28. It is no small tribute to her spiritual guide that Elizabeth walked four miles to her class meeting in spite of frequent ridicule for devotion to the Methodists; see Taft, *Holy Women,* 2:121. On the work of Ann Gilbert, see pp. 145–46 above.
29. Quoted in Taft, *Holy Women,* 2:121–22, from Richard Collett's manuscript account of her life.
30. Taft, *Holy Women,* 2:122; cf. Church, *More about Early Methodist People,* p. 158. The reference to Balaam's ass should not be missed here. See Numbers 22:21–35, where a donkey reproves Balaam for acting contrary to the will of Yahweh.
31. Quoted in Taft, *Holy Women,* 2:125. This fact led Church to write: "She combined the work of a mother and housewife with that of a preacher. She had eleven children, seven of whom survived her. Forty years of happy, married life, in a home which was a model, gave answer to the critics who said a woman's place was her home. . . . It is because she proved that a woman may perform most important public functions and yet remain devoted to her home that she is important to any survey of Methodist preaching" (*More about Early Methodist People,* p. 159).
32. Through her efforts a chapel was built at Veryan for the growing society. The site of her final appearance as a preacher in St. Erme was a chapel constructed by her husband and opened in April 1804. In St. Erme she conducted private devotional exercises at two secluded and retiring spots which she called "Gethsemane" and "Calvary"; see Taft, *Holy Women,* 2:125–30.
33. Quoted in Taft, *Holy Women,* 2:116. Likewise, a powerful letter regarding her experience of holiness and seeking perfection, which she had written to Rev. Benjamin Rhodes on February 5, 1792, appeared in the *Arm. Mag.* in June 1794, but her identity was shrouded by assigning it to "Mr." instead of "Mrs. E. C."
34. Taft, *Holy Women,* 2:137.
35. Wesley, *Journal,* 6:338–39. Cf. Telford, *Wesley's Veterans: Lives of Early Methodist Preachers,* 7 vols. (London: Robert

Cully, C. H. Kelly, 1909–14), 3:245–48; and Simon, *John Wesley: The Last Phase,* p. 181. Wells was 12 miles north of Fakenham.

36. A. B. Lawson claimed that this event "would sweep away any remaining prejudices on the part of Wesley" (*John Wesley and Christian Ministry,* p. 179).

37. There is no evidence to support the idea that any of these preachers was formally related to any Methodist organization. Lawson's statement that Mrs. Parker of Fakenham "was instrumental in Miss Sewell taking up the work" would seem to be totally unfounded (ibid.).

38. Taft, *Holy Women,* 1:326–28. Such ambiguity or lack of specificity on Taft's part generally indicates that nothing is known about her early life. It is dangerous simply to accept his statements on face value. See Appendix A for details.

39. Wesley, *Journal,* 6:338n. Lamb lived in and apparently heard her preach in the neighboring village of Haddiscoe. Curnock dates this event about 1779. Mary was born toward the end of the 1750s.

40. J.B.B. Clarke, editor of Adam Clarke's biography, observes that "he thought then, this is God's work,—and if he choose to convert men by employing such means, who am I that I should criticise the ways of God!" (*An Account of the Infancy, Religious and Literary Life of Adam Clarke, LL.D., F.A.S.,* 3 vols. [London: Printed and published by T. S. Clarke, 1833], 1:215).

41. From the journal of Adam Clarke, quoted in J.B.B. Clarke, *Account of Adam Clarke,* 1:215–16. This portion of Clarke's journal was also reprinted in *Bible Christian Magazine* 5, 4(April 1833): 142–43. It is important to note the reference to Balaam's ass and its affinity to Joseph Taylor's remark to Elizabeth Collett (see p. 187 above). Such responses were becoming standard with reference to women's preaching by this time.

42. Taft, *Holy Women,* 1:328; Mellis = modern spelling.

43. J. Conder Nattrass, "Some Notes from the Oldest Register of the Great Yarmouth Circuit," *W.H.S.* 3 (1902): 74. Cf. Wesley F. Swift, "The Women Itinerant Preachers of Early Methodism," *W.H.S.* 28, 5(March 1952): 89; Simon, *John Wesley: The Last Phase,* p. 181; Wearmouth, *Methodism and Common People,* p. 228; and Church, *More about Early Methodist People,* pp. 169–70. This is the earliest known entry of this kind in any Methodist society records. Mary Sewell's

name appeared for the last time in the list of society members for 1786, as she died on October 29, 1786.

44. Taft, *Holy Women,* MS notations, facing p. 328.
45. J.B.B. Clarke, *Account of Adam Clarke,* 1:216; cf. *Bible Christian Magazine* 5:143. This quotation reveals as much about the transformation of attitude in the reporter as it does the work of the preacher.
46. Taft, *Holy Women,* 2:27. Cf. Hellier, "Mother Chapel of Leeds," p. 64; and Church, *More about Early Methodist People,* p. 145.
47. Wesley, *Journal,* 7:226–27. Wesley published an account of her life, written by her uncle, William Mallitt [*sic*], in *Arm. Mag.* 11 (1788): 91–93, 130–33, 185–88, 238–42. See bibliographical data in Appendix A.
48. In a letter to her uncle she states that she was born on this day in 1768, but all other evidence, including age references to specific months and years, lead to the conclusion that she was born in 1764; see *Arm. Mag.* 11:91, 130, 132.
49. *Arm. Mag.* 11:92.
50. Ibid., pp. 186–87.
51. In later years she wrote: "It was so deeply impressed on my mind, 'Woe to me if I preach not the Gospel,' that my distress of soul almost destroyed my body" (quoted in Hellier, "Some Methodist Women Preachers," p. 66).
52. *Arm. Mag.* 11:92. See Wesley's account of this, pp. 192–93 above.
53. Her texts on these occasions included: Mark 16:16 (January 15); Isaiah 58:1 (January 24); 1 Peter 4:18 (January 27); and Isaiah 55:1 (January 30) (ibid., p. 93).
54. Sarah's uncle described the nature and progress of these seizures: "About five in the morning, she felt a pain in her stomach. Afterwards it seized her head. Then she lost her senses. In about an hour and a half she began speaking. When she had ended her sermon, she usually prayed about ten minutes. In about a quarter of an hour after, she began to groan, and then in a short time opened her eyes and came to herself. Her behaviour all the time she was with me was unreprovable." On the basis of her own testimony, Sarah was able to recall the place where she was preaching and the words from which she spoke (ibid., p. 238).
55. Ibid., p. 239. Similarly, she confesses that "often, sensible of the importance of the work, I said, 'Why me, Lord? What am I, or my father's house?'"

56. Sarah's journal does indicate that she preached on December 4, the day of Wesley's visit, but there is no indication either from her account or his that he actually heard her preach. Perhaps, still under the influence of her interview with Wesley, Sarah wrote about her gift on December 12: "I saw more clearly than ever the danger of trusting in any gift I had received. I saw, I must give an account, how I use every gift, and that gifts are not for *me*, but for the benefit of others. It is not gifts that make me alive to God, but grace. Therefore I desire He would increase my gifts, for the good of others, and my grace for the good of my own soul: that when he calls me to give an account of my stewardship, I may give up my account with joy" (ibid., p. 241). Sarah's paroxysms are clearly uncharacteristic of the general experience of the women preachers, even exhibiting some of the qualities of spirit possession described by Lewis in *Ecstatic Religion,* but Wesley does not seem to have been overly concerned about such supernatural manifestations if they bore good fruit.

57. Hellier, "Some Methodist Women Preachers," p. 66.

58. Quoted in Taft, *Holy Women,* 1:84.

59. In the early nineteenth century, Zechariah Taft possessed the original document and reproduced it in his *Holy Women,* 1:84. Nattrass reprinted a version of the letter in *W.H.S.* 3 (1902): 74, which was dated October 27, 1787, contained several minor textual variations, was signed by "Josh. Harper," and included a postscript reading: "You receive this by order of Mr. Wesley and the Conference." Cf. Simon, *John Wesley: The Last Phase,* pp. 181–82; Hellier, "Mother Chapel of Leeds," p. 64; Church, *More about Early Methodist People,* p. 170; J. F. Hurst, *The History of Methodism: British Methodism,* 3 vols. (London: Charles H. Kelly, 1901), 2:917–18; and Wesley, *Letters,* 8:15n.

60. Quoted in Taft, *Holy Women,* 1:84–85. Cf. Hellier, "Some Methodist Women Preachers," pp. 66–67. The local preacher whom she married was a Mr. Boyce of Norfolk. His name has appeared incorrectly in related materials as both Boyle and Royce. Taft afforded the following notation concerning the inclusion of her name on Methodist preaching plans: "Why not? If the people were fully satisfied *she* was one of those whom the Lord had called to prophesy or preach in his name—why not put her on the printed plan? The ground I have taken is this—that some few women have an *extraordinary* call to ministerial service." Later in the nineteenth

century, Taft included his own wife, Mary, on the plan by placing a star in the plan where she was expected to preach.

61. Wesley, *Letters*, 8:15.
62. March 11, 1788, Bath, in ibid., p. 44.
63. Ibid. In a note on the back of the letter, Sally says that she worked with her own hands so as to lay no charge on the people.
64. Ibid., pp. 77–78; cf. pp. 108–9.
65. Ibid. Wesley frequently found it necessary to counter the charge that Methodist preaching was illegal because neither their preachers nor their preaching houses had been registered under the terms of the Toleration Act. See in particular, his *Farther Appeal to Men of Reason and Religion,* in Wesley, *Oxford Edition,* 11:180–85. Cf. Baker, *John Wesley and the Church of England,* pp. 95, 163, 173–77, 198–99, 316–19.
66. Ibid., pp. 118–19.
67. For pertinent resources, see Appendix A. Church incorrectly refers to her residence in the village of Redgrove, which error stems from a misprint in Taft's *Holy Women,* corrected by his notation in the personal copy.
68. Wesley referred to her in a letter of July 31, 1790, to Sarah Mallet. "It is well that you are acquainted with our sister *that likewise is sometimes* employed in the same labour of love; Providence has marked you out for friends to each other, and there should be no reserve between you. Pour all your thoughts and troubles and temptations into each other's bosom. . . . *If you go on in the work to which God has called you,* you will experience trials upon trials" (Wesley, *Letters,* 8:229). He also mentions Betty Reeve in his last letter to Sally on December 13, 1790 (*Letters,* 8:250).
69. Taft, *Holy Women,* 1:92. In June 1795 she married a Mr. W. Wright of Redgrave and died from a "consumption" at Diss on August 3, 1797, aged 32. No other information is available concerning her life and ministry. She is not to be confused with another Elizabeth Reeve who died at Diss in 1804 and whose obituary appears in *Meth. Mag.* 28 (1805):281.
70. Wesley, *Letters,* 8:190.
71. December 13, 1790, Near London, in ibid., p. 250. In actuality, this was Wesley's penultimate letter, for a final piece of correspondence between Wesley and Mallet was known to Taft, but not included in his *Holy Women* due to the fact that it was written in a hand other than Wesley's. This note was dictated "a few days only before his death" (Taft, *Holy Women,* 1:90).

72. Quoted from her journal in Hellier, "Some Methodist Women Preachers," p. 66. There is no information available revealing the date or place of her death.
73. Wesley, *Journal,* 7:247. In spite of Wesley's failure to persuade Mary to move to Bristol following her husband's death, she made frequent trips to the west country at his request. Miss Elizabeth Flamanck, later Mrs. Shaw, heard her preach at Miss Bishop's School at Keynsham on one of her visits in February 1786. "It was during my stay at Keynsham," wrote the impressionable student, "that I had the honour and privilege of hearing Mrs. Fletcher give an exhortation in the chapel to the young people" (Robert C. Barratt, *Memorials of Mrs. Elizabeth Shaw,* [London: Wesleyan Conference Office, 1875], pp. 8–9).
74. Ibid., p. 249.
75. Mary Fletcher wrote a brief sketch of her life, entitled *An Account of Sarah Lawrence* (London: Printed by Thomas Cordeux, 1800), which provided the basis for all subsequent biographies. See Appendix A.
76. See pp. 126 and 199 above.
77. Fletcher, *Account of Sarah Lawrence,* pp. 8–9; cf. Taft, *Holy Women,* 1:43; and Stevens, *Women of Methodism,* p. 89.
78. A portion of Mary Fletcher's funeral sermon on the occasion of Sarah's death on December 3, 1800, reads: "My dear friend, Sarah Lawrence, was many years weak and infirm, but her ardent desire for the salvation of souls carried her frequently beyond her strength, and many times, when she was speaking to sinners with a view to bring them to repentance, her poor body was fitter for bed, than any other place. It might be truly said, 'the zeal of the Lord did eat her up' " (ibid., p. 20); cf. Taft, *Holy Women,* 1:46.
79. Ibid., pp. 12–13.
80. Ibid., p. 13; cf. Taft, *Holy Women,* 1:44. Note the similarity to Susanna Wesley's practices.
81. Ibid., p. 14. Unfortunately, no other record of these activities has been preserved. On one occasion, however, Sarah expressed the depth of her feelings for that community: "If ever I was called any where, I surely was to that place. It seemed at times, as if my whole soul were drawn out in their behalf; and, when I think of the dear children, and grown persons too, who used to come through such deep roads to meet me, I cannot help turning my eyes, with tears and prayers, many times towards that spot" (p. 21). The ancient tar tunnel and china mill of Coalport are still open.

82. Ibid.
83. Hellier, "Mother Chapel of Leeds," p. 64. The chapel took its name from the willowy field in which it was constructed.
84. *W.H.S.* 19, 7(September 1934): 173–74. The letter was apparently hand delivered to her in Leeds. Wesley also expressed his hope that the preachers would not suffer the wife of Thomas Brisco "to bury her talent in the Earth!"
85. Hellier, "Mother Chapel of Leeds," p. 64. Cf. Baker, *Friends and Early Methodism,* p. 21, for the note; and Baker, "Wesley and Crosby," p. 81. The insufficiency of records and the lack of reliable data make it difficult to determine the precise composition of this group. It would seem likely that Elizabeth Hurrell and Sarah Stevens participated in the endeavor, and it would be surprising if, in later years, Mary Barritt did not play some part in their enterprise. Very little can be gleaned from original sources even about the life and work of Ann Tripp. Her obituary in *Wes. Meth. Mag.* 46 (1823): 706, contains no reference to her preaching, as might well be expected at that time. It does refer, however, to her lengthy connection with Methodism in Leeds. "She had the spirit, piety, and exemplary conduct of a primitive Christian; and being one of the oldest leaders in the Leeds Society, many females who had the privilege of meeting in her Classes, or enjoyed the happiness of her acquaintance, imbibed the same spirit, and learned from her instructions and example to be the humble, active, and zealous servants of Christ. The last time she attended the public meeting of the Bands, she spoke much longer than usual, and in a most pleasing and profitable way." Cf. Taft, *Holy Women,* 2:112–15; and the similar work of Hannah Harrison and Ruth Hall in the consolidation of Methodist women in York, in Lyth, *Methodism in York,* pp. 64–71.
86. See Ibid. There is no clear indication as to why the women had formed such a strong opinion against the noted biblical scholar who exhibited some sympathy for their work.
87. To this situation, Dr. Clarke replied: "The same principle must guide my movements, on this, as on the former occasion; my call, I conceived, not extending to any locality in which women were the governors, for that I was certain Christ had not the proper management, where women held the reins!" (James Everett, *Adam Clarke Portrayed,* 3 vols. [London: Published by Hamilton, Adams, 1843–44, 1849], 1:232–33). Wesley had written to Clarke the previous November, encouraging him to see that his wife was fully employed, "that she

fulfill the office of a deaconess" (November 5, 1788, London, Wesley, *Letters,* 8:101–2); cf. Wesley, *Journal,* 7:446n. Mary Clarke had been extremely influential in the development of Methodism at Trowbridge in Wiltshire. For her life and work, see *Mrs. Adam Clarke: Her Character and Correspondence* (London: Partridge and Oakey, 1851). Tension was beginning to mount between the men who were assuming responsibility for the future of the movement and the women, especially the women preachers, who were expanding the range of their influence.

88. See Cocking, *Methodism in Grantham,* pp. 180–84, 189–205, 242.
89. February 16, 1783, Deptford, Wesley, *Letters,* 7:167.
90. April 25, 1783, Dublin, in ibid., pp. 175–76. See n. 80 above.
91. Henrietta F. Gilbert, *Memoirs of the Late Mrs. Mary Gilbert,* (London: Printed by Thomas Cordeux, 1817), pp. 19–20. Cf. Bretherton, *Methodism in Chester,* pp. 73–79. Mary was born at St. Albans on February 24, 1733, married Francis Gilbert on November 17, 1767, at Chester, and died on April 21, 1816, having returned to England in 1791. One of the preachers called her a stewardess as she had assumed responsibility for receiving subscriptions for the Methodist chapel.
92. Charles Pollard, "John Wesley and Robert Carr Brackenbury: Some Unpublished Letters," *W.H.S.* 28, 4(December 1951): 68. Later that year, on Saturday, August 25, Wesley interviewed this young prodigy: "This morning I had a particular conversation (as I had once or twice before) with Jeannie Bisson of this town; such a young woman as I have hardly seen elsewhere. She seems to be wholly devoted to God, and to have constant communion with Him. She has a clear and strong understanding; and I cannot perceive the least tincture of enthusiasm. I am afraid she will not live long. . . . I doubt whether I have found her fellow in England. Precious as my time is, it would have been worth my while to come to Jersey, had it been only to see this prodigy of grace" (Wesley, *Journal,* 7:319); cf. Tyerman, *Life of John Wesley,* 3:599–600, 609–610. For Wesley's opinion of her in a letter to Hester Ann Rogers, dated October 12, 1787, see *Letters,* 8:17.
93. On June 7, 1783, Wesley wrote to Hannah Ball of High Wycombe, acknowledging the indispensable work of women. "Four young women were made the chief support of four Societies. One of them [Miss Hartly?] quitted her post at Henley, and both she and the Society sank into nothing. The

other three by the grace of God stand their ground; and so do the Societies at Wycombe, Watlington, and Witney. And I trust my dear friends Hannah Ball, Patty Chapman, and Nancy Bolton will never be weary of well doing!" (Wesley, *Letters*, 7:180). For the work of Mary Lowe in Cheshire, see "Memoir of Mrs. Mary Lowe, Written by Herself," photocopy of typescript in Meth. Arch. For the establishment and leadership of cottage prayer meetings in and around Haslingden by Alice Maudsley, see John Stott, *Notices of Methodism in Haslingden* (London: Printed by Hayman, Christy and Lilly, [1898]), pp. 23–24. The work of Mrs. Edwards of Purfleet, who was instrumental in the conversion of John Valton, and of Miss Marsh, who frequently made excursions to Bristol, may be gleaned from Joseph Sutcliffe, ed., *The Life and Labours of the Late Rev. John Valton* (London: Published by John Mason, 1830), pp. 11–26.

94. See pp. 159–61 above.
95. See Appendix A for a biographical outline and bibliographical details.
96. Crookshank, *Memorable Women*, p. 195; cf. Taft, *Holy Women*, 1:269.
97. January 31, 1791, London, Wesley, *Letters*, 8:258–59; cf. Crookshank, *Memorable Women*, pp. 195–96; Lawson, *John Wesley and Christian Ministry*, pp. 180–81; and Church, *More about Early Methodist People*, p. 174.
98. Stevenson, *City Road Chapel*, p. 109.
99. According to Crookshank, *Memorable Women*, p. 197.
100. See pp. 232–33 below. Two lesser-known women preachers of Ireland were Mrs. Anne Brown of Femanagh and Jane Newland of Dublin. Anne married one of Wesley's itinerant preachers, George Brown, in 1782 and later became involved in the debate concerning women preachers in Ireland along with Miss Cambridge. For bibliographical and biographical details on all of these women, consult Appendix A.
101. June 20, 1790, Kirkstall-Forge, Zechariah Taft, *Original Letters, Never Before Published, On Doctrinal, Experimental, and Practical Religion* (Whitby: Printed at the Office of George Clark, 1821), pp. 66–67. This letter was written to Mrs. Holder, the wife of an itinerant preacher, who thereafter carried on the work of preaching.

PART III

Women Preachers in an Evolving Church, 1791–1803

THE
WONDERFUL WOMAN

OF

Strong Faith & Mighty Prayer,

EXEMPLIFIED IN THE

PIOUS AND USEFUL LIFE

OF

ANN CUTLER,

COMMONLY CALLED

PRAYING NANNY.

BY THE LATE

REV. W. BRAMWELL,
Minister of the Gospel.

TO WHICH IS ADDED,

A plain account of the great Revival of the work of God in Burslem Circuit,

STAFFORDSHIRE POTTERIES,

IN THE YEAR 1820-21.

FOURTH EDITION.

WEDGWOOD, PRINTER, TUNSTALL.

1821.

7

FROM RECOGNITION TO REPRESSION AFTER WESLEY

J OHN WESLEY DIED on the morning of Wednesday, March 2, 1791, at the advanced age of eighty-seven.[1] In 1784 the Deed of Declaration had legally incorporated the Methodist Societies and created the Legal Hundred. This executive body of governing clergy was to oversee the work of the vast Connection and ensure its perpetuity. But the question remained in many a person's mind, Would the connectional discipline be maintained and the work of God continue to prosper and expand? It is not surprising that the event of Wesley's death created a crisis within the Methodist Connection, a crisis that would not be resolved in a number of respects for years to come.

Dissension quickly arose in the succession of conferences immediately following the death of Methodism's founder. In 1797 Alexander Kilham and his contingent seceded from the Wesleyans and established a so-called New Connection within the Methodist family.[2] This was but the first of a number of schisms which led to the disintegration of the movement into several major and some minor groups. In addition to these internal problems, certain external factors contributed to the critical nature of this period in the life of the newly emerging church. The French Revolution greatly affected the political outlook of the English, stiffening their conservatism and later deepening their insularity. And on the domestic scene, radical social changes brought about by the Industrial Revolution created a sense of instability and uncertainty.

In spite of all these hindrances, Wesleyan Methodism continued to expand by leaps and bounds during the 1790s.[3]

Moreover, the expansion of the public ministry of women seems to have approached its zenith within that body toward the close of the eighteenth century. At the same time, however, the question of women's preaching became a point of bitter controversy. It contributed substantially to later schisms within Methodism, antagonists and protagonists marshaling their arguments for and against the practice, and all aspects of the debate reflecting the larger connectional crisis following Wesley's death.

Therefore, even though it is beyond the scope of this study, a concluding word must be said about the developments within Wesleyan Methodism up to 1803. For, in little more than a decade following Wesley's death, women were either formally forbidden from functioning as preachers (as was the case in the Irish Methodist Conference) or were restricted in their activities in such a way as to severely impede their influence within the societies (as was the case in England). Developments at the turn of the century reveal that the women preachers of the Methodist revival lost much by the death of Wesley.

AN ERA OF CONNECTIONAL CRISIS

Certainly by 1784, if not long before that momentous year, the Methodist Societies under Wesley's direction had entered into an evolutionary process by which a closely knit connection of societies, or *ecclesiolae in ecclesia,* were being gradually transformed into a distinct church, separate from the Church of England.[4] The removal of the guiding hand and comprehensive outlook of John Wesley served to heighten the tensions which this process naturally entailed. Methodism during Wesley's lifetime had been characterized by a dynamic interrelation of a strong personal urge toward holiness, an evangelistic missionary impulse, and adherence to a distinctive form of church order and discipline. These theological and ecclesiological emphases necessarily became the center of concern and debate during the period of institutional consolidation after 1791. With regard to the question of ministry—the area most affecting the women preachers of Methodism—two opposing ideas emerged.[5]

At this critical turning point, Methodism was a movement in search of a coherent doctrine of the church and ministry. And the development of a "Wesleyan doctrine of the Pastoral Office," as Bowmer has described it, was essentially a growing awareness of status.[6] The growth of Methodism from a federation of societies into a church involved a concomitant transformation in self-understanding as Wesley's successors thought of themselves increasingly as ordinary ministers rather than extraordinary—even emergency—preachers. Influenced greatly by a growing church consciousness, the Methodist hierarchy began to articulate a conception of pastoral responsibility and authority that was foreign to the democratic spirit and leveling sentiment which pervaded some of the societies.

Professor Ward has demonstrated how the leaders of the movement, increasingly concerned with matters of institutional stability and security, were caught up in a difficult and socially explosive situation as they entered the nineteenth century.[7] The "high" view of the ministry which emerged as a part of their program, therefore, emphasized ministerial control and discipline as a necessary bulwark against disaster.[8] This view, with its concern for the connectional dimensions of the emerging church and the pastoral-didactic function of the clergy was clarified and tightened in its confrontation with an apparently antithetical point of view.

On the part of Methodists who held a "low" view of the church and ministry, who tended to emphasize the local or congregational aspects of their Methodist heritage and the part played by lay persons in its development, there was a reluctance to follow this evolving pattern of Wesleyan Methodism after 1791. According to the proponents of this view, the itinerant was, as Wesley had originally styled him, an "extraordinary messenger."[9] The minister was conceived first and foremost as a "missioner," whose office "existed simply as the agency of a special mission, and required no complicated background of 'ordination' or 'succession.' The minister was essentially an itinerant evangelist."[10]

There is little doubt that this "low" view was produced in part by the dissenting background of a large number of the later converts to Methodism. But it also appealed to those who viewed the "normal" ministry as flat and uninviting. Jabez Bunting, the dominant figure in Wesleyan Methodism during the first half of the nineteenth century and an outspoken proponent of the "high" view, is reported to have said: "I do not think we can be proved to be evangelists. Our proper office is pastors and teachers. . . . I believe that we are teachers to instruct and pastors to govern the people."[11] The process of institutionalization, which Bunting considered to be the necessary consolidation of gains from the revivals of the previous century, his critics construed to be a bureaucratic hardening into unevangelical respectability.[12] One coalition created the impression that revivalism rather than denominationalism was the fundamental antidote to the tensions of Church and Society, while the other, awakening to a broader role for Methodism and its ministry, viewed growing church consciousness as an inevitable and necessary development, a safeguard of Wesleyan Methodism in a turbulent reform epoch.

At a deeper level, this debate represents the perennial tension between the charismatic and authoritarian views of the Church which Wesley had attempted to balance throughout his lifetime with varying degrees of success. This volatile legacy broke apart after Wesley's death. It seems that the left wing of the Wesleyan tradition retained a stress upon the autonomy of the Spirit in the life of the Church, but tended to denegrate the role of institutional structures. The conservatives, represented to a large degree by the leadership, were able to preserve Wesley's conception of institutional authority, but in the process rejected the egalitarian legacy he had embraced. The instability of Methodist ecclesiology during this era goes far to explain why members of the Wesleyan hierarchy reacted as they did to the activities of the women preachers. The idea that what was extraordinary, irregular, or even shocking was the hallmark of genuine Methodism stood in diametrical opposition to the inflexibility, formality, and respectability of the emerging Wesleyan Methodist church.

Proponents of a charismatic view of the church, who conceived itinerants as "extraordinary messengers" engaged in an extraordinary mission, generally supported the evangelistic activities of women, especially those which were bearing much fruit. This explains, in large measure, the proliferation of women preachers during a period of unprecedented growth and revivalism following Wesley's death. On the other hand, those who were in key leadership positions advocated a more authoritarian view of the church and supported a normal ministry, and quickly moved to restrict the function and influence of "unauthorized women preachers."

Wesleyans who felt thwarted in their evangelistic purpose by the rigid organization of the mother church and who sought to recover the more flexible, free, and egalitarian ethos which had marked the movement originally, were obliged to follow one of two courses. They could either conform to the standards and expectations of the Methodist institution, or, as a form of "new dissent," establish sects of their own.[13] The unbounded movements of God's grace, so dear to these revivalists, would evoke a powerful echo in persons who were at the losing end of institutions, as most women still were, and chilled the marrow of those with a stake in institutional stability.

FEMALE PREACHERS IN AN ERA OF REVIVAL

During the revivalistic period immediately following Wesley's death, there were many women who openly exercised their gifts in the ministry of preaching.[14] It was not the fissiparousness of revivalism but its capacity to unite these women in a common mission which contributed to the restrictive mood of subsequent conferences. The first reports of substantial advancement among the societies came from those developing industrial areas of West Yorkshire where the women preachers had been most active. In 1791 William Bramwell was sent to Dewsbury as an agent of reconciliation to repair the damage of a secession led by John Atlay. Little progress was made until Ann Cutler, one of Bramwell's early

converts in Lancashire, arrived to assist the aspiring revivalist in 1792.

"Nothing appeared very particular," he reports, "till
under Nanny Cutler's prayers, one soul received a clean
heart."[15] Her "simple and artless yet powerful and awakening" prayers seemed to pour new life into the floundering
society. Through such efforts Praying Nanny became well
known throughout Yorkshire and Lancashire as a herald of
revival.[16]

It is not surprising that a number of traveling preachers'
wives became engaged in similar activities at this time. Many
of them exhorted, a good number "prophesied" following
the preaching of their husbands, and some preached in the
more technical sense. The wife of George Holder, formerly
Mary Woodhouse of Whitby, received strong encouragements in this work from her close friend Sarah Crosby:

> Our reverend and dear Father's direction to me used to be,
> "Do all you can for God." I believe it would be the same to
> you, because Moses like Mr. Wesley, would say, "Oh, that all
> the Lords people were Prophets."[17]

Mrs. Hainsworth, who had preached prior to her marriage
to an itinerant, frequently accompanied her husband on his
journeys and assisted him in his work.[18] Likewise, Mrs. Mary
Wiltshaw would occasionally supply the place of her husband
and frequently visited the country villages in his circuit to
expound the word of God.[19] One of the effects of Mrs. Sarah
Stevens' preaching became a matter of public record when
the Reverend Mr. Lomas proclaimed to the Conference of
1824:

> I also am the fruit of female preaching. Mrs. Stevens was the
> instrument of my conversion to God; I went to hear her under
> the sense of Godly fear—but I returned feeling the love of
> God shed abroad in my heart.[20]

These women, like their predecessors, struggled with the
matter of a call into the ministry. In spite of strong
intimations to proclaim the word of God publicly, Sarah Cox
kept her call a secret. Only after sharing the conviction of her

mind with another female preacher was she able to break through her aversion to public ministry. Thereafter she preached with great acceptance and success throughout Nottingham and Leicestershire.[21] Similarly, Sarah Eland of Hutton, in the North Riding of Yorkshire, responded in her journal to the censure of those who did not think it to be the province of women to speak in public:

> Ah! had they known the inward travail of my soul, and the great aversion I always felt to publicity; they must have concluded it to have been no ordinary operation of the Spirit. . . . I am as certain as to my call from God to speak in his name, as I was clear in a sense of his pardoning mercy, through Christ my Saviour.[22]

Mrs. Mary Harrison preached on Sunday evenings at her native Wishall in Nottinghamshire;[23] Miss Margaret Watson, who had been converted under the preaching of George Whitefield, awakened the slumbering society at Redcar where she preached regularly in the Methodist chapel;[24] and Hannah Parker of Ampleforth preached in barns and in the open air throughout the North Riding of Yorkshire.[25] Charles Allen's manuscript "Service Register" for Houghton-Le-Spring near Sunderland reveals that a certain Mary Goulden preached from 2 Thessalonians 1:7–9 at Wapping on February 27, 1803.[26] And Mrs. Jane Treffry, the wife of a noted itinerant preacher, who had been bounced on the knee of John Wesley in her childhood, often preached in her husband's circuit with his approval.[27]

About this same time Elizabeth Dickinson created considerable excitement in Bingley where she preached in the open air and fell into ecstatic trances.[28] A biographical sketch of this Yorkshire lass from Staveley, near Knaresborough in the West Riding, was appended to Bramwell's *Account of Ann Cutler.* According to Taft, her biographer, she experienced seizures very similar to those reported by Sarah Mallet.[29] In her preaching she often referred to her visions and trances, and many were skeptical of her labors in spite of the abundant fruit which resulted from them. One eyewitness, however, testified to the nature of her ministry:

> Her motto was *holiness to the Lord.* She has often said we
> must not only preach the gospel, but live the gospel, or we
> shall do more harm than good: . . . I have heard her give out
> hymns, sing, and pray, and exhort the people to flee from the
> wrath to come, in such a pathetic manner, that I have seen
> tears like showers, flow from the eyes of crowded audiences.[30]

Such paroxysms, however, were alien to the ordered
spirituality of the emerging Wesleyan Methodist church and
mitigated against the acceptance of women involved in
revivalistic endeavors.

MARY BARRITT: A STORM CENTER
OF CONTROVERSY

In his later years, Wesley preferred to believe that prejudice
against women preachers was declining among his adherents.
In this confidence, however, he was mistaken. In the decade
following his death, hardening antifeminist sentiment fo-
cused increasing upon the ministry of one woman in
particular: Miss Mary Barritt.[31] This Lancashire woman was
born at Hay, near Colne, in 1772, and was unquestionably
the most famous female evangelist of the early nineteenth
century. In 1827 she published an extensive account of her
work as a revivalist in an autobiography which demonstrates
her preeminence as an itinerant preacher of unparalleled
ability and success.[32] The opposition she encountered,
however, was often her greatest grief:

> All that I have suffered from the world in the way of reproach
> and slander, is little in comparison with what I have suffered
> from some professors of religion, as well as even ministers of
> the gospel.[33]

Mary joined the Methodist Society at Colne and soon
followed the pattern set by her fellow laborers. Prayer in
class meetings, and testimony and exhortation at the
lovefeasts soon led to preaching. But her actions aroused
immediate hostilities, especially among the local preachers.
When a noted itinerant, Lancelot Harrison, was first

appointed to that circuit, his prejudice against women's preaching was very strong. William Sagar of Southfield, however, cautioned him with regard to this young prodigy. "It is at the peril of your soul," he warned, "that you meddle with Mary Barritt: God is with her—fruit is appearing wherever she goes."[34] Even her brother, another traveling preacher, seemed annoyed at her behavior and gave only grudging approval to Walton's request that she preach with him in the chapel at Hexham. Upon hearing her, however, all prejudice melted away.

Indeed, invitations for her to preach were many and came from some of the most prominant ministers in Methodism— John Pawson, Alexander Mather, Thomas Vasey, Samuel Bradburn, William Bramwell, Thomas Shaw, and many others.[35] She traveled from place to place, therefore, as invited, and in 1794 began a series of preaching pilgrimages that continued for many years. A revival spread throughout the whole district when she began her work at Pateley Bridge.[36] In Whitehaven she supplied for her brother, and during her stay some one hundred eleven persons were added to the society.[37] During a prolonged campaign in the Nottingham Circuit no fewer than five hundred were added to that society in one quarter.[38] Mary's journal reveals something of her own reaction to this unprecedented growth:

> In the Yorkshire Dales, extending from Ripon to Bainbridge, Reeth, and Richmond, the Lord enabled me, and others, to gather the harvest, in handfuls, and everywhere he gave us fruit: for, at that time, those circuits had but little help from the travelling preachers. . . . Suffice it to say, that the Almighty, in a most extraordinary manner, removed my scruples, answered my objections, and thrust me out into his vineyard. Indeed, nothing but a powerful conviction that God required it at my hand. . . could have supported me in it.[39]

But Mary's brand of evangelism was no mere revivalism. Like Wesley she provided meticulous care for her converts and made every attempt to see that they were established in classes and properly assimilated into the life of the societies. Moreover, Mary's preaching was well balanced and theologically sound. Alexander Suter once raised objections to her work at the Quarterly Meeting held at Leeds, observing that "a raw girl had come into the circuit, who had made a great hubbub." But when he intimated that she proclaimed a shallow gospel based on one or two obscure texts, Edward Wade of Sturton Grange rose to her defense and summarily dismissed such erroneous charges. "I have now heard *Miss Barritt,* twenty-seven or twenty-eight times," he retorted, "and have never heard her speak twice from the same text."[40] It is not surprising that among the many hundreds of converts ascribed to her ministry are included the names of several prominent preachers—Thomas Jackson, William Dawson, Joseph Taylor, Thomas Garbutt, and Robert Newton, D.D.[41]

The support and encouragement which Mary received from laypersons, fellow laborers, and eminent preachers throughout the Connection was a source of gratification, especially in the face of mounting opposition.[42] Thomas Smith, a leader and local preacher in the Nottingham Circuit wrote a characteristic letter to her from Long Eaton on April 20, 1801:

> We approve of your preaching the gospel: we have come so to do, for God has blest your labours amongst us, and made you a lasting blessing to this day. We know *that God has called you to preach his word,* therefore, fear not; cry aloud, and spare not; lift up your voice like a trumpet, and tell the people the error of their doings. I shall ever love the thought of a woman preaching the gospel. I myself went to hear one out of curiosity, and God made it his opportunity to bless me with his grace, nineteen years ago. . . . May you devote body, and soul, and spirit to his glory, and never tire till death your soul remove.[43]

The revivalist William Bramwell was undoubtedly her most enthusiastic supporter among the itinerant preachers. On the eve of her marriage to Zechariah Taft in 1802, Bramwell expressed fears concerning the restrictions which such a change would impose upon her ministry:

From a full persuasion of your call in an extraordinary way, and believing that the design of God concerning you, is, to spread the flame of heavenly love in our connexion,—I write to you with all freedom on a certain subject, which has given me much concern. I understand you have some serious thoughts about marrying. I am led to think that this proceeding would prevent the design of the Almighty concerning you. . . . I think it would prevent in you the answering that great end of your call.

In the *first* place, your situation would become *local*. . . . In the *next* place, you may have the cares of a family; but you would not have that influence amongst numbers of your own sex.

I conceive you can only think of altering your state upon one ground,—and that is, "I am become obsolete! My work is done! I am shut out! I can do no more! I am called to give it up!" If you think so, I think differently. A number of places will yet receive you; and I think your way is more open this Conference than ever it has been.[44]

As Michael Fenwick had reminded her toward the outset of her ministry, "God himself has sent you, like the great Wesley, and the great Whitfield [*sic*]; namely, as a blessing to the nation."[45]

Mary's passionate desire to save souls, however, often led her to defy the conventions of the more conservative societies. Her revivalistic spirit and leveling sentiment created anxiety among some of the faithful members of the established chapels. Her opponents were quick to criticize what appeared to be the excesses of emotionalism which often swept through her spellbound congregations. Miss Monkhouse's perceptive account of the revival in her society reveals something of the latent tensions within many circuits:

We have had a Miss Mary Barritt in this circuit. . . . she has been made very useful in the hands of God at many places; indeed at Darlington, they attribute the great revival there chiefly to her instrumentality; and I believe, there might have been many more saved here, had not some of us been too prejudiced to suffer a woman to teach in public—too orderly to detain the people at the prayer-meetings, past such a time of night.[46]

The stage was set for an explosive confrontation.

THE RESTRICTION AND PROHIBITION OF WOMEN PREACHERS

In the summer of 1802 Joseph Entwisle wrote to his colleague Jonathan Edmondson concerning the situation in his new circuit at Macclesfield:

> We have *no female preachers* in this part of the country. I think women might with propriety exercise their gifts in a private way, or amongst their own sex; but I never could see the propriety of their being public teachers. Under the Patriarchal dispensation, the oldest male was the priest of the family. Under the Law, all the priests were men. The seventy preachers sent out by our Lord were all men. So were the twelve Apostles. Nor do we ever read of a woman preaching, in the Acts of the Apostles. Hence I conclude, women are not designed for public teachers.[47]

As Methodism entered into the nineteenth century, this conservative, restrictive attitude seemed to become increasingly dominant.

At the Dublin Conference for Irish Methodism, in July 1802, a serious debate took place on the question of women's preaching and even exhorting in public assemblies. Hostility to female preaching had become so strong, in spite of the overwhelming success of women such as Alice Cambridge and Anne Brown, that the Irish clergy took extreme and immediate action to suppress their activities:

> It is the judgment of the Conference, that it is contrary both to Scripture and prudence that women should preach, or should exhort in public: and we direct the Superintendent to refuse a Society Ticket to any woman in the Methodist Connexion who preaches, or who exhorts in any public congregation, unless she entirely cease from so doing.[48]

By this action Miss Cambridge was immediately excluded from the society and prohibited from utilizing any Methodist chapel or premises for her evangelistic services.[49] On July 29, 1802, Zechariah Taft informed his colleague Mary Barritt of this momentous decision:

> I was thankful to hear of your success in Grimsby Circuit— what would the *Irish Brethren* say to this—they have passed an act in their conference held the 2 of this month that no *Woman* should preach or exhort in public upon pain of *Excommunication*.[50]

Less than a month later, on August 17, 1802, Miss Barritt married this young suitor who was then emerging as Methodism's most vocal protagonist of the women preachers.[51] At the English Methodist Conference of this year, held at Bristol, George Sykes submitted his report on the Grimsby Circuit with the comment, "I left 530 members;—how many there are now, I cannot tell,—for Mary Barritt is knocking them down like rotten sticks."[52] A different life now awaited Mrs. Taft, however, as she traveled with her husband to Canterbury and then on to Dover where he had been stationed. On Saturday evening, September 18, Mary spoke at Dover, "for the first time, in a public place of worship."[53] She took as her text, "suffer me that I may speak; and after that I have spoken, mock on."

Word of the evangelistic successes of the couple soon spread throughout the district and several invitations were extended to Taft and his wife from the societies at Canterbury. On October 7, 1802, the *Kentish Herald* published a favorable report of Mrs. Mary Taft's labors in that cathedral city:

> On Monday evening, a sermon was preached in King-Street chapel, in this city, by Mrs. Taft, a female preacher, in the connexion of the late Rev. John Wesley. The novelty of a female preacher naturally excited great curiosity; many hundreds of persons were present, and others were prevented from getting in for want of room. The text of her discourse was from the first epistle of St. John, the first chapter, and the ninth verse—"If we confess our sins, he is faithful and just to

forgive us our sins, and to cleanse us from all unrighteous-ness"; which she supported with many judicious and well-grounded remarks; and being possessed with great fluency of speech, she attracted great attention from the whole of the congregation.[54]

Joseph Benson was outraged by these developments and wrote a caustic letter to Mary's husband expressing his displeasure. He claimed that the conference was ignorant about Taft's "taking a female to assist him in the ministry." He then added:

What the District Meeting or the Conference may say to you for deceiving them in this manner, I am not certain. . . . Mrs. Taft should decline ascending the pulpits of the chapels unless Mr. Sykes, Mr. Rogers, and you be *less sufficient* for your work than the Conference supposed you to be.[55]

George Sykes, who was the newly appointed superintendent, countered with a strong letter of defense:

We find two Mary Apostlesses to the Apostles. I have had a personal acquaintance with Mary Barritt for more than eight years. I *dare* not oppose her. . . . More than a year and a half ago, Mary Barritt was strongly pressed by our Hull friends to visit them; the elders of the Society sat in counsel . . . the conclusion was *not to admit her into the pulpit,* but allow her to stand by the little desk in the chapel. But after once hearing this ram's horn, prejudices fell down like the walls of Jericho, the pulpit-door gave way, and this King's daughter entered, the chapel could not contain the people, hundreds stood in the street. She then preached abroad to thousands, and solemn reverence sat on their countenances to the very skirts of the huge assembly.[56]

Ironically, on the same day that Benson sent his protest to Taft, the aged John Pawson wrote to the society at Dover, expressing his pleasure at the providence which stationed Mary among them. In this important letter, which helped pave the way for the realization of a female ministry in that circuit, Pawson explained how "the Lord is pleased to go out of his common way sometimes for the good of his poor creatures." "I have been no great friend to women preaching among us," he continued, "but when I evidently see that good is done, I dare not forbid them." He testified to the fact that God had blessed Mrs. Taft's labors and brought many souls to a saving knowledge of God through her preaching. In striking contrast to the attitude of his antagonistic colleague, he wrote:

> I would therefore advise you by no means oppose her preaching, but let her have full liberty, and try whether the Lord will not make her an instrument of reviving his work among you.[57]

Pawson wrote to the Tafts again at the beginning of the new year and expressed his regret concerning the storm that had arisen over their initial ministry in Kent. The storm having blow over, however, he encouraged them both to press on in hopes of spiritual renewal and growth in that place. He rejoiced to learn that the leaders at Dover had responded as they did to his intervention on Mary's belief:

> I am very glad that those good men at Dover were not offended with my letter, and much more so to find that the door was now opened wide for the partner of your life, to use the gifts which the Lord hath given her, for the enlargement of his kingdom. He will send by whom he will send, and it does not become us to say to the infinitely wise and blessed God,—"What doest thou?" but rather to rejoice when we have reason to believe that he doth good by the instrumentality of any one. An apostle could rejoice, even when Christ was preached out of envy and strife. I have long been convinced that the Lord takes such methods, and uses such instruments in reviving, increasing, and carrying on his work, as hath a direct tendency to hide pride from man, and so convince every one that this is the work of God,—so that no flesh may glory in his sight, but that he who glorieth, may glory in the Lord.[58]

The whole controversy surrounding her labors erupted once again, however, when the preachers gathered at Manchester for the Conference of 1803. When the question whether women should be permitted to preach among the

Methodists was posed, the conference responded with the following restrictive resolution:

> We are of the opinion that, in general, they ought not. 1. Because a vast majority of our people are opposed to it. 2. Because their preaching does not at all seem necessary, there being a sufficiency of Preachers, whom God has accredited, to supply all the places in our connexion with regular preaching. But if any woman among us think she has an extraordinary call from God to speak in public, (and we are sure it must be an *extraordinary* call that can authorize it,) we are of opinion she should, in general, address her *own sex*, and *those only*. And, upon this condition alone, should any woman be permitted to preach in any part of our connexion; and, when so permitted, it should be under the following regulations: 1. They shall not preach in the Circuit where they reside, until they have obtained the approbation of the Superintendant [*sic*] and a Quarterly Meeting. 2. Before they go into any other Circuit to preach, they shall have a *written* invitation from the Superintendant of such Circuit, and a recommendatory note from the Superintendant of their own Circuit.[59]

For all practical purposes, the women preachers had received the official condemnation of the Wesleyan Methodist leaders who were now in place to direct the course of the institution over the next half century. Women were formally forbidden from even functioning as public exhorters in Irish Methodism. And now, in England, they were restricted in their activities in such a way as to impede severely their influence within the hardening institution. After 1803 increasing numbers of aspiring women preachers found it necessary to sever their ties with the parent body of Methodism, finding sanction for their activities within the larger pale of the Methodist tradition, among the later Primitive Methodists and Bible Christians for instance.[60] Still others found a home within the Society of Friends.

Those devoted Wesleyans who chose to conform to the new regulations, and those who indulged in what was now "irregular preaching," found it increasingly difficult to assert their charismatic view of the ministry against the authoritarianism of the Wesleyan Methodist church. In spite of the fact that the Conference of 1804 was sore pressed for preachers and restored the shortage only by means of a benevolent press-gang, the leadership was resolute in the stand it had taken against the women. Shortly after the momentous Conference of 1803, Mary Taft's faithful supporter, William Bramwell expressed his regret over the decisive action of his ministerial colleagues:

> That rule should not have been submitted to. This I advised, and had all the friends stood firm, it would never have been made. But as it is made, and complied with, I would advise you to act according to it in every thing, whilst in the connexion. This is right,—whilst in the Body, to submit to all rules made by that Body.[61]

Within the Wesleyan Methodist church, the question of female preaching never became a live issue again until the twentieth century, and the conference was never pressed to change its mind until general cultural attitudes were changed.

THE LEGACY OF THE WOMEN PREACHERS OF EARLY METHODISM

The women preachers of early Methodism frequently defied powerful social and religious conventions. In their efforts to proclaim the gospel they rose above the backstage role commonly assigned to and accepted by women in the eighteenth century. After having been blown about by the winds of cultural change and ecclesiological reformulation within Wesleyan Methodism, the question of women preachers was supposedly laid to rest at the beginning of the nineteenth century. The rich legacy of the women preachers was to live on, however, only to be resurrected a century later. The factors which contributed to the empowerment of women in Methodism, the process of institutionalization which eventually led to their repression, and the fascinating biographies of the women themselves all combine in a unique way to reveal the nature of the Wesleyan revival and its leader.

As we have seen, the earlier experiences of sectarian women in the seventeenth century conditioned the way in which the activities of the Methodist women were perceived. The egalitarian impulse of the Wesleyan revival was founded upon certain principles held in common with a number of church renewal movements: the value of individual souls, the possibility of direct communion with God, the emphasis on the present activity of the Holy Spirit in the life of the believer, the importance placed upon shared Christian experience, the rights of conscience, and the Reformation doctrine of the priesthood of all believers. These notions all combined to create a theological environment conducive to the empowerment of women. Likewise, the influence of Susanna Wesley, the legacy of the Puritan heritage, the rediscovery of primitive Christianity, and Wesley's close relationship with Continental Pietism fostered a conviction within the founder of Methodism that no one, even a woman, ought to be prohibited from doing God's work.

Two factors in particular, however, combined to pave the way toward the full realization of a female ministry within Methodism during Wesley's lifetime. The first important factor was the theological dynamic of Wesley's basic program of reform. Wesley's goal was personal, religious experience and its power to transform both individuals and society, and he would utilize any method to accomplish this divine mission. Extraordinary situations demanded extraordinary actions, and while Wesley attempted to champion an authoritarian, institutional view of the Church, he formulated views of the Church and ministry that were charismatic and functional in their emphasis. While Wesley was raised in a highly chauvinistic Anglican tradition, he moved in a liberationist direction, first in practice and then in theory.[62]

His dynamic view of salvation and the Christian life, evoked by a gift of grace, tended to transcend sexual and social differences. His stress on charismatic leadership fostered a leveling sentiment among the Methodists which tended to undercut social stereotypes about the propriety of women functioning in this kind of a role. Viewing his movement as an extraordinary dispensation of God's grace, Wesley was led by the logic of events to embrace the ministry of exceptional women who were convinced of their calling, gifted for their work, and productive of abundant fruit. The phenomenon of women preachers, therefore, was a natural progression, a logical extension of the Wesleyan theology of religious experience.

Second, the Methodist societies provided an environment which was conducive to the empowerment of women who were called to a public ministry. The pioneering work of women in the nascent revival, their participation and leadership in the bands and classes, their activities among the sick and imprisoned, and the free expression of their experiences and feelings within the context of distinctively Methodist settings of worship all contributed to the later acceptance of their expanded public ministry within the movement. These various networks were an invaluable support system for women who sought to engage in activities reserved for men in a male-dominated world. It was only natural that intimate fellowship, prayer, and testimony should evolve into exhortation, scriptural exposition, and formal preaching.

And so, Wesley's evolving theology of the Church and ministry, the extraordinary nature of the revival, and the unique environment of the Methodist societies led to the acceptance and empowerment of women as "extraordinary messengers" of the evangelical revival. The lives and work of these women provide striking evidence that despite the social controls and religious conventions of the eighteenth century, many women managed to exert a substantial influence upon Methodism during its formative period.

It was not long after Wesley's death, however, that the phenomenon of institutionalization and its reversion to patriarchal patterns of leadership became evident within the life of the evolving Wesleyan Methodist church. This whole process was somewhat retarded during the eighteenth century because of Wesley's longevity. And the eventual transformation of the ethos of the movement was impeded by his authoritarian rule. A very different set of theological principles emerged, however, among the immediate successors of Wesley. And these principles were much less friendly to the egalitarian sentiments embraced by the founder. In place of an emphasis upon the freedom of the Holy Spirit to empower and revive, there was a stress on authority, ministerial discipline, and control within the Church. The socially transforming character of early Methodism was fundamentally altered.

In the place of a community ideal embodying the values of revivalism and democracy, there was an increasing tendency to urge conformity to societal expectations and to limit leadership to men. It is very evident, particularly in this period of institutional consolidation, that the conflicts which developed around the issue of female preaching were closely correlated with theological issues. And those values which had a tendency to encourage growth in the direction of sexual equality were increasingly set aside by the Wesleyans as they were embraced by offshoots of the parent body.

The women preachers of early Methodism came from every walk of life. Many were the wives of itinerant preachers, but others were single or widowed and employed in a variety of ways. While some had the privilege of a well-rounded education, others were barely literate; but they all sought to use the knowledge they had for the glory of God. While some enjoyed all the comforts of life, others struggled to survive in the brutal world of eighteenth-century Britain; but they all devoted the entirety of their resources to the work of the evangelical revival. While some of the women preached in the solitude of Cornish villages or on the trackless moors of Yorkshire, others proclaimed their message in the burgeoning cities of the industrial north; but they all sought out the people in need—the poor, the hungry, and the neglected. Their message was the same as Wesley and their male colleagues in the revival, namely, that of faith working by love leading to holiness of heart and life.[63]

Their message was one of urgency, of renewal, and of love. On one occasion, when Mary Fletcher was unable to fulfill a preaching obligation due to an illness late in her life, she summed up her evangel in a brief letter to be read at the society meeting:

> O that you would therefore do as Jacob did, be earnest with the Lord, that his love may fill your heart, as the Scripture expresses it, the love of God, shed abroad in your hearts by

the Holy Ghost, given unto you. If you get your hearts full of the love of God, you will find that is the oil by which the lamp of faith will be ever kept burning; love makes all our duty easy; a soul united as one spirit to the Lord, if temptation presents, has a ready answer; such a one instantly cries out, How shall I do this great wickedness, and sin against God? against Him in whom my soul delighteth? Pray, my friends, pray much for this love; and remember that word, "He that dwelleth in love dwelleth in God, and God in him!"[64]

In life and in death they offered the fullness of God's grace in Christ for all, and that is the richest legacy of the women preachers of early Methodism.

And I ask you also, true yokefellow, help these women, for they have labored side by side with me in the gospel together with Clement and the rest of my fellow workers, whose names are in the book of life. (Philippians 4:3).

NOTES

1. For a general survey of developments within Methodism during this period, consult Davies and Rupp, eds., *History of the Methodist Church,* vol. 2; John Kent, *The Age of Disunity* (London: Epworth Press, 1966); W. R. Ward, *Religion and Society in England, 1790–1850* (London: B. T. Batsford, 1972); Maldwyn Edwards, *After Wesley: A Study of the Social and Political Influences of Methodism in the Middle Period (1791–1849)* (London: Epworth Press, 1935), all of which may be supplemented by two important social histories: Wellman J. Warner, *The Wesleyan Movement in the Industrial Revolution* (London: Longmans, Green, 1930); and Robert F. Wearmouth, *Methodism and the Working-Class Movements of England, 1800–1860* (London: Epworth Press, 1957).
2. On the various dimensions of this schism, see John T. Wilkinson, "The Rise of Other Methodist Traditions," in *History of the Methodist Church,* ed. Davies and Rupp, pp. 280–94. Cf. two standard biographies of the founder, J. Blackwell, *The Life of the Rev. Alexander Kilham, formerly a preacher under the Rev. J. Wesley* (London: Darton and Harvey, 1838) and W. J. Townsend, *Alexander Kilham, the First Methodist Reformer* (London: Hamilton, Adams, 1889).

3. Wesleyan membership as recorded in the Conference *Minutes* grew during the decade from 58,318 to 90,619. Yorkshire, a county in which Methodism had always experienced great success, exemplifies the revivalistic atmosphere of the age. See John C. Hartley, "After Wesley: Expansion in Yorkshire Methodism, 1791–1800," *W.H.S., Yorkshire Branch* 36 (April 1980): 2–9.

4. See the important discussion of this transition in Baker, *John Wesley and the Church of England*, pp. 283–303.

5. The development of a doctrine of ministry within Methodism is discussed with great clarity and persuasiveness by John C. Bowmer, in *Pastor and People: A Study of Church and Ministry in Wesleyan Methodism from the Death of John Wesley (1791) to the Death of Jabez Bunting (1858)* (London: Epworth Press, 1975), a revised and abbreviated form of his Ph.D. thesis. Cf. the succinct presentation of his views in an article entitled "The Wesleyan Conception of the Ministry," *Religion in Life* 40, 1(Spring 1971): 85–96. This theme is also taken up by the historian John H. S. Kent in *Jabez Bunting, the Last Wesleyan: A Study in the Methodist Ministry after the Death of John Wesley* (London: Epworth Press, 1955), esp. pp. 7–16.

6. See Bowmer, *Pastor and People*, pp. 202–4.

7. See Ward, *Religion and Society in England*, particularly chap. 1–3.

8. The attitude of the Wesleyan hierarchy toward evangelists and unconventional, evangelical movements is reflected in the tightening of disciplinary controls related to the local preachers, such as the following restrictive rules enacted at the Conference of 1796: "Q. 22. What can be done to bring certain Local Preachers more fully to observe our discipline? A. 1. Let no one be permitted to preach, who will not meet in Class, and who is not regularly planned by the Superintendent of the Circuit where he resides. 2. Let no Local Preacher be allowed to preach in any other Circuit, without producing a recommendation from the Superintendent of the Circuit where he lives. . . . 3. Let no Local Preacher keep love-feasts without the appointment of the Superintendent" (*Minutes*, 11:344).

9. See Wesley's sermon, "The Ministerial Office," in *Works*, 7:273–81, with specific references to this term on pp. 277 and 280. Cf. pp. 78, 81, and 106 above.

10. Kent, *Age of Disunity*, p. 68; cf. Kent, *Jabez Bunting*, p. 39.

11. Benjamin Gregory, *Side Lights on the Conflicts of Meth-*

odism during the Second Quarter of the Nineteenth Century, 1827–1852 (London: Cassell, 1898), p. 83.

12. Margaret Batty has attempted to document some of the effects of this process: "The Methodist leaders tried to make Methodism respectable. Outspoken local preachers were expelled, those who tried to establish a means of mutual education and support were snubbed. Women preachers, who had become a joke to magazine editors, were banned. Any growth in new forms of religious expression, like camp meetings, was suppressed" ("Local Preaching in Wesleyanism in the Nineteenth Century," *W.H.S., N.E. Branch* 19 [April 1973]: 5). While all of these actions may certainly be documented with ease, it is also very easy to cast the Wesleyan ministers surreptitiously as the villains of this piece. This, however, is one of the stereotypes of early-nineteenth-century Methodism that is being qualified, if not revised, by the work of scholars such as Bowmer and Ward.

13. As the lines between the two schools became more sharply drawn in the early nineteenth century, reactions to the respectability and unadventurous evangelism of the establishment led to division. The offshoots, among which the Primitive Methodists, Bible Christians, and Arminian Methodists were prominent, embodied the "low" view of the church and ministry, and all employed women preachers to a large degree in their development and expansion. These "offshoots," which were concerned more with matters of evangelism and revivalism, are generally distinguished from the "secessions"—i.e., Methodist New Connection, Protestant Methodists, Wesleyan Methodist Association, and Wesleyan Reformers—which were schisms occasioned by constitutional issues. See the essay by John T. Wilkinson, "The Rise of Other Methodist Traditions," in *History of the Methodist Church*, ed. Davies and Rupp, 2:276–329; and Robert Currie, *Methodism Divided: A Study in the Sociology of Ecumenism* (London: Faber and Faber, 1968), as well as subsequent notes in this chapter.

14. Women such as Mary Fletcher, Sarah Crosby, and Sarah Lawrence continued their preaching throughout this period, but began to recede into the background as a new generation of women preachers took their place. On their continuing ministry, see in particular, Moore, *Fletcher,* pp. 268, 273–79, 283–86, 295–96, 307, 317–19, 324, 326–27, 334–39, 370–73, 375, 378, 386–90. Toward the close of Mrs. Fletcher's active ministry she reflected on the effects of one particular service:

"I thought what I had said was so short of what ought to have been spoken,—that all the next week I felt a deep conviction, that unless the Lord put words into my mouth, and gave power with them, no good would be done. I even feared that the Lord did not approve of my calling the people together, when there was no one but me to speak to them. Yet I knew well that 'all the good done upon the earth is the Lord's doing,' and that he can work by the meanest instrument. However, this was the conclusion, I must ask and wrestle for every meeting, public and private, and hang by faith on Christ alone, believing that word: 'It is not you that speak, but the Spirit of your Father which speaketh in you.' . . . I had great freedom, and I cannot tell how many have since praised God for the blessing brought into their souls that night" (pp. 338–39). See Appendix A for further details on the closing years of these women.

15. Bramwell, *Account of Ann Cutler*, p. 15. See Appendix A for biographical details and sources related to her life and work. For the revival at Dewsbury, see Robinson, *Methodism in Dewsbury*, pp. 80–85.

16. From Dewsbury her evangelistic crusades took her through the Greatland, Birstal, Leeds, Bradford, and Otley circuits. The following portion of a letter to her friend in Leeds, dated December 8, 1794, from Derby, reveals the extent of her final itinerary and the great revival which followed in her wake: "I have seen many souls convinced and converted to God. I was above a week in Oldham circuit. We believed there were near a hundred souls brought to God. I have been above a fortnight at Manchester . . . in Leek circuit. . . . in Derby circuit. In this week above forty souls were set at liberty: some cleansed of sin. . . . I am going for Macclesfield. They have sent for me. I have had a very happy time in my own soul" (ibid., pp. 19–20). Ann died in Macclesfield and was buried at Christ Church, where her epitaph reads: "Underneath lies the remains of Ann Cutler, Whose simple manners, solid piety, and extraordinary power in prayer, distinguished and rendered her eminently useful in promoting a religious revival wherever she came. She was born near Preston, in Lancashire, and died here December 29th, 1794, AE. 35." Bramwell preached a funeral sermon for his faithful coadjutor at Kirskstall Forge on February 11, 1795, based upon 1 Corinthians 1:27–29. See Sigston, *Memoirs of William Bramwell*, 2:164.

17. Taft, *Original Letters*, p. 66. Kirkstall-Forge, June 20, 1790. She reported her modest labors to Zechariah Taft in a letter

dated February 11, 1825, from Whitby: "I have studiously avoided speaking of my poor labours in the work of the Lord, the reason of this is—I have done so little, that it is not worth a name or place among those holy and useful females, who have *laboured much in the Lord*. . . . My method, as you know, was to give a word of exhortation after my dear husband had finished his sermon" (Taft, *Holy Women,* 1:127–28).

18. Taft reports that "her manner of address is very pleasing; her voice melodious; her views of scripture truth clear; and her ministrations are often attended with much of the divine unction and power" (Taft, *Holy Women,* 2:226).

19. "Her talents for preaching were very good," says Taft, "and her sermons not only showed that she had received a good education, but that she was in possession of that salvation which she recommended to others. She was well acquainted with the scriptures, in the constant reading of which she took great delight; and to which she would refer at all times in support of her arguments with the greatest propriety; but keeping principally in view the essential doctrines of Christian religion. On one occasion she received a very unkind letter relative to her public work; upon reading it she retired—like good Hezikiah, and laid it before the Lord—from whom she received an assurance of his approbation" (ibid., p. 190). Cf. Taft, *Memoirs,* p. 114.

20. Mr. Marshland, who was also received into full connection at that conference in Leeds, had been awakened under the ministry of Mrs. Taft, at Birstal. In 1797 Mr. Stevens wrote to Mr. Carlill concerning his wife and explained that "she does not yet presume to mount the Rostrum, but gives a word of exhortation in company and in class, which I presume you will tolerate!!" (November 3, 1797, Egglescliff, Taft, *Original Letters,* p. 134). Like Mrs. Wiltshaw, she frequently supplied her husband's place in the circuit when he was incapable of exercising his public functions.

21. Taft, *Holy Women,* 1:70–74. She sought the counsel of Mary Harrison, who is mentioned above.

22. Quoted from her journal in Taft, *Holy Women,* 2:197. Apparently, the first time that she spoke from a text was at Nottingham when she preached to some 2,000 persons from "be ye clean that bear the vessels of the Lord" (p. 198). For further details concerning Miss Eland, afterward Mrs. De Putron, see Appendix A.

23. Taft, *Holy Women,* 1:76–79.

24. Ibid., 2:178–81; cf. Taft, *Memoirs,* pp. 114–15.
25. Ibid., 1:202–3. Taft testifies that "there was scarcely ever a love-feast held in her neighbourhood in which several did not stand forth and acknowledge her as the instrumental cause of their conversion" (p. 202).
26. Frank Young, "Houghton-Le-Spring," *W.H.S.* 16, 3–4 (September-December 1927): 74. This register also records three instances of Mary Taft's preaching in October 1816 at Shiney Row and Chatershough.
27. She had come under the influence of Quakers early in life and emulated them in many ways. See the account of her activities as remembered by her son, in Richard Treffrey [*sic*], Jun., *Memoirs of Mrs. Jane Treffrey* (London: Published by John Mason, 1830), pp. 68–71. Some women preachers of this period had their start in the Methodist societies but extended their influence into other Christian bodies. See, for example, the work of Dorothy Ripley of Whitby who became an unaffiliated itinerant evangelist. In 1801 she felt called to labor among the Negro slaves in America, secured an interview with President Jefferson to discuss the issue of slaveholding, and in 1806 received his permission to preach before Congress. See Appendix A for biographical and bibliographical data. Likewise, see the biographical outline of Hannah Kilham, second wife of the Methodist secessionist, who also joined the Quakers and was eminent as a preacher among them, in the same Appendix.
28. According to John Ward, thousands flocked to hear her and many professed their conversions through her instrumentality. See *Historical Sketches of the Rise and Progress of Methodism in Bingley* (Bingley: John Harrison and Son, 1863), p. 46.
29. See pp. 192–96 above, as well as Appendix A.
30. Quoted in Zechariah Taft, "Some Account of Elizabeth Dickinson," in Bramwell, *Account of Ann Cutler,* p. 32. One of her brothers, John Dickinson, seemed to make light of her revelations until she told him of some circumstance in his private life unknown to anyone else. He was convinced of the authenticity of her experience by this inexplicable occurrence and afterward became the "first *seal* God gave to her mission."
31. Only the barest outline of her extensive labors can be afforded here. A definitive biography of this influential preacher remains a desideratum despite a number of studies which recount the story of her early career. See Appendix A for a

biographical outline and survey of pertinent primary and secondary materials.

32. A second edition of this work was considerably enlarged in 1828, and a third part added to this two-part volume in 1831, which extended her life story to the year 1827. These two volumes were bound together in one volume in the possession of Dr. Frank Baker, which volume has been cited throughout.

33. Taft, *Memoirs,* 1: vi.

34. Ibid., p. 30. Note the similarity to Susanna Wesley's words of advice to her son concerning the ministry of Thomas Maxfield, Wesley's first "son in the gospel."

35. See Appendix F for a selected list of such invitations. Wherever Mary traveled she was scrupulous in observing the regulations of the conference and in respecting the authority of superintendent ministers. "It has always been a rule with me," she wrote, "never to go to any place to labour, without a previous invitation from the travelling preacher, as well as the friends of the circuit I visit. As a member of the Methodist Connexion, I conceived this to be my bounden duty; . . . I do not know that I have ever deviated from this rule, excepting in a few instances, when I have been so sensible of its being my duty, and the will of God, for me to go, that I durst not at the peril of my soul neglect going" (Taft, *Memoirs,* 1:viii-ix). During the fall of 1798 she wrote: "Mr. James Wood, the superintendent preacher, makes my appointments, and I feel led to act according to his direction" (ibid., pp. 102–3). Cf. his letter to her of July 21, 1798, in Appendix F.

36. See *Arm. Mag.* 13 (1795): 473–79; cf. Taft, *Memoirs,* 1:38.

37. Taft, *Memoirs,* 1:111.

38. Ibid., p. 163. Mary's influence in the north of England is incalculable. Wherever she went, she experienced similar success. At Aysgarth her ministrations led to the conversion of Ann Thompson who thereafter followed in Mary's footsteps as a noted preacher in the Yorkshire Dales. See ibid., p. 55; John Ward, *Methodism in Swaledale and the Neighbourhood* (Bingley: Harrison and Son, 1865), pp. 62–64; and Appendix A. Cf. p. 102 above.

39. Ibid., p. 64.

40. Ibid., pp. 86–87. Indeed, Mary possessed a wide-ranging knowledge of the Bible and based her preaching on a wide variety of biblical materials. See a representative selection of these texts in Appendix H. Slanderous rumors about her were

reported by John Braithwaite in the letter of April 11, 1795, which reads in part: "Floods of reproach and approbrious epithets are heaped upon her, and she suffers with magnanimity and seeming indifference; . . . Some say, 'She has been married and has run away from her husband and children,' and others again affirm, 'She is a man in woman's clothes.' Her strong rough voice, brawny arms, and masculine appearance, increase the number of those who favour the last hypothesis" (quoted in Robert Dickinson, *The Life and Labours of the Rev. John Braithwaite* [London: Printed for John Broadbent, 1825], pp. 242–43).

41. See the manuscript record of Mrs. Waites's conversion in J. Ward, *Methodism in the Thirsk Circuit* (Thirsk: David Peat, 1860), 29–30. Cf. Gordon Rupp, *Thomas Jackson: Methodist Patriarch* (London: Epworth Press, 1954), p. 11; Swift, "Women Itinerant Preachers," p. 91; Dr. Waller, "A Famous Lady Preacher," *Wes. Meth. Mag.* 130 (1907): 538–44. For a description of her "methodical preaching," see Thomas Jackson's account in Hellier, "Some Methodist Women Preachers," p. 67.

42. See Appendix G for a sampling of supportive letters.

43. Taft, *Memoirs*, 2:11–12. It is very probable that the woman preacher under whom he was converted was Mrs. Sarah Crosby.

44. Sigston, *Memoir of William Bramwell*, pp. 206–7.

45. Letter of March 10, 1796, Cold-kirby, *Arm. Mag. (B.C.)* 3, 12(December 1824): 431. In words reminiscent of John Wesley, he advised her with regard to her pulpit style: "Preach within yourself, and beware of extraordinary exertions; provided this is attended unto, you will last the longer. Never strain your voice. Never keep your congregation too long. Never sit up too long. Never converse too long. In all things watch and pray, so shall you in all things gain ground."

46. Miss Monkhouse to Mrs. Holder, June 28, 1794, Bouse, Taft, *Original Letters*, p. 103.

47. Entwistle [*sic*], *Memoir of the Rev. Joseph Entwistle, Fifty-four Years a Wesleyan Minister* (Bristol: Printed and sold for the author, 1848), p. 231.

48. *Minutes, Ireland*, p. 152. Nightingale claims to have been informed "that this motion was carried by a very small majority" (*Portraiture of Methodism*, p. 455).

49. Alice continued in her work, was readmitted as a member of the Methodist Society by a special resolution of the conference

in 1811, devoted herself entirely to a ministry of evangelism after 1813, and appears to have had her greatest success in the north of Ireland where she preached to enormous crowds of eight to ten thousand persons. See Crookshank, *History of Methodism in Ireland,* 2:400; 3:78–79; and *Memorable Women,* pp. 198–203. Crookshank provides no supporting documentation for these claims however. Cf. William Smith, *A Consecutive History of Wesleyan Methodism in Ireland* (Dublin: T. W. Doolittle, 1830), pp. 85–86.

50. MS Letter, Meth. Arch.
51. Taft published his views on the validity of female preaching in several tracts later in the nineteenth century. These include *Thoughts on Female Preaching* (Dover: Printed for the author, 1803); *A Reply to an Article Inserted in the Methodist Magazine, for April 1809, Entitled Thoughts on Women's Preaching, Extracted from Dr. James M'Knight* (Leeds: Printed at the Bible-Office, by G. Wilson, 1809); *Scripture Doctrine of Women's Preaching* (1809); and "Thoughts on a Proper Call to the Christian Ministry," *Arm. Mag. (B.C.)* 5, 2(February 1826): 42–48. *Holy Women* (1825, 1828), as we have seen throughout, provided biographical sketches of women preachers within the Methodist and other traditions.
52. Taft, *Memoirs,* 2:39. Her success among the people of Grimsby was very great, with a large number added to the society.
53. Ibid., p. 48.
54. Cf. ibid., pp. 49–50.
55. Joseph Benson to Z. Taft, October 25, 1802, Meth. Arch. Cf. Helliers, "Some Methodist Women Preachers," p. 67.
56. George Sykes to Joseph Benson, [October 1802], Dover, Meth. Arch.
57. October 25, 1802, Bristol, Meth. Arch. This letter, the postscript of J. S. Pipe supporting Pawson's views, and the letter of George Sykes to Mary Taft, which provides some additional details regarding this debate, are included in Appendix G. Apparently, sometime during the course of this extended controversy, Mary Taft preached before the conference by request of several senior members. Dr. Adam Clarke is reported to have patted her on the back as she descended from the pulpit and said, "Well done, Mary; go on with your preaching, and the Lord will own and bless your efforts" (cited in Taylor, *Apostles of Fylde Methodism,* p. 59). This particular hagiographical detail, however, requires more thorough examination and research.

58. Taft, *Memoirs,* 2:77–79; cf. *Arm. Mag. (B.C.)* 4, 1 (January 1825): 34–36.
59. *Minutes,* 2:188–89. Cf. Swift, "Women Itinerant Preachers," p. 90; Philip Garrett, *A Digest of the Methodist Conferences* (Halifax: Printed by Thomas Walker, 1827), pp. 96–97; Samuel Warren, *A Digest of the Laws and Regulations of the Wesleyan Methodists* (London: Published by John Stephens, 1835), p. 178. This regulation remained in effect until it was revised in 1910 by the deletion of the words restricting the preaching of women to their own sex, and by a proviso restricting such activities to areas where there was little or no opposition. This then was the official position of Wesleyan Methodism until the Methodist Union of 1932. Church, in his *More about Early Methodist People,* pp. 137, 172, claimed that the conference expressed its strong disapproval of "female preaching" in 1835 and considered this date to be something of a terminus ad quem for the whole question of women's ministry in early Wesleyan Methodism. It is very possible that Church was simply reflecting the unsubstantiated statement in one of the standard histories of Methodism which he nearly reproduced verbatim. See W. J. Townsend, H. B. Workman, and George Eayers, eds., *A New History of Methodism,* 2 vols. (London: Hodder and Stoughton, 1909), 1:413. There is absolutely no evidence that the issue of female preaching was even raised at the Conference of 1835, as a close examination of the daily proceedings and the journals of prominent participants reveals. See *The Watchman: A Weekly Journal, of News, Politics, Religion, and Literature, for the Year 1835* (London: Published by William Gawtress, 1835). The matter was raised, however, in 1832 with regard to the Derby Faith Folk and the Arminian Methodists of whom the famed Elizabeth Evans was a shining light, but no formal action was taken on the part of the conference. Church may have been referring to this conference or even the action of the conference of 1803, mistakenly assigning a date of 1835 to the prohibition. See Gregory, *Side Lights on Conflicts,* pp. 127–28; Church, *More about Early Methodist People,* pp. 159–63; Stevens, *Women of Methodism,* pp. 129–34; and Valentine Cunningham, *Everywhere Spoken Against: Dissent in the Victorian Novel* (Oxford: Clarendon Press, 1975), pp. 143–71.
60. See Swift, "Women Itinerant Preachers," pp. 76–83, for a judicious summary of developments in these traditions. For the pioneering work of female preachers in Primitive Meth-

odism, see in particular, Joseph Ritson, "Of Its Women Preachers," in *The Romance of Primitive Methodism* (London: Edwin Dalton, Primitive Methodist Publishing House, 1909), pp. 133–59; H. B. Kendall, *The Origin and History of the Primitive Methodist Church*, 2 vols. (London: Edwin Dalton, n.d.), 1:142–46, 176–78, 194–95, 202–8, 232–33, 370–71, 402–3; John Petty, *The History of the Primitive Methodist Connexion from Its Origin to the Conference of 1860*, 2d ed., revised and enlarged (London: Published by R. Davies, Conference Offices, 1864), passim; B. Aquila Barber, "A Group of Noble Women," in *A Methodist Pageant: A Souvenir of the Primitive Methodist Church* (London: Holborn Publishing House, 1932), pp. 101–14. For an excellent sketch of the life and work of Sarah Kirkland, the first woman traveling preacher in Primitive Methodism, see George Herod, *Biographical Sketches of Some of Those Preachers Whose Labours Contributed to the Origination and Early Extension of the Primitive Methodist Connexion* (London: Published by T. King, n.d.), pp. 305–36. At the originating conference of the Bible Christians in 1819, fourteen of the itinerant preachers were women. For the work of Mary Ann Werrey, Mary Toms, and Catherine O'Bryan, among others, see F. W. Bourne, *The Bible Christians: Their Origin and History (1815-1900)* (London: Bible Christian Book Room, 1905), pp. 119–45; Richard Pyke, *The Early Bible Christians* (London: Epworth Press, 1941), pp. 26–30; and Richard Pyke, *The Golden Chain: The Story of the Bible Christian Methodists from the Formation of the First Society in 1815 to the Union of the Denomination in 1907 with the Methodist New Connexion and the United Methodist Free Churches in Forming—The United Methodist Church* (London: Henry Hooks, n.d.), pp. 41–57. Cf. Oliver A. Beckerlegge, "Women Itinerant Preachers," *W.H.S.* 30, 8(December 1956): 182–84; and Olive Anderson, "Women Preachers in Mid-Victorian Britain: Some Reflexions on Feminism, Popular Religion and Social Change," *Historical Journal* 12, 3(1969): 467–84.

61. Sigston, *Memoir of William Bramwell*, 2:214–15.
62. Wesley's intellectual pilgrimage is not dissimilar from that of a contemporary Episcopalian priest with regard to the ordination of women to the priesthood. "Ten years ago," he writes, "the idea was repugnant to me and I know the reasons why. Five years ago the idea was still repugnant to me, but my reasons no longer 'held water.' I was thinking differently. Now

my feelings have followed good reasons for the ordination of women to the priesthood" (Urban T. Holmes, *Ministry and Imagination* [New York: Seabury Press, 1976], p. 215).

63. See some accounts of their evangelical preaching in John Hodson, *A Widow Indeed. A Sermon Occasioned by the Lamented Death of Mrs. Fletcher* (Wednesbury: Printed and sold by J. Booth, 1816), pp. 44–46 in particular; and Treffrey, *Memoir of Jane Treffrey,* pp. 68–71. Cf. Appendix H for a list of all the known texts of the early women preachers.

64. Quoted in Mary Tooth, *A Letter to the Loving and Beloved People of the Parish of Madeley* (Shiffnal: Printed by A. Edmonds, n.d.), pp. 17–18.

APPENDIX A: BIOGRAPHICAL OUTLINES OF METHODIST WOMEN PREACHERS

T HIS APPENDIX IS INTENDED to be a research tool for further study in the area of the women preachers of early Methodism. While data concerning some of these women are readily available to the researcher, basic biographical detail is completely lacking in the case of others. The research required to recover the facts about the women of early Methodism is often difficult and tedious, but the work must be done in order to reclaim this important legacy.

Material related to the women preachers is arranged in the following manner:

NAME

A. Pertinent Biographical Details
B. Publications (if any)
C. Primary Sources
D. Secondary Sources

While every effort has been made to be as comprehensive as possible, many lacunae remain to be filled.

BISSON, JEANNIE (*afterward* MRS. COCK)

A. Member of the Methodist Society, St. Heliers, Jersey.

C. Charles Pollard, "John Wesley and Robert Carr
Brackenbury" *W.H.S.* 28:68–69.

Wesley *Journal* 7:317D, 318D, 319, 456D; letters
noted, 7:306, 325, 348, 356, 390, 439, 458, 484,
524; 8:22, 42, 69, 81, 112.

D. Tyerman, *Life of Wesley,* 3.599–600, 609–10.

BROWN, MRS. ANNE (NEE DEVLIN)

A. 1750   Born at Fermanagh, Ireland; raised Roman
        Catholic.

    1772   Awakened under preaching of James Perfect
        in Enniskillen Circuit.

    1782   M. Rev. George Brown, itinerant preacher.

    1808   July 8, died at Monaghan.

D. Church, *More about Early Methodist People,* p. 174.

Crookshank, *History of Methodism in Ireland,* 2:201,
229–30.

Crookshank, *Memorable Women,* pp. 94–103.

CAMBRIDGE, ALICE

A. 1762   January 1, born at Bandon, Ireland.

   1778–79?   Moved by preaching of William Myles,
             itinerant preacher stationed at Cork.

   1780   Death of her mother.
             Joined the Methodist Society.

   1798   Instrumental in revival at Charles Fort.

   1802   Expelled from Methodist Society by ac-
             tion of Irish Methodist Conference.

   1811   Readmitted to membership by special
             resolution of conference.

   1813   Devoted herself entirely to work of
             itinerant evangelist.

   1815   First visit to Northern Ireland; great
             success.

   1825   Led revival at Nenagh.

   1829   January 1, died.

C. MS Memoirs, location unknown.

Taft, *Holy Women*, 1:269–70.
Tyerman, *Life of Wesley*, 3:645.
Wesley, *Journal*, 7:494D; 8:124n.
Wesley, *Letters*, 8:258–59.
D. Church, *More about Early Methodist People*, pp. 21, 173–74.
Crookshank, *History of Methodism in Ireland*, 1:353–54; 2:30–31, 153, 229–30, 332, 400; 3:78–79.
Crookshank, *Memorable Women*, pp. 191–203.
Robert H. Gallagher, *Pioneer Preachers of Irish Methodism* (Belfast: Nelson and Knox [N.I.], 1965), pp. 37, 157.
Garlow, "John Wesley's Understanding of Laity," p. 98.
Lawson, *John Wesley and Christian Ministry*, pp. 180–81.
O'Malley, *Women in Subjection*, p. 133.
Stevenson, *City Road Chapel*, p. 109.

COX, SARAH

A. 1773　March 6, born at Wishall, near Nottingham.
Awakened under preaching of James Bogie.
Deeply affected by preaching of John Leppington.
Preached throughout Leicestershire and Nottinghamshire; colleague of Mary Harrison.
　1808　Desisted from preaching for health reasons.
C. Taft, *Holy Women*, 1:70–76.

CROSBY, MRS. SARAH

A. 1729　November 7, born.
　1749　October 29, converted.
　1750　February, heard John Wesley preach.
October, interviewed by Wesley, received membership ticket, and joined Society.
　1757　February 2, deserted by her husband.

May, met Mary Bosanquet.

1761 January 7, accompanied Mrs. Dobinson to Derby.

February 1, held class meeting.

February 8, "preached" to enlarged class of 200.

February 14, wrote to Wesley seeking advice.

April, returned to London.

1763 March 24, moved to orphanage with Mary Bosanquet and Sarah Ryan at Leytonstone.

1768 June 7, left London for Yorkshire with Mary and Sarah and settled at Cross Hall.

1769 March 18, important letter from John Wesley concerning her preaching.

1772 July, traveled with Wesley and Elizabeth Hurrell in Yorkshire.

1804 October 29, died at Leeds.

C. "Account of Mrs. Crosby," *Meth. Mag.* 29:418–23, 465–73, 517–21, 563–68, 610–17.

Arm. Mag. 2:300–301, 304–8.

Bramwell, *Account of Ann Cutler,* pp. 47–48.

Agnes Bulmer, ed., *Memoirs of Mrs. Elizabeth Mortimer: With Selections from Her Correspondence,* 2d ed. (London: J. Mason, 1836), pp. 136, 190–91.

Everett, *Methodism in Sheffield,* pp. 153–54.

Moore, *Fletcher,* pp. 27–29, 30, 69, passim.

MS Letterbook, Duke University.

MS Letters, Meth. Arch.

Sarah Crosby Papers, Perkins Library, Duke University.

Seckerson, "Account of Mrs. Dobinson," pp. 558–60.

Sutcliffe, *Experience of Frances Pawson,* pp. 27, 32–33, 54, 62, 84, 96–98, 104–5.

Taft, *Holy Women,* 1:vi, 104, 114, 127, 2:23–115.

Taft, *Original Letters,* pp. 62–71.

Taft, *Scripture Doctrine,* pp. 18–24.

Wesley: Autograph Letters and Manuscripts, ff. 46–65.

Wesley, *Journal*, 4:243n, 525n; 5:54n, 306n, 376n, 418n; 7:521D; letters noted, 4:220, 434; 5:206, 306; 6:278; 7:30.

Wesley, *Letters*, 3:216–17; 4:132–33; 5:46, 130–31, 257–58; 6:184–85, 192, 290–91; 6:329, 331, 383; 8:105.

Wesley, *Oxford Edition*, 25:86.

W.H.S. 5:241; 8:166, 196; 10:70; 15:48; 19:173–74; 21:122; 28:161.

Taft reported that Mrs. Crosby "left behind her three or four books in manuscript, each of them containing two or three hundred closely written pages; . . . it evidently appears that she intended them for publication. After the death of Mrs. Crosby, these journals fell into the hands of her intimate friend and companion, Mrs. Tripp, and from thence to Mrs. Mortimer, who had made a few extracts for the Methodist Magazine, but she did this very sparingly. . . . Having obtained the loan of part of these journals I have made some very considerable extract of this Memoir" (*Holy Women*, 1:23–24). These manuscripts must be extant, but their location is unknown. No fewer than 24 of John Wesley's letters to her are extant, the earliest letter dated June 14, 1757. The full text of these letters, now available only in Wesley, *Letters*, (21 letters), *W.H.S.* 19:173–74 (1 letter), and Crosby, MS Letterbook (2 letters), will appear in Wesley, *Bicentennial Edition*, vols. 27ff.

D. Frank Baker, *A Charge to Keep: An Introduction to the People Called Methodists* (London: Epworth Press, 1947), p. 136.

Baker, *John Wesley and the Church of England*, pp. 203–4, 381.

Baker, "John Wesley and Sarah Crosby," pp. 76–82.

Brown, "Standing in the Shadow," pp. 26–28.

Brown, "Women in Church History," pp. 129–30.

Brown, "Women of the Word," pp. 69–87.

J. M. Buckley, "What Methodism Owes to Women," in *Proceedings, Sermons, Essays, and Addresses of the Centennial Methodist Conference,* ed. H. K. Carroll (Cincinnati: Cranston and Stowe, 1885), pp. 305–6.

Church, *Early Methodist People,* p. 34.

Church, *More about Early Methodist People,* pp. 139, 149–54, 159.

J. Edward Cooper, " 'Dinah Morris' and 'Seth Bede,' and the Early Days of Derby Methodism," *Methodist Recorder Winter Number* 37 (Christmas 1896): 35.

Crookshank, *Memorable Women,* p. 192.

Cunningham, *Everywhere Spoken Against,* p. 158.

Edwards, *My Dear Sister,* pp. 91–94.

Fletcher, "Derby," pp. 109–12.

Garlow, "John Wesley's Understanding of Laity," pp. 97–100.

Gregory, *History of Methodism,* 1:311.

Harmon, *Encyclopedia,* 1:607.

Harrison, "Early Woman Preacher," pp. 104–9.

Harrison, "New Light on Methodism in the Isle of Man," *W.H.S.* 19, 8 (December 1934): 198.

Hellier, "Mother Chapel of Leeds," pp. 64–65.

Hellier, "Some Methodist Women Preachers," pp. 65–66.

Hurst, *History of Methodism,* 2:899–902.

Lawson, *John Wesley and Christian Ministry,* pp. 176–77, 179.

Lyth, *Methodism in York,* p. 71.

Morrow, *Early Methodist Women,* pp. 7, 9–26, 46, 54, 81.

O'Malley, *Women in Subjection,* p. 132.

Ruether, *Women of Spirit,* p. 228.

Theodore Runyon, ed., *Sanctification and Liberation Theologies in Light of the Wesleyan Tradition* (Nashville: Abingdon Press, 1981), p. 166.

Schmidt, *John Wesley,* 3:142–46, 165.

Simon, *John Wesley: The Master Builder,* pp. 292–94.

Smith, *History of Methodism,* 1:420–21; 2:388.

Stevens, *History of Methodism,* 2:207.

Stevens, *Women of Methodism,* pp. 79–87.

Swift, "Women Itinerant Preachers," p. 89.
Townsend, *New History of Methodism,* 1:321.
Tyerman, *Life of Wesley,* 2:286, 289, 398–99, 436–
37, 565; 3:41, 68–69.
Tyerman, *Wesley's Designated Successor,* pp. 28, 33,
400, 467, 473.

CROSS, MRS. ALICE

A. 1709   Born, Cheshire.
           M. John Cross (d. February 28, 1795).
  1744   Moved to Booth-Bank.
           Pioneered Methodism, starting a Methodist
           Society in home.
  1752   Probably hosted first Quarterly Meeting in
           Cheshire.
  1774   May 29, died at home in Booth-Bank.
C. Everett, *Methodism in Manchester,* pp. 63–66.
  Swift, "Methodism in Northwich," pp. 39–40.
  Wesley, *Journal,* 3:296n; 4:59n.
  Wes. Meth. Mag. 66:26–28, 376–82.
D. Buckley, "What Methodism Owes to Women," p.
  306.
  Rose, *Methodism in Cheshire,* p. 33.
  Tyerman, *Life of Wesley,* 1:546–47.
  W.H.S. 7:78–81.

CUTLER, ANN ("PRAYING NANNY")

A. 1759   Born at Thornley, near Preston.
  1785   First experienced forgiveness of sins.
  1792   Instrumental in reviving Methodism in
              Dewsbury in conjunction with the work
              of William Bramwell.
  1793–94 Traveled extensively throughout the north
              of England on evangelistic missions.
  1794   December 29, died at Macclesfield; bur-
              ied in Christ Church yard.

C. Bramwell, *Account of Ann Cutler.*

Thomas Harris, *The Christian Minister in Earnest: Exemplified in a Memoir of the Rev. William Bramwell,* 2d ed. (London: Sold by John Mason, 1847), pp. 41–42.

Sigston, *Memoir of William Bramwell,* 1:41, 74–75, 153; 2:19–20, 164–65.

Taft, *Holy Women,* 1:301–24.

Wesley, *Journal,* letter noted, 8:60n.

Wesley, *Letters,* 8:214–15.

D. Brown, "Women of the Word," pp. 72, 81.

Church, *More about Early Methodist People,* pp. 140, 155–56.

Dyson, *Methodism in Leek,* p. 34.

Hellier, "Some Methodist Women Preachers," pp. 68–69.

Pilkington, *Methodism in Preston,* p. 25.

Robinson, *Methodism in Dewsbury,* p. 80.

Smith, *History of Methodism,* 2:225–26.

Smith, *Methodism in Macclesfield,* pp. 222–23.

Stevens, *History of Methodism,* 3:83–84.

Taylor, *Apostles of Fylde Methodism,* pp. 33, 57–67, 131.

Townsend, *New History of Methodism,* 1:321–22.

Tyerman, *Life of Wesley,* 3:606.

Waller, "Famous Female Preacher," p. 539.

Wearmouth, *Methodism and Common People,* p. 228.

DAVIDSON, MARGARET

A. Born at Ballybredagh, Killinchy, Ireland.

1758	Converted under preaching of James Oddie.
1766–67	Moved to Lisburn.
1776	First experience at preaching at Dunsford, under the direction of Rev. Edward Smyth.

The first woman preacher of Irish Methodism.

Totally blind from birth.

C. Smyth, *Experience of Margaret Davidson.*
Wesley, *Journal,* 5:113n.
D. Church, *More about Early Methodist People,* p. 173.
Crookshank, *History of Methodism in Ireland,* 1:124,
151, 182–83, 188–89, 231, 301–2.
Crookshank, *Memorable Women,* pp. 63–72.

DICKINSON, ELIZABETH

A. 1773   Born at Staveley, near Knaresborough.
1792–93 Experienced seizures or trances in which
she preached.
1793   Is reported to have preached to thousands in and around Leeds.
Instrumental in the conversion of Wel-
bourne, an itinerant preacher.
1793   June 17, died suddenly at the age of 20.
C. Taft, *Account of Elizabeth Dickinson.*
Taft, *Holy Women,* 1:181–86.
D. Hellier, "Some Methodist Women Preachers," p. 67.
Ward, *Methodism in Bingley,* p. 46.

ELAND, SARAH (*afterward* MRS. DE PUTRON)

A. Born at Hutton, near Stokesley, Yorkshire.
One of eleven children in a Methodist home.
1802   January 1, converted under the preaching
of Warrener in a Methodist covenant service.
1802–3 First preached in Nottingham.
Became associated with the Leeds Revivalists, Ann Carr and Martha Williams.
1824   M. Rev. John De Putron, Wesleyan
Methodist missionary to America.
Moved to Guernsey.
1825   Moved to Jersey.
C. Taft, *Holy Women,* 2:194–200.
Martha Williams, *Memoirs of the Life and Character*

of Ann Carr (Leeds: Sold by H. W. Walker, 1841), pp. 65–71.

D. Hellier, "Some Methodist Women Preachers," p. 67.

FLETCHER, MRS. MARY (NEE BOSANQUET)

A. 1739   September 1, born at Leytonstone, Essex.

    1746   Impressed by Methodist servant girl.
Influenced in her childhood by the writings of Mrs. Lefevre.

    1757   Summer, became closely related to the Foundery Society in London.

    1762   Left home and moved to Hoxton Square where she began her benevolent work.
Experienced "evangelical conversion" during the prayer of Joseph Guildford.
Joined in her work by Mrs. Sarah Ryan who had vacated her post as housekeeper at Kingswood.

    1763   March 24, moved to "The Cedars," Leytonstone.
Established an orphanage and school on the Kingswood prototype.
Ann Tripp secured as governess for children.
Began public services of worship on Thursday evenings.

    1768   June 7, moved to Yorkshire with entire family including Sarah Ryan and Sarah Crosby.

    1768   August, purchased Cross Hall farm, near Morley and Leeds.

    1768   August 17, Sarah Ryan died.

    1771   June, important letter from Mary to John Wesley defending the preaching of women.

    1771   June 13, Wesley's reply defining the "extraordinary call" which she possessed.

    1773   February 2, first explicit reference to a sermon text utilized by a Methodist woman preacher.
Preached throughout the north of England,

making some excursions to Bristol and London.

1776   September 17, famous account of her preaching at Goker and Huddersfield.

1781   November 12, m. Rev. John Fletcher, vicar of Madeley.

1782   January 2, removed to Madeley, Shropshire. Functioned as Fletcher's "co-pastor."

1785   August 14, death of John Fletcher. She remained in the vicarage until her own death and carried on religious work in the neighborhood, frequently preaching in the several chapels built by her husband and herself; the tithe barn became a noted site for her preaching where she proclaimed her message to both laity and clergy.

1815   September 15, died at her home in Madeley.

B. *Account of Sarah Lawrence* (1820).

An Aunt's Advice to a Niece, 2d ed. (Leeds: printed by J. Bowling, 1780).

Jesus, Altogether Lovely (Bristol, 1766).

A Legacy to the People of Madeley, revised by Joseph Entwisle (London: Printed by Thomas Cordeux, 1819).

A Letter to the Rev. John Wesley (1764).

Thoughts on Communion with Happy Spirits (Birmingham: Printed by William Rickman King, n.d.).

C. *Arm. Mag.* 7:470; 8:393, 437, 522–25; 9:518; 10:218; 11:47; 13:390.

Arm. Mag. (B.C.) 3:286–88.

Christian Miscellany 1847:381.

Crosby, MS Letterbook, pp. 55–61.

Hodson, *A Widow Indeed.*

Benjamin Hopkins, *The Life of the Reverend Robert Hopkins* (Sheffield: Printed by J. C. Platt, 1828), pp. 47–50.

Jackson, *Lives of Early Methodist Preachers*, 6:102.

Thomas Jackson, *Recollections of My Own Life and*

Times, ed. B. Frankland (London: Wesleyan Conference Office, 1874), p. 46.

John Lightfoot, *The Power of Faith and Prayer Exemplified in the Life and Labours of Mrs. Mary Porteus* (London: Published by R. Davies, Conference-Offices, 1862), p. vi.

Meth. Mag. 22:602–4; 29:295; 39:80; 40:527; 42:690; 44:240.

Moore, *Fletcher.*

MS Letters, Meth. Arch.

Sigston, *Memoir of William Bramwell,* 1:156–57, 2:176–78.

Sutcliffe, *Experience of Frances Pawson,* pp. 45, 65.

Sutcliffe, *Life of John Valton,* pp. 103–4.

Taft, *Holy Women,* 1:iv–vi, 19–40, 43, 104, 127, 294; 2:131–33.

Taft, *Original Letters,* pp. 79–86, 140–41, 142.

Taft, *Scripture Doctrine,* pp. 19–24.

Tooth, *Letter to the People of Madeley.*

Treffrey, *Memoirs of Joseph Benson,* p. 131.

Charles Wesley, *Journal,* 2:3, 9, 204, 246, 311.

Wesley, *Journal,* 4:243n, 244n, 274; 5:7n, 102, 152, 226n, 262n, 375, 484n; 6:4n, 11n, 30n, 71, 177n, 210, 272n, 345; 7:150D, 161n, 247, 249, 367, 368, 480; letters noted, 5:227, 296, 331, 360, 448, 522; 6:4, 5, 10, 291, 301, 361, 7:115, 118, 121, 133, 135, 194, 204, 227, 352.

Wesley, *Letters,* 3:216–17, 220, 239–41; 5:61, 257–58; 6:50, 290–91, 306–7; 7:29, 94–95, 128, 264, 297.

Wesley, *Oxford Edition,* 25:86.

W.H.S. 5:241; 8:22, 29–33; 17:71; 19:155; 21:197–98.

Wes. Meth. Mag. 48:330; 60:900–903; 63:825; 68:981–82; 69:58–59; 70:553–54.

Williams, *Memoirs of Ann Carr,* p. 22.

D. Baker, *A Charge to Keep,* p. 136.

Baker, *Friends and Early Methodism,* p. 21.

Baker, *John Wesley and the Church of England,* pp. 203–4, 381.

Baker, "John Wesley and Sarah Crosby," pp. 77, 81.

Barber, *Methodist Pageant,* p. 102.

Brooke, "Journal of Isabella Mackiver," p. 161.

E. K. Brown, "Archetypes and Stereotypes: Church Women in the Nineteenth Century," *Religion in Life* 43, 3 (Autumn 1974); 325–26.

Brown, "Standing in the Shadow," pp. 24–26.

Brown, "Women of the Word," pp. 70, 73–77, 79–80, 84–87.

Buckley, "What Methodism Owes Women," pp. 308–9.

Samuel Burder, *Memoirs of Eminently Pious Women of the British Empire,* new ed., revised and enlarged, 3 vols. (London; Printed for Ogle, Duncan, 1823), 3:365–412.

Burns, *Life of Mrs. Fletcher.*

Church, *More about Early Methodist People,* pp. 138–39, 141–50, 175, 187–90.

Stephen Cox, ed., *Holiness unto the Lord. Illustrated in the Character and Life of Miss Bosanquet, of Leytonstone* (London: Wesleyan Conference Office, 1876).

Crookshank, *Memorable Women,* pp. 14, 191.

Cunningham, *Everywhere Spoken Against,* pp. 157–66.

Dawson, *Yorkshire Methodism,* p. 6.

D. C. Dews, "Nonconformity in Morley," *W.H.S., Yorkshire Branch* 38 (April 1981): 12.

Edwards, *My Dear Sister,* pp. 85–99.

William E. Farndale, *The Secret of Mow Cop: A New Appraisal of Primitive Methodist Origins* (London: Epworth Press, 1950), p. 48.

Garlow, "John Wesley's Understanding of Laity," pp. 97–100.

Thomas E. Gill, *The Life of Mrs. Fletcher, Relict of the Rev. John Fletcher, Late Vicar of Madeley* (Easingwold: T. Gill, 1844).

Gregory, *History of Methodism,* 1:114–15, 309–11.

Harmon, *Encyclopedia,* 1:852–53.

Hellier, "Mother Chapel of Leeds," p. 64.

Hellier, "Some Methodist Women Preachers," pp. 65–66.

Hurst, *History of Methodism,* 2:895–99, 902–4, 905–13.

Annie E. Keeling, *Susanna Wesley and Other Eminent Methodist Women,* 3d ed. (London: Charles H. Kelly, 1897).

Kendall, *Primitive Methodist Church,* 1:140–41.

Lawson, *John Wesley and Christian Ministry,* pp. 178–79.

Dorothy McConnell, "The Women of Early Methodism," in *Forever Beginning, 1766–1966,* ed. Albea Godbold (Lake Junaluska, N.C.: Association of Methodist Historical Societies, 1967), pp. 179–80.

Morrow, *Early Methodist Women,* pp. 13, 64–105.

Nightingale, *Portraiture of Methodism,* pp. 454–55.

Eric M. North, *Early Methodist Philanthropy* (New York: Methodist Book Concern, 1914), pp. 99–102.

O'Malley, *Women in Subjection,* pp. 133–41.

Ritson, *Romance of Primitive Methodism,* p. 133.

Robinson, *Methodism in Dewsbury,* p. 65.

Ruether, *Women of Spirit,* pp. 228–29.

Runyon, *Sanctification and Liberation,* pp. 166–67, 170, 172.

Schmidt, *John Wesley,* 3:143, 157.

Simon, *John Wesley: The Master Builder,* pp. 187, 205, 272, 275, 292n.

Simon, *John Wesley: The Last Phase,* pp. 36, 60, 62, 182, 185.

Smith, *History of Methodism,* 1:347–48, 362–63, 420–23, 446; 2:388.

Stevens, *History of Methodism,* 2:94, 203–8, 381; 3:172–74.

Stevens, *Women of Methodism,* pp. 56–74.

Swift, "Women Itinerant Preachers," pp. 89, 93.

Thomas, *Life of Robert Gate,* pp. 32–36.

Townsend, *New History of Methodism,* 1:321, 396.

Tyerman, *Life of Wesley,* 2:286, 289, 517–18, 588–89; 3:68, 111–12, 206, 208, 213, 240–41, 329.

Tyerman, *Wesley's Designated Successor,* passim, esp. pp. 475–83, 502–3.

Walker, *Methodism in Halifax,* pp. 135–38, 145–48.

John T. Wilkinson, *Hugh Bourne, 1772–1852* (London: Epworth Press, 1952), p. 58.

GILBERT, MRS. ANN

A. Born in Cornwall, probably at Gwinear.
- 1743 Decided to become a Methodist upon hearing "Captain Dick" Williams in Gwinear.
- 1754? This first Cornish woman preacher was apparently blinded near Redruth.
- 1760 Joined the society when it was formed there.
- 1771 Began exhorting and thereafter preaching in Cornish villages. She preached in the Methodist Chapel at Redruth to some 1,400 people.
- 1790 July 18, died at Gwinear.

C. "The Experience of Ann Gilbert."
Taft, *Holy Women,* 1:ii, 49–51.

D. Brown, "Women of the Word," p. 76.
Church, *More about Early Methodist People,* p. 157.
Garlow, "John Wesley's Understanding of Laity," p. 100.
Hellier, "Some Methodist Women Preachers," p. 67.
Hurst, *History of Methodism,* 2:918.

GILBERT, MRS. MARY (NEE WALSH)

A. 1733 February 24, born at St. Albans.
- 1750 M. Mr. Leadbetter.
- 1767 November 17, m. Francis Gilbert, missionary to Antigua.

Following her husband's death, Mary contin-
ued his work among the native Antiguans.
1791 Returned to England.
Served as steward of Methodist Society at
Chester.
1816 April 21, died.
C. Gilbert, *Memoirs of Mrs. Mary Gilbert.*
D. Bretherton, *Methodist in Chester,* pp. 73–79.

GOULDEN, MARY

A. The only reference to this woman is that within
Charles Allen's service register for the Houghton-
Le-Spring Circuit, where she preached at Wapping
in 1803.
C. Young, "Houghton-Le-Spring," p. 74.

GRETTON, ELLEN (*afterward* MRS. CHRISTIAN)

A. 1757 Born (Lincolnshire); daughter of clergyman.
1777 Moved to Grantham where she became a
focal point of the society.
1783 April, m. Mr. William Christian of Skillington.
After her marriage Ellen continued her pioneering work with Wesley's blessing.
1793 June 3, died at her home in Skillington.
C. Wesley, *Letters,* 7:90, 167, 175–76.
D. Cocking, *Methodism in Grantham,* pp. 180–84,
189–205, 242.

HAINSWORTH, MRS. (NEE HARGREAVES)

A. No biographical information other than the fact that
she was the wife of a Methodist itinerant preacher,
Rev. William Hainsworth and the leader of men's
classes.

C. Taft, *Holy Women,* 2:224–26.
D. Jessop, *Methodism in Rossendale,* p. 293.

HARRISON, HANNAH

A. 1734　Born at York.
　　1747　Blinded.
　　1750　November, awakened under the preaching of J. Maskew.
　　1751　May, experienced forgiveness of sins while receiving the Lord's Supper.
　　　　　Became a leading pioneer of Methodism in York.
　　1768　Instrumental as a reconciler in Beverley.
　　　　　Became close friend and associate of Sarah Crosby.
　　　　　Held services at Malton.
　　　　　Later in life, moved to London where she made excursions into the country during the summer months.
　　1801　December 19, died at London; Joseph Benson preached her funeral sermon on December 27.
　　　　　John Atlay was awakened under her preaching and later became an itinerant preacher.
C. "Account of Mrs. Hannah Harrison."
　　Taft, *Holy Women,* 1:203–4.
　　Wesley, *Journal,* 5:239.
　　Wesley, *Letters,* 5:59–60, 113.
D. Jessop, *Methodism in Rossendale,* p. 94.
　　Lawson, *John Wesley and Christian Ministry,* pp. 177, 179.
　　Lyth, *Methodism in York,* pp. 64–68.
　　Simon, *John Wesley: The Master Builder,* p. 294.
　　Tyerman, *Life of Wesley,* 2:421; 3:41.
　　Hellier, "Some Methodist Women Preachers," p. 67.

HARRISON, MRS. MARY

A. 1751–52 Born.
Awakened under the preaching of
Samuel Davenport.
Pioneered Methodism in Wishall.
1808 October 19, died at Wishall.
C. Taft, *Holy Women,* 1:73, 76–79.
D. Brown, "Women of the Word," p. 74.

HOLDER, MRS. MARY (NEE WOODHOUSE)

A. 1751 Born at Whitby.
1767 Admitted to the Methodist Society by
William Brammah.
1775–76? Involved in revival led by J. Blades.
Became a friend of Sarah Crosby, Mary
Bosanquet, and Elizabeth Ritchie.
1788 August, m. Rev. George Holder, itiner-
ant preacher.
Set out for Isle of Man.
Assisted her husband throughout his
ministry.
1836 June 20, died.
C. George Holder, *A Short Account of the Life of Mrs.
Mary Holder. Mostly Taken from Her Journal*
(Whitby, 1836).
Taft, *Holy Women,* 1:100–128; 2:89–93, 95–97,
99–100, 106–7.
Taft, *Original Letters,* pp. 50–57, 63–71, 100–103.
D. Brown, "Women of the Word," p. 73.
Harrison, "Methodism in Isle of Man," pp. 193–202.
Hellier, "Some Methodist Women Preachers," p. 67.

HURRELL, ELIZABETH

A. 1740 Born.
Awakened under preaching of Rev. J. Berridge.

1775 October 22, preached in the Methodist Chapel at Sunderland and became embroiled in a controversy over the propriety of her actions.

Exchange of letters among Joseph Benson, John Wesley, and Robert Empringham concerning her work.

Became closely associated with Sarah Crosby, Mary Bosanquet, and the other women preachers of the north; traveled extensively throughout Yorkshire, Lancashire, and Derbyshire.

1780 June, desisted from preaching for unknown reasons.

Moved to London where she resided thereafter in Queen Square.

1798 March 13, died in London; interred at City Road Chapel.

The conversions of William Warrener and John Lancaster, among others, are ascribed to her ministry.

C. Crosby, MS Letterbook, pp. 69–71.
Taft, *Holy Women,* 1:127, 175–81; 2:101–3.
Taft, *Scripture Doctrine,* p. 22.
Wesley, *Journal,* 7:446D; 8:109D.
Wesley, *Letters,* 6:169, 192, 269, 286; esp. 184–85.
W.H.S. 5:241.
Meth. Mag. 44:361–62.

D. Baker, *Friends and Early Methodism,* p. 21.
Hellier, "Mother Chapel of Leeds," p. 64.
Hellier, "Some Methodist Women Preachers," p. 67.
Hurst, *History of Methodism,* 2:918.
Laycock, *Methodist Heroes of Haworth,* p. 300.
Stevenson, *City Road Chapel,* p. 361.
Tyerman, *Wesley's Designated Successor,* p. 400.

KILHAM, MRS. HANNAH (NEE SPURR)

A. 1774 August 12, born at Sheffield.
1794? Joined the Methodist Society.

1796   Began keeping a journal.
       M. Rev. Alexander Kilham—his second wife.
       Left Methodism to become a Quaker.
       Later served as a missionary to Africa.
1832   March 31, died at sea.
C. Sarah Biller, ed., *Memoirs of the Late Hannah Kilham, Chiefly Compiled from Her Journal, and edited by Sarah Biller* (London: Darton and Harvey, 1837).
D. Baker, *Friends and Early Methodism,* p. 21.
   E. A. Rose, "Sarah Kilham and Hannah Kilham," *W.H.S.* 39, 6 (October 1974): 185–86.
   J. K. Sanders, "Mrs. Hannah Kilham," *W.H.S.* 39, 3 (October 1973): 93–94.
   Smith, *Catalogue of Friends' Books,* 2:58–61; *Supplement,* pp. 213–14.

LAWRENCE, SARAH

A. 1760? Born; the niece of Mrs. Sarah Ryan.
   1763   Orphaned and became a part of the Leytonstone family.
   1768   June 7, moved with Mary Bosanquet to Cross Hall, Yorkshire.
   1768   August 17, her aunt, Sarah Ryan, died and Mary Bosanquet became her adoptive mother.
   1781   January 2, moved with the Rev. and Mrs. Fletcher to Madeley, Shropshire.
          She began evangelistic work in Madeley.
          She responded to a call to preach at Coalport and continued preaching there every other Sunday evening for several years.
          Assisted Mary Fletcher in her work.
   1800   December 3, died at Madeley.
C. Fletcher, *Account of Sarah Lawrence.*
   Moore, *Fletcher,* pp. 49, 124, 142, 296, 307, 317, 324.
   Taft, *Holy Women,* 1:41–48.
D. Brown, "Women of the Word," pp. 73, 85.

Crookshank, *Memorable Women,* p. 192.
Hellier, "Some Methodist Women Preachers," p. 67.
Stevens, *Women of Methodism,* pp. 87–92.
Tyerman, *Wesley's Designated Successor,* p. 477.

MALLET, SARAH

A.	1764	February 18, born at Loddon, Norfolk. First exposure to Methodism—preaching of Mr. Floyd.
	1780	January 1, whole family became Methodists and Sarah received her first membership ticket.
	1780	January 3, she moved to Long Stratton to live with her Uncle William.
	1781	May 27–28, experienced first of many seizures.
	1782–84	Moved back and forth between Loddon and Long Stratton.
	1785	March, experienced a "call" to preach.
	1785	December 15, began having seizures once again. December 25, preached for the first time during one of the seizures. These activities continued into January of 1786.
	1786	January 15, Long Stratton Society invited to hear her preach in a trance.
	1786	February, Sarah submitted to her call to preach and began preaching regularly at the chapel and at her uncle's house.
	1787	August, received formal authorization to preach within the Methodist Connection from the conference and John Wesley via a letter delivered by Joseph Harper.

M. Mr. Boyce, a Methodist local preacher, who regularly included her in his plan.

Little information is available concerning her life and work beyond this point.

C. Mallitt, "Account of Sarah Mallitt."

Taft, *Holy Women,* 1:iv, 79–90, 91.

Taft, *Scripture Doctrine,* pp. 18–19.

Wesley, *Journal,* 6:338n; 7:226, 455n; letter noted, 7:331, 361, 455, 458, 470, 8:31, 83, 116.

Wesley, *Letters,* 8:15, 43–44, 77, 108–9, 190, 228–29, 250.

W.H.S. 3:74.

D. Baker, *Friends and Early Methodism,* p. 21.

Brown, "Women of the Word," pp. 74, 76, 78.

Church, *More about Early Methodist People,* pp. 140, 170–72.

William L. Doughty, "George J. Stevenson: A Letter to Zechariah Taft," *W.H.S.* 28, 2(June 1951): 36–37.

William L. Doughty, *John Wesley, Preacher* (London: Epworth Press, 1955), p. 148.

Garlow, "John Wesley's Understanding of Laity," p. 100.

Hellier, "Mother Chapel of Leeds," p. 64.

Hellier, "Some Methodist Women Preachers," pp. 66–67.

Hurst, *History of Methodism,* 2:916–18.

Knox, *Enthusiasm,* p. 536.

Lawson, *John Wesley and Christian Ministry,* pp. 179–80.

Morrow, *Early Methodist Women,* p. 15.

Ritson, *Romance of Primitive Methodism,* p. 133.

Ruether, *Women of Spirit,* p. 229.

Runyon, *Sanctification and Liberation,* pp. 166–67.

Simon, *John Wesley: The Last Phase,* p. 182.

Swift, "Women Itinerant Preachers," p. 89.

Townsend, *New History of Methodism,* 1:321.

Wearmouth, *Methodism and Common People,* p. 228.

NEWLAND, JANE

A. 1757 October 25, born at Dublin, Ireland.

1779 Attended the Methodist Society for the first time and joined shortly thereafter.

1780   Established prayer meetings which grew so rapidly that she found it necessary to have three each week.

1789   October 22, died prematurely, prior to thirty-second birthday.

C. *A Short Account of the Life and Death of Miss Jane Newland* (Dublin, 1790).

Wesley, *Letters,* 8:191.

D. Crookshank, *Memorable Women,* pp. 170–79.

NEWMAN, PENELOPE (*afterward* MRS. COUSSINS)

A. Born at Cheltenham, date unknown; sister of Mr. Thomas Newman, a mercer, draper, and tailor.

1771   August 1, converted under the preaching of John Wesley.

Became the proprietor of a bookshop in Cheltenham.

Entered fully into life of society.

1776   October 24, instrumental in the conversion of Jonathan Coussins, later to become her husband and an itinerant preacher.

1782   Coussins stationed in Gloucester Circuit.

1782   October, m. Jonathan Coussins.

After her marriage Penelope curtailed many of her preaching activities; she was well known in her native town as well as Tewkesbury and the Cotswolds.

C. *Arm. Mag.* 8:434–37; 9:171–72.

Taft, *Holy Women,* 1:290–95.

Taft, *Scripture Doctrine,* pp. 21–22.

Richard Waddy, "Account of Mr. Jonathan Coussins," *Meth. Mag.* 29 (1806): 289–92, 296, 344.

Wesley, *Journal,* 6:215n.

Wesley, *Letters,* 5:310–11; 6:307; 7:143, 324–25.

W.H.S. 8:165–68; 17:164; 25:86–88.

Wes. Meth. Mag. 50:392; 57:902.

D. Dyson, *Methodism in Isle of Wight,* p. 115.

Green, "Jonathan and Penelope Coussins," pp. 58–60.

Lawson, *John Wesley and Christian Ministry,* pp. 179–80.
Tyerman, *Life of Wesley,* 2:560.

PARKER, HANNAH (*afterward* MRS. FISHER)

A. Born at Cold-Camb, near Thirsk, date unknown.
M. John Fisher of Ampleforth.
Began preaching at thirty years of age, mainly in North Riding of Yorkshire.
1811   Died at Ampleforth.
C. Taft, *Holy Women,* 1:202–3.

PERROTT, MADAME

A. No information other than Taft's reference to her preaching on the Isle of Jersey, in *Holy Women,* 1:170–72.

PROUDFOOT, MRS.

A. No biographical data. She preached in the Norwich Circuit where Adam Clarke heard her expound Exodus 3:3 in the spring of 1784.
C. J.B.B. Clarke, *Account of Adam Clarke,* 1:216.
Bible Christian Magazine 13 (1833): 143.

RIPLEY, DOROTHY

A. 1767   April 24? born at Whitby; daughter of Rev. William Ripley.
Deeply impressed by Methodist preachers in early years.
Came under Quaker influences.
1801   Felt call to become missionary in America.
Secured interview with President Jefferson to discuss issue of slavery.

1805   Returned to England.
      Returned to America to preach among Indians.
1806   Preached before Congress in Washington.
      Developed a center in Charleston, S.C., for evangelistic/benevolent activities.
1818   Engaged in evangelistic tour of England with Lorenzo Dow.
      Crossed Atlantic eight or nine times in her preaching missions.
1831   December 23, died at Mecklenburg, Va.

B. *An Account of Rose Butler* (New York: Printed by John C. Totten, 1819).

An Address to All in Difficulties (Bristol: Rose, Printer, [1821?]).

The Bank of Faith and Works United, 2d ed. (Whitby: Printed for the authoress, by G. Clark, 1822).

The Extraordinary Conversion, and Religious Experience, of Dorothy Ripley, 2d ed. (London: Printed for the Authoress, by Darton, Harvey, 1817).

Letters, Addressed to Dorothy Ripley (Chester: Printed by J. Hemingway, 1807).

Memoirs of William Ripley, Minister of the Gospel (Philadelphia: J. H. Cunningham, 1827).

C. William Clowes, *The Journals of William Clowes, A Primitive Methodist Preacher* (London: Published by Hallam and Holliday, 1844), p. 191.

Taft, *Holy Women*, 1:205–41.

D. Baker, *Friends and Early Methodism*, p. 23.

"Dorothy Ripley, Unaccredited Missionary," *Journal of the Friends Historical Society* 22 (1925): 33–51; 23 (1926): 12–21, 77–79.

Church, *More about Early Methodist People*, pp. 199, 206–7.

Arthur Mounfield, "Dorothy Ripley," *W.H.S.* 7, 2 (June 1909): 31–33.

Arthur Mounfield, *The Quaker Methodists* (Nelson: Independent Methodist Book Room, 1924), p. 14.

Smith, *Catalogue of Friends' Books*, 2:496; *Supplement*, pp. 286–87.

W.H.S. 6:37–44.

Wilkinson, *Hugh Bourne,* p. 107.

RYAN, MRS. SARAH

A. 1724 October 20, born.

 1741–42 Converted under the preaching of George Whitefield in London.

     Heard Wesley preach at the Foundery and later joined the society.

     Became involved in a number of unsuccessful marriages.

 1757 Appointed housekeeper at Bristol and later at Kingswood.

 1762 Joined Mary Bosanquet in her works of benevolence in London.

 1763 March 24, moved with Miss Bosanquet to "The Cedars" and helped organize the Leytonstone Orphanage and School.

 1768 June 7, moved with the family to Yorkshire.

 1768 August 17, died at Cross Hall, Yorkshire.

C. "Account of Mrs. Sarah Ryan," *Arm. Mag.* 2 (1779): 296–310.

 Arm. Mag. 5:passim (eleven letters).

 Meth. Mag. 21:494.

 Moore, *Fletcher,* pp. 28–29, 30, 41–44, 45–47, 49, 69–70, 72, 80–85.

 Charles Wesley, *Journal,* 2:230, 256.

 Wesley, *Journal,* 4:243n, 244n, 274; 5:226n; letters noted, 4:245, 246, 248, 249, 258; 5:172.

 Wesley, *Letters,* 3:239–41; 4:4.

 Wesley, *Oxford Edition,* 25:86.

D. Stanley Ayling, *John Wesley* (Nashville: Abingdon Press, 1979), 227.

 Baker, *Friends and Early Methodism,* p. 21.

 Baker, "John Wesley and Sarah Crosby," pp. 77, 81.

 Brown, "Women of the Word," pp. 84–85.

 Church, *More about Early Methodist People,* pp. 149–50.

Crookshank, *Memorable Women*, pp. 14, 191.
Cunningham, *Everywhere Spoken Against*, p. 159.
Edwards, *My Dear Sister*, pp. 50–57.
Hellier, "Mother Chapel of Leeds," pp. 64–65.
T. F. Hulme, *Voices of the New Room* (London: Epworth Press, 1933), pp. 100–107.
Ives, *Kingswood School*, pp. 50–51.
McConnell, "Women of Early Methodism," p. 180.
Morrow, *Early Methodist Women*, pp. 13, 74–75, 81.
O'Malley, *Women in Subjection*, pp. 134–38.
Runyon, *Sanctification and Liberation*, p. 172.
Harmon, *Encyclopedia*, 2:2061.
Schmidt, *John Wesley*, 3:142, 165–66, 168.
Simon, *John Wesley: The Master Builder*, p. 205.
Stevens, *History of Methodism*, 2:205–6.
Stevens, *Women of Methodism*, pp. 75–79.
Tyerman, *Life of Wesley*, 2:109–10, 285–89, 517, 562–63.
Tyerman, *Wesley's Designated Successor*, pp. 28, 33, 43–44, 476–77.

SEWELL, MARY

A. 1750s (Late) Born at Thurlton.
Joined Methodist Society at an early age.
Began preaching in 1770s.
1779 Possibly preached for first time at Haddiscoe.
1784 April 28, Adam Clarke heard her preach on Ephesians 2:8 at Thurlton.
1785 Listed as a "local preacher" on the Norwich Circuit preaching plan.
1786 October 29, died at her home in Thurlton.
C. *Bible Christian Magazine* 5, 4(April 1833): 142–43.
J.B.B. Clarke, *Account of Adam Clarke*, 1:215–16.
Nattrass, "Great Yarmouth Circuit," pp. 73–77.
Taft, *Holy Women*, 1:326–28.
Wesley, *Journal*, 6:338n.
D. Church, *More about Early Methodist People*, pp. 169–70.

Lawson, *John Wesley and Christian Ministry*, p. 179.
Simon, *John Wesley: The Last Phase*, p. 181.
Swift, "Women Itinerant Preachers," p. 89.
Wearmouth, *Methodism and Common People*, p. 228.

STEVENS, MRS. SARAH (NEE WILLIS)

A. 1770   February 26? born at Bristol.
   1786   April, first admitted to Methodist Society.
   1788   M. Rev. Stevens, itinerant preacher.
          Later began Benevolent Society at Kingswood.
          Rev. John Lomas converted under her preaching.
          Traveled with her husband and assisted him in his services.
   1824   April 6, died.
B. *Meth. Mag.* 43 (1820): 46–53, 127–36.
   Taft, *Holy Women*, 1:159–69.
   Taft, *Original Letters*, pp. 133–34.
D. Baker, *Friends and Early Methodism*, p. 21.
   Hellier, "Mother Chapel of Leeds," p. 64.
   Hellier, "Some Methodist Women Preachers," p. 67.

STOKES, MARY (*afterward* MRS. DUDLEY)

A. 1750   June 6, born at Bristol.
          Joined Methodist Society at the New Room.
          Intimate friend of Elizabeth Johnson.
   1777   M. Robert Dudley of Clonmel, Ireland.
          Later became a noted Quaker preacher for some fifty years.
   1823   September 24, died at her home in Peckham, London, and was buried in the Friends' Cemetery near Bunhill Fields.
B. *An Extempore Discourse*
C. *Arm. Mag.* 18:99–101.

Dudley, *Life of Mary Dudley.*
Taft, *Holy Women,* 2:149–77.
Wesley, *Journal,* 6:185, 254n; 5:482n.
Wesley, *Letters,* 5:230, 302, 305, 335.
D. Baker, *Friends and Early Methodism,* pp. 19, 23.
Jones, *Later Periods of Quakerism,* 1:63–64, 198–99,
    210–11, 237–42, 274–78.
Smith, *Catalogue of Friends' Books,* 1:546.

TAFT, MRS. MARY (NEE BARRITT)

A. 1772   August, born at Hay, near Colne, Lan-
               cashire.
   1772   August 12, baptized in parish church of
               Colne.
               Led somewhat wild childhood, being
               nicknamed "Mad Poll."
               Awakened under preaching of Samuel
               Bardsley.
   1791   Held prayer meeting with exhortation at
               Rimmington.
               Much opposed to female preaching.
   1792   Called to exhort at Todmorden.
   1792–93?   Interviewed by Lancelot Harrison who
               was much opposed to women's preaching.
               Assisted Ann Cutler in Ackrington re-
               vival.
   1793   Christmas, preached at Hexham by re-
               quest of Walton and with grudging ap-
               proval of her brother, John Barritt.
               Experienced strong call to preach.
   1794   Began series of preaching pilgrimages
               and became a noted itinerant evangelist.
               Frequently assisted William Bramwell
               and other revivalists throughout the
               north of England.
   1798   Spring, her preaching challenged and
               defended at Leeds Quarterly Meeting.
   1802   August 17, m. Rev. Zechariah Taft, itin-

erant preacher and strong advocate of women's
preaching.

Removed to Kent where her husband was
stationed.

1802 September 18, preached in Methodist Chapel
at Dover.

1802 October, invited to preach in Canterbury.

1802 October 25, caustic letter of Joseph Benson
and letter of support by John Pawson.

1803 Restricted her work to conform to the prohibitive resolutions of the conference.

Hereafter she was scrupulous in following
conference regulations, confining her work to
the circuits in which Taft was stationed.

The remaining years of her life require much more
solid research in order to document her movements
and activities. She was frequently included in the
preaching plans of many circuits after 1803.

1851 March 26, died at Sandiacre, Derbyshire.

B. *Memoirs of the Life of Mrs. Mary Taft* (1827, 1828,
1831).

C. *Arm. Mag. (B.C.)* 4:430–32; 5:34–36, 105–6; 6:359;
7:178–80, 214–16, 395.

Dickinson, *Life of John Braithwaite*, pp. 242–43, 318.

James Everett, *Memoirs of the Life, Character, and
Ministry of William Dawson, Late of Barnbow,
near Leeds* (London: Published by Hamilton,
Adams, 1842), p. 115.

J. R. Gregory, ed., *Benjamin Gregory, D.D.,
Autobiographical Recollections* (London: Hodder
and Stoughton, 1903), pp. 12–13, 274–75.

Harris, *Memoir of William Bramwell*, pp. 189,
222–23.

Jackson, *Recollections*, pp. 42–48.

John Lyth, *The Blessedness of Religion in Earnest: A
Memorial of Mrs. Mary Lyth, of York* (London:
Book Society, 1861), p. 21.

MS Letters, Meth. Arch.

*Memorials of Mary, the Beloved Wife of the Rev.
James Henshaw; Including Extracts from Her*

Correspondence (London: William Cooke, 1870), pp. 14–16.

Obituary of Mrs. Mary Taft, *Wes. Meth. Mag.* 74 (1851): 604.

Sigston, *Memoir of William Bramwell,* 1:154–57, 158–59, 161–62, 190–92, 204–17; 2:40–41, 44, 65–66, 67–71, 99, 100, 117–18, 181–82.

Taft, *Holy Women,* 1:127.

Taft, *Scripture Doctrine,* pp. iii–iv.

Wesley, *Journal,* 6:115n.

Wes. Meth. Mag. 105:552–53; 119:538–44.

D. Church, *More about Early Methodist People,* pp. 146, 163–69, 175.

Doughty, "G. J. Stevenson," pp. 36–37.

William Garner, *The Life of the Rev. and Venerable William Clowes* (London: Published by William Lister, 1868), p. xxv.

Gregory, *Side Lights on Conflicts,* pp. 127–28.

George H. Harwood, *The History of Wesleyan Methodism in Nottingham and Its Vicinity,* new and enlarged ed. (Nottingham: Printed and Published by John Ellis, 1872), pp. 99–100, 125–26.

Hellier, "Mother Chapel of Leeds," p. 64.

Hellier, "Some Methodist Women Preachers," pp. 67–68.

Hurst, *History of Methodism,* 3:1301–4.

Jessop, *Methodism in Rossendale,* p. 269.

Kendall, *Primitive Methodist Church,* 1:194–95.

Lawson, *John Wesley and Christian Ministry,* p. 179.

Lyth, *Methodism in York,* p. 284.

Nightingale, *Portraiture of Methodism,* p. 456.

Pilkington, *Methodism in Preston,* pp. 24–25.

Ruether, *Women of Spirit,* p. 229.

Rupp, *Thomas Jackson,* pp. 11–13.

Swift, "Women Itinerant Preachers," pp. 90–92.

Taylor, *Apostles of Fylde Methodism,* pp. 57–67, 131.

Edwin Thompson, "This Remarkable Family: A Study of the Barritt's of Foulridge, 1750–1850," privately circulated, St. Andrew's Manse, Barnoldswick, Colne, Lancs., June 1981, pp. 8–11.

Ward, *Methodism in Swaledale,* pp. 62–64.
Ward, *Methodism in Thirsk,* pp. 27, 29–30, 37–38.
Young, "Houghton-Le-Spring," p. 74.

THOMPSON, ANN (*afterward* MRS. COATES)

A. Born at Aysgarth, Yorkshire.
Converted under preaching of Mary Barritt in 1795.
Preached throughout the Dales, especially at Reeth.
M. Thomas Coates.
C. Taft, *Memoirs,* 1:55.
Taft, *Holy Women,* 2:218–19.
D. Ward, *Methodism in Swaledale,* pp. 63–64.

TONKIN, ELIZABETH (*afterward* MRS. COLLETT)

A. 1762 May 9, born at Gwinear, Cornwall.
1776 First experienced forgiveness.
1778 Invited to and joined Methodist Society.
Came under influence of Ann Gilbert, the first woman preacher in Cornwall.
1782 March 12, moved to Feock.
Pressed into preaching when an appointed itinerant preacher was unable to attend.
Preached regularly in Roseland and was permitted to continue in such irregularities by Joseph Taylor.
1785 December, m. Mr. Collett.
Mother of eleven children.
1786 Moved to Veryan and continued her labors.
1800 Moved to St. Erme.
1804 May, preached for the last time in a chapel built by her husband at St. Erme.
1820 Moved to Warliggan.
1825 Died.
C. *Arm. Mag. (B.C.)* 3:286–88.
Taft, *Holy Women,* 2:115–39.
D. Brown, "Women of the Word," p. 73.

Church, *More about Early Methodist People,* pp. 156–59.
Hellier, "Some Methodist Women Preachers," p. 67.
Shaw, *History of Cornish Methodism,* pp. 28, 58.

TREFFRY, MRS. JANE (NEE HAWKEY)

A. 1761 March, born in Cornwall.
Awakened under preaching of Joseph Benson.
1797 September 25, received first Class Ticket.
1800 Summer, m. Rev. Treffry, itinerant preacher. Preached at Helston.
Assisted her husband, supplying his place on occasion.
1829 December 13, died at Leeds where she was interred at Brunswick Chapel.
C. Treffry, *Memoirs of Mrs. Jane Treffry.*
Wes. Meth. Mag. 53:693.
D. Church, *Early Methodist People,* pp. 224–25.
Church, *More about Early Methodist People,* pp. 169–70.

TRIPP, ANN

A. 1745 Born (London?).
Awakened under preaching of Thomas Maxfield.
Experienced forgiveness by influence of John Wesley's preaching.
1763 Became governess for children of the Leytonstone orphanage and close associate of Mary Bosanquet and Sarah Ryan.
1768 June 7, moved to Yorkshire with Leytonstone family.
Continued as governess of Cross Hall school.
1781 Following Mary Bosanquet's marriage to John Fletcher moved to Leeds with Sarah Crosby and formed nucleus of the "Female

Brethren" at the Old Boggard House, the mother chapel of Leeds.

Became one of the central figures in Leeds Methodism.

1823   September 16, died at Leeds; buried at Old Parish Church.

C. Moore, *Fletcher,* p. 49.

Sutcliffe, *Experience of Frances Pawson,* p. 96.

Taft, *Holy Women,* 2:112–15.

Wes. Meth. Mag. 46:706.

D. Baker, *Friends and Early Methodism,* p. 21.

Baker, "John Wesley and Sarah Crosby," pp. 76, 81.

Brown, "Women of the Word," p. 85.

Church, *More about Early Methodist People,* pp. 149–50.

Harrison, "Early Woman Preacher," p. 108.

Hellier, "Mother Chapel of Leeds," pp. 64–65.

Morrow, *Early Methodist Women,* p. 77.

Tyerman, *Life of Wesley,* 2:289.

Tyerman, *Wesley's Designated Successor,* p. 477.

WALTON, GRACE

A. No biographical data.

C. Wesley, *Letters,* 4:164. Cf. Appendix C.

D. Brown, "Women of the Word," pp. 75–76.

Church, *More about Early Methodist People,* p. 139.

Cunningham, *Everywhere Spoken Against,* p. 158.

Lawson, *John Wesley and Christian Ministry,* p. 178.

Swift, "Women Itinerant Preachers," p. 89.

WATSON, MARGARET

A. Born at Stockton, daughter of Captain George Watson who had been converted under George Whitefield.

Joined Methodist Society, but left because of controversy over her work.

Returned to Methodism under influence of Stephen Potter.

1790s Moved to Redcar where she was influential in reviving the society.

C. Taft, *Holy Women*, 2:178–81.

WILTSHAW, MRS. MARY (NEE CHAPMAN)

A. 1763 Born at Spalding, Linconshire.

1785 M. first husband who died shortly thereafter.
Became governess to a family that moved to Gibraltar.
Returned to England to become her brother's housekeeper.

1790s Moved to Holbeach where she established a boarding school with her sister.
M. Rev. John Wiltshaw, itinerant preacher (retired 1809; died July 27, 1818).
Began preaching after her marriage.

1819 April 28, died.

C. Taft, *Holy Women*, 2:184–93.

WRIGHT, MRS. ELIZABETH (NEE REEVE)

A. 1765–66? Born in Suffolk.

1784 Nearly blinded in an accident.

1786 Death of her mother greatly affected her.

1790s Began preaching in Redgrave, Suffolk.

1795 June, m. Mr. W. Wright of Redgrave.

1797 August 3, died at Diss.

C. *Arm. Mag.* 22:386–88.
Taft, *Holy Women*, 1:89, 91–92.

D. Church, *More about Early Methodist People*, pp. xiv–xv.

APPENDIX B: LETTERS RELATED TO THE QUESTION OF WOMEN'S PREACHING IN EARLY METHODISM

I NFORMATION IN THE FOLLOWING LIST includes the names of the correspondents, the place of writing, date, and the primary source in which the letter may be found. This list does not include all letters written by or to each of the women preachers, but is restricted to those pieces of correspondence which address the question of women's preaching or provide information concerning the activities of women preachers.

The following abbreviations have been employed with regard to the correspondents:

EH	Elizabeth Hurrell
JW	John Wesley
MB	Mary Bosanquet
MBar	Mary Barritt
MF	Mary Fletcher
MS	Mary Stokes
MT	Mary Taft
SC	Sarah Crosby
SM	Sarah Mallet
WB	William Bramwell
ZT	Zechariah Taft

Abbreviations for primary sources, which differ from those utilized throughout the text, include:

Crosby	Crosby, MS Letterbook, q.v.
JWL	Wesley, *Letters*, q.v.
Sigston	Sigston, *Memoir of William Bramwell*, q.v.
Taft, *HW*	Taft, *Holy Women*, q.v.
Taft, *Mem*	Mary Taft, *Memoirs*, q.v.
Taft, *OL*	Taft, *Original Letters*, q.v.
Tyerman	Tyerman, *Life of John Wesley*, q.v.

FROM	TO	PLACE	DATE	SOURCE
		1761		
JW	SC	London	Feb. 14	*JWL* 4:133
JW	Grace Walton	London	Sept. 8	Appendix C
		1763		
SC	James Oddie	London	Jan. 28	Meth. Arch.
		1765		
SC	Mrs. ——		July 7	Crosby, 37–38
		1769		
JW	SC	Chester	Mar. 18	*JWL* 5:130
		1770		
SC	Mr. Mayer	Stump Cross	July 13	Meth. Arch.
		1771		
MB	JW	Cross Hall	(June)	Appendix D
JW	MB	Londonderry	June 13	*JWL* 5:257
JW	SC	Londonderry	June 13	*JWL* 5:257–58
Mary Stokes	Thomas Rankin		Oct. 12	*Arm. Mag.* 18:101
		1772		
JW	Mary Stokes		(Jan.)	*JWL* 5:302
JW	Mary Stokes	London	Feb. 11	*JWL* 5:305

FROM	TO	PLACE	DATE	SOURCE
		1773		
SC	JW	Cross Hall	Jan. 26	Crosby, 48–53
		1774		
SC	EH	Cross Hall	July 2	Crosby, 69–71
SC	Mrs. Cayley	Whitby	Oct.	Crosby, 74–76
		1775		
Joseph Benson	Robert Empringham		(Oct.)	Appendix E Watkinson Col.
Joseph Benson	JW		(Oct.)	*JWL* 6:184 Benson, MS Life, 1:376
JW	Joseph Benson	London	Oct. 30	*JWL* 6:184–85
JW	SC	Norwich	Nov. 29	*JWL* 6:192
		1777		
John Fletcher	MB	Madeley		Tyerman, *Wesley Successor,* 400–401
JW	Jane Barton		July 29	*JWL* 6:269
JW	Jane Barton	London	Oct. 28	*JWL* 6:286
JW	SC	London	Dec. 2	*JWL* 6:290–91
		1778		
SC	Mary Woodhouse	Hagget	July 9	Crosby, 65
JW	SC	Dover	Dec. 9	*JWL* 6:331
		1779		
EH	SC	Derby	May 18	Taft, *HW,* 1:178–9
		1780		
JW	George Robinson	Manchester	Mar. 25	*JWL* 7:8–9
SC	Mrs. ———		June	Taft, *HW,* 1:181

FROM	TO	PLACE	DATE	SOURCE
		1782		
JW	MF	Birmingham	July 12	*JWL* 7:128
JW	Penelope Newman	Bristol	Oct. 1	*JWL* 7:143
		1783		
JW	Elizabeth Gretton	Deptford	Feb. 16	*JWL* 7:167
JW	Elizabeth Gretton	Dublin	Apr. 25	*JWL* 7:175–76
		1785		
JW	SC	Manchester	Apr. 3	*WHS* 19:173–74
		1787		
JW	Robert Brackenbury		Feb. 16	*WHS* 28:68
JW	SM	Bristol	Oct. 6	*JWL* 8:15–16
Joseph Harper	SM		Oct. 27	Taft, *HW*, 1:84
		1788		
JW	SM	Bath	Mar. 11	*JWL* 8:43–44
JW	SM	London	Aug. 2	*JWL* 8:77–78
JW	SM	London	Dec. 26	*JWL* 8:108–9
		1789		
JW	SM	London	Feb. 21	*JWL* 8:118–19
JW	SM	Canterbury	Dec. 15	*JWL* 8:190–91
		1790		
SC	Mary Holder	Kirkstall-Forge	June 20	Taft, *OL*, 66
JW	SM	Bristol	July 31	*JWL* 8:228–29
JW	SM	Near London	Dec. 13	*JWL* 8:250

FROM	TO	PLACE	DATE	SOURCE
		1791		
JW	Alice Cambridge	London	Jan. 31	*JWL* 8:258–59
JW	SM	London	Feb./ Mar.	Taft, *HW*, 1:90
Miss Monkhouse	Mary Holder	Bouse	July 10	Taft, *OL*, 100–102
		1794		
Thomas Pullan	Mrs. Barritt	Pateley-Bridge	June 6	Taft, *Mem*, 1:43
Miss Monkhouse	Mary Holder	Bouse	June 28	Taft, *Mem*, 1:50–51
		1795		
John Braithwaite			Apr. 11	Dickinson, *Life of J.B.*, 242–43
EH	Frances Pawson	London	Apr. 21	Meth. Arch.
		1796		
T. Ogilvie	MBar			Taft, *Mem*, 1:63
Michael Fenwick	MBar	Cold-Kirby	Mar. 10	Taft, *Mem*, 1:65
Philip Hardcastle	MBar	Middleham	Nov. 15	Taft, *Mem*, 1:67
Philip Hardcastle	MBar	Cravenholn	Dec. 31	Taft, *Mem*, 1:70
		1797		
Mr. Burrows	MBar	Near Leeds	Feb. 27	Taft, *OL:* 123–24
Mr. Stevens	Mr. Carlill	Egglescliff	Nov. 3	Taft, *OL:* 133–34
W. Jackson	Barritts	Harewood	Dec. 2	Taft, *Mem*, 1:75
Robert Richardson	Mary Holder	Whitby	Dec. 26	Taft, *Mem*, 1:80

FROM	TO	PLACE	DATE	SOURCE
		1798		
WB	Joseph Drake		1798–99?	Sigston, 2:38–39
Alexander Mather	MBar	Leeds	Mar. 16	Taft, *Mem,* 1:85
Thomas Vasey	MBar	Whitby	Apr. 12	Taft, *Mem,* 1:82
Mr. Blackborne	MBar	Tadcaster	May 17	Taft, *Mem,* 1:83
WB	MBar	Coverton	May 30	Sigston, 2:65–66
Sarah Baisden	MBar	Leeds	June 6	Taft, *Mem,* 1:87–88
James Wood	MBar	Sheffield	June 12	Taft, *Mem,* 1:98
William Allen	MBar	Sherborn	July 21	Taft, *Mem,* 1:104
James Wood	MBar	Sheffield	July 21	Taft, *Mem,* 1:103
William Blackborne	MBar	Bristol	Aug. 7	Taft, *Mem,* 1:108
Jonathan Brown	MBar	Whitby	Sept. 11	Taft, *Mem,* 1:101–2
WB	MBar	Nottingham	Sept. 22	Sigston, 1:161–62
George Levick	MBar	Sheffield	Oct. 2	Taft, *Mem,* 1:106
Jonathan Brown	MBar	Whitby	Oct. 7	Meth. Arch.
WB	MBar	Nottingham	Nov.	Sigston, 2:40–41
George Lomas	MBar	Manchester	Nov. 22	Taft, *OL,* 129–30
Samuel Hoole	MBar	Sheffield	Dec. 17	Meth. Arch.
		1799		
Richard Elliot & T. Moses	MBar	Brampton	Jan. 18	Taft, *Mem,* 1:110
Mr. Burrows	MBar	Scott-Hall	Jan. 22	Taft, *OL,* 124–25
WB	MBar	Nottingham	Mar. ?	Taft, *Mem,* 1:115

FROM	TO	PLACE	DATE	SOURCE
Edward Wade	MBar	Sturton Grange	Mar. ?	*Arm. Mag. (B.C.)* 6:395
WB	MBar	Nottingham	Mar. 19	Sigston, 1:67–68
William Allen	MBar		(Aug.)	Taft, *Mem,* 1:123
M. Stephenson	MBar	Northwich	Sept. 19	Taft, *Mem,* 1:125
Thomas Shaw	MBar	Hinkley	Nov. 16	Taft, *OL,* 118–19
Birchenall	MBar	Macclesfield	Dec. 24	Meth. Arch.
WB	MBar	Calverton	1799–1800	Sigston, 2:44

1800

Isabella Wilson	Mr. & Mrs. Wilson	Nottingham	Jan. 2	Pipe, *Life of Wilson,* 136
Thomas Shaw	MBar	Hinkley	Mar. 26	Taft, *OL,* 119
T. Rutherford	MBar	Sheffield	Mar. 31	Meth. Arch.
Sarah Baisden	MBar	Leeds	Apr. 30	Taft, *Mem,* 1:151
William McAllum	MBar	Thrumaston	July 15	Taft, *OL,* 120–21
WB	MBar	Nottingham	Sept. 27	Sigston, 1:190–91
WB	MBar	Taghill	Oct. 16	Sigston, 1:191–92

1801

William McAllum	MBar	Lockington		Taft, *Mem,* 2:6
SC	Mary Holder	Leeds	Feb. 14	Taft, *OL,* 70–71
John Brandreth	MBar	Boxton	Mar. 22	Taft, *OL,* 74
Thomas Smith	MBar	Long Eaton	Apr. 20	Taft, *Mem,* 2:11–12
Thos. Scott	MBar	Manchester	Nov.	Taft, *Mem,* 2:22–24
WB	ZT	Thorner	Nov. 9	Sigston, 2:70
WB	MBar	Thorner	Nov. 17	Sigston, 1:204–6

FROM	TO	PLACE	DATE	SOURCE
		1802		
WB	MBar			Sigston, 1:206–8
John Braithwaite	MBar	Carlisle	Mar. 17	Taft, *Mem,* 2:28–29
John Braithwaite	MBar	Carlisle	May 25	Taft, *Mem,* 2:32
WB	ZT	Leeds	May 27	Sigston, 1:209
Joseph Entwisle	Jonathan Edmondson	Macclesfield	Summer	Entwisle, *Memoirs,* 231
ZT	MBar	Bristol	July 29	Meth. Arch.
William McAllum	MT	Church-Fenton	Sept. 26	Taft, *Mem,* 2:59–60
MT	ZT	Margate	Oct. 16	Taft, *Mem,* 2:53
Joseph Benson	ZT		Oct. 25	Meth. Arch.
John Pawson, J. S. Pipe	Dover Stewards	Bristol	Oct. 25	Meth. Arch.
George Sykes	Joseph Benson		Oct. (30)	Meth. Arch.
George Sykes	ZT	Margate	Nov. 6	Meth. Arch.
MT	ZT	Tenterdon	Nov. 26	Taft, *Mem,* 2:63–64
WB	MT	Leeds	Nov. 30	Sigston, 1:211–13
Ann Parnel	MT	Canterbury	Dec. 9	Taft, *Mem,* 2:67
Wm. Greathead & John Sole	ZT	Sheerness	Dec. 9	Taft, *Mem,* 2:66
Mrs. F. Bate	MT	Sitterbourne	Dec. 26	Taft, *OL,* 47–48
		1803		
Ann Parnel	MT	Canterbury	Jan. 5	Taft, *Mem,* 2:74
John Pawson	ZT	Bristol	Jan. 24	Meth. Arch.
ZT	MT	Dover	Mar. 21	Taft, *Mem,* 2:76
Mrs. F. Bate	MT	Sitterbourne	Apr. 4	Taft, *Mem,* 2:81
George Lees	MT	Ashfor	Apr. 5	Meth. Arch.
Isbella Wilson	MT	Sinethwhite	May 25	Taft, *Mem,* 2:85–86
WB	MT	Wetherby	July ?	Sigston, 1:214–15

APPENDIX C: A JOHN WESLEY LETTER OF SEPTEMBER 8, 1761

J OHN TELFORD ATTEMPTED TO RECONSTRUCT a defective letter from John Wesley to an aspiring woman preacher, dated September 8, 1761, which he included in Wesley, *Letters,* 4:164. In 1940 E.G.H. Bryant made a transcript of the original manuscript which was somewhat fuller than Telford's but still unsatisfactory. In a letter of May 1, 1949, to F. F. Bretherton, Bryant wrote:

> I have just seen, and been allowed to copy, a fragment of a Wesley letter which may interest you. I haven't access to the Standard "Letters," so do not know if it has been noted before.
>
> The writing of the vertical part and of the address is alike: that of the horizontal part is fainter and smoother. A different pen may account of the difference: there is no join in the paper.

Where there are deficiencies in the manuscript, Bryant shows them, while Telford fills them in without indicating that they are his insertions. Bryant retains a method of capitalization, underlining, and abbreviation which is consonant with Wesley's general practices. He includes two sentences carelessly omitted by Telford, and also provides a line-by-line text; all of which gives his transcript better evidential value.

The discovery of the original manuscript, which is surely about somewhere, would answer a number of puzzling questions, especially those about the actual format of the letter or letters involved. Bryant's notes may very well suggest a double letter. Telford tentatively identified the recipient of the second letter, dated November 12, 1761, as Mrs. Ryan. But as this portion of the manuscript does not deal with the question of women's preaching, we must focus attention on Wesley's letter to the aspiring woman preacher.

This portion of the manuscript clearly lacks a strip down the left margin of the first page. An examination of the original would provide the basis for a better supplying of more exact wording, along with the careful measurement of the likely missing components. Telford undoubtedly identified Grace Walton as the recipient of this letter on the basis of Wesley's subsequent letter of March 18, 1769, to Sarah Crosby, which reads in part: "I advise you as I did Grace Walton formerly, . . ." While there is some similarity between these letters, there is not enough evidence to identify positively Grace Walton as the recipient of the earlier correspondence.

The letter was apparently addressed to "Mr. John Smith's/Writer in Gally-gate/Aberdeen/Scotland," and may have been written in such a way as to let the addressee deliver it to the unnamed recipient, surely a woman and possibly Grace Walton. Until the original is rediscovered, however, insertions and identifications must be made conjecturally. The provisional text based upon Bryant, which may be used in Wesley, *Bicentennial Edition,* volume 27, follows with annotations indicating pertinent textual variations.

London, Sept. 8, 1761

[My dear sis]ter,

If a few more Persons come in when you are meeting, [you may] either enlarge four or five Minutes on [ye][1] Question you had [or give][2] a short Exhortation (perhaps for five or six minutes) [and then] sing & pray: This is going as far as I think any Woman[3] [should do.] For the Words of the Apostle are clear.[4] I think & [?as] always, [that his][5] meaning is this: "I suffer not a woman to teach in a [public congr]egation, nor thereby to usurp Authority over the man." [The man] God has invested with this Prerogative: whereas teaching [Some later lines are missing, surely because of a strip missing from the outer margin, not (apparently) affecting the address. This strip may have contained the postmark.]

NOTES

1. Bryant, "a"; Telford, "the."
2. Bryant, "d"; Telford, "with."
3. & 4. Sentences omitted by Telford.
5. Bryant, "-"; Telford, "its."

APPENDIX D: A MARY BOSANQUET LETTER TO JOHN WESLEY, JUNE 1771

C OPY IN CROSBY, MS LETTERBOOK. Duke University. The location of the original manuscript is unknown. A transcript was first published in Taft, *Scripture Doctrine of Women's Preaching* (1820), pp. 19–21. A full transcript is also included in *A History of the Methodist Church in Great Britain* (1988), 4:168–71. For sources other than those herein noted, see p. 172, n. 4, above.

Cross Hall, near Leeds, 1771

Very dear & Honoured Sir,

Various have been my hindrances in writing, but none sufficient to have kept me so long silent to you, had I not been at a loss on one particular subject. I wanted your advice and direction in an important point, viz to know if you approved my light in it. Yet I have been toss'd between the temptations of Satan and the arguments of men, that I really could not tell what I thought myself nor how to state the case fairly at all; but at present I think, both outward and inward circumstances tend to bring me to a crisis, and my light been [being?] clearer, I will now open all my mind: and I feel a faith God will make you my Director in this thing, so as to remove my scruples one way or the other.

My soul desires peace & would follow after it with all, especially with God's children, and more particularly with those that act as heads among us. I would hold up their hands in every point that lays within the short limits of my power, and perhaps can say more strongly than many, I honour them for their works' sake. Yet that word of the prophets has oft come to my mind, "Woe is me that my mother has borne me a man of contention"; how painful is it to be forced to contend with those with whom one desires above all things to live in peace, is well known to you, Sir, by experience. My present situation is very peculiar—

When we first settled at Leytonstone, Sr. Ryan & I began with little kind of prayer meetings, and they were productive of a blessing. Afterwards, on coming into Yorkshire, Sr. Crosby, Br. S. & I did the same now and then, till the people desiring us to come to such and such of their houses the number of these meetings increased so as to return sometimes three or four times a week; the numbers of persons that came to them increased also, hundreds of carnal persons coming to them, who would not go near a preaching-house; and it is enough to say God was with us and made it known by the effects in many places.

However, about a month ago, one of our preachers began to express great dislike to it many ways. We conversed on it in a friendly manner and I asked him, if my abstaining from any more meetings in a particular place would satisfy him (tho' Mr. O. had desired me to come there). He said no. He thought it quite unscriptural for women to speak in the Church & his conscience constrained him to prevent it. We had a good deal more conversation but got no nearer, tho' were very friendly. Afterwards some others conversed with me on the same point, alledging the same objections and Satan strongly persuaded me to swallow them down altogether, and I found it very comfortable and easy to nature. However, on weighing the thing before the Lord, I think it appears to me thus: I believe I am called to do all I can for God, and in order thereto, when I am asked to go with Br. T. to a prayer meeting, I may both sing, pray and converse with them, either particularly, or in general, according to the numbers. Likewise when Br. T. goes to preach in little country places, after he has done, I believe I may speak a few words to the people and pray with them. Twice it has happened, thro' the zeal of the people, that they gave out a meeting in a preaching house, because they had no private house that would hold the people, nor one quarter of them. When we came I was sorry, but could not tell what to do; hundreds of unawakened persons were there, & my heart yearned over them. I feared my Master should say, "Their blood will I require of you." So after Br. T. had preached I spoke to them. I believe I may go as far as I have mentioned above. But several object to this in our own round, & out of it, saying, "A woman ought not to teach, nor take authority over the man." I understand that text to mean no more than that a woman shall not take authority over her husband, but be in subjection, neither shall she teach at all by usurping authority, she shall not meddle in Church discipline, neither order nor regulate anything in which men are concerned in the matters of the Church; but I do not apprehend it means she shall not entreat sinners to come to Jesus, nor say, Come, and I will tell you what God hath done for my soul.

Ob:—But the Apostle says, I suffer not a woman to speak in the Church—but learn at home. I answer—was not that spoke in reference to a time of dispute and contention, when many were striving to be heads and leaders, so that his saying, She is not to speak, here seems to me to imply no more than the other, she is not to meddle with Church Government.

Ob:—Nay, but it meant literally, not to speak by way of Edification, while in the Church, or company of promiscuous worshippers.

An:—Then why is it said, Let the woman prophesy with her head covered, or can she prophesy without speaking? or ought she to speak but not to edification?

Ob:—She may now and then, if under a peculiar impulse, but never else.

An:—But how often is she to feel this impulse? Perhaps you will say, two or three times in her life; perhaps *God* will say, two or three times in a week, or day—and where shall we find the Rule for this? But the consequences (here I acknowledge is my own objection, that all I do is *lawful,* I have no doubt, but is it expedient? that, my dear Sir, I want your light in) but what are the consequences feared?

Ob:—Why, for forty that comes to hear the preaching, one hundred & fifty will come to your meetings. Will not this cause their hands to hang down?

An:—That only forty comes to preaching, I am sorry for, but that perhaps a hundred careless carnal sinners comes to our meetings (who would not otherwise hear at all) I am not sorry for, neither should I think this would make the hands of any sensible, gracious man hang down. He must know tis no excellence in us that draws them, but the novelty of the thing; and does it not bring many to preaching, let any impartial person judge.

Ob:—But a worse consequence than this is to be feared: will not some improper woman follow your example?

An:—This I acknowledge I have feared; but the same might be said of preachers that come out, will not some improper man follow them?

Ob:—But if an improper man comes out, the Church has power to stop his mouth, but you will not let yours be stopped.

An:—Yes, on the same condition I will. You would not say to him, no *man* must speak, therefore be silent; but only, *You* are not the proper man. Now allowing women may speak, prove to me, it is not my personal call, and I will both lovingly and cheerfully obey.

Ob:—But is it safe to trust women to teach? Does not the Apostle say, She was first in the transgression, therefore let her take no authority, and does not Mr. Wesley observe, She is more easily deceived, and more easily deceives?

An:—He does, and there is much truth in it. On this supposition, the man's understanding is stronger, and his passions harder, consequently not so easily wrought on; and on the other hand, supposing the woman's understanding weaker, & her passions more tender, she is certainly more liable to be deceived; and probably speaking more to the affections than to the understanding, she is more likely to deceive; so far I allow. But may not all this objection be removed by this single caution: Let no woman be allowed to speak among the people any longer than she speaks and acts according to the Oracles of God; and while she speaks according to the truth she cannot lead the people into an error.

Ob:—Well, but is it consistent with that modesty the Christian religion requires in a woman professing godliness?

An:—It may be, and is, painful to it, but I do not see it inconsistent with it, and that for this reason: does not Christian modesty stand in these two particulars, Purity and Humility? 1st I apprehend it consists in cutting off every act, word and thought that in the least infringes on the purity God delights in. 2dly in cutting off every act, word, and thought, which in the least infringes on *humility*, knowing throughly our own place, and rendering to every one their due. Endeavouring to be little, and unknown, as far as the order of

God will permit, and simply following that order, leaving the event to God. Now I do not apprehend Mary sinned against either of these heads, or could in the least be accused of immodesty, when she carried the joyful news of her Lord's Resurrection and in that sense taught the Teachers of Mankind. Neither was the woman of Samaria to be accused of immodesty when she invited the whole city to come to Christ. Neither do I think the woman mentioned in the 20th chapter of the 2nd Samuel could be said to sin against modesty, tho' she called the General of the opposite army to converse with her, and then (verse the 22nd) went to all the people, both Heads and others, to give them her advice and by it the City was saved. Neither do I suppose Deborah did wrong in publicly declaring the message of the Lord, and afterwards accompanying Barak to war, because his hands hung down at going without her.

Ob:—But all these were extraordinary calls; sure you will not say yours is an extraordinary call?

An:—If I did not believe so, I would not act in an extraordinary manner. I do not believe every woman is called to speak publicly, no more than every man to be a Methodist preacher, yet some have an extraordinary call to it, and woe be to them if they obey it not.

Ob:—But do you believe you have this public call?

An:—Not as absolute as some others, nevertheless, I feel a part of it, and what little I see to be my call, I dare not leave undone.

Ob:—But if the people are continually coming to your Meetings, they will not have time to attend the stated ones.

An:—That I have often thought of, and therefore, I know no place except home where I meet more than once a month, and sometimes not that, as there is so many places to go to, and that caution, not to multiply meetings, I see very necessary.

Now, my dear Sir, I have told you all my mind on this head, and taken the freedom to incroach a deal on your time and I find a liberty to say, I believe your exact direction I shall be enabled to follow, and shall be greatly obliged to you for the same.

Mr. Oliver is very desirous of our doing all the good we can; and indeed I am pained for the trouble he has had on our account. But it is not only on ours, for various difficulties have, I believe, interrupted some of his comfort this year; if he stays another year with us, I hope he will see more fruit of his labours: the Lord gives him a patient, loving spirit, and his preaching is very animating and profitable.

I praise my God I feel Him very near, and I prove His faithfulness every day, but I want to live as I do not, and to feel every moment that word, My God and my all. I am &c. M.B.

APPENDIX E:
A JOSEPH BENSON LETTER

THE FOLLOWING TEXT IS THE transcript of a letter/draft in the handwriting of the Reverend Joseph Benson, Number 167 in the W. L. Watkinson Collection, New Room, Bristol. The manuscript contains no postal markings of any kind and is most certainly a draft of a letter sent to a Methodist itinerant preacher. It would seem to be most likely that the draft was produced in response to the controversy surrounding the labors of Elizabeth Hurrell, and may be assigned a provisional date of October 1775. While it is impossible to identify the recipient with any measure of certainty, the most likely candidate would seem to be Robert Empringham, one of Benson's colleagues who was sympathetic to the cause of women's preaching. On these questions, see pp. 176–77, n. 72, above.

My very dear friend,

I should not so soon have troubled you again with [this] a letter, had not some particulars in your last very acceptable favour seem'd to call for [my] speedy attention. Passing over some things less material, I hasten to assure you I am very sorry you should be so far overseen as to allow any *female* whatsoever to take your place in the pulpit. I wonder where was your conscience & prudence? *Conscience* I say, for does

---

Portions of the text enclosed in square brackets [] indicate editorial changes made by Benson in the text. Where the text is obscure, question marks have been inserted so as to indicate conjectural insertions.

not an inspired Apostle, expressly forbid a woman to speak in the church? "God (says he) is not the author of confusion but of peace" [& the Spirits of the Prophets are subject to the prophets."] Having laid down this general preposition he proceeds to infer from it the absolute necessity of imposing silence on women in the congregation; well know^g w^t confusion w^d ensue if they were permitted to speak in public. [It follows] "Let your women be silent in the churches (εν ταιζ εκκλησιαιζ) in the assemblies for it is not permitted them to speak, but to be in subjection as the Law also saith. And if they would learn any thing let them ask their own husbands at home. For it is a shame (αισχρον) tis indecent, unbecoming the modesty of the sex for a woman to speak in the church or assembly." Now my dear Sir, may we not, with as much reason, & as good a grace, set aside any other part of scripture as the passage before us? May we not with as good reason neglect & disobey every apostolical [command] injunction & divine command as this here given? Sure St. Paul authorises us to thinks so, for he immediately adds vs 37 "If any one think himself a Prophet or Spiritual, let him take knowledge that the things which I write to you are the COMMANDMENTS OF THE LORD. But if any one is ignorant, let him be ignorant." as if he had s^d his ignorance is wilful & therefore inexcusable. [As M^r W^y says in his notes], "at his peril."

Now dear friend, can you tell me why those who set aside this command^t of the L^d do not set aside all his other command^ts? Can you tell me why those [fema] daring females, who seem['d] to have stript themselves of the[ir] chief ornament of their sex, I mean chaste & humble modesty, & made themselves naked to their shame do not also commit fornication, & adultery, get drunk & swear? Surely you will not alledge "these vices are forbidden in Sirit [sic], & their consciences will not suffer them to [plunge] give into them." For 'tis plain, by their conduct they pay little regard to the word of God or the dictates of conscience, in as much as in direct oposition to both they have [impudence] effrontery enough, to ascend [into] a pulpit & harange a promiscuous congregation for an hour together, [with] when they are by God himself expressly forbid to so much as speak (by way of teach^g) in a[n] public assembly, yea or to ask questions *there,* but are to inquire of their husbands at home.

And what excuse can they offer for their most manifest & flagrant violation of God's *Law?*—Sure they will not say that souls are perishing for want of *preaching,* & because the Lord raises up no witnesses of the contrary sex, therefore they think themselves authoris'd to take upon them this ministry?—For 1st supposing it was so. Supposing souls were destroy'd for lack of knowledge & there were no men [to] endow'd by him from whom every good & perfect gift cometh with gifts & graces, to warn a guilty people to flee from the wrath to come, yet even then, I do not [supp] conceive they w^d have authority "to do evil that good might come," to commit open sin, by breaking a plain command of God, that they might call others to repentance for their sins. But why sh^d we suppose what has no existence? God does now (as he has done in all ages) he raises up preachers of ye superior sex to declare his gospel, & thus we may still pray the Lord of ye harvest to send [others?], yet we must acknowledge to the glory of his grace, there are now abundance of preachers. [But that is not the case There is no want of preaching or of preachers] at least as *able* & as *gracious* as they can pretend to be, as I imagine they themselves allow. They do not, I suppose, presume to say they have more grace or greater gifts than [other] the generality of our preachers. What then in the name of wonder do they say for themselves? On what principle do they act? What are the motives of their conduct? Let them tell us this.—Sure they must produce some very extraordinary reasons for so extraordinary a conduct, or [no reasonable man will be satisfied otherwise] we must conclude, not humility, the love of Jss. & a concern for the salvation of souls, but pride, self love & a concern for their own honour have induced them to assume their present employ^t.—an extraordinary conduct I say, for sure it cannot be parallel'd in any age of the Church of X^t. Did our Lord appoint & commission any female Apostles, or evangelists? Did any of [that] this weaker sex presume to take upon them any such office? At least was any such thing allow'd of in the earliest & purest ages of the Church? That there were Prophetesses [in the] among the primitive Chris^s is granted & that there sometimes (viz. when under an extraordinary & immediate impulse) utter'd their prophecies in the assemblies. But this is nothing to those, who do not even pretend to be under any immediate impulse or to have any new revelation to communicate. Nay I grant further that a few daring & immodest women in the church at Corinth (a place noted for lewdness) presumed to take upon them the office of teachers, but the Apostle knowing the confusion wch was likely to ensue if a stop was not put to such proceedings, if a general liberty of that kind was given to that aspiring sex, who are seldom content wth the station [providence] God has assign'd them, but are ever usurping authority over the [men] man; as well as knowing it contrary to the will of God & the order of providence, expressly [for] bids them *be silent.* And thus sh^d M^r W^y act [if] with respect to our [fe] heroines. He & the Conference sh'd bid them *be silent.*

But I fear they w^d hardly obey. Having already disregarded X^t & his inspired Apostles, & [now] counter to the stream of all antiquity 'tis no wonder if they sh^d pour contempt on the order of M^r W^y & his preachers. Tho' I must say, I hope better things of them & things that accompany salvation. I w^d not rank them wth the lew'd & imprudent whores & actresses at Corinth, who after their conversion, still retained too much of their former boldness & effrontery. They, I trust, have still a spark of modesty & humility left, wch tho' burried under the [noise & din] ashes of popular clamour & self admiration, is still capable of being excited & kindled into a divine flame.—I am quite sincere & serious in all this & I add, I do surely believe—it is a desire of Satan to cast an odium upon the spreading [work] revival of religion begun & carried on by [the] M^r W^y & others in Eng^d & of consequence to hinder its [progress?——for their part of the thing?] If it was but [?] in [?] that such proceedings were allow'd of among us, we might I fear bid adieu to it. Our usefulness in all probability w^d soon be at an end.

—I wish M^r W^y & the Brethren w^d take the matter into serious consideration. It is now high time to do it.—If it is winked at for a few years, we shall have female preachers in abundance, more I dare say than men. This we may infer from what has happen'd among the Quakers; (tho to do their women justice they never ascend a pulpit, but modestly stand on a level wth the men) they [not] allowing of this at first, the evil has spread by little & little, till behold the sexes have changed places, the woman is become the head of the man, the men almost all, learn in subjection & the women teach wth authority! These things ought not so to be!

APPENDIX F: SELECTED INVITATIONS TO MARY BARRITT

T HE FOLLOWING FIVE LETTERS, given in part or in their entirety, are representative of numerous letters Mary Barritt received both from itinerant preachers and friends requesting her to preach.

Sheffield, July 21, 1798

My Dear Sister,

I am sorry to inform you that my dear fellow labourer, Mr Bramwell, is not able to supply his places through lameness by a wound in his leg. I must therefore request you to go to Chesterfield tomorrow for him. If there be any one from that place at Hanley to-morrow morning, send a message by that friend to turn their own preaching into a prayer meeting, and publish for you in the evening. I must also beg you to make the collection for Kingswood School, at Hanley and Chester-field.—Brother Pinder can inform our friends at Ridgeway of your not going to-morrow evening. I will endeavour for you to be there at some future period, for *you must stay with us a great while longer.* Our friends at Doncaster are very urgent for you to be at their love-feast to-morrow week. I have therefore consented: they are to come for you that morning. If I can get away on Tuesday, I purpose spending a night with my friends at Chesterfield, and going by the coach the next morning; if so, I hope to see you again before I go off to Bristol;—but if not, I wish you much of God in all places, and much fruit of your labour. I bless God that so far from envying you, I rejoice in your success. If good be done, I will praise the Lord. I feel love to precious souls, and am thankful when any of them are taken from the snare of the devil, and brought into the fold of Christ. Pray for me: I do for you. May God keep you like *Mary* at his feet, till he shall take you to his throne! Farewell!

I am your affectionate friend,
James Wood

Source: Taft, *Memoirs,* 1:103.

A portion of a letter from Jonathan Brown to Mary Barritt, Whitby, October 7, 1798:

As soon as you can let me know when you will be with us and w^t way you will come. N.B. *You must stay one month at least*—We still find that God is with us.

Source: Meth. Arch.

A portion of a letter from Mr. Lomas to Miss Barritt, Manchester, November 22, 1798:

My Dear Friend,

I desired Mr. W—— to tell you, that a great many friends would be glad to see you in Manchester, and that the Pulpits would be opened unto you; but being informed that you are gone to Whitehaven, our friends, with myself, are desirous you should be wrote to, and invited to come and spend a little time amongst us.

Source: Taft, *Original Letters,* pp. 129–30.

Sheffield, March 31, 1800

Dear Sister,

I told you in Manchester, that I should be glad to see you in Sheffield, and am still of the same mind. I therefore beg you will, as soon as possible, come over and help us. The friends in Sheffield, and all thro' the circuit will be glad to see and hear you. There is an open door and a large field for usefulness, and I shall greatly rejoice to see you made the Instrument of a Revival of the work of God amongst us. Mr. Longden from whom I expect you will receive this, will second my request.—Wishing you much happiness and prosperity, I am

Your's in our Lord Jesus,
Thos Rutherford

Source: Meth. Arch.

A portion of a letter from Mr. McAllum to Miss Barritt, Thurmaston, July 15, 1800:

In looking over your plan, I am glad to find that you are going to many of my old hospitable friends houses. . . . On the twenty-ninth, you will not be a great way from one part of our Circuit. If you are willing to come from S——, on Tuesday the twenty-ninth, into our Circuit . . . I will . . . go back to H——with you the next day.

Source: Taft, *Original Letters,* pp. 120–21

APPENDIX G: SELECTED LETTERS OF ENCOURAGEMENT TO MISS MARY BARRITT (AFTERWARD MRS. TAFT)

M ARY BARRITT RECEIVED COUNTLESS letters of support and encouragement both before and after her marriage to the great protagonist of women's preaching, Zechariah Taft. This appendix consists of six letters of this nature or the pertinent segments from these pieces of correspondence.

A portion of a letter from Mrs. Baisden to Miss Barritt, Leeds, June 6, 1798:

> I trust you will be made (under God) a blessing in Sheffield. May the Lord stand by you, and make you very simple, and very lively, and when you have done your work in that part of his vineyard, may it please him to send you to us again. Many will rejoice to see you.

> *Source:* Taft, *Memoirs,* 1:87–88.

A portion of a letter from Edward Wade to Mary Barritt, Sturton Grange, March 1799:

> I rejoice to hear that the Lord is carrying on His blessed work at Whitehaven, and that you keep so happy and valiant. O! how am I ashamed that I have been such a coward; that I have not been more valiant for my Master. . . . The Lord bless you Mary, and make you as happy as an Angel, and keep you in the very dust, and loosen your tongue, and enlarge your heart.

> *Source: Arm. Mag. (B.C.)* 6:395.

A portion of a letter from I. & R. Birchenall to Mary Barritt, Macclesfield, December 24, 1799:

. . . the Cry in general is When will Miss Barritt Come again—will she ever Come—may the God of Heaven open your way soon. Amen.

Source: Meth. Arch.

Taghill, Nottingham, October 16, 1800

My Dear Sister,

I was much affected when I came home and found you were gone; especially as we had both promised for Dunington circuit and Leicester, and thousands were waiting for you at Mount Sorrel. There is such an opening for you in that country as I never saw before.

I bless God that you ever came amongst us. Were it in the order of God, I should not have the least objection to stand by you in every place till we take our seats in Glory. Pray for us every day. I trust I shall ever pray for you.

I have had a powerful season at Bulwell; several souls saved. The same at Watnal, and last night at Eastwood— Glory, glory, glory to God!—Please write to me soon, and tell me of your journeys and labours in every place. The Lord bless you all; and may thousands be saved!

Your's &c.
Wm Bramwell

Source: Sigston, *Memoir of William Bramwell,* 1:191–92.

Bristol, October 25th, 1802

My dear unknown Friends,[1]

It is now about 33 years since I was at Dover or any place in that neighbourhood, so that I suppose there is no person now living who has any remembrance of me, yet nevertheless I cannot help wishing the prosperity of the work of God among you; it is but too well known that this has been for some considerable time at a very low ebb in Dover. I therefore could not help thinking that it was a kind providence that

Mary Barritt was stationed among you, and that by the blessing of God she might be the instrument of reviving this blessed work among you. Perhaps there never was an age in which the Lord so greatly condescended to the curiosity of mankind in order to do them good than in the present. He has been pleased to raise up and send forth all sorts of instruments—men, almost of all descriptions, poor men, rich men, learned and unlearned, yea black as well as white men, and if he is pleased to send by a woman also, who shall say unto him, "What doest Thou?"

The late Mr. Wesley was very much opposed to women preaching, yet when he saw that the Lord owned and blessed the labours of Mrs. Crosby, Mrs. Fletcher and the late Miss Horral[2] he was obliged to allow that the Lord is pleased to go out of his common way sometimes for the good of his poor creatures and therefore he would say nothing against women preaching in extraordinary cases.

As to myself, I have long thought that it is far more difficult to prove that women ought not to preach than many imagine. Let anyone seriously consider I Cor. 11:5, "Prophesieth with her head uncovered." Now prophesying there has generally been understood preaching. If then, the women never did preach at all, why did the Lord by the Apostle give these instructions respecting their heads being covered or uncovered.

I have been no great friend to women preaching among us, but when I evidently see that good is done, I dare not forbid them.

I seriously believe Mrs. Taft to be a deeply pious, prudent, modest woman. I believe the Lord hath owned and blest her labours very much, and many, yea very many souls have been brought to the saving knowledge of God by her preaching. Many have come to hear her out of curiosity who would not come to hear a man, and have been awakened and converted to God. I do assure you there is much fruit of her labours in many parts of our Connexion. I would therefore advise you by no means oppose her preaching, but let her have full liberty, and try whether the Lord will not make her an instrument of reviving his work among you.

I am an old man and have been long in the work, and I do seriously believe that if you yourselves do not hinder it, God will make Mrs. Taft the instrument of great good to you. Take care you do not fight against God. Many will come to hear her everywhere who will not come to hear your preachers. Let these poor souls have a chance for their lives; do not hinder them.

I am, though unknown, your affectionate
friend and brother in Christ,
J. Pawson

Please to give this to your Leaders and Stewards.

My Dear Brethren,

From a pretty long acquaintance with Mrs. Taft, I most heartily unite with our honoured Father, Mr. Pawson, in beseeching you not to hinder her exercising her talents among you; for I most assuredly believe that God has called her to declare the glad tidings of salvation to the world and that he has already honoured her in the conversion of multitudes.

Yours affectionately,
J. S. Pipe

Source: Meth. Arch.

Ashfor Apr 5th 1803

Dear Mrs. Taff

My heart and views is not changed for the worse Nor agains you But Do Consider it Duty to Speak of your Usefullness and allways Did when their was no Probility of ever seeing You hear or have an oppertunity telling of You Being the Means of my Conversion to your Selfe. O my Dear Friend While You was Use to be Speaking and Praying in York it was to my Soul as though I was on the Boarders of Heaven And not to Me But many more. I Never shall forget York Tadcaster and Weatherby Love Feast And the very Many Precious Souls that Asembled With me to Tell Of what the Lord had Done for our Souls through Your Instrumentality. Bless His Holy Name for Bringing you into this Part that the People may see And hear What I have so Long Aserted And Mentioned Aboute You. Doo come with Mr. Cobb to Tenterdon And I will Meet You their. the People are all Enquiring After You and to know When you come. And you Will see If I have canged for the worse my Soul Regoice at Your Name Being Mentioned and Doo oppose all that come in my way Bouth People and Preachers that Speak Against You. Bless the Lord I Silence all When I Begin to Tell how You was the Means of My Conversion and Talk Aboute the Love of God Shed Abroad in my Heart. They see and own it is the Work of God or I had not Continued Serious 4 Years. When a Souldier even to the Present time Through the Desire of the Presbatarians I Rote to Mr. Rogers to come And see them not Me. But if He comes I am Ready Prepared to Talk Aboute You as I have Done With many others this is not to Flatter You But is my Duty and I is Always Ready to Doo it Now Bless You and Bless Mr. Taff. may you Engoy every Happiness I can wish You Is the Desire

Your son in the Lord
George Lees

Source: Meth. Arch.

NOTES

1. This letter was not directed to Mary Taft, but to the stewards and leaders of the Dover Society to pave the way for her work among them.
2. Elizabeth Hurrell

APPENDIX H: A SERMON REGISTER OF THE WOMEN PREACHERS

T HE FOLLOWING REGISTER IS an exhaustive list of all known texts employed by the women preachers of early Methodism up to the time of John Wesley's death in 1791. The listing has been extended, however, to July 1803 so as to include a representative sampling of the scriptural material utilized by subsequent preachers, primarily Mary Barritt (afterward Mrs. Taft), who left a more complete record of her preaching activities in her *Memoirs*.

Wherever ascertainable, the following information is also included: preacher's last name, date, place, and source. The following abbreviations have been used with regard to source material:

Clarke	J.B.B. Clarke, *Account of Adam Clarke*, q.v.
Fletcher	Fletcher, *Account of Sarah Lawrence*, q.v.
Memoirs	Taft, *Memoirs*, q.v.
Moore	Moore, *Fletcher*, q.v.
Sutcliffe	Sutcliffe, *Experience of Frances Pawson*, q.v.
Taft	Taft, *Holy Women*, q.v.

TEXT	PREACHER	DATE	PLACE	SOURCE
		1773		
Dan. 3:16	Bosanquet	Feb. 2	A——	Moore, 98
		1774		
1 Cor. 13	Crosby	Dec. 1		Sutcliffe, 33
		1775		
Matt. 4:17	Bosanquet	Sept. 10	D——	Moore, 108
		1776		
John 11:28	Bosanquet	Apr.	B——	Moore, 113
Job 22:21	Bosanquet	June 11	B——	Moore, 114
1 Sam. 15:22a	Bosanquet	Aug. 30		Moore, 115–16
1 Sam. 15:22b	Bosanquet	Sept. 15	Goker	Moore, 117
Isa. 33:22	Bosanquet	Sept. 15	Huddersfield	Moore, 118–20
		1778		
Deut. 6:15	Bosanquet	Nov. 15	Daw-green	Moore, 130
		1784		
Eph. 2:8	Sewell	Apr. 28	Thurlton	Clarke, 1:215–16
Exod. 3:3	Proudfoot	Apr./May		Clarke, 1:216
		1785		
Matt. 25	Fletcher		Bristol	Moore, 201
Rev. 3:20	Mallet	Dec. 25	Long Stratton	*Arm. Mag.* 11:92
John 7:37	Mallet	Dec. 26	Long Stratton	*Arm. Mag.* 11:92
		1786		
Mark 16:16	Mallet	Jan. 15	Long Stratton	*Arm. Mag.* 11:93
Isa. 58:1	Mallet	Jan. 24	Long Stratton	*Arm. Mag.* 11:93
1 Pet. 4:18	Mallet	Jan. 27	Long Stratton	*Arm. Mag.* 11:93
Isa. 55:1	Mallet	Jan. 30	Long Stratton	*Arm. Mag.* 11:93
Ps. 142:7	Fletcher	July 21	Madeley	Moore, 222

TEXT	PREACHER	DATE	PLACE	SOURCE
		1787		
Ps. 130:7	Fletcher	Dec. 17		Moore, 236
		1793		
Jer. 50:5	Fletcher	May 5	The Dale	Moore, 283–84
		1797		
1 Chron. 16:10	Barritt	(Aug.)	Keswick	*Memoirs*, 1:74
		1798		
2 Kings 10:1	Barritt	May 21	Sheffield	*Memoirs*, 1:90
Luke 24:25	Barritt	June 10	Bamford	*Memoirs*, 1:92
Rev. 6:17	Barritt	June 10	Eyam	*Memoirs*, 1:93
Luke 19:10	Barritt	June 13	Bradwell	*Memoirs*, 1:94
Isa. 42:18	Barritt	June 14	Bradwell	*Memoirs*, 1:95
Luke 6:47	Barritt	June 15	Eyam	*Memoirs*, 1:96
1 John 1:9	Barritt	June 18	Bakewell	*Memoirs*, 1:99
Acts 2:47	Barritt	June 20	Towark	*Memoirs*, 1:100
Luke 19:10	Barritt	Sept. ?	Barnsley	*Memoirs*, 1:102
		1799		
Mal. 3:16	Barritt	June 30	Tadcaster	*Memoirs*, 1:118
Heb. 9:27	Barritt	June 30	Tadcaster	*Memoirs*, 1:118
Mal. 3:2	Barritt	July 18	Ferrybridge	*Memoirs*, 1:120
Mark 5:34	Barritt	July 24	Skipton	*Memoirs*, 1:121
Heb. 4:9	Barritt	Aug. 2	Manchester	*Memoirs*, 1:123
Rom. 6:22	Barritt	Aug. 2	Manchester	*Memoirs*, 1:123
John 5:17	Barritt	Aug. 8	Shude-Hill	*Memoirs*, 1:123
Rev. 6:17	Barritt	Aug. 10	Shude-Hill	*Memoirs*, 1:123
Ps. 16:3	Barritt	Sept. 8	Northwich	*Memoirs*, 1:124
Matt. 19:25	Barritt	Sept. 8	Northwich	*Memoirs*, 1:124
Matt. 3:10	Barritt	Sept. 10	Northwich	*Memoirs*, 1:125
Exod. 17:7	Barritt	Sept. 22	Manchester	*Memoirs*, 1:131
Exod. 14:13	Barritt	Sept. 22	Manchester	*Memoirs*, 1:131
Jon. 1:6	Barritt	Sept. 30	Bury	*Memoirs*, 1:131
John 3:14	Barritt	Nov. 17	Macclesfield	*Memoirs*, 1:132
John 1:46	Barritt	Nov. 17	Macclesfield	*Memoirs*, 1:132
John 1:46	Barritt	Nov./ Dec.	Lower-Ease	*Memoirs*, 1:132

TEXT	PREACHER	DATE	PLACE	SOURCE
Dan. 5:27	Barritt	Dec. 4	Buxton	*Memoirs*, 1:133
Ps. 37:4	Barritt	Dec. ?	Halifax-Lane	*Memoirs*, 1:137

1800

Rev. 6:17	Barritt	Feb. 16	Great Leek	*Memoirs*, 1:147
1 Pet. 4:18	Barritt	Feb. 20?	Wimeswold	*Memoirs*, 1:147
Ps. 40:2	Barritt	(June ?)	Calverton	*Memoirs*, 1:158
Acts 2:47	Barritt	Oct. 12	Normanton	*Memoirs*, 1:163
Acts 16:31	Barritt	Dec. 1	Robstom	*Memoirs*, 1:166
Esther 6:9	Barritt	Dec. 9	Wighill	*Memoirs*, 1:167
Matt. 7:13	Barritt	Dec. 10	Warton	*Memoirs*, 1:167
Ps. 1:6	Barritt	Dec. 11	Spofforth	*Memoirs*, 1:167
Gen. 19:17	Barritt	Dec. 12	Kirkby	*Memoirs*, 1:167
Luke 19:17	Barritt	Dec. 23	Church-Fenton	*Memoirs*, 1:168

1801

Rom. 8:32	Barritt	Apr. 12	Preston	*Memoirs*, 2:13
Rev. 14:13	Barritt	July 20	Tanfield	*Memoirs*, 2:18

1802

1 Pet. 4:7	Barritt	Mar. 15	Nessall	*Memoirs*, 2:26
Job 21:3	Taft	Sept. 18	Dover	*Memoirs*, 2:48
1 John 1:9	Taft	Oct. 4	Canterbury	*Memoirs*, 2:49
John 11:36	Taft	?	York	*Memoirs*, 2:50
2 Cor. 5:11	Taft	Oct. ?	Sandwich	*Memoirs*, 2:53
Ps. 51:10	Taft	Nov. 21	Hamstreet	*Memoirs*, 2:63

1803

Isa. 38:1	Taft	Feb. 8	Sandwich	*Memoirs*, 2:71
2 Thess. 1:7–9	Goulden	Feb. 27	Wapping	*W.H.S.* 16:74
Mal. 3:16	Taft	Mar. 14	Sittingburn	*Memoirs*, 2:73
1 Cor. 6:19–20	Taft	Apr. 23	Deal	*Memoirs*, 2:83
Isa. 52:11	Eland	nd	Nottingham	Taft, 2:198
Acts 27:29	Fletcher	nd		Moore, 405

APPENDIX I: TEXT OF A SERMON BY MARY FLETCHER

THE FOLLOWING TEXT HAS BEEN copied from Moore, *Fletcher,* pp. 405–9, and is the only extant sermon of its type.

ACTS xxvii. 29.

They cast four anchors out of the stern, and wished for the day.

The situation of the ship wherein Paul and his companions were, seems to me to illustrate the state and situation of many of us here.—We are told,—"There arose a tempestuous wind called, in that country, Euroclydon;"—a kind of hurricane, not carrying the ship any one way, but driving her backwards and forwards with great violence. So it is in general with those who enter on the voyage of life. Satan, who is called "the Prince of the power of the air, and who ruleth in the hearts of the children of disobedience," keeps the mind in a continual agitation. Sometimes they are sunk, and almost crushed, under a weight of care; and again raised high in the waves of some expected pleasure. One while they are filled with resentment, on account of some slight from a neighbour, or an unjust accusation from an enemy; while the mind is harassed with the imagination, how it shall be cleared. Sometimes the most idle and extravagant fancies so deeply involve it, that no message from heaven could find any more entertainment than the Saviour could find in the Inn at Bethlehem. By all this, the soul becomes restless, and knows not where it is, nor which way it is going. It does not feel that it is in a state of probation, and that this trial is to fix its eternal lot. Dear souls, is not this

321

the case with some of you? You do not know where you are,—you do not consider this may be your last night, perhaps your last hour. Your eternal state will then be fixed for ever. If the Lord should call you this hour, are you ready? O, remember it is the word of Jehovah himself,—"The ox knoweth his owner, and the ass his master's crib, but Israel doth not know,—my people do not consider." Again, do you know where you are going? Why, you are going "the broad road," you are going to hell as fast as you can. It is a "narrow way" that leads to heaven, and you do not know one step of it. You have not begun to walk therein, nor perhaps to think about it. "O that you were wise, that you understood this, that you would consider your latter end!" It may be you find a great many things to divert and take up your mind; it is employed by Satan from hour to hour. You are like the disobedient Prophet, "asleep in the ship when a great storm lay upon them." You neither see nor know your danger. Are you the safer for this? Would not those who are awake cry out to such, "Awake, thou sleeper, and call upon thy God." Thou art on the very brink of destruction. Well then, permit me so to call upon you, lest when we meet at the great day, you should upbraid me, that I had once an opportunity of warning you, and that I did it but by halves; and so the blood of your souls shall be found in my skirts. I fear for many in this Parish. My soul oft weeps in secret for them, lest the word which to others proves "the savour of life," should to them become "the savour of death," and rise up in judgment against them.

But I hope you who are this night within the reach of my voice, are in a degree awakened, and most of you earnestly longing to be brought out of the storm into the quiet harbour of Jesu's breast. To these I chiefly feel my message to be, though I was not willing to leave the sleepers wholly disregarded. Well, let us see what they did in this great danger, that we may do likewise. Paul says,—"As we were exceedingly tossed with a tempest, the next day we lightened the ship, and the third day we cast out with our hands the tackling of the ship. And as neither sun nor stars appeared for many days,* and no small tempest lay on us, all hope of our being saved was taken away." Observe, first, they lightened the ship;—lighten your hearts! There is too much of the world in them.—They cast out their merchandise,—cast away your idols! You will say, perhaps, "I cannot." True, I know you cannot yourselves; but if you will "call on the Lord in the time of trouble," He hath said, "I will hear thee, and thou shalt glorify me." If you will begin to pray in good earnest, and persevere therein, as the Lord is true, you shall know "the liberty of his children," and have power to "cast all your idols to the moles and to the bats." Well, but "on the third day they cast out the tackling of the ship;"—the very thing which we might think they would have kept, in order to manage the vessel.—No, all must go! Cast away your false confidence in any thing of your own; despair of any help but from the Lord Jesus. Yet obey his word; "Look," remember He says, "Look unto me, and be saved," yea, "look unto him as the author and finisher of your faith." "Wait upon him;" and remember the mind is the mouth of the soul,—therefore, according as you feed your mind with thoughts, so will the state of your soul be discovered. "Look," I say, "unto him," and your soul shall ride out the storm.

And now a gleam of hope appears. Paul stood up and said, "Be of good courage,—for there shall be no loss of any life among you. The Angel of that God, whose I am, and whom I serve, stood by me this night, and said, Fear not, Paul, thou must be presented before Caesar, and, lo, I have given thee all them that sail with thee."—So may hope spring up to thee this present moment, whether thou art a poor backslider, or one of the ship's company, who till this very hour hast been fast asleep; but if now awake, if now in earnest, and willing to be saved,—come a step further yet, and observe what they did next.—"They cast four anchors out of the stern, and wished for day." There is no day to the soul till Christ manifests his cheering presence. In order to wait for that, follow their example,—"they cast out four anchors."—Let us do so this night. Remember it is your part to "believe," and it is the Lord's to give the "peace and joy" consequent on believing. Let us then make repeated acts of faith, so "casting our anchor" further and further within the veil, and we shall draw up our souls nearer and nearer to God.

Well, let us try to cast out one anchor now. I am sensible your cable is short; therefore we must seek for some ground as *near* you as we can. We will try, if we can, to find it in the "Creating love of God," surrounding us on every side. Look through the creation,—observe the tender love of the birds towards their young, yea, even the most savage beasts! From whence does this spring? It is from God. It is a shadow of that infinite compassion which reigns in His heart. Rise a little higher. Fix your eye on man. How does he love a stubborn son who will neither serve God nor him? True, he frowns on him, and corrects him, lest it should be said to him as to Eli, "Thou preferrest thy son before me."—But if that son shed but a tear of sorrow,—raise but a sigh of repentance,—if he but come a few steps, how do the father's bowels yearn towards him! How doth he run to meet him! Now carry the idea a little higher;—are ye not the offspring of God? Has he not said, "I have created thee for my glory, I have formed thee for my praise?" Is not "his mercy over all his works?" Believe, then, that "this Author of all love is more ready to give the Holy Spirit to you, than you are to give good gifts to your children." Will not this anchor take? Does it still come home? Well, the ground is good, but your cable is too short. Let us try another anchor;—and we will drop it on "Redeeming love."

Lift up your eyes of faith,—behold your bleeding Saviour! See all your sins laid on his sacred head! Behold him as your surety before the Throne, and hear him plead,—"I have tasted death for every man. Thou, Father, wast in me, reconciling the world to thyself, not imputing their trespasses to them." I stood before thee charged with them all. If this poor soul, who cries for mercy, is deeply in debt to thee, "place it to my account; I will repay." Now ventue on him! Venture freely. He hath drunk all the bitter cup for *you,* and he offers this night to take you into fellowship and communion with himself. "He was delivered for your offences!" He hath cancelled all the charge against you; yea, "He was raised again for your justification." Your Surety is exalted, in proof that your debt is paid. Come, let me hear some voice among you giving praise, and saying with the Christian Poet,—

> Now I have found the ground, wherein
> *Sure* my soul's anchor may remain;
> The wounds of Jesus, for my sin,
> Before the world's foundation slain.

Methinks this anchor will hold.—Is there not an increase of hope? Hearken! You shall hear his voice. Himself hath said, "Hear, O my people, and I will speak!" Heaven is never dumb, but when man hardens his heart.

But, perhaps, there are some poor trembling souls still left behind. For the sake of such we will try to find firm ground a little nearer yet. We will drop our third anchor on the

Promises. Here are some quite within your reach: "He that cometh unto me, I will in no wise cast out. Whosoever will, let him take of the water of life freely. I came not to call the righteous but sinners to repentance."—Yes,—"He came to seek and to save that which is lost." Are *you* lost? Lost in your own estimation? Then he came to *save you*. Yes, and to *seek* you too;—and he seeks you this night as diligently as ever shepherd sought his lost sheep. Will you be found of him? Yes, if you will believe in his love. Remember he "willeth not the death of a sinner; but had rather he would turn from his wickedness and live." And though it should appear to thee as if a mountain stood in the way, yet this is the word of truth,—"If thou canst believe, all things are possible to him that believeth. Thou shalt say to this mountain, Depart; and it shall be done." There is no getting one step forward in the heavenly road without courage, or, in other words, faith; and I trust there are here many whose anchor has held in the first ground, "Creating love;" more in the second, "Redeeming love;" and surely trembling sinners have found some hold in the *Promises.* The "Word of God" is full of them, and they are all for *you.* All belong to a wounded conscience,—to sinners seeking the power of faith, to conquer their sins, and bring them to God. But yet I fear there may be a feeble-minded one who is still left behind, and I am unwilling any should remain in darkness, when Christ offers them light. But, perhaps, such will say,—"O, I am an ungrateful sinner. I have turned away my eyes from Jesus. The world, and the wild imaginations of my polluted affections have stolen between me and the Saviour. Once 'the candle of the Lord did shine upon my head.' But now he is gone; 'my beloved hath withdrawn himself; and I am again 'shorn of my strength,' and feeble as another man." Well, do not despair. Thy soul shall yet ride the storm. There is yet one anchor more, but it is possible you will not all admire it. Some will cry out, Is that all? O, it is too low. But let me tell you, low as you esteem it, because it seems within your reach, it will rise to the highest mansion in Heaven. It is, I own, a little dark at the first view, but the more you look upon it, the brighter it will grow. Remember it was the "sound of a ram's horn, and the shout of human voices," that shook the "mighty walls of Jericho." God delights to do great things by little means.

The name then of my fourth anchor is *Resignation,* and there is a motto engraved thereon: "In quietness and confidence shall thy strength be." You that are asleep have nothing to do with this: but you who are awake, and groaning for the salvation you have forfeited,—you are invited, nay, *commanded* to cast it out. You have fallen by a worldly spirit, and by indulging a busy and idolatrous imagination. Come, then, let this be the moment! Now cast your whole soul,— your everlasting concerns, on the free unmerited love of the Saviour, and live upon,—"Thy will be done!" Let your soul cry out, "I will bear the indignation of the Lord, because I have sinned against him." Abandon yourself, as a victim, into his hand, and there lie as "clay before the potter." If you are tempted because you cannot pray, let this be your prayer,—let the constant cry of your heart be,—"Thy will be done on earth, as it is done in heaven." And take knowledge, while you are so doing, your prayer is echoed by the highest Archangel in heaven, for the glory of that bright abode is a perfect resignation, fully consistent with the most faithful activity. You are permitted to pray,—"Father, let this cup pass from me:"—Yet, while you add, "Not my will, but Thy will be done," you join in spirit with the "Saviour and Captain of your salvation." I have often found, in an hour of temptation, when no other anchor seemed to hold, that thought, "The Lord reigneth,"—his will and glory shall be accomplished, and in that I will rejoice,—has brought peace, and laid the storm. Lie down at his dear feet, and remember, "Whom he loveth, he chasteneth, and correcteth every son whom he receiveth." He brings your sins to your remembrance, that your soul may be brought to know its misery and wants, and in order that he may burn them up with the purifying fire of his love. Take courage then, and, with one voice, let us all unite in the cry,—"Thy will be done! Thy will be done!" And our song shall be echoed through all the courts above. Here then drop your anchor. It is sound ground, and it will not come home. With this patient faith, therefore, be found in all the means of grace, walking humbly, while you do his will. "And pleading the promises, which are yea and amen in Christ. Blessed are all they who wait for him."

We read of Paul's company,—That "they cast out four anchors, and wished for the day." Do you the same, for that is a wish very pleasing to the Lord. I observed before,—That it is not day-light with the soul till that promise is accomplished: "I will manifest myself unto him." Here is the great design of the wonderful plan of salvation,—to restore man to his original communion with God; and he who hath said, "I will give unto him that is athirst of the water of life freely,"—now waits to make your soul his loved abode, the temple of indwelling God. There is a rest which remains for the people of God; and you who love the Lord, remember, "He came not only that you might have life," but that "you may have it more abundantly." Cry, my beloved friends, day and night, that you may "enter into the land of uprightness, on which the eyes of the Lord are continually" from the beginning of the year to the end. But when the people of Israel slighted the rest of Canaan, and had lost that courage by which alone they could enter,—how greatly did it offend the Lord! And will he approve lazy, dull seekers of that spiritual Canaan, that "Baptism of the Spirit" to which every believer is expressly called? We often talk of the time when "righteousness is to overspread the earth," but this millennium must overspread our own hearts, if we would see the face of God with joy. For the very end of our creation is, that we may become "the habitation of God through the Spirit."

NOTE

* Which was the more terrible, the use of the compass not being then discovered.

APPENDIX J: DISTRIBUTION OF WOMEN PREACHERS THROUGHOUT BRITAIN

SELECTED BIBLIOGRAPHY

T HIS IS NOT A COMPLETE bibliography of the subject, but only a listing of some of the more important works to which reference has been made in the text and notes. Citation of the extensive manuscript material which has been used throughout this study, especially epistolary sources, has been limited to important individual works or collections of particular interest.

PRIMARY MATERIALS

MANUSCRIPT SOURCES

An Account of the Rise & Progress of the Work of God in Latonstone, Essex, 1763. This Hath God Wrought. Meth. Arch.

Bulmer, Agnes. Memoirs of Elizabeth Ritchie. Meth. Arch.

Crosby, Sarah. MS Letterbook, 1760–74. Perkins Library, Duke University.

Crosby, Sarah. Papers, 1760–1804. Perkins Library, Duke University.

Wesley, John. Autograph Letters and Manuscripts. Meth. Arch.

Wesley, Susanna. MS Journal. Wesley College, Bristol.

PRE-EIGHTEENTH-CENTURY SOURCES

Astell, Mary. *An Essay in Defence of the Female Sex. In Which are Inserted the Characters of a Pedant, a Squire, a Beau, a*

Vertuoso, a Poetaster, a City-Critick, &c. London: Printed for A. Roper and E. Wilkinform, and R. Clavel, 1696.

———. *A Serious Proposal to the Ladies, for the Advancement of their True and Greatest Interest. By a Lover of Her Sex.* London: Printed for R. Wilkin, 1694.

Baillie, Robert. *A Dissvasive from the Errours of the Time.* London: Printed for Samuel Gellibrand, 1645.

Beda Venerabilis. *Bede's Ecclesiastical History of the English People.* Edited by Bertram Colgrave and R.A.B. Mynors. Oxford: Clarendon Press, 1969.

A Discoverie of Six Women Preachers in Middlesex, Kent, Cambridgeshire, and Salisbury. London, 1641.

Edwards, Thomas. *The First and Second Part of Gangraena; or, A catalogue and discovery of many of the errors, heresies, blasphemies, and pernicious practices of the sectaries of this time.* 2d ed., corrected and much enlarged. 2 vols. London: Printed by T. R. and E. M. for Ralph Smith, 1646.

Fell, Margaret. *A Touch-Stone; or, A Perfect Tryal by the Scriptures.* London: Printed in the year 1667.

———. *Womens Speaking Justified, Proved and Allowed of by the SCRIPTURES, . . . And how WOMEN were the first that preached the Tidings of the Resurrection of JESUS.* London: Printed in the year 1666.

The Females Advocate; or, An Essay to Prove that the Sisters in every Church of Christ, have a Right to Church-Government as well as the Brethren. British Museum.

Fox, George. *A Collection of Many Select and Christian Epistles, Letters and Testimonies.* London: Printed and sold by T. Sowle, 1698.

———. *Gospel-Truth Demonstrated, In a Collection of Doctrinal Books.* London: Printed and sold by T. Sowle, 1706.

———. *The Journal of George Fox.* Edited by Norman Penney. 2 vols. Cambridge: At the University Press, 1911.

Foxe, John. *The Acts and Monuments of John Foxe.* Edited by George Townsend and Stephen Reed Cattley. 8 vols. London: R. B. Seeley and W. Burnside, 1837–41.

Lake, Arthur. *Sermons with Some Religious and Divine Meditations.* London: Printed by W. Stansby for N. Butler, 1629.

Locke, John. *The Educational Writings of John Locke.* Edited by James L. Axtell. Cambridge: At the University Press, 1965.

Luther, Martin. *Luther's Works.* Jaroslav Pelikan and Helmut T. Lehmann, general editors. 53 vols. Philadelphia: Fortress Press, 1958–67.

Robinson, John. *The Works of John Robinson, Pastor of the Pilgrim Fathers.* Edited by Robert Ashton. 3 vols. London: John Snow, 1851.

Rogers, John. *Ohel or Beth-shemesh. A Tabernacle for the Sun; or, Irenicum Evangelicum, an Idea of Church Discipline.* London: R. I. and G. and H. Eversden, 1653.

EIGHTEENTH-CENTURY SOURCES

"Account of Mrs. Sarah Ryan." *Arm. Mag.* 2 (1779): 296–310.

Anderson, James. *A Sermon Preached on Sunday Evening, Jan. 24, at the Methodist Chapel, Lowestoft, Upon the Death of Mrs. Tripp, of that Place.* Yarmouth: Printed for the author, by F. Bush, 1796.

Arminian Magazine: Consisting of Extracts and Original Treatises on Universal Redemption. Edited by John Wesley. London: Fry et al., 1778–79; continued as *Methodist Magazine,* 1798–1821, and *Wesleyan Methodist Magazine,* 1822–1913.

Bate, James. *Quakero-Methodism; or, A Confutation of the First Principles of the Quakers and Methodists.* London: John Carter, [1740].

Bosanquet, Mary. *An Aunt's Advice to a Niece, In a Letter to Miss + + + + + + + + + + +.* 2d ed. Leeds: Printed by J. Bowling, and sold by J. Binns, in Briggate, 1780.

———. *Jesus, Altogether Lovely: or A Letter to Some of the Single Women in the Methodist Society.* Bristol, 1766.

———. *A Letter to the Rev. Mr. John Wesley. By a Gentlewoman.* London: Sold at the Foundery, in Upper Moorfields, 1764.

Bowman, William. *The Imposture of Methodism Display'd.* London: Joseph Lord, 1740.

Buller, James. *A Reply to the Rev. Mr. Wesley's Address to the Clergy.* Bristol: S. Farley, 1756.

Cooper, Jane. "Christian Experience." *Arm. Mag.* 5 (1782): 408–9, 489–90.

Cranz, David. *The Ancient and Modern History of the Brethren.* Translated by Benjamin LaTrobe. London: Printed by W. and A. Strahan, 1780.

Deacon, Thomas. *A Compleat Collection of Devotions, Both Publick and Private.* London: n.p., 1734.

"Excerpts from John Valton's MS Journal." *W.H.S.* 8 (1911–12): 21–23, 33–36, 67–69, 100–102, 150–52, 191–94.

"The Experience of Mrs. Ann Gilbert, of Gwinear, in Cornwall." *Arm. Mag.* 18 (1795): 42–46.

"An Extract from the Diary of Mrs. Bathsheba Hall." *Arm. Mag.* 4 (1781): 35–40, 94–97, 148–52, 195–98, 256–59, 309–11, 372–75.

Fleetwood, William. *The Perfectionists Examined, . . . in A Letter to Mr. Wesley.* London: J. Roberts, 1741.

Fletcher, John William. *Letters of the Rev. John Fletcher.* Edited by Melville Horne. New York: Lane and Scott, 1849.

———. *Works of the Rev. John Fletcher.* 8 vols. London: Printed by Richard Edwards, 1807.

Fletcher, Mary. *An Account of Sarah Lawrence.* London: Printed by Thomas Cordeux, 1820.

———. *A Legacy to the People of Madeley.* Revised by Joseph Entwisle. London: Printed by Thomas Cordeux, 1819.

———. *Thoughts on Communion with Happy Spirits.* Birmingham: Printed by William Rickman King, n.d.

The Gentlemen's Magazine: Or, Monthly Intelligencer, 1731–1914.

Gisbourne, Thomas. *An Enquiry into the Duties of the Female Sex.* 5th ed. London: Printed by A. Strahan for T. Cadell, Jr., and W. Davies, 1801.

Grubb, Sarah. *Some Account of the Life and Religious Labours of Sarah Grubb.* Edited by Lindley Murray. Dublin: Printed for R. Jackson, 1792.

Helton, John. *Reasons for Quitting the Methodist Society; Being a Defence of Barclay's Apology.* London: Printed by J. Fry, 1778.

Hill, George Birkbeck, ed. *Boswell's Life of Johnson.* Revised and enlarged by L. F. Powell. 6 vols. Oxford: At the Clarendon Press, 1934.

An Impartial Hand. *The Progress of Methodism in Bristol: or, The Methodist Unmask'd.* 2d ed. Bristol: J. Watts, 1743.

Jackson, Thomas, ed. *The Lives of the Early Methodist Preachers. Chiefly Written by Themselves.* 4th ed. 6 vols. London: Wesleyan Conference Office, 1875.

Lackington, James. *Memoirs of the Forty-five First Years of the Life of James Lackington, the Present Bookseller in Finsbury Square, London.* New ed. London: By the author, 1794.

[Lavington, George]. *The Enthusiasm of Methodists and Papists Compared. Part 2.* London: J. and P. Knapton, 1749.

[Lefevre, Mrs.]. *Letters upon Sacred Subjects, by a person lately deceased.* London, 1757.

London Magazine. 1732–85.

Mallitt, William. "An Account of S. Mallitt." *Arm. Mag.* 11 (1788): 91–93, 130–33, 185–88, 238–42.

Minutes of the Methodist Conferences, from the First, Held in London, by the Late Rev. John Wesley, A.M. in the Year 1744. London: Printed at the Conference Office, 1812–.

Minutes of the Methodist Conferences in Ireland. Dublin: Religious and General Book Co., 1864.

The Mock-Preacher: A Satyrico-Comical-Allegorical Farce. London: C. Corbett, 1739.

A Plain and Easy Road to the Land of Bliss. London: W. Nicholl, 1762.

Pope, Alexander. *The Poems of Alexander Pope.* General editor, John Butt. 11 vols. New Haven: Yale University Press, 1939–69.

A Review of the Policy, Doctrines and Morals of the Methodists. London: J. Johnson, 1791.

A Short Account of God's Dealings with Mrs. Elizabeth Maxfield, Wife of the Rev. Thomas Maxfield. London: Printed by J. W. Pasham, 1778.

A Short Account of the Life and Death of Miss Jane Newland. Dublin, 1790.

Smollett, Tobias. *The Expedition of Humphrey Clinker.* Harmondsworth: Penguin Books, 1978.

Smyth, Edward, ed. *The Extraordinary Life and Christian Experience of Margaret Davidson, as Dictated by Herself.* Dublin: Dugdale, 1782.

Some Account of the Lives and Relgious Labours of Samuel Neale, and Mary Neale, Formerly Mary Peisley, Both of Ireland. New ed., enlarged. Edited by A. R. Barclay. London: C. Gilpin, 1845.

Stokes, Mary. "The Experience of Miss Mary Stokes, in a Letter to Mr. Tho. Rankin." *Arm. Mag.* 18 (1795): 99–101.

[Tailfer, Patrick]. *A True and Historical Narrative of the Colony of Georgia.* Charleston: n.p., 1741.

Taylor, D. *A Sermon Occasioned by the Death of Mrs. Elizabeth Taylor, Who Departed This Life October 22, 1793.* London: Printed for the author, 1794.

Told, Silas. *An Account of the Life and Dealings of God with Silas Told, Late Preacher of the Gospel.* 3d ed., corrected. London: George Whitfield, 1786.

[Weller, Samuel]. *The Trial of Mr. Whitefield's Spirit in Some Remarks Upon his Fourth Journal.* London: T. Gardner, 1740.

Wesley, Samuel, Jr. "The Battle of the Sexes." In *Poems on Several Occasions*. 2d ed., with additions. Cambridge: Printed by J. Bentham, 1743.

[Wesley, Susanna]. *Some Remarks on a Letter from the Reverend Mr. Whitefield to the Reverend Mr. Wesley, in a Letter from a Gentlewoman to her Friend.* London: Printed for John Wesley, 1741.

Wollstonecraft, Mary. *A Vindication of the Rights of Women: With Strictures on Political and Moral Subjects.* London: Printed for J. Johnson, 1792.

WESLEY SOURCES

Clarke, Adam. *Memoirs of the Wesley Family.* 4th ed., enlarged. 2 vols. London: W. Tegg, 1860.

Green, Richard. *An Itinerary in Which are Traced the Rev. John Wesley's Journeys from October 14, 1735 to October 24, 1790.* Burnley: Printed by B. Moore, n.d.

Stevenson, G. J. *Memorials of the Wesley Family.* London: S. W. Partridge, [1876].

Wesley, Charles. *The Journal of the Rev. Charles Wesley, M.A.* Edited by Thomas Jackson. 2 vols. London: John Mason, 1849.

Wesley, John. *Explanatory Notes upon the New Testament.* London: Printed by Bowyer, 1755.

———. *Explanatory Notes upon the Old Testament.* 3 vols. Bristol: Printed by William Pine, 1765.

———. *An Extract of Letters by Mrs. L****. London, 1769.

———. "A Female Course of Study, Only Intended for Those, Who have a good understanding and much leisure: In a letter to Miss L——." *Arm. Mag.* 3 (1780): 602–4.

———. *The Journal of the Rev. John Wesley, A.M.* Edited by Nehemiah Curnock. 8 vols. London: Epworth Press, 1909–16.

———. *The Letters of the Rev. John Wesley, A.M.* Edited by John Telford. 8 vols. London: Epworth Press, 1931.

———. *Letters Wrote by Jane Cooper: To which is Prefixt, some Account of Her Life and Death.* London: Strahan, 1764.

———. *The Nature, Design, and General Rules of the United Societies in London, Kingswood, and Newcastle Upon Tyne.* Newcastle upon Tyne: Printed by John Gooding, 1743.

———. "Ought We to Separate from the Church of England?" In

John Wesley and the Church of England, pp. 326–40. By Frank Baker. New York: Abingdon Press, 1970.

———. *Sermons on Several Occasions.* 3 vols. New York: Published by J. Soule and T. Mason, 1818.

———. "Some Account of Sarah Peters." *Arm. Mag.* 5 (1782): 128–36.

———. *The Standard Sermons of John Wesley.* Edited by E. H. Sugden. 2 vols. London: Epworth Press, 1921.

———. *The Works of the Rev. John Wesley, M.A.* Edited by Thomas Jackson. 14 vols. London: Mason, 1829–31.

———. *The Works of John Wesley.* Edited by Frank Baker. Vol. 11: *The Appeals to Men of Reason and Religion and Certain Related Open Letters.* Edited by Gerald R. Cragg. Oxford: At the Clarendon Press, 1975.

———. *The Works of John Wesley.* Edited by Frank Baker. Vols. 25–26: *Letters I* and *Letters II.* Edited by Frank Baker. Oxford: At the Clarendon Press, 1980, 1982.

EARLY-NINETEENTH-CENTURY SOURCES

"An Account of Mrs. Crosby, of Leeds." *Meth. Mag.* 29 (1806): 418–23, 465–73, 517–21, 563–68, 610–17.

"An Account of Mrs. Hannah Harrison." *Meth. Mag.* 25 (1802): 318–23, 363–68.

Atmore, Charles. *The Methodist Memorial; Being an Impartial Sketch of Lives and Characters of the Preachers.* Bristol: Printed by Richard Edwards, 1801.

Barratt, Robert C. *Memorials of Mrs. Elizabeth Shaw.* London: Wesleyan Conference Office, 1875.

Bennet, William. *A Gospel Treatise on the Gospel Constitution.* London: Sold by B. I. Holdsworth, 1822.

———. *Memoirs of Mrs. Grace Bennet.* Macclesfield: Printed and sold by E. Bayley, 1803.

Bible Christian Magazine. Formerly the *Arminian Magazine,* 1821–.

Biller, Sarah, ed. *Memoirs of the Late Hannah Kilham.* London: Darton and Harvey, 1837.

Bramwell, William. *A Short Account of the Life and Death of Ann Cutler.* New ed. with an appendix by Z. Taft, containing *An Account of Elizabeth Dickinson.* York: Printed by John Hill, 1827.

Bulmer, Agnes. *Appendix to the Memoirs of Mrs. Elizabeth Mortimer.* London: Printed by James Nichols, 1836.

Bulmer, Agnes, ed. *Memoirs of Mrs. Elizabeth Mortimer.* 2d ed. London: J. Mason, 1836.

Bunting, William M., ed. *Select Letters of Mrs. Agnes Bulmer.* London: Published and sold by Simpkin and Marshall, 1842.

Burder, Samuel. *Memoirs of Eminently Pious Women of the British Empire.* New ed., revised and enlarged. 3 vols. London: Printed for Ogle, Duncan, 1823.

Carvosso, Benjamin. "The Dairyman's Daughter." *Wes. Meth. Mag.* 61 (1838): 102–9.

Clarke, J.B.B., ed. *An Account of the Infancy, Religious and Literary Life of Adam Clarke, L.L.D., F.S.A.* 3 vols. London: Printed by T. S. Clarke, 1833.

Clowes, William. *The Journals of William Clowes, a Primitive Methodist Preacher.* London: Published by Hallam, 1844.

Cole, Joseph, ed. *Memoir of Hannah Ball, of High-Wycombe, in Buckinghamshire.* Revised and enlarged by John Parker. London: Published by John Mason, 1839.

Crowther, J. *A True and Complete Portraiture of Methodism; or the History of the Wesleyan Methodists.* New York: Published by Daniel Hitt and Thomas Ware, 1813.

Dickinson, Robert. *The Life of the Rev. John Braithwaite.* London: Printed for John Broadbent, 1825.

Dudley, Elizabeth, ed. *The Life of Mary Dudley.* London: Printed for the editor, and sold by J. and A. Arch, 1825.

Dudley, Mary. *An Extempore Discourse, Spoken at a Public Meeting, Held at the Friends' Meeting House, at Epping.* London: Printed for R. Hunter, 1823.

Entwistle. *Memoir of the Rev. Joseph Entwistle, Fifty-four Years a Wesleyan Minister.* Bristol: Printed and sold for the author, 1848.

Everett, James. *Adam Clarke Portrayed.* 3 vols. London: Published by Hamilton, Adams, 1843, 1844, 1849.

———. *Memoirs of the Life, Character, and Ministry of William Dawson.* London: Published by Hamilton, Adams, 1842.

Gardner, James. *Memoirs of Christian Females; with an Essay on the Influence of Female Piety.* 3d ed. Edinburgh: John Johnstone, 1847.

Garrett, Philip. *A Digest of the Methodist Conferences, from the First, Held in London, by the Late Rev. John Wesley.* Halifax: Printed by Thomas Walker, 1827.

Gilbert, Henrietta F. *Memoirs of the Late Mrs. Mary Gilbert.*

London: Printed by Thomas Cordeux, 1817.

Harris, Thomas. *The Christian Minister in Earnest: Exemplified in a Memoir of the Rev. William Bramwell.* 2d ed. London: Sold by John Mason, 1847.

Hodson, John. *A Widow Indeed. A Sermon Occasioned by the Lamented Death of Mrs. Fletcher.* Wednesbury: Printed and sold by J. Booth, 1816. Cf. *Meth. Mag.* 41 (1818): 685–87.

Holder, George. *A Short Account of the Life of Mrs. Mary Holder, Mostly Taken from her Journal.* Whitby, 1836.

Hopkins, Benjamin. *The Life of the Reverend Robert Hopkins,* Sheffield: Printed by J. C. Platt, 1828.

Jackson, Thomas. *Recollections of my Own Life and Times.* Edited by B. Frankland. London: Wesleyan Conference Office, 1874.

Kilham, Hannah. *A Brook by the Way; Extracts from the Diary of Hannah Kilham.* London: Charles Gilpin, 1844.

———. *Scripture Selections on the Attributes of the Divine Being.* Sheffield: Printed by William Todd, 1813.

———. *Scripture Selections on the Principles of the Christian Religion.* 4th ed. Sheffield: Printed and sold by Christopher Bentham, 1816.

MacDonald, James. *Memoirs of the Rev. Joseph Benson.* London: Sold by T. Blanshard, 1822.

Moore, Henry. *The Life of Mrs. Mary Fletcher, Consort and Relict of the Rev. John Fletcher, Vicar of Madeley, Salop: Compiled from her Journal and Other Authentic Documents.* 6th ed. London: Published and sold by J. Kershaw, 1824.

Myles, William. *A Chronological History of the People Called Methodists.* 4th ed., enlarged. London: Printed at the Conference Office, 1813; 3d ed.: London: Sold by the author, 1803.

Nightingale, Joseph. *A Portraiture of Methodism.* London: Longman, Hurst, Rees, and Orme, 1807.

Pipe, John. "Memoir of Miss Isabella Wilson." *Meth. Mag.* 31 372–75, 410–15, 461–69, 516–18, 562–67, 595–97.

"Recollections of the Rev. John Eyton, A.M., Formerly Vicar of Wellington, Salop." *Wes. Meth. Mag.* 70 (1847): 551–59.

Ripley, Dorothy. *An Account of Rose Butler.* New York: Printed by John C. Totten, 1819.

———. *An Address to All in Difficulties. God is Love. A Hymn from My Nativity.* Bristol: Rose, Printer, 1821.

———. *The Bank of Faith and Works United.* 2d ed. Whitby: Printed for the authoress, by G. Clark, 1822.

————. *The Extraordinary Conversion, and Religious Experience, of Dorothy Ripley.* 2d ed. London: Printed for the authoress, by Darton, Harvey, 1817.

————. *Letters, Addressed to Dorothy Ripley, from Several Africans & Indians.* Chester: Printed by J. Hemingway, 1807.

————. *Memoirs of William Ripley, Minister of the Gospel.* Philadelphia: J. H. Cunningham, 1827.

Seckerson, Anthony. "An Account of Mrs. Dobinson." *Meth. Mag.* 26 (1803): 557–66.

————. *Memoirs of the Experience, Life, and Death, of Mrs. Mary Prangnell, of Merston, in the Isle of Wight.* Newport: Printed by W. W. Yelf, 1827.

Sigston, James. *A Memoir of the Life and Ministry of Mr. W. Bramwell, Lately An Itinerant Methodist Preacher.* 2 vols. London: Printed for James Nichols, 1821, 1822.

Sutcliffe, Joseph. *The Experience of the Late Mrs. Frances Pawson, Widow of the Late Rev. John Pawson.* London: Printed at the Conference Office, by T. Cordeux, 1813.

————. *The Life and Labours of the Late Rev. John Valton.* London: Published by John Mason, 1830.

Taft, Mary. *Memoirs of the Life of Mrs. Mary Taft; Formerly Miss Barritt.* 2d ed., enlarged. York: Printed for and sold by the author, 1828; Devon: Published and sold by S. Thorpe, 1831.

Taft, Zechariah. *Biographical Sketches of the Lives and Public Ministry of Various Holy Women, Whose Eminent Usefulness and Successful Labours in the Church of Christ, Have Entitled Them to be Enrolled Among the Great Benefactors of Mankind.* 2 vols. London: Published for the author, and sold in London by Mr. Kershaw, 1825; Leeds: Printed for the author by H. Cullingworth, and sold in London by J. Stephens, 1828.

————. *Original Letters, Never Before Published, On Doctrinal, Experimental, and Practical, Religion.* Whitby: Printed at the Office of George Clark, 1821.

————. *A Reply to An Article Inserted in the Methodist Magazine, For April 1809, Entitled Thoughts on Women's Preaching, Extracted from Dr. James M'Knight.* Leeds: Printed at the Bible-Office, by G. Wilson, 1809.

————. *The Scripture Doctrine of Women's Preaching: Stated and Examined.* York: Printed for the author, by R. and J. Richardson, 1820.

————. "Some Account of Elizabeth Dickinson." In *A Short*

Account of the Life and Death of Ann Culter, pp. 27–34. By William Bramwell. York: Printed by John Hill, 1827.

————. *Thoughts on Female Preaching.* Dover: Printed for the author, 1803.

————. "Thoughts on a Proper Call to the Christian Ministry. *Arm. Mag. (B.C.)* 5, 2(February 1826): 42–48.

Tooth, Mary. "Further Account of Mrs. Fletcher's Death." *Meth. Mag.* 39 (1816): 157–59.

————. *A Letter to the Loving and Beloved People of the Parish of Madeley.* Shiffnal: Printed by A. Edmonds, n.d.

Treffry, Richard, Jr. *Memoirs of Mrs. Jane Treffry.* London: Published by John Mason, 1830.

————. *Memoirs of the Rev. Joseph Benson.* London: Published by John Mason, 1840.

Waddy, Richard. "Account of Mr. Jonathan Coussins." *Meth. Mag.* 29 (1806): 289–96, 337–44, 385–89.

Warren, Samuel. *A Digest of the Laws and Regulations of the Wesleyan Methodist Church.* London: Published by John Stephens, 1835.

————. *Memoirs and Select Letters of Mrs. Anne Warren: With Biographical Sketches of Her Family.* 2d ed. London: Printed for the author, sold by John Mason, 1832.

The Watchman: A Weekley Journal, of News, Politics, Religion, and Literature, for the Year 1835. London: Printed and published by William Gawtress, 1835.

Williams, Martha. *Memoirs of the Life and Character of Ann Carr; Containing an Account of her Conversion to God.* Leeds: Sold by H. W. Walker, 1841.

SECONDARY MATERIALS

LOCAL HISTORIES

Bretherton, F. F. *Early Methodism in and around Chester, 1749–1812.* Chester: Phillipson and Golder, 1903.

Cocking, Thomas. *The History of Wesleyan Methodism in Grantham and Its Vicinity.* London: Simpkin, Marshal, 1836.

Dyson, J. B. *A Brief History of the Rise and Progress of Wesleyan Methodism in the Leek Circuit.* Leek: Printed by Edward Hallowes, [1853].

————. *Methodism in the Isle of Wight*. Ventnor: George M. Burt, 1865.

Everett, James. *Wesleyan Methodism in Manchester and Its Vicinity*. Manchester: Printed by the Executors of S. Russell, 1827.

Graham, J. J. *A History of Wesleyan Methodism in Sheffield Park*. Sheffield: Sir W. C. Leng, 1914.

Harwood, George H. *The History of Wesleyan Methodism in Nottingham and Its Vicinity*. New ed., enlarged. Nottingham: Printed and published by John Ellis, 1872.

Hatton, W. *A History of Methodism in Halifax and Its Vicinity from Its Commencement in 1741 to 1824*. Halifax: T. Walker, 1824.

Jackson, George. *Wesleyan Methodism in the Darlington Circuit*. Darlington: Printed by J. Manley, 1850.

Jessop, William. *An Account of Methodism in Rossendale and the Neighbourhood*. Manchester: Tubbs, Brook, and Chrystal, [1880].

Laycock, J. W. *Methodist Heroes in the Great Haworth Round, 1734 to 1784*. Keighley: Wadsworth, 1909.

Lester, George. *Grimsby Methodism (1743–1889) and the Wesleys in Lincolnshire*. London: Wesleyan-Methodist Book-Room, 1890.

Lyth, John. *Glimpses of Early Methodism in York and the Surrounding District*. York: Williams Sessions, 1885.

Pilkington, W. *The Makers of Wesleyan Methodism in Preston*. London: Charles H. Kelly, 1890.

Richardson, W. F. *Preston Methodism's Two Hundred Fascinating Years, 1776–1976*. Preston: Printed at Adelphi Chambers by Henry L. Kirby, 1975.

Robinson, John R. *Notes of Early Methodism in Dewsbury, Birstal, and Neighbourhood*. Batley: J. Fearnsides and Sons, 1900.

Rose, E. A. *Methodism in Cheshire to 1800*. Wilmslow: Published by Richmond Printers, [1979].

Smith, Benjamin. *The History of Methodism in Macclesfield*. London: Wesleyan Conference Office, 1875.

Stamp, William W. *Historical Notices of Wesleyan Methodism, in Bradford and Its Vicinity*. Bradford: Henry Wardman, n.d.

————. *The Orphan-House of Wesley; with Notices of Early Methodism in Newcastle-upon-Tyne*. London: Published by J. Mason, 1863.

Steele, Anthony. *History of Methodism in Barnard Castle and the*

Principle Places in the Dales Circuit. London: George Vickers, 1857.

Taylor, John. *The Apostles of Fylde Methodism.* London: T. Woomer, 1885.

Tuck, Stephen. *Wesleyan Methodism in Frome, Somersetshire.* Frome: Printed by S. Tuck, 1837.

Walker, J. U. *A History of Wesleyan Methodism in Halifax.* Halifax: Hartley and Walker, 1836.

Ward, John. *Historical Sketches of the Rise and Progress of Methodism in Bingley.* Bingley; John Harrison and Son, 1863.

———. *Methodism in Swaledale and the Neighbourhood.* Bingley: Harrison and Son, Printers, 1865.

———. *Methodism in the Thirsk Circuit.* Thirsk: David Peat, Printer, 1860.

Watmough, Abraham. *A History of Methodism in the Neighbourhood and City of Lincoln.* Lincoln: Printed by R. E. Leary, sold by J. Mason, 1829.

West, George. *Methodism in Marshland.* London: Wesleyan Conference Office, [1886].

GENERAL WORKS

Abbey, C. J., and Overton, J. H. *The English Church in the Eighteenth Century.* London: Longmans, Green, 1887.

Armytage, W.H.G. *Heavens Below: Utopian Experiments in England, 1560–1960.* London: Routledge and Kegan Paul, 1961.

Ayling, Stanley. *John Wesley.* Nashville: Abingdon Press, 1979.

Baker, Frank. *A Charge to Keep: An Introduction to the People Called Methodists.* London: Epworth Press, 1947.

———. *John Wesley and the Church of England.* New York: Abingdon Press, 1970.

———. *Methodism and the Love-Feast.* London: Epworth Press, 1957.

———. *The Relations between the Society of Friends and Early Methodism.* London: Epworth Press, 1949.

Barber, B. Aquila. *A Methodist Pageant: A Souvenir of the Primitive Methodist Church.* London: Holborn Publishing House, 1932.

Barclay, Robert. *The Inner Life of the Religious Societies of the Commonwealth.* London: Hodder and Stoughton, 1879.

Beard, Mary. *Woman as Force in History: A Study in Traditions and Realities*. New York: Macmillan, 1946.

Bebb, E. Douglas. *Wesley: A Man with a Concern*. London: Epworth Press, 1950.

Bett, Henry. *The Early Methodist Preachers*. London: Epworth Press, 1935.

Blackwell, J. *The Life of the Rev. Alexander Kilham, Formerly a Preacher under the Rev. J. Wesley*. London: Darton and Harvey, 1838.

Blease, Walter Lyon. *The Emancipation of English Woman*. London: Benjamin Blom, 1910.

Boulding, Elise. *The Underside of History: A View of Women through Time*. Boulder, Colo.: Westview Press, 1976.

Bourne, F. W. *The Bible Christians: Their Origin and History (1815–1900)*. London: Bible Christian Book Room, 1905.

Bowmer, John C. *Pastor and People: A Study of Church and Ministry in Wesleyan Methodism from the Death of John Wesley (1791) to the Death of Jabez Bunting (1858)*. London: Epworth Press, 1975.

Brailsford, Mabel R. *Quaker Women*. London: Duckworth, 1915.

———. *Susanna Wesley: The Mother of Methodism*. London: Epworth Press, 1938.

Braithwaite, William C. *The Beginnings of Quakerism*. London: Macmillan, 1912.

———. *The Second Period of Quakerism*. London: Macmillan, 1919.

Bready, J. Wesley. *England, before and after Wesley: The Evangelical Revival and Social Reform*. London: Hodder and Stoughton, 1938.

Brown, Earl Kent. *Women of Mr. Wesley's Methodism*. New York: E. Mellen Press, 1983.

Bunting, T. P. *The Life of Jabez Bunting, D.D.* 2 vols. London: T. Woolmer, 1887.

Buoy, Charles W. *Representative Women of Methodism*. New York: Hunt and Eaton, 1893.

Burns, Jabez. *Life of Mrs. Fletcher*. London: J. Smith, 1843.

Carpenter, S. C. *Eighteenth-Century Church and People*. London: John Murray, 1959.

Carroll, Berenice A., ed. *Liberating Women's History: Theoretical and Critical Essays*. Urbana: University of Illinois Press, 1976.

Carwardine, Richard. *Trans-Atlantic Revivalism: Popular Evangelicalism in Britain and America, 1790–1865*. Westport, Conn.: Greenwood Press, 1978.

Church, Leslie F. *The Early Methodist People*. London: Epworth Press, 1948.

———. *More about the Early Methodist People*. London: Epworth Press, 1949.

Clark, Alice. *Working Life of Women in the Seventeenth Century*. New York: E. P. Dutton, 1919.

Clarke, Eliza. *Susanna Wesley*. Boston: Roberts Brothers, 1891.

Cohn, N. *The Pursuit of the Millennium*. London: Secker and Warburg, 1957.

Coles, George. *Heroines of Methodism; or, Pen and Ink Sketches of the Mothers and Daughters of the Church*. New York: Published by Carlton and Porter, 1857.

Collins, William E. *Typical English Churchmen from Parker to Maurice*. London: SPCK, 1902.

Cook, Alice I. *Women of the Warm Heart*. London: Epworth Press, 1952.

Cox, Stephen, ed. *"Holiness unto the Lord." Illustrated in the Character and Life of Miss Bosanquet, of Leytonstone*. London: Wesleyan Conference Office, 1876.

Crookshank, C. H. *History of Methodism in Ireland*. 3 vols. Belfast: R. S. Allen, Son and Allen, 1885.

———. *Memorable Women of Irish Methodism in the Last Century*. London: Wesleyan-Methodist Book-Room, 1882.

Cross, F. L., ed. *The Oxford Dictionary of the Christian Church*. London: Oxford University Press, 1957.

Cunningham, Valentine. *Everywhere Spoken Against: Dissent in the Victorian Novel*. Oxford: Clarendon Press, 1975.

Currie, Robert. *Methodism Divided: A Study in the Sociology of Ecumenicalism*. London: Faber and Faber, 1968.

Davies, Rupert, and Rupp, E. Gordon, eds. *A History of the Methodist Church in Great Britain*. 4 vols. London: Epworth Press, 1965–88.

Dawson, Joanna, and Kellet, Arnold. *People and Places in Yorkshire Methodism*. Harrogate Conference, 1971.

Dimond, Sidney. *The Psychology of the Methodist Revival: An Empirical and Descriptive Study*. Oxford: Oxford University Press, 1926.

Doughty, William L. *John Wesley, Preacher*. London: Epworth Press, 1955.

Dryden, John. *The Poems of John Dryden*. Edited by James Kinsley. 4 vols. Oxford: Clarendon Press, 1958.

Edwards, Maldwyn. *After Wesley: A Study of the Social and*

Political Influence of Methodism in the Middle Period (1791–1849). London: Epworth Press, 1935.

———. *John Wesley and the Eighteenth Century: A Study of His Social and Political Influence.* London: Allen and Unwin, 1933.

———. *Laymen and Methodist Beginnings.* Nashville: Methodist Evangelistic Materials, 1963.

———. *My Dear Sister: The Story of John Wesley and the Women in His Life.* Manchester: Penwork (Leeds), n.d.

Farndale, William E. *The Secret of Mow Cop: A New Appraisal of Primitive Methodist Origins.* London: Epworth Press, 1950.

Fritz, Paul, and Morton, Richard, eds. *Women in the Eighteenth Century and Other Essays.* Toronto: Samuel Stevens Hakkert, 1976.

Funk, Theophil. *Die Anfänge der Laienmitarbeit im Methodismus.* Bremen: Anker-Verlag und Druckerei, 1941.

Gallagher, Robert H. *Pioneer Preachers of Irish Methodism.* Belfast: Nelson and Knox (N.I.), 1965.

Garner, William. *The Life of the Rev. and Venerable William Clowes.* London: Published by William Lister, 1868.

Gill, Thomas E. *The Life of Mrs. Fletcher, Relict of the Rev. John Fletcher, Late Vicar of Madeley.* Easingwold: T. Gill, 1844.

Gollin, Gillian Lindt. *Moravians in Two Worlds: A Study of Changing Communities.* New York: Columbia University Press, 1967.

Goncourt, Edmond de, and Goncourt, Jules de. *The Woman of the Eighteenth Century: Her Life, from Birth to Death.* Translated by Jacques le Clerq and Ralph Roeder. New York: Minton, Balch, 1927.

Green, V.H.H. *The Young Mr. Wesley: A Study of John Wesley and Oxford.* London: Arnold, 1961.

Gregory, Benjamin. *Side Lights on the Conflicts of Methodism during the Second Quarter of the Nineteenth Century, 1827-1852.* London: Cassell and Company, 1898.

Gregory, J. Robinson, ed. *Benjamin Gregory, D.D.: Autobiographical Recollections.* London: Hodder and Stoughton, 1903.

———. *A History of Methodism.* 2 vols. London: Charles H. Kelly, 1911.

Halévy, Elie. *The Birth of Methodism in England.* Translated by Bernard Semmel. Chicago: University of Chicago Press, 1971.

———. *England in 1815.* London: E. Benn, 1949.

————. *A History of the English People, 1815–1830.* Translated by E. I. Watkin. New York: Harcourt, Brace, 1926.

Hall, Joseph. *Hall's Circuits and Ministers: An Alphabetical List of the Circuits in Great Britain, with the Names of the Ministers Stationed in Each Circuit, from 1765 to 1885.* London: Wesleyan Methodist Book Room, 1886.

Hamilton, J. Taylor, and Hamilton, Kenneth G. *History of the Moravian Church.* Bethlehem, Pa.: Interprovincial Board of Christian Education, 1967.

Harmon, Nolan B., ed. *The Encyclopedia of World Methodism.* 2 vols. Nashville: United Methodist Publishing House, 1974.

Harmon, Rebecca L. *Susanna, Mother of the Wesleys.* Nashville: Abingdon Press, 1968.

Harrison, G. Elsie. *Son to Susanna: The Private Life of John Wesley.* London: I. Nicholson and Watson, 1937.

Hill, Christopher. *The World Turned Upside Down: Radical Ideas during the English Revolution.* London: Temple Smith, 1972.

Hill, Georgiana. *Women in English Life.* 2 vols. London: Richard Bentley and Son, 1894, 1896.

Hill, William. *An Alphabetical and Chronological Arrangement of the Wesleyan Methodist Ministers and Preachers on Trial in Connexion with the British and Irish Conferences.* London: Methodist Publishing House, 1819.

Hobhouse, Stephen. *William Law and Eighteenth-Century Quakerism.* London: George Allen and Unwin, 1927.

Hobshawn, H. E. *Labouring Men: Studies in the History of Labour.* New York: Basic Books, 1964.

Holmes, Urban T. *Ministry and Imagination.* New York: Seabury Press, 1976.

Hulme, T. Ferrier. *Voices of the New Room.* London: Epworth Press, 1933.

Hunter, Frederick. *John Wesley and the Coming Comprehensive Church.* London: Epworth Press, 1968.

Hurst, John F. *The History of Methodism: British Methodism.* 3 vols. London: Charles H. Kelly, 1901.

Hutton, J. E. *History of the Moravian Church.* 2d ed. London: Moravian Publication Office, 1909.

Irwin, Joyce L. *Womanhood in Radical Protestantism, 1525–1675.* New York: Edwin Mellen Press, 1979.

Isichei, Elizabeth. *Victorian Quakers.* London: Oxford University Press, 1970.

Ives, A. G. *Kingswood School in Wesley's Day and Since.* London: Epworth Press, 1970.

Jones, Rufus M. *The Later Periods of Quakerism.* 2 vols. London: Macmillan, 1921.

Kanner, Barbara, ed. *The Women of England from Anglo-Saxon Times to the Present: Interpretive Bibliographical Essays.* London: Mansell, 1980.

Keeling, Annie E. *Susanna Wesley and Other Eminent Methodist Women.* 3d ed. London: Charles H. Kelly, 1897.

Kendall, H. B. *The Origin and History of the Primitive Methodist Church.* 2 vols. London: Edwin Dalton, n.d.

Kent, John H. S. *The Age of Disunity.* London: Epworth Press, 1966.

———. *Jabez Bunting, the Last Wesleyan: A Study in the Methodist Ministry after the Death of John Wesley.* London: Epworth Press, 1955.

Kirk, John. *The Mother of the Wesleys: A Biography.* London: H. J. Tresidder, sold by J. Mason, 1864.

Knox, Ronald A. *Enthusiasm: A Chapter in the History of Religion with Special Reference to the Seventeenth and Eighteenth Centuries.* Oxford: Oxford University Press, 1950.

Lawson, A. B. *John Wesley and the Christian Ministry: The Sources and Development of His Opinions and Practice.* London: SPCK, 1963.

Leach, Robert J. *Women Ministers: A Quaker Contribution.* Wallingford, Pa.: Pendle Hill, 1979.

Leger, Augustin. *Wesley's Last Love.* London: J. M. Dent and Sons, 1910.

Lewis, A. J. *Zinzendorf, the Ecumenical Pioneer: A Study in the Moravian Contribution to Christian Mission and Unity.* Philadelphia: Westminster Press, 1962.

Lewis, I. M. *Ecstatic Religion: An Anthropological Study of Spirit Possession and Shamanism.* Harmondsworth: Pelican Books, 1971.

Lightfoot, John. *The Power of Faith and Prayer Exemplified in the Life and Labours of Mrs. Mary Porteus.* London: Published by R. Davies, Conference-Offices, 1862.

Lloyd, Arnold. *Quaker Social History, 1669–1738.* London: Longmans, Green, 1950.

Luder, Hope Elizabeth. *Women and Quakerism.* Wallingford, Pa.: Pendle Hill, 1974.

Lyles, A. M. *Methodism Mocked: The Satiric Reaction to Methodism in the Eighteenth Century.* London: Epworth Press, 1960.

Lyth, John. *The Blessedness of Religion in Earnest: A Memorial of Mrs. Mary Lowe, of York.* London: Book Society, 1861.

McBeth, Leon. *Women in Baptist Life.* Nashville: Broadman Press, 1979.

McCulloh, Gerald O., ed. *The Ministry in the Methodist Heritage.* Nashville: Board of Education, Methodist Church, 1960.

Manners, Emily. *Elizabeth Hooten: First Quaker Woman Preacher.* London: Headley Brothers, 1914.

Marshall, Dorothy. *Eighteenth-Century England.* New York: David McKay, 1962.

Mathews, Donald G. *Religion in the Old South.* Chicago: University of Chicago Press, 1977.

Memorials of Mary, the Beloved Wife of the Rev. James Henshaw. London: William Cooke, 1870.

Monk, Robert C. *John Wesley: His Puritan Heritage.* New York: Abingdon Press, 1966.

Moore, Henry. *The Life of the Rev. John Wesley, A.M.* 2 vols. London: Kershaw, 1824–25.

Moore, Katharine. *She for God: Aspects of Women and Christianity.* London: Allison and Busby, 1978.

Moore, Robert L. *John Wesley and Authority: A Psychological Perspective.* American Academy of Religion Dissertation Series, No. 29. Missoula, Mont.: Scholars Press, 1979.

Morrow, Thomas M. *Early Methodist Women.* London: Epworth Press, 1967.

Mounfield, Arthur. *The Quaker Methodists: Stories of the Early Independent Methodist Churches.* Nelson: Independent Methodist Book Room, 1924.

Mrs. Adam Clarke: Her Character and Correspondence. London: Partridge and Oakey, 1851.

Newton, John A. *Methodism and the Puritans.* London: Dr. Williams's Trust, 1964.

———. *Susanna Wesley and the Puritan Tradition in Methodism.* London: Epworth Press, 1968.

North, Eric McCoy. *Early Methodist Philanthropy.* New York: Methodist Book Concern, 1914.

Norwood, Frederick A. *The Story of American Methodism.* New York: Abingdon Press, 1974.

Nuttall, Geoffrey F. *The Holy Spirit in Puritan Faith and Experience.* Oxford: Basil Blackwell, 1946.

———. *Studies in Christian Enthusiasm: Illustrated from Early Quakerism.* Wallingford, Pa.: Pendle Hill, 1948.

————. *Visible Saints: The Congregational Way, 1640–1660.* Oxford: Basil Blackwell, 1957.

O'Faolain, Julia, and Martines, Laurel, eds. *Not in God's Image: Women in History from the Greeks to the Victorians.* New York: Harper and Row, 1973.

O'Malley, Ida B. *Women in Subjection: A Study of the Lives of English Women before 1832.* London: Duckworth, 1933.

Penney, Norman, ed. *"The First Publishers of Truth." Being Early Records (Now First Printed) of the Introduction of Quakerism into the Countries of England and Wales.* London: Headley Brothers, 1907.

Petty, John. *The History of the Primitive Methodist Connexion.* 2d ed., revised and enlarged. London: Published by R. Davies, Conference Offices, 1864.

Phillips, Margaret, and Tomkinson, W. S. *English Women in Life and Letters.* New York: Oxford University Press, 1927.

Pinchbeck, Ivy. *Women Workers in the Industrial Revolution, 1750–1850.* London: Routledge, 1930.

Plumb, J. H. *England in the Eighteenth Century.* Harmondsworth: Penguin Books, 1953.

Pyke, Richard. *The Early Bible Christians.* London: Epworth Press, 1941.

————. *The Golden Chain: The Story of the Bible Christian Methodists.* London: Henry Hooks, n.d.

Richmond, Legh. *The Dairyman's Daughter.* Edinburgh: Oliphant, Anderson and Ferrier, 1869.

Ritson, Joseph. *The Romance of Primitive Methodism.* London: Edwin Dalton, 1909.

Rogers, Edward. *Some Account of the Life and Opinions of a Fifth-Monarchy-Man. Chiefly Extracted from the Writings of John Rogers, Preacher.* London: Longmans, Green, Reader, and Byer, 1867.

Ross, Isabel. *Margaret Fell: Mother of Quakerism.* London: Longman's, Green, 1949.

Rowbotham, Sheila. *Hidden from History: Rediscovering Women in History from the Seventeenth Century to the Present.* New York: Pantheon Books, 1974.

Rowe, Kenneth E. *Methodist Women: A Guide to the Literature.* Lake Junaluska, N.C.: General Commission on Archives and History, United Methodist Church, 1980.

Ruether, Rosemary R., ed. *Religion and Sexism: Images of Woman in the Jewish and Christian Traditions.* New York: Simon and Schuster, 1974.

Ruether, Rosemary, and McLaughlin, Eleanor, eds. *Women of Spirit: Female Leadership in the Jewish and Christian Traditions.* New York: Simon and Schuster, 1979.

Runyon, Theodore, ed. *Sanctification and Liberation: Liberation Theologies in Light of the Wesleyan Tradition.* Nashville: Abingdon Press, 1981.

Rupp, Gordon. *Thomas Jackson: Methodist Patriarch.* London: Epworth Press, 1954.

Schmidt, Martin. *John Wesley: A Theological Biography.* 2 vols. Translated by Norman Goldhawk and Denis Inman. New York: Abingdon Press, 1962–66.

Seed, Thomas A. *John and Mary Fletcher: Typical Methodist Saints.* London: C. H. Kelly, 1906.

Semmel, Bernard. *The Methodist Revolution.* New York: Basic Books, 1973.

Shaw, Thomas. *A History of Cornish Methodism.* Truro: Bradford, Barton, 1967.

Simon, John S. *John Wesley and the Advance of Methodism.* London: Epworth Press, 1925.

———. *John Wesley and the Methodist Societies.* London: Epworth Press, 1923.

———. *John Wesley and the Religious Societies.* London: Epworth Press, 1921.

———. *John Wesley: The Last Phase.* London: Epworth Press, 1934.

———. *John Wesley: The Master Builder.* London: Epworth Press, 1927.

Smith, Florence M. *Mary Astell, 1666–1739.* New York: Columbia University Press, 1916.

Smith, George. *History of Wesleyan Methodism.* 2d ed. rev. 3 vols. London: Longman, 1862.

Smith, Joseph. *A Descriptive Catalogue of Friends' Books.* 2 vols. London: Joseph Smith, 1867; *Supplement,* London: Edward Hicks, 1893.

Smith, William. *A Consecutive History of the Rise, Progress, and Present State of Wesleyan Methodism in Ireland.* Dublin: T. W. Doolittle, 1830.

Southey, Robert. *The Life of Wesley: and the Rise and Progress of Methodism.* New ed. 2 vols. London: Longman, Green, Longman, Roberts, and Green, 1864.

Stenton, Doris Mary. *The English Woman in History.* London: Allen and Unwin, 1957.

Stevens, Abel. *The History of the Religious Movement of the*

Eighteenth Century Called Methodism. 3 vols. London: Wesleyan Methodist Book Room, 1878.

————. *The Women of Methodism: Its Three Foundresses—Susanna Wesley, the Countess of Huntingdon, and Barbara Heck.* New York: Published by Carlton and Porter, 1866.

Stevenson, George J. *City Road Chapel, and Its Associations.* London: George J. Stevenson, [1872].

Tavard, George H. *Woman in Christian Tradition.* Notre Dame: University of Notre Dame Press, 1973.

Taylor, Ernest E. *The Valiant Sixty.* Revised edition. London: Bannisdale Press, 1951.

Telford, John. *Wesley's Veterans: Lives of Early Methodist Preachers.* 7 vols. London: Robert Cully, Ch. H. Kelly, 1909–14.

Thomas, George G. S. *The Life of Mr. Robert Gate, with some Notices of Early Methodism in the Penrith Circuit.* London: Elliot Stock, 1869.

Thomas, Hilah F., and Keller, Rosemary Skinner, eds. *Women in New Worlds: Historical Perspectives on the Wesleyan Tradition.* 2 vols. Nashville: Abingdon Press, 1981, 1982.

Thompson, E. P. *The Making of the English Working Class.* New York: Pantheon Books, 1964.

Towlson, Clifford W. *Moravian and Methodist: Relationships and Influences in the Eighteenth Century.* London: Epworth Press, 1957.

Townsend, W. J. *Alexander Kilham, the First Methodist Reformer.* London: Hamilton, Adams, 1889.

Townsend, W. J., Workman, H. B., and Eayrs, George, eds. *A New History of Methodism.* 2 vols. London: Hodder and Stoughton, 1909.

Turberville, A. S., ed. *Johnson's England: An Account of the Life and Manners of His Age.* 2 vols. Oxford: Clarendon Press, 1933.

Tyerman, Luke. *The Life and Times of the Rev. John Wesley, M.A.* 3 vols. London: Hodder and Stoughton, 1870–71.

————. *The Oxford Methodists.* London: Hodder and Stoughton, 1873.

————. *Wesley's Designated Successor: The Life, Letters, and Literary Labours of the Rev. John William Fletcher, Vicar of Madeley, Shropshire.* London: Hodder and Stoughton, 1882.

Underwood, A. C. *A History of the English Baptists.* London: Baptist Union Publication Department, 1947.

Ward, W. Reginald. *Religion and Society in England, 1790–1850.* London: B. T. Batsford, 1972.

Warner, Wellman J. *The Wesleyan Movement in the Industrial Revolution.* London: Longmans, Green, 1930.

Watson, David L. *The Early Methodist Class Meeting: Its Origins and Significance.* Nashville: Discipleship Resources, 1985.

Wearmouth, Robert F. *Methodism and the Common People of the Eighteenth Century.* London: Epworth Press, 1945.

————. *Methodism and the Working-Class Movements of England, 1800–1860.* London: Epworth Press, 1957.

Whitehead, John. *The Life of the Rev. John Wesley.* 2 vols. London: Couchman, 1793, 1796.

Whitely, J. H. *Wesley's England: A Survey of Eighteenth-Century Social and Cultural Conditions.* London: Epworth Press, 1938.

Wiggins, James. *The Embattled Saint: Aspects of the Life and Thought of John Fletcher.* Macon, Ga.: Wesleyan College, 1966.

Wilkinson, John T. *Hugh Bourne, 1772–1852.* London: Epworth Press, 1952.

Williams, Basil. *The Whig Supremacy, 1714–1760.* Oxford: Clarendon Press, 1939.

Wilson, Bryan, ed. *Patterns of Sectarianism: Organization and Ideology in Social and Religious Movements.* London: Heinemann, 1967.

Wilson, D. Dunn. *Many Waters Cannot Quench: A Study of the Sufferings of Eighteenth-Century Methodism and Their Significance for John Wesley and the First Methodists.* London: Epworth Press, 1969.

CHAPTERS AND ARTICLES

Anderson, Olive. "Women Preachers in Mid-Victorian Britain: Some Reflexions on Feminism, Popular Religion and Social Change." *Historical Journal* 12, 3(1969): 467–84.

Baker, Frank. "John Wesley and Sarah Crosby." *W.H.S.* 27, 4(December 1949): 76–82.

————. "John Wesley's Churchmanship." *L.Q.R.* 185, 3(July 1960): 210–15; 185, 4(October 1960): 269–70.

————. "John Wesley's First Marriage." *L.Q.R.* 192, 4(October 1967): 305–15.

————. "Salute to Susanna." *Meth. Hist.* 7, 3(April 1969): 3–12.

————. "Susanna Wesley, Apologist for Methodism." *W.H.S.* 35, 3(September 1965): 68–71.

———. "Susanna Wesley: Puritan, Parent, Pastor, Protagonist, Pattern." In *Women in New Worlds,* 2:112–31. Nashville: Abingdon Press, 1982.

———. "Thomas Maxfield's First Sermon." *W.H.S.* 27, 1(March 1949): 7–15.

Bates, E. Ralph. "Sarah Ryan and Kingswood School." *W.H.S.* 38, 4(May 1972): 110–14.

Batty, Margaret. "Local Preaching in Wesleyanism in the Nineteenth Century." *W.H.S., North East Branch* 19 (April 1973): 4–8.

Beadle, Harold. "Methodism in Barnard Castle and Upper Teesdale before 1880." *W.H.S., North East Branch* 21 (March 1974): 4–8; 22 (September 1974): 15–18; 23 (March 1975): 6–9.

Beckerlegge, Oliver A. "Women Itinerant Preachers." *W.H.S.* 30, 8(December 1956): 182–84.

Blanchard, Rae. "Richard Steele and the Status of Women." *Studies in Philology* 26 (1929): 325–55.

Bowmer, John C. "The Wesleyan Conception of the Ministry." *Religion in Life* 40, 1(Spring 1971): 85–96.

Brackenbury, Thomas. "Methodism in Sevenoaks," *Methodist Recorder Winter Number* 41 (Christmas 1900): 91–93.

Bretherton, F. F. "Quarterly Meetings." *W.H.S.* 7 (1910): 78–81.

Brooke, Susan C. "The Journal of Isabella Mackiver." *W.H.S.* 28, 8(December 1952): 159–63.

Brown, E. K. "Archetypes and Stereotypes: Church Women in the Nineteenth Century." *Religion in Life* 43, 3(Autumn 1974): 325–36.

———. "Standing in the Shadow: Women in Early Methodism." *Nexus* 17, 2(Spring 1974): 22–31.

———. "Wesley and Women Preachers." *Circuit Rider* 6, 1(January 1982): 6–7.

———. "Women in Church History: Stereotypes, Archtypes and Operational Modalities." *Meth. Hist.* 18, 2(January 1980): 109–32.

———. "Women of the Word." In *Women in New Worlds,* 1: 69–87. Nashville: Abingdon Press, 1981.

Brown, R. A. "Review of Mary Beard's *Woman as Force in History*" *Christian Science Monitor,* April 17, 1946.

Buckley, J. M. "What Methodism Owes to Women." In *Proceedings, Sermons, Essays, and Addresses of the Centennial Methodist Conference.* Edited by H. K. Carroll. Cincinnati: Cranston and Stowe, 1885.

Cannon, William. "John Wesley's Years in Georgia." *Meth. Hist.* 1, 4(July 1963): 1–7.

Chandler, Douglas R. "John Wesley and His Preachers." *Religion in Life* 24, 2(Spring 1955): 241–48.

Church, Leslie F. "The Call to Preach in Early Methodism." *L.Q.R.* 179 (July 1954): 185–91.

Coomer, Duncan. "The Influence of Puritanism and Dissent on Methodism." *L.Q.R.* 175, 4(October 1950): 346–50.

———. "The Local Preacher in Early Methodism." *W.H.S.* 25, 3(September 1943): 33–42.

Cooper, J. Edward. "Dinah Morris and Seth Bede, and the Early Days of Derby Methodism." *Methodist Recorder Winter Number* 37 (Christmas 1896): 35–38.

Crippen, T. G. "The Females Advocate." *Transactions of the Congregational Historical Society* 8, 2(1921): 96–101.

———. "A Forgotten Chapter of Early Nonconformist History." *Transactions of the Congregational Historical Society* 1, 3(1902): 192–94.

Curnock, N. "The Loves and Friendships of John Wesley." *Methodist Recorder Winter Number* 42 (Christmas 1901): 19–27; 43 (Christmas 1902): 21–32.

Davies, Horton. "Epworth's Debt to Geneva: A Field of Research." *Livingstonian* (1960): 5–6.

Dayton, Donald W., and Sider, Lucille. "Women as Preachers: Evangelical Precedents." *Christianity Today* 19, 17 (May 23, 1975): 822–25.

Dews, D. C. "Nonconformity in Morley." *W.H.S., Yorkshire Branch* 38 (April 1981): 10–18.

"Dorothy Ripley, Unaccredited Missionary." *Journal of the Friends Historical Society* 22 (1925): 33–51; 23 (1926): 12–21, 77–79.

Doughty, W. L. "George J. Stevenson: A Letter to Zechariah Taft." *W.H.S.* 28, 2(June 1951): 33–38.

Eichler, Margrit, and Nelson, Carol Avin. "History and Historiography." *Historian* 40, 1(November 1977): 1–15.

Fletcher, G. Arthur. "Derby: The Old Chapel in St. Michael's Lane." *W.H.S.* 15, 4(December 1925): 109–12.

Green, W. A. "Jonathan and Penelope Coussins." *W.H.S.* 34, 3(September 1963): 58–60.

Grubb, John H. "The Conference Town." *Wes. Meth. Mag.* 121 (1898): 483–94.

Harrison, A. W. "An Early Woman Preacher: Sarah Crosby." *W.H.S.* 14, 5(March 1924): 104–9.

————. "New Light on Methodism in the Isle of Man." *W.H.S.* 19, 8(December 1934): 195–202.

————. "Wesley's Reading during the Voyage to Georgia." *W.H.S.* 13, 2(June 1921): 25–29.

Hartley, John C. "After Wesley: Expansion in Yorkshire Methodism, 1791–1800." *W.H.S., Yorkshire Branch* 36 (April 1980): 2–9.

Hellier, J. E. "The Mother Chapel of Leeds." *Methodist Recorder Winter Number* 35 (Christmas 1894): 62–67.

————. "Some Methodist Women Preachers." *Methodist Recorder Winter Number* 36 (Christmas 1895): 65–69.

Judge, G. H. Bancroft. "The Beginnings of Methodism in the Penrith District." *W.H.S.* 19, 7(September 1934): 153–60.

Keller, Rosemary S. "Alternative Forms of Leadership by Women in the Protestant Tradition." Paper delivered at Berkshire Conference of Women Historians, Mount Holyoke College, August 12, 1978.

Kent, John H. S. "M. Elie Halévy on Methodism." *W.H.S.* 29, 4(December 1953): 84–91.

Lewis, Idwal. "Early Methodist Societies in Glamorgan and Monmouthshire." *Bathafarn* 11 (1956): 57–65.

McConnell, Dorothy. "The Women of Early Methodism." In *Forever Beginning, 1766–1966.* Edited by Albea Bodbold. Lake Junaluska; N.C.: Association of Methodist Historical Societies, 1967.

"Mary Astell: A Seventeenth-Century Advocate for Women." *Westminster Review* 149 (January-June 1898): 440–49.

Miller, William F. "Episodes in the Life of May Drummond." *Journal of the Friends Historical Society* 4 (1907): 55–61, 103–14.

Moers, Ellen. "Vindicating Mary Wollstonecraft." *New York Review of Books* 23 (1976): 38–42.

Mounfield, Arthur. "Dorothy Ripley." *W.H.S.* 7, 2(June 1909): 31–33.

Nattrass, J. Conder. "Some Notes from the Oldest Register of the Great Yarmouth Circuit." *W.H.S.* 3, 3(1901): 73–77.

Newton, John A. "Susanna Wesley (1669–1742): A Bibliographical Survey." *W.H.S.* 37, 2(June 1969): 37–40.

Norwood, Frederick A. "The Shaping of Methodist Ministry." *Religion in Life* 45, 3(August 1974): 348–49.

Parlby, William. "Diana Thomas, of Kington, Lay Preacher in the Hereford Circuit, 1759–1821." *W.H.S.* 14, 5(March 1924): 110–11.

Rogal, Samuel J. "John Wesley's Lady Preachers." *United Methodists Today/Today's Ministry Section* 1, 9(September 1974): 78–81.

——. "John Wesley's Women." *Eighteenth-Century Life* 1 (1974): 7–10.

Rose, E. A. "Sarah Kilham and Hannah Kilham." *W.H.S.* 39, 6(October 1974): 185–86.

Rosen, Beth. "Sexism in History, or Writing Women's History Is a Tricky Business." *Journal of Marriage and the Family* 33, 3(August 1971): 541–44.

Sanders, J. Kingsley. "Mrs. Hannah Kilham." *W.H.S.* 39, 3(October 1973): 93–94.

Schnorrenberg, Barbara B. "The Eighteenth-Century English-woman." In *The Women of England from Anglo-Saxon Times to the Present: Interpretive Bibliographical Essays.* Edited by Barbara Kanner. London: Mansell, 1980.

Shipley, David C. "Methodist Ministry in the Eighteenth Century." *Perkins School of Theology Journal* 13, 1(Fall 1959): 5–14.

Smith, C. Ryder. "The Ministry of Women." In *Methodism: Its Present Responsibilities.* London: Epworth Press, 1929.

Stein, Stephen J. "A Note on Anne Dutton, Eighteenth-Century Evangelical." *Church History* 44, 4(December 1975): 485–91.

Swift, Wesley F. "Early Methodism in Northwich." *W.H.S.* 22, 2(June 1939): 38–45.

——. "The Women Itinerant Preachers of Early Methodism." *W.H.S.* 28, 5(March 1952): 89–94; 29, 4(December 1953): 76–83.

Taylor, Ernest E. "The First Publishers of Truth: A Study." *Journal of the Friends Historical Society* 19 (1922): 66–81.

Thomas, Keith V. "Women and the Civil War Sects." *Past & Present* 13 (April 1958): 42–62.

Thompson, Edwin. "This Remarkable Family: A Study of the Barritt's of Foulridge, 1750–1850." Privately circulated, St. Andrew's Manse, Barnoldswick, Colne, June 1981.

Todd, Janet M. "The Biographies of Mary Wollstonecraft: Review Essay." *Signs: Journal of Women in Culture and Society* 1 (1976): 721–34.

Tranter, William. "Methodism in Madeley." *Wes. Meth. Mag.* 60 (1837): 900–903.

Waller, Dr. "A Famous Lady Preacher." *Wes. Meth. Mag.* 130 (1907): 538–44.

Walmsley, Robert. "John Wesley's Parents: Quarrel and Reconciliation." *W.H.S.* 29, 3(September 1953): 50–57.

Whitley, W. T. "The Rise of Lay Preaching in Holland." *Transactions of the Congregational Historical Society* 5, 5(1912): 282–89.

Williams, Ethyn Morgan. "Women Preachers in the Civil War." *Journal of Modern History* 1, 4(December 1929): 561–69.

Wood, A Skevinton. "John Wesley's Reversion to Type: The Influence of His Nonconformist Ancestry." *W.H.S.* 35, 4(December 1965): 88–93.

Young, Frank. "Houghton-Le-Spring." *W.H.S.* 16, 3–4(September-December 1927): 72–74.

"Zinzendorf and the Moravians." *Christian History* 1, 1(1982): 7–35.

ACADEMIC THESES AND DISSERTATIONS

Batty, Margaret. "The Contribution of Local Preachers to the Life of the Wesleyan Methodist Church until 1932, and to the Methodist Church after 1932 in England." M.A. thesis, University of Leeds, 1969.

Bennett, E. Fay. "The Call of God in the Ministry of John Wesley: A Study of Spiritual Authority in Methodist History." Dissertation, Southwestern Baptist Seminary, 1963.

Blackmore, J. H. "Lay Preaching in England from the Reformation to the Rise of Methodism: A Study in Its Development, Nature and Significance." Ph.D. dissertation, University of Edinburgh, 1951.

Butler, H. M. "The 'Pious Sisterhood': A Study of Women's Roles in English Methodism, c. 1740-c. 1840." B.A. thesis, LaTrobe University, 1978.

Carruth, Samuel E. "John Wesley's Concept of the Church." Th.D. dissertation, Iliff School of Theology, 1952.

Gadt, Jeanette Carter. "Women and Protestant Culture: The Quaker Dissent from Puritanism." Dissertation, University of California at Los Angeles, 1976.

Garlow, James L. "John Wesley's Understanding of the Laity as Demonstrated by His Use of the Lay Preachers." Ph.D dissertation, Drew University, 1979.

Greaves, B. "Methodism in Yorkshire, 1740–1851." Ph.D. dissertation, University of Liverpool, 1968.

Harder, Robert C. "The Ministry of the Laity and the People of God." Th.D. thesis, Boston University School of Theology, 1958.

Heitzenrater, Richard. "John Wesley and the Oxford Methodists, 1725–1735." Ph.D. dissertation, Duke University, 1972.

Kent, John H. S. "The Clash between Radicalism and Conservatism in Methodism, 1815–1848." Ph.D. dissertation, University of Cambridge, 1951.

Kirkham, Donald H. "Pamphlet Opposition to the Rise of Methodism: The Eighteenth-Century English Evangelical Revival under Attack." Ph.D. dissertation, Duke University, 1973.

Ludlow, Dorothy. " 'Arise and Be Doing': English 'Preaching' Women, 1640–1660." Ph.D. dissertation, Indiana University, 1978.

Lynn, James D. "The Concept of the Ministry in the Methodist Church, 1784–1844." Dissertation, Princeton Theological Seminary, 1973.

MacKenzie, P. D. "The Methodist Class Meeting: A Historical Study." Th.M. thesis, St. Andrews University, 1969.

Score, John N. R., II. "A Study of the Concept of the Ministry in the Thought of John Wesley." Ph.D. dissertation, Duke University, 1963.

Shipley, David C. "Methodist Arminianism in the Theology of John Fletcher." Ph.D. dissertation, Yale University, 1942.

Watson, David Lowes. "The Origins and Significance of the Early Methodist Class Meeting." Ph.D. dissertation, Duke University, 1978.

Wilder, James Simpson. "Early Methodist Lay Preachers and Their Contribution to the Eighteenth-Century Revival in England." Ph.D. dissertation, University of Edinburgh, 1948.

GENERAL INDEX

Only select matter in the notes is indexed, not the authorities cited. The appendixes have not been indexed, except for the names of the women preachers in Appendix A and the scriptural references in Appendix H. Some titles of works appear abbreviated.

Aberystwyth (Wales) 26
Account of Ann Cutler 227
"Account of Hannah Harrison" 131
"Account of Latonstone" 126
Act of Toleration 214
Act of Uniformity (1662) 15
Adams, Thomas 80
Addison, Joseph 12
Aldersgate Street (London) 45
Aldersley, Mary 50
Allen, Charles 227
Allinson, Mary 49
America 246
Ampleforth 227
Anabaptists 5, 8, 28
Anglicans 45–46, 54, 56, 68, 78, 141, 189, 199, 238
Annesley, Samuel 17
Anticlericalism 5
Antigua 202
Apology (Barclay) 57, 163
Apostolic Constitutions 22–23, 40
Appeal to All Men of Common Sense 180
Appeals to Men of Reason and Religion 89
Arminian Magazine 3

Arminian Methodists 243, 250
Arminianism 79, 206–7
Ars Moriendi 101
"Assistants" 68, 132, 148, 157, 181, 202
Astell, Mary 13
Athlone (Ireland) 54, 97
Atlay, John 132, 173, 225
Atmore, Charles 190
Attaway (Mrs., Baptist preacher) 8, 30
Avison, Edward 140
Axminster 110
Aysgarth 247

Baildon 165
Baillie, Robert 6
Bainbridge 229
Baker, Frank 77, 79, 98–99, 121, 247
"Balaam's Ass" 190, 210
Baldock 51
Baldwin St. Society (Bristol) 58, 110
Ball, Hannah 64, 147–48, 217–18
Ballinderry (Ireland) 160
Ballybredagh (Ireland) 160

Ballyculter (Ireland) 160
Bandon (Ireland) 203
Band meeting 46–50, 68–72, 74, 82, 92, 97, 99, 103, 128, 149, 152, 181, 204, 216, 239
Band select 149
Baptism 23
Baptists 8, 10, 29, 154
Barber (Mr., Irish itinerant) 204
Barclay, Robert 57, 163
Barnard Castle 62, 103
Barritt, John 229
Barritt, Mary 146, 216, 228–34, 281–84. *See also* Mary Taft
Barrowist 28
Barton, Jane 111, 170, 176
Barton, William 131
Bartram, James 174
Bath 7, 139, 148, 150, 161, 174, 178
Batley 183
Batty, Margaret 84, 243
Baxter, Richard 18
Bayley Hill 26
Bealey, Mary 64
Beard, Mary 1
Beauty's Triumph 14
Beccles 191
Bedminster 146
Beeston 152
Bell, George 124
Belton (Mrs., of Walkeringham) 64
Bennet, John 86–87, 89
Bennis, Elizabeth 50, 70, 99, 132–33, 148, 159–60
Benreken, Solomon 137
Benson, Betty 180
Benson, Joseph 139–40, 157–59, 234
Beresford, Judith 53
Berkshire 174
Bernard (Dr., Puritan author) 28
Berridge (Rev., of Everton) 156
Best, Sibyll 103
Bethel 135

Beverley 131, 156, 170
Bible Christians 236, 243, 251
Biggleswade 51
Bilsdale 153
Bilston 65
Bingley 156, 227
Bird, Mary 65
Birmingham 208–9
Birstal 50, 62, 98, 156, 244–45
Bishop, Mary 148, 174, 215
Bishopscastle 26
Bisson, Jeannie 202–3, 253–54
Blocker, Ruth 62
Blow, Elizabeth 50
Boggard House (Leeds) 175, 200
Bolton, Ann ("Nancy") 147, 218
Book of Common Prayer 38, 41
Booth-Bank 105
Bosanquet, Mary 119, 122, 123–31, 142–44, 150–51, 156, 161, 165–70, 182, 183–86, 262–67. *See also* Mary Fletcher
Boston (Mass.) 10
Boswell, James 117
Bourke, Richard 132
Bouse 248
Bowman, William 55–56, 58
Bowmer, John 223
Boyce (Mr., husband of Sarah Mallet) 213
Bracebridge 52
Brackenbury, Robert 203
Bradburn, Samuel 207, 229
Bradford 61, 110, 112, 154–56, 244
Bradwell 93
Braithwaite, John 230
Bramhall, John 8
Brammah, William 140, 175
Bramwell, William 94–95, 102–3, 172, 225–26, 227, 229, 230–31, 237
Bransdale 153
Brasenose College (Oxford) 41
Brethren 42
Bridlington 169
Briestfield 62

Brilley (Wales) 26
Brisco, Thomas 216
Bristol 29, 45–46, 48, 53, 55, 57, 59–60, 65, 68, 87, 97, 125, 137–38, 140, 144, 146, 148, 158, 162–63, 174, 178, 196, 198–99, 208, 218, 233
Broadmead (Bristol) 29
Brown, Anne 218, 232, 254
Brown, George 218
Brownist 5, 28
Buckinghamshire 64
Builth (Wales) 26
Buller, James 48
Bunhill Fields (London) 179
Bunting, Jabez 88, 188, 224, 242
Bunyon, John 29
Burlington 157
Burns, Jabez 172
Burnside, Margaret (née Bovey) 22
Butterfield, Herbert 12
Byrom (Mrs., of Liverpool) 106
Byron (Mr., of Long Stratton) 194

Calder, Hannah 52
Call 21–22, 50, 72–73, 76, 78–84, 90, 94, 103–4, 120, 133, 143, 146–47, 151, 168–69, 171, 184, 186, 194–95, 197, 200–202, 204, 226–27, 230–31, 238–39; extraordinary, 76, 78, 80–81, 141–45, 161, 171–72, 213, 231, 236, 238–39; inward, 80–81; ordinary, 76, 78, 80–81, 171; outward, 80–81
Calvinistic Methodists 178, 206
Calvinists 30
Cambridge, Alice 203–4, 232–33, 254–55
Cambridge 12
Camp meeting 243
Canterbury 124, 197, 233
Cappoquin (Ireland) 204
Carey, Mary 62
Carlill (Mr., husband of preacher) 245

Carroll, Berenice 3
"Caution against Bigotry" 80
Cayley (Mrs., friend of Sarah Crosby) 154
"Cedars, The" 126, 127
Chapel, Methodist 51–52, 58, 62, 64, 102–3, 105, 107, 134–35, 146, 154–55, 165, 178, 185, 188, 194–96, 202, 210, 227, 229, 231, 233–34
Chapman, Martha ("Patty") 148, 217
Chapone, Sally 13
Chatershough 246
"Checks on Antinomianism" 206
Cheltenham 103, 148
Cheshire 105, 140, 218
Chester 64, 130, 217
Chickward (Ireland) 26
Chinley 61
Chinton (Ireland) 26
Christian, William 202
"Christian Perfection" 53, 68, 102, 174
Christopher's Alley 119
Church, Leslie 82, 250
Church: authoritarian view, 76–77, 224–25, 237–38, 239; charismatic view, 6–7, 76–77, 96–98, 225, 237–39; of England, 15, 54, 68, 76–77, 80, 97, 141, 144, 147, 189, 206, 222
Churwell 154
Circuit 127, 132–33, 135, 146, 157, 171, 174, 177, 187–91, 200–201, 226–27, 229–35, 242, 244–45
Clark, Mary 119
Clarke, Adam 190–91, 201, 203, 249
Clarke, Mary 216–17
Clarkson, Lawrence 30
Class meeting 47, 49, 68–72, 74, 81, 83, 92–93, 97, 103, 120–21, 149, 151, 153–54, 186–88, 199, 201–2, 228–30, 239, 242, 245
Clayton, John 40–41

Clinker, Humphrey   47
Clonmel (Ireland)   132, 179
Clulow, Elizabeth   51
Clun (Wales)   26
Coalbrookdale   186
Coalport   186, 200, 215
Cock, Benjamin   166
Collection of Hymns   112
Collett (Mr., husband of Eliza-
   beth)   188
Collett, Elizabeth   211, 285–86.
   See also Elizabeth Tonkin
Collett, Richard   188, 210
Colne   228
Colston, Sally   101
Comber (Ireland)   160
Commonwealth   5
*Compleat Collection of Devo-
   tions*   23
Conference, English Method-
   ist   52, 80, 127–28, 134, 155,
   182, 192, 196, 201–2, 213, 221,
   225, 229, 231–37, 249; (1744),
   54, 89; (1745), 89; (1746), 79–
   80; (1747), 89; (1748), 89;
   (1755), 106; (1765), 127;
   (1770), 134; (1784), 192;
   (1787), 195, 205; (1789), 201;
   (1796), 242; (1802), 234;
   (1803), 235–7; (1804), 237;
   (1824), 226; Irish Methodist,
   232, 237
Confession   46, 68, 233
Congregationalism   28, 96,
   148
Congress   246
Conscience   6, 19–20, 29, 100,
   158, 238
Constantine   81
Conventicle   8, 20
Conversion   3, 7, 23, 50, 52, 74,
   80, 94–96, 98, 102, 117–20, 137,
   145, 148–49, 163, 165, 181–82,
   197, 211, 217, 226–27, 230, 244,
   246, 248
Conway, Lord   8
Cooper, Jane   99–100
Cork (Ireland)   204

Cornwall (Cornish)   83, 138,
   145–46, 182, 186–89, 240
Cotswolds   22, 184
Coussins, Jonathan   102, 149,
   174, 184
Coussins, Penelope   174, 275–
   76. *See* also Penelope Newman
Covenant service   97
Cownley, Joseph   158
Cox, Sarah   227, 255
Crookshank, C. H.   203–4
Crosby, Sarah   50, 72, 94, 99,
   118–31, 133–34, 142, 144, 149,
   151–55, 157, 161–62, 169–71,
   200–201, 205–7, 226, 243, 248,
   255–59
Cross, Alice   105–6, 118, 259
Cross, John   105–6, 112
Cross Hall (Yorkshire)   129–31,
   145, 152, 154, 172–73, 175,
   182–83, 199, 206
Crosse, Alice   112
Crosse, John   112
"Culamite Preachers"   131
Curnock, Nehemiah   211
Cutler, Ann ("Praying
   Nanny")   94–95, 102, 225–26,
   259–60

Dairyman's Daughter, The   107
Dale, Peggy   133
Dales, The   62, 103, 229
Darlaston   65
Darlington   50, 231
Davenport, Hannah   54
Davidson, Margaret   159–62,
   203, 260–61
Dawgreen   156
Dawson, Joanna   175
Dawson, William   230
Deacon, Thomas   23
Deaconess   22–23, 72, 201
Deacons   7, 72, 88, 106, 206
Deed of Declaration (1784)   132,
   221
Defoe, Daniel   13, 17
Deism   163
Denny, Mary   49

Denominationalism   172
Deptford   217
DePutron, Sarah   227, 261–62.
   See also Sarah Eland
Derby   50, 65, 121–4, 142, 156,
   244
Derby Faith Folk   250
Derbyshire   156
Derryaghy (Ireland)   160
Deschamps, Esther   46
"Devotionalists"   56
Dewsbury   62, 225–26
Dickinson, Elizabeth   108, 227–
   28, 261
Dickinson, John   228
Diss   174, 197, 214
Dissvasive from Errours   6
Dobinson (Mrs., Derby pioneer)
   50, 120–21
Donaghadee (Ireland)   51, 62
Doncaster   103, 156
Dover   181, 233–35, 249
Down, county (Ireland)   160,
   203
Downes, Dorothy   71–72, 119,
   183. *See also* Dorothy Furly
Downpatrick (Ireland)   177
Driffield   156
Drummond, May   15–16
Drury, Sarah   103
Dryden, John   15
Dublin (Ireland)   10, 174, 177,
   204, 217, 232
Dudley, Mary   179, 280. *See also*
   Mary Stokes
Dudley, Robert   179
Duffrin (Wales)   26
Dunsford   161, 177
Dutton, Anne   25

Eardisland (Wales)   26
Easter   136
Ecclesiolae in Ecclesia   45, 222
Ecclesiology   25, 47, 54, 58, 75–
   77, 171, 222, 224, 237, 239
Edmondson, Jonathan   232
Edwards (Mrs., of Purfleet)   218
Edwards, Thomas   29–30

Egalitarianism   6–7, 178, 224–
   25, 238–40
Egglescliff   245
Eland, Sarah   226–27, 261–62.
   See also Sarah DePutron
Elder   7
"Eldress"   23
Embden, Synod of (1571)   7
Empringham, Robert   158, 174,
   176–77
Enquiry into the Duties   12
Enthusiasm   4, 15, 54–57, 125,
   148–49, 218
Enthusiasm of Methodists   57–58
Entwisle, Joseph   209, 231–32
Episcopal Church   251
Epistles (Fox)   10
Epping   179
Epworth   16–20, 90, 109, 122,
   136, 142
Equality   6, 9–11, 14, 53, 58, 71,
   73, 98, 178, 239
Ernest (Duke) the Pious   138
Essex   124
Evangelism   3, 79, 81, 106, 186,
   189, 223–25, 227–28, 246
Evans, Elizabeth   250
Everton   61, 156
Evesham   56
Excommunication   233
Exegesis   7
Exeter   57
Exhortation   7, 47, 70, 73–74,
   77, 82–84, 92, 95–6, 100–106,
   118, 121–23, 130–31, 133, 142,
   144–45, 149–50, 160–61, 170,
   190–91, 193, 200, 203–4, 226,
   228, 232, 236, 239, 245
Exposition (expounding)   6–7,
   28, 55, 82, 88, 96, 127, 185–86,
   202, 226, 239
"Extraordinary Messengers"
   79, 89, 165, 171, 223–25, 239

"Faithful Ambassador, The"
   104
Fakenham   189
Falmouth   188

Familist 5
Farther Appeal 214
Fell, Margaret 10–11, 142–43, 180
"The Female Brethren" 198, 201, 205
Fermanagh (Ireland) 218
Feminism 13–14, 17, 27, 47, 178, 228, 251
Fenwick, John 157–58, 177, 180
Fenwick, Michael 231
Feock 8, 187
Fetter Lane Society 45–46, 48, 53, 55
Field preaching 45–46, 76–77, 154–55, 165, 180, 191, 195, 227–28
Fielding, Henry 34
Finsbury Square 48
Fisher, Dorothy 51–52
Fisher, Mary 31
Flamanck, Elizabeth 199
Fleetwood, William 48
Fletcher, John 170–71, 174, 183–86, 215
Fletcher, Mary 150, 183–86, 198–201, 205, 240, 243–44, 262–67. *See also* Mary Bosanquet
Foard, Ann 131
Foster, Henry 157
Foundery, The (London) 48–49, 74, 95, 118–19, 121, 125
Foundery, The (Norwich) 99
Fox, Elizabeth 23
Fox, George 9–11
Fox, Thomas 23
Foy, Captain 68
Francke, A. H. 138
Franklin (Miss) 189. *See also* (Mrs.) Parker (church builder of Fakenham)
"French Prophetesses" 16, 54–55
French Revolution 34–35, 221
Friars, The (Bristol) 162
Frome 60
"Full Connection" 80

Furly, Dorothy 119. *See also* Dorothy Downes
Furness, Isabella 93
Fylde, The 63

Galway (Ireland) 61
Gamblesby 62, 180
Garbutt, Thomas 230
Gate, Robert 180
"Gathered Church" 6, 96, 109
Gayer, Henrietta 51
Geneva (University of) 109, 206
Gentlemen's Magazine 16
George, Amy 51
Georgia 22–23, 78
Germany 28
Gilbert, Ann 145–46, 186, 267
Gilbert, Francis 202
Gilbert, Mary 202, 267–68
Gilbert, Nathaniel 217
Gilbert, Mrs. Robert 22
Gildersome 129
Gillamore 153
Gisbourne, Thomas 12
Glamorgan (Wales) 60
Glass (Mrs., Irish exhorter) 97
Glorious Revolution (1688/89) 15
Gloucester 174
Goddard (Mrs., Chinley pioneer) 49
Goker 166–67
Good Friday 122
Goodwin, John 6
Gore, The (Wales) 26
Gotha (Germany) 138
Goulden, Mary 227, 268
Governesses 126, 138
Gowt's Bridge 52
Grantham 62, 201
Granville (family) 39
Graves, Catherine 103, 118
Gray, Betty 16
Gonerby, Great 52, 62
Greatland 244
Green, V. H. H. 21
Gretton, Ellen 201–2, 268

Grevil (Mrs., early London band member) 46
Grimsby 50, 181, 233
Grubb, Sarah 179
Guisborough 153
Guiseley 156
Gwennap 83
Gwinear 145, 186

Hadderson 193
Haddiscoe 211
Hainsworth (Mrs., Rakefoot class leader) 71, 226, 268–69
Halévy thesis 35
Halifax 49, 150, 154–55, 201
Hall, Bathsheba 146
Hall, Ruth 50, 216
Hallam 93
Halle (Germany) 138
Hampson, J. 122, 135
Hanby, Thomas 54
Hargreaves, John 86
Harper, Joseph 195–96
Harrison, Ebeneezer 140
Harrison, Hannah 63, 130–32, 216, 269–70
Harrison, Lancelot 52, 140, 229
Harrison, Mary 227, 245, 268–69
Harrogate 150, 154
Hartly (Miss, of Henley) 217–18
Harvey (Miss, Hertfordshire chapel builder) 51
Haslingden 218
Haworth 63, 156
Hay (Wales) 26
Hay (Lancashire) 228
Hazzard, Dorothy 29
Healy, John 54
Hebrides (Scotland) 134
Heck, Barbara 37
"Helpers" 68
Helton, John 163–65
Henley 217–18
Henry, Matthew 164
Hereford 26
Herrnhut (Germany) 23
Hertfordshire 51

Hexham 229
High Wycombe 64, 147, 217
Higham 110
High Churchman 117
Highton-dale 153
Hill, Christopher 9
Hilton, Jane 111, 131
Hinxworth 51
History of Cornish Methodism 186
Holder, George 226
Holder, Mary 103, 169–70, 226, 248, 270. *See also* Mary Woodhouse
Holiness 46, 70, 109, 170, 210, 222, 228, 240
Holland 7
Holland (Lincolnshire) 8
Holmes (Mrs., pioneer of Halifax) 49
"Holy Club" 39, 41
Holy Spirit 6, 10–11, 19, 76, 79–80, 92, 94, 97–98, 104, 117, 120, 123, 128, 152, 163–64, 186, 196, 206, 224, 227, 238, 240–41, 244
Holy Women 191, 205
Hoo Hoyle 112
Hooker, Richard 88, 90
Hooten, Elizabeth 10
Hopper (Mrs., Yorkshire preacher's wife) 156
Hopper, Christopher 176
Horne, Melville 209
Horsefair, The (Bristol) 58, 161
Hosmer (Mrs., pioneer of Darlington) 50
Houghton-Le-Spring 227
Housekeeper 68, 74–75, 125
Howe, Margaret 93
Hoston Square 125, 138
Huddersfield 133, 166–68, 173
Hudson (Rev., Irish itinerant) 160
Hull 50, 234
Hunt (Mr., of Norwich) 197
Huntingdon, Selina, Countess of 37, 178

Hurrell, Elizabeth 156–59, 169–
70, 175, 180, 216, 270–71
Hutton, James 42, 46
Hutton 227

Imposture of Methodism 55
Impressment 83
Independents 6
Industrial Revolution 14, 63,
221
Ingham, Benjamin 42
Inman, Godfrey 20
Ireland 50–51, 54, 62, 75, 97,
107, 127, 130, 132, 159–61, 179,
203, 204, 206, 222, 232–33, 236
Isle of Wight 60–61, 93
Israel 94

Jackson, Thomas 3, 230
"Jansenist Convulsionaries" 55
Jefferson, Thomas 227
Jersey, Isle of 173, 202–3
Johnson, Elizabeth 179
Johnson, John 53
Johnson, Samuel 117
Jones, Rebecca 16
Journal (Wesley) 53, 94
Justification 57, 164

Keighley 156
Kellet, Arnold 175
Kempis, Thomas à 22
Kent 235
Kentish Herald 233
Kerry, Mary 62
Keyley, Elizabeth 52
Keynsham 148, 215
Kilham, Alexander 221, 246
Kilham, Hannah 246, 271–72
Killinchy (Ireland) 160
Killinghall 154
King-Street Chapel (Canter-
bury) 233
Kingswood 87, 161, 178
Kingswood School 87, 125–26,
138, 178
Kington (Wales) 26
Kinsale (Ireland) 204

Kirkham, Betty 39
Kirkham, Lionel 39
Kirkham, Robert 39
Kirkham, Sally ("Varanese")
22, 39
Kirkland, Sarah 251
Kirkstall-Forge 218, 244–45
Knaresborough 227
Knighton 26
Knox, Alexander 21
Knox, Ronald 3

Lackington, James 48
Lake, Arthur 7, 28–29
Lamb, William 190
Lancashire 105, 156, 225–26,
228
Lancaster, John 96
Lancaster, John 157
Lancaster 11
Land, Judith 104
Lastingham 153
Laud, William 8
Lavington, George 57–58
Law, William 36
Lawrence, Sarah 126, 199–200,
207–8, 243, 272–73
Laws of Ecclesiastical Polity 88,
90
Lawson, A. B. 211
Leade (Mrs., foundress of Phila-
delphians) 17
Leaders: band, 46, 59, 68–72,
74–75, 95, 239; class, 59, 68–72,
74–75, 103, 118, 120, 239
Ledbury (Wales) 26
Ledsham 156
Lee, Ann 17
Leeds 50, 118, 129, 138, 151,
154–56, 158, 165, 172, 181, 182,
192, 198–201, 205, 230, 244, 245
Leek 65, 244
Lefevre (Mrs, feminist
writer) 124
Legal Hundred 221
Leicestershire 227
Lerner, Gerda 3
Letter to a Quaker 57, 162–63

Letterbook (Crosby) 99–100, 120
Letters upon Sacred Subjects 137
Levellers 5
Lewen, Margaret 133
Leytonstone 123–24, 126–29, 133, 147, 199
Leytonstone Orphanage 123–29
License (for preaching) 105, 196
Lightcliffe 61
Ligwardine (Wales) 26
Limerick (Ireland) 50, 132, 148, 160, 204
Lincoln 52–53, 64
Lincolnshire 52, 63, 132
Lisburn (Ireland) 51, 160
Liverpool 106
Lives of Early Methodist Preachers 3
Llandaff (Wales) 16
Llansantffraed (Llansaintfraid) (Wales) 96
Llansomefried (Llansomeffraed) (Wales) 26
Llanvihangel (Wales) 26
Lloyd, Arnold 15
Locke, John 37
Loddon 193
Lollard 5, 7
Lomas (Rev.) 226
London 8, 10, 16, 24, 28, 45–46, 48, 52, 55, 60, 65, 71–74, 85, 95, 98, 100, 118–19, 121–24, 127, 132–33, 173–76, 179, 183, 214, 218
Londonderry (Ireland) 143
Long Eaton 230
Long Stratton 191–95
Longmore, Elizabeth 53
Lopham 191
Lord's Supper 132
Lovefeast 47, 97–98, 161, 199, 228, 242, 246
Lowe, Mary 64, 218
Lowes, Matthew 158
Lowestoft 191–94
Luther, Martin 5

Lutherans 22
Luton 173
Lyonshall (Wales) 26

Macclesfield 50–51, 232, 244
Machynlleth (Wales) 26
Mackiver, Isabella 181
McKnight, (Dr.) James 249
Madeley 170, 182–86, 200, 252
Maldon 49
Mallet, Sarah ("Sally") 192–98, 201, 205, 227–28, 273–74
Mallitt (Mallet), William 193–94
Malton 132
Manchester 41, 61, 64, 105, 127, 171, 195, 200, 235, 244
Marsh (Miss, pioneer in Bristol) 218
Marshall (Mrs., Yorkshire Methodist) 156
Marshland 62
Marshland (Rev.) 245
Martyrs 47, 53–54
Maskew, Jonathan 132
Mather, Alexander 229
Maude, Mary 50
Maxfield, Elizabeth 101
Maxfield, Thomas 78, 88, 90, 101, 124, 138, 247
Maudsley, Alice 218
Mayer, (Mr., correspondent of Sarah Crosby) 134, 140
Maylont (Wales) 26
Mellis (Melless) 191
Merston 107
Merton College (Oxford) 39
Methodist Archives 126
Methodist Magazine 131, 187
Methodist New Connection 221, 243, 251
Middleton 154
Midlands 65
Millenarians 17
Millennialists 16
"Ministerial Office, The" 78, 81, 113, 242
"Ministers" 68, 85

Ministry, Doctrine of   54, 57, 75–77, 136, 223–24, 236, 238–39
Mission (-aries)   31, 78, 176, 179, 202, 222–25
"Misuse of the Mass"   5
Mitchell, Thomas   192
Monkhouse (Miss, of Darlington)   231, 248
Monmouthshire   60
Montagu, Lady   13
Moor(e), Sarah (of Sheffield)   93, 135
Moore, Henry   172
Moorfields   119, 124
Moravians   22–24, 48, 68, 97, 109. *See also* Brethren
Morley   129
Mortimer, Elizabeth   94, 207. *See also* Elizabeth Ritchie
Mortimer, Frances   155. *See also* Frances Pawson
Muncy, Jane   71
Murlin (Rev., London itinerant)   127
Murray, Grace   21, 74–75, 119
Myles, William   134
Mysticism   162–63

Nattrass, Conders   213
Neale, Mary   113. *See also* Mary Peisley
Neale, Samuel   113
Nebuchadnezzar   150
Nelson, John   50, 65, 113
New Radnor   26
New Room (Bristol)   58, 68, 87, 137, 158, 162, 199
Newark   65
Newcastle   74, 102, 133, 139, 157–58, 177
Newgate Prison   95
Newington   176
Newland, Jane   218, 274–75
Newman, Penelope   102–3, 148–49, 184, 275–76. *See also* Penelope Coussins
Newman, Thomas   174
Newport (Isle of Wight)   60–61

Newport (Wales)   60–61
Newton, Robert   230
Newton   153
Newtownards (Ireland)   160
Nicholas Street Society   58
Nitschmann, Anna   42
Nonconformity   5, 8, 15, 18, 54, 109, 196, 223
Non-Jurors   15, 23
Nonsense of Common Sense   13
Norfolk   104, 110, 174, 189–92, 195, 197, 205
Norman (Mrs., early Methodist in London)   46
Normanton   50
North Riding (Yorkshire)   152, 227
Northallerton   153
Northampton   7
Northwich   112
Norwich   99, 107, 176, 189–91, 195, 197, 208
Notes (Wesley)   22, 122–23
Nottingham   65, 227, 229–30
"Nurses"   23
Nuttall, Geoffrey   6–7
Nyon (Switzerland)   206

O'Bryan, Catherine   251
Oddie, James   137, 160
"Offshoots"   240, 243
Ohel or Beth-shemesh   9
Oldham   244
"On Trial"   80
Ordination   28, 73, 79, 80–81, 88, 206, 223, 251–52
Orphan-House, The (Newcastle)   74
Orphan-School (Halle)   138
Otley   147, 171, 244
"Ought We to Separate?"   113
Oxford   21, 23, 38–41, 45

Pacifism   54
Page, Mary Ann   46
Pannal   150, 154
Panou (Mrs., early Methodist in London)   46

Parker (Mrs., chapel builder of Fakenham) 189. *See also* (Miss) Franklin
Parker, Hannah 227, 276
Parkgate 156
Parks, Joan 53
Parrot, Sarah 52
Pateley Bridge 229
Paterson, Alexander 157
Pauline prohibitions 8–10, 28, 56–57, 123, 127–28, 142–43, 158–59, 163–64
Paulton 57
Pawson, Frances 72, 94
Pawson, John 86, 105–6, 131, 155, 229, 234
Pearson, George 51
Peckham 179
Peisley, Mary 107. *See also* Mary Neale
Pembridge (Wales) 26
Penrith 62, 165, 180
Pentre (Wales) 26
Peacock, John 171
People's Plea for Prophecy 7
Percival (Mr.) 93
"Perfect Love" 102
Perfection 68, 102, 152, 202, 210
Perfectonists 48, 55
Perronet (Miss, of Shoreham) 147
Perronet, Vincent 72, 208
Perrott, Madame 148, 276
Peters, Hugh 8
Peters, Sarah 86, 95–96
Phebe (Phoebe) 72
Philadelphia 140
Philadelphians 16–17
Phillips, Catherine 16
Pickering 157
Pietas Hallensis 126
Pietism 22, 42
Pietism, Continental 138, 238
"Pilgrim's Inn" 51
Pim, James 113
Pioneers 45, 47, 49–53, 58, 62, 67, 74, 92, 95, 131, 201, 210, 239, 250

Pipe, J. S. 249
Plain Account of Christian Perfection 152
Plain Account of Methodists, The 72
Plewit, Mary 55
Plummer, Stephen 57
Pocklington 156
Pope, Alexander 12, 16
Portarlington 174
Portwood Hall 140
Potter, Miss 40
Potto 153
Prangnell, Mary 93
Prayer 7, 19, 22, 24, 45–47, 49–50, 56, 75, 82, 92–96, 98, 102–4, 119–23, 127, 130, 139, 145, 151, 154, 160, 185–86, 193, 198, 200, 202–3, 207, 215, 226, 228, 239
Prayermeeting 92–93, 102–3, 130, 152, 154, 177, 218, 232
Preachers: itinerant, 70–71, 85, 127, 131–33, 135, 144–46, 149, 155–58, 170, 176, 184–85, 193, 195–96, 211, 218, 223–25, 226–28, 230, 240, 251; lay, 7, 15, 26, 76–85, 101, 117–18, 130, 143, 171; local, 68, 82–83, 91, 106, 157, 174, 191, 196, 213, 228, 230, 242–43; traveling, 82, 84, 168, 196, 226, 229, 251
Presbyterians 29, 37
Presteigne (Wales) 26
Preston 50, 244
Priests 45, 54, 56, 78, 80–81, 206, 232, 238
Priesthood of All Believers 5, 76, 238
Primitive Methodism 236, 243, 251
Priscilla 174
Prisons 73, 95–96
Prophesying 6–8, 27, 57, 91, 101, 104, 106, 143, 164, 171, 196, 226
Prophetesses 8, 16–17, 29, 55–56
Prophets 81, 83, 226

"Prophet's Chamber" 51
Protestant Methodists 243
Proudfoot (Mrs, preacher of Norwich) 191, 276
Psychohistory 38
"Pudding Pie Moll" 16
Pulpit 7–8, 151–52, 159, 177, 198, 201, 234, 248–49
Purfleet 218
Puritanism 4, 7, 17–19, 23, 27, 29, 91, 96–97, 103, 238

Quakers (Society of Friends) 5, 9–11, 15–17, 29, 48, 56–57, 60, 107, 112, 144, 154, 161–65, 169, 175, 204, 227, 236
Quarterly Meeting 26, 70, 112, 230, 236
Queen Square 176
Quietism 15, 48

Radcliffe 64
Rakefoot 71
Rankin, Thomas 140, 162
"Ranter" 30
Rationalism 163
Ray, Ann 176
Reading 174
Reasons against Separation 46
Redcar 227
Redgrave 197
Redruth 146
Reeth 229
Reeve, Elizabeth 197, 287. *See also* Elizabeth Wright
Reformation 5–6, 28, 82, 203, 238
Reigate 174
Reproof 84, 101, 190, 193, 200
Rhayader (Wales) 26
Rhodes, Benjamin 210
Richards, Thomas 78
Richardson (Miss, of Ryefield) 64
Richardson, Samuel 34
Richmond 229
Ripley, Dorothy 246, 276–78
Ripon 229

Ritchie, Elizabeth 111, 138, 147, 170. *See also* Elizabeth Mortimer
Robin Hood's Bay 153
Robinson, George 171
Robinson, John 7
Roe, Robert 182
Rogers (Rev.) 234
Rogers, Hester Ann 217
Rogers, John 9
Roman Catholicism 203
Roseland 188
Rosen, Beth 2
Rossendale 86
Rufforth 50
Rules of the Band-Society 68
Ryan, Sarah 87, 119, 124–30, 138, 162, 199, 278–79
Ryefield 64
Ryle, Martha 63

Sacraments 81, 106
Sagar, William 229
Saint Albans 217
Saint Austell 188
Saint Ermme 188
Saint Heliers (Isle of Jersey) 202
Saint Hilda 5
Saint Ives 138
Saint Mawes 188
Saint Michael's Lane (Derby) 135
Saint Peter's (Leeds) 139
Saint Teresa 16
Salkeld, Jane 147
Samaria, woman of 143
Sanctification 53
Savannah (Ga.) 45
Scarborough 124, 153, 156, 170
Schismatick Sifted, The 8
Scotland 103
"Secessions" 226
Seckerson, A. B. 93
Second Letter to Author of Enthusiasm 58
Sectarianism 4–6, 8, 10, 15–17, 19, 30, 54, 56, 58, 77, 225, 238

Select Society 49, 74
Self-authentication 79
Serious Proposal, A 13
Sermon 6, 122, 150, 166, 191, 233
"Sermon Preached at St. Cuth-berts" 8
Sevenoaks 51
Sewell, Mary 189–93, 279
Shakers 17
Shaman 16–17
Shaw, Elizabeth 215. *See also* Elizabeth Flamanck
Shaw, Thomas 186
Shaw, Thomas 229
Sheffield 93, 135, 156, 179
Sheffield Park 93
Shent, Mary 50
Sheriff Hutton 154
Shiney Row 246
Shipley, David 80
Shoreham 51, 147, 208
"Short History of Methodists" 45
Shrigley-fold 50
Shropshire 181, 206, 252
Sierra Leone 209
Skillington 202
Slaves 246
Sligo (Ireland) 128
Smith (Mr.) 158
Smith, John 77
Smith, Thomas 230
Smith House (Halifax) 49
Smollett, Tobias 47
Smyth, Agnes 160–61
Smyth, (Rev.) Edward 160–61
Smyth, (Dr.) F. A. 177
Soddon 191
Soteriology 79
Southcott, Joanna 17
Southfield 229
Southwark 131
Spencer (Mrs.) 151
Spirituality 110
Stamp, William 75
Stanton 22
Staveley 227

Steed, Ann 53
Steele, Richard 12
Stevenage 51
Stevens, Abel 18
Stevens, George 245
Stevens, Sarah 111, 216, 226, 280
Stevenson, G. J. 204
Steward 68, 83, 201, 217
Stockport 140
Stokes, Joseph 179
Stokes, Mary 144, 179–84, 280–81. *See also* Mary Dudley
Stokesley 153
Stump Cross 140
Sturton 52
Sturton Grange 230
Suffolk 189–92, 195, 197, 205
Sunderland 157, 177, 227
Superintendents 26, 232, 234, 236, 242
Sutcliffe, Samuel 112
Suter, Alexander 229
Sutton-Common 200
Swaledale 229
Swarthmore Hall 10–11
Swindells, Robert 50
Sykes, George 234, 249

Taft, Mary 213–14, 233–37, 245–46, 281–84. *See also* Mary Barritt
Taft, Zechariah 94, 103, 117, 132, 148, 155–57, 171–72, 190–91, 197, 204–5, 213, 214, 227, 230, 233–35, 244–46
Talgarth (Wales) 26
Tattershall (Mr., itinerant preacher) 198
Tavistock 147
Taylor, Elizabeth 72
Taylor, Jeremy 22, 110
Taylor, Joseph 187, 211
Taylor, Joseph 230
Taylor, Richard 129, 167–68
Teesdale 49, 111
Telford, John 140
Tersteegen, Gerhard 112

Testimonies 7, 47, 73, 76, 82–
84, 92, 95–100, 102, 119–20,
131, 136, 182, 191, 192, 228,
239
Tewkesbury 149
"Theodoras" 8
Thirsk 248
Thomas, Diana 26
Thompson, Ann 102, 229, 284
Thompson, Martha 50
Thompson, Martha 50
Thornton, John 139
Thoughts on Communion 208–9
Thurlton 190
Tickets, class 70, 93, 193, 232
Todmorden 91
Told, Silas 95
Toms, Mary 251
Tonkin, Elizabeth 186–89, 205,
284–85. *See also* Elizabeth Col-
lett
Torshell, Samuel 9
Tranter, William 185
Treffry, Jane 111, 227, 252, 285
Tripp, Ann 126, 129, 135, 139,
200–201, 285–86
Trowbridge 217
Truro 188
Turkey 31
Tyerman, Luke 131, 149

United Methodist Church 251
United Methodist Free Church
251
"United Societies" 45–46

Valton, John 183, 218
Vanderplank, Mary 22
Vandome, Elizabeth 110
Varty, William 165
Vasey, Thomas 229
Vazeille, Mary 21
Veryan 188
Vicars, John 8
Victorian England 179
Vindication of Rights 14
Visiting the sick 22–23, 68, 72–
75, 108

Wade, Edward 230
Waddy, Richard 150
Waites (Mrs., of Thirsk) 248
Wales 26, 60, 96, 117
Walker, Samuel 89
Walkeringham 64
Wallbridge, Elizabeth 107
Walsall 65
Walton (Rev.) 229
Walton, Grace 123, 130, 286
Wapping 227
Ward, John 246
Ward, W. R. 223
Wardley, "Mother Jane" 17
Warren, Anne 93, 110
Warrenner, William 157
Watchnight 97
Waterford (Ireland) 132, 160
Watkinson, W. L., Collection
158
Watlington 218
Watson, Margaret 227, 286–87
Weardale 147
Wearmouth, Robert F. 14, 67
Weddale, Mary 50
Wednesbury 53, 65
Wells 7
Wells (by-the-Sea) 189
Werrey, Mary Ann 251
Wesley, Charles 41, 55–56, 68,
72, 75, 83, 101, 208
Wesley, Mehetabel ("Hetty")
39
Wesley, Samuel, Sr. 19–20
Wesley, Susanna 17–21, 24, 90,
122, 136, 142, 215, 238, 247
Wesleyan Methodist Association
243
Wesleyan Reformers 243
West Indies 157
West Riding (Yorkshire) 98,
129, 152, 227
Westall, Thomas 78
Whitby 5, 99, 153–54, 157, 170,
226, 246
White Hart Motel 175
Whitefield, George 46, 59, 103,
118, 124, 227, 231

Whitehaven 229
Whitehead, Thomas 66
"Widows" 23
Williams, Anne 59
Williams, "Captain Dick" 145
Wilson, Isabella 93
Wiltshaw, Mary 226, 245, 287
Wiltshire 217
Wishall 227
Witnesses 6, 53–54, 82, 96–97,
 100, 102, 104, 120, 129, 133,
 136, 141, 150, 153, 160–61, 163,
 182, 188
Witney 147, 218
Wolfe, Francis 173
Wollstonecraft, Mary 13–14
Woman Learning in Silence 10
Womans Glorie, The 9
Womens Speaking Justified 10,
 142

Wonton (Wales) 26
Wood, James 247
Woodhouse, Mary 169, 270. *See
 also* Mary Holder
Wortham 191
Wright, Elizabeth 287
Wright, W. 214

Yarborough, Lady 19
Yarmouth 190–91
York 50, 62, 132, 140, 154, 156,
 216
Yorkshire 8, 55, 91, 93, 98, 102,
 129–32, 150–52, 156, 165, 170,
 182–84, 199, 201, 225–27, 229,
 240, 242
Youghal (Ireland) 204

Zinzendorf 42

INDEX OF SCRIPTURAL REFERENCES

Genesis
19:17   320
Exodus
3:3   191, 318
7:1–2   180
14:13   319
15:20   28
17:7   319
Numbers
22:21–35   190, 210–11
Deuteronomy
6:15   318
Judges
4:4   28
1 Samuel
15:22a   318
15:22b   318
2 Samuel
6:22   180
20   143
1 Chronicles
16:10   319
2 Kings
10:1   319
Esther
6:9   320
Job
21:3   233, 320
22:21   165, 318
Psalm
1:6   320
16:3   319
37:4   320
37:37   208

40:2   320
51:10   320
130:7   319
142:7   318
Isaiah
33:22   168, 318
38:1   320
42:18   319
52:11   227, 320
55:1   212, 318
58:1   212, 318
Jeremiah
50:5   319
Daniel
3:16   318
5:27   320
Joel
2:28–29   10, 57, 106, 180–81
Jonah
1:6   319
Malachi
3:2   319
3:16   319, 320
Matthew
3:10   319
4:17   318
7:13   320
19:25   319
25   318
25:36   73
Mark
16:16   212, 318
Luke
1:67   180

2:36   28
2:38   180
6:47   319
19:10   319
19:17   320
24:25   319
John
  1:46   319
  3:14   319
  5:17   319
  7:37   194, 318
  11:28   165, 318
  11:36   320
  20:17   32
  21:16   119–20
Acts
  2:17–9   10, 28, 57
  2:28   180–81
  2:47   319, 320
  15:33   180
  16:31   320
  20:9   180
  21:9   10
  27:29   321
Romans
  6:22   319
  8:32   320
  16:1   86
  16:11   180
1 Corinthians
  6:19–20   320
  11:5   10, 57, 143, 180

13   155, 318
14   8, 28, 31, 143
14:3–5   180
14:31   180
14:34–5   57, 113, 123, 128,
    136–37, 158, 164
2 Corinthians
  5:11   320
Galatians
  3:28   73
Ephesians
  2:8   190, 318
Philippians
  4:2–3   180, 241
2 Thessalonians
  1:7–9   227, 320
1 Timothy
  2   8, 31, 143
  2:12   57, 123, 128, 136–37,
    164
  2:13   136–37
Hebrews
  9:27   319
1 Peter
  4:7   320
  4:18   212, 318, 320
1 John
  1:9   233–34, 319, 320
Revelation
  3:20   194, 318
  6:17   319, 320
  14:13   320